War Games

WAR GAMES

Inside the World of
Twentieth-Century War Reenactors

Jenny Thompson

Smithsonian Books
Washington

Copy editor: Gregory McNamee
Production editor: Robert A. Poarch
Designer: Brian Barth

Library of Congress Cataloging-in-Publication Data
Thompson, Jenny, 1966–
    War games : inside the world of 20th-century war reenactors / Jenny
Thompson.
        p.   cm.
    Includes bibliographical references and index.
    ISBN 1-58834-128-3 (alk. paper)

    1. United States—History, Military—20th century—Miscellanea.
2. Historical reenactments—United States. 3. War and society—United
States. I. Title.
    E745.T47 2004
    796.1—dc   2003067214

British Library Cataloguing-in-Publication Data available

Manufactured in the United States of America
10 09 08 07 06 05 04   5 4 3 2 1

Contents

For Donald

Acknowledgments

The reenactors who are described and quoted in this book are its most important contributors. I thank them for their generosity in talking with me, for sharing their experiences, and for helping me every step of the way in my research. I also thank them for their friendship. They made life interesting, fun, and much better than it would have been had I not met them. I am indebted to each and every one of them. In particular, I would like to thank the members of the 4th Armored, Grossdeutschland, the 4th Middlesex, the Russian Guards, the 27th Division, the 5th Sturmpioniere, and the Great War Association. Thanks especially to Bryan Grigsby, Scott Farb, Wayne L. Pierce, and Jonathan Krieger. I would also like to thank the more than three hundred reenactors who responded to my questionnaire. I am grateful for their time and effort. And, for such a rich and lively exchange of ideas, I would like to thank the moderators and members of the various reenactor newsgroups. Thanks also to the veterans who shared their experiences with me, the people at Great War Militaria, and the members of the Western Front Association.

Many others beyond the hobby's borders also helped me with their encouragement and efforts. I would like especially to thank my former professors at the University of Maryland, College Park. In particular, I want to thank John

Caughey for his insight, friendship, and support. I have learned a lot from him. I am indebted to Larry Mintz for being such a great teacher and friend. I am grateful to Myron Lounsbury, Mark Leone, Gordon Kelly, and Hasia Diner for their help, guidance, and instruction. Many thanks to Ann Denkler, Nicole DeWald, Diana Turk, Jerry Yates, and David Zurawik, each of whom contributed in important ways to this book. I would also like to thank the participants in the Life Writing Workshop at the University of Maryland and David Segal and Mady Segal for their seminar on military sociology. I am grateful to Valerie Brown, who has done so much for me and is such a good friend. I also want to thank my former students for their insights and questions. They always energized me.

For helping me fill in the gaps of this study, I thank Richard E. Lemmurs, site ranger of the Eisenhower National Historic Site; John C. Blanda, US Army Public Affairs Officer at Fort Indiantown Gap; Fred Pierce, Publicity and Promotions Director for the Mid Atlantic Air Museum; and Dan Grekitis and Steve Meserve of the North-South Skirmish Association. The various conferences at which I presented my research, including those sponsored by the American Studies Association, the Oral History Association, and the Popular Culture Association, provided a wonderful forum for the exchange of ideas. Thanks to those organizations and conference participants. Thanks to the staff at Quality Data and at the Survey Research Center at the University of Maryland, College Park, who read through a draft of my questionnaire and offered some important suggestions. Thanks especially to David Rohall, who went beyond the call of duty. Without his expertise, I would not have completed such a successful questionnaire.

I am indebted to Jeff Hardwick for his fantastic editing and wonderful energy. I could not have asked for a finer editor; this book has truly benefited from his skills and insights. Thanks to Nicole Sloan for all her terrific work and important comments and to Gregory McNamee for his careful reading of the manuscript. Thanks also to everyone at Smithsonian Books. It has been a great pleasure to work with so many talented and enthusiastic people.

I owe a great deal to Michael Ames for his support and for helping me make this book stronger and leaner. Jay Mechling made many excellent suggestions, and I thank him for being so encouraging. Thanks also to Nina Graybill, who has helped me on many occasions and is very talented at what she does. For their help and instruction over the years, I also want to thank Albert "Cap" Lavin, Rodger Birt, Ted Keller, Mike Lunine, Marvin Nathan, Stan Anderson, Tim Drescher, Judith Breen, Clarence Mondale, David Bjelajac, and Andrzej Ceynowa.

Thanks also to my friends, Jessica White, Tom Yanni, and Colin Weil. I would also like to pay tribute to the memory of Timothy James Van Brunt, a truly extraordinary individual. And I wish to remember my dear lost friend, Jim Daneu. I am grateful to my family for their love, their many talents, and their insatiable interest in the world: My father, Ted Thompson; my stepmother, Mary Hart Thompson; my mother, Barbara Thompson; my stepfather, Gary Armor; my sister, Victoria Thompson, and her partner Deborah Hamilton; and my grandmother, Jane Thompson. And thanks to all the many and extended members of the Souhrada family. Much more than thanks are owed to my husband, Donald Souhrada, for all that he does for me. He is truly my heart, my love, and my best friend. This book is dedicated to him.

"Those Guys Need Therapy"

The Hobby of War Reenacting

In an episode of the NBC television drama *ER*, a middle-aged "general" decked out in a Union Army uniform is rushed in for treatment of a battlefield injury. More anxious about missing the reenactment of the battle of Malvern Hill than he is about his injured toe, he tells the doctor, "Just saw it off and throw it in a basket. I've got to get back to the field." When told that amputation is unnecessary, he appears disappointed. Next he requests ether to dull the pain. "We haven't used ether as an anesthetic for over forty years," the doctor replies, rolling his eyes. The general responds, "Just give me a bullet to bite on." The scene ends with the reenactor, bullet between his teeth, grimacing in pain.

From Jessica Yu's 1996 documentary about American Civil War reenactors *Men of Reenaction* to the 2003 feature film *The Battle of Shaker Heights*, the media have been drawn to a phenomenon that seems to have emerged out of nowhere: war reenacting. Reenacting itself is not new. Historically, the US military has reenacted past battles to train soldiers, and war reenactments have long been part of commemorative ceremonies. As early as 1822, twenty American Revolutionary War veterans engaged in a reenactment of their 1775 clash with British troops at Lexington; in 1902, Crow Indians and state militiamen reenacted "Custer's Last Stand" near Sheridan, Wyoming. But what reenactors themselves simply refer to as "the hobby" has grown into a popular leisure activity in the United States, Canada, Europe, Australia, and Japan in the last two decades.

By now, most people have at least heard of the hobby by virtue of its largest and most public segment: American Civil War reenacting. Throughout the United States, crowds of spectators venture to various sites to watch Civil War battles re-created by reenactors. Some of the largest of these battles involve tens of thousands of reenactors charging across fields, firing artillery, and even riding on horseback. But what many people have yet to hear about is the hobby's lesser-known branch: the twentieth-century-war reenacting hobby. With a far lower profile than the Civil War hobby, this branch of reenacting involves men and some women who regularly dress up like more modern soldiers and gather together to re-create the combat of World War I, World War II, and, more recently, the Korean and Vietnam Wars.

Twentieth-century war reenacting is far smaller in membership than the Civil War hobby, which boasts tens of thousands of members in the United States. By my own estimate, based in part on the educated guesses of participants, there are roughly six thousand twentieth-century war reenactors who belong to established war reenacting units across the United States. With their stated goal of honoring history's real soldiers and creating an "authentic" war experience for themselves, twentieth-century war reenactors portray not only American soldiers, but also German, Australian, Russian, Scottish, Japanese, Canadian, French, British, and Vietnamese troops, for example. Throughout the year, they conduct private weekend-long reenactments, known to them as "private events," which are neither advertised nor open to the public.

In California, Wisconsin, and Oklahoma, for example, World War I reenactments are attended by hundreds of reenactors who join their established units in the field for these weekend-long events. And, on a remote site in Pennsylvania, the largest group of World War I reenactors in the United States meets twice a year. Meticulously "kitted out" in period uniforms, they spend the weekend in an intricate network of trenches, firing rifles and machine guns, conducting raids, launching mortar, grenade, and gas attacks, and "killing" each other as well as "dying" themselves (usually several times in a given event). When not in combat, they sit in the bunkers they have constructed or in period camps, eating hardtack, singing songs, and talking about their (real) lives.

Many of these same reenactors also participate in World War II reenactments, which are hosted across the country by reenactors themselves at privately owned sites, as well as state parks and federal military installations. World War II events range in size from a dozen to well over fifteen hundred reenactors and also involve "tactical battles" that employ period firearms, jeeps, and even tanks.

Korean War events, far more recently having taken off, are generally small; they include public displays and tactical reenactments of historical events such as General Douglas MacArthur's landing of American and Allied forces at Inchon. Vietnam events also include public displays of uniforms and equipment as well as privately reenacted patrol missions where American grunts search for Vietcong reenactors.

Being a member of the twentieth-century war reenacting hobby involves much more than putting on a period uniform and doing an "impression," the word reenactors use to describe a portrayal of a particular soldier. Nearly half of these reenactors claim reenacting to be their primary leisure activity, and, along with participation in their private events, nearly all engage in a wide variety of other hobby-related activities, often spending large amounts of time, effort, and money on them. They collect and restore firearms, equipment, and uniforms, known collectively as "militaria"; they conduct historical research; they reproduce period uniforms; they craft replicas of period leather and paper goods; they restore original military vehicles and aircraft; they tour battlefields; they interview veterans of the wars they reenact; and some even parachute out of planes in order to authenticate their airborne impressions.

Although some reenactors are quite guarded about their involvement in the hobby, the hobby also has what one reenactor calls its "public face." Citing a need to instruct people about the wars they reenact and to commemorate the sacrifices of veterans, most reenactors also participate in what they refer to as "public events," such as mock battles, parades, and commemoration ceremonies. At schools, museums, historical sites, and conventions, they set up living history displays of their militaria collections and serve as history instructors to the public at large.

Whenever reenactors move into the public spotlight, they are well aware of the criticism and even outrage they can evoke, especially in response to their portrayal of Nazis, their use and display of weapons, and their apparent desire to recreate wars whose memories are still painful and survivors plentiful. After a century marked by multiple wars in which tens of millions of people were killed, injured, or emotionally scarred, the use of war as a personal pastime strikes many as distasteful at best. Spending one's leisure time waging mock combat, firing a gun, wearing a uniform, and playing war can surely be seen as a bizarre if not wholly disturbing pastime. After all, according to the view of many outsiders to the hobby, only a child or warmonger would want to pretend to be a soldier. But reenactors are the first to acknowledge that, unlike, say, golf or ceramics, their hobby places them within the realm of a potentially heated debate over whether reenacting is a proper way to represent war.

Such a debate is not new, of course. Efforts to express collective war memories—from the Vietnam Veterans Memorial to the Smithsonian's Enola Gay exhibit—often stir controversy. "Americans," historian G. Kurt Piehler observes, "remain troubled and divided over the most appropriate way to remember and commemorate the past." Writer and Vietnam veteran Tobias Wolff acknowledges the particularly difficult task of representing war. "How do you tell such a terrible story?" he asks. "As soon as you open your mouth you have problems, problems of recollection, problems of tone, ethical problems." Such problems are central to the question of how the troubling memories of war should be represented. And it is this question that determines many outsiders' less than enthusiastic responses to the hobby.

After I presented a paper on reenacting at an American Studies Association conference, one of my panel members identified himself as a veteran and commented: "Those guys need therapy." (Laughter from the audience.) "If they want to know what it's like to be a real soldier, I'll show them." Like many outsiders to the hobby, this veteran based his opposition to reenacting on the fact that reenactors are not soldiers, and therefore deserve little more than dismissal as observers note their obvious, even laughable failure to reach their purported goal: to re-create war authentically. They're not soldiers. They're not really in a war. They can't know what it was like. Those who find reenacting to be weird, sick, or, as the *ER* episode asked viewers to believe, mildly crazy, find their reactions affirmed by most serious assessments.

Ironically, at a time when many bemoan Americans' "ignorance" of history, some critics simply oppose the efforts of laypeople to take history into their own hands through their hobby. Assuming that the primary goal of reenacting is to re-create war authentically, critics argue that reenactors might get some of the details of war right, but they leave war's larger truths behind—its complex historical and social implications—and do nothing more than trivialize it. Cultural critic Kevin Walsh, for example, argues that reenactments "are nothing but mere titillation, meaningless amateur dramatics promoting the post-modern simulacrum, a hazy image of a manipulated and trivialized past." Former National Park Service official Dwight F. Rettie remarks, "battle reenactments are by their nature an inaccurate portrayal of a dirty, deadly, bloody event. [They] trivialize the horror and reality of war and, for young people and children in particular, they convey a false impression of war's terrible effects."

Reenactors are well aware of such criticism. Some even agree with one charge. "We do somewhat trivialize [war]," one reenactor admits, "because you don't have the real pain" and "you don't have bullets whizzing by you." But almost universally, they dismiss the other charges as stemming from "public ignorance" or "academic arrogance." "I can understand the resentment of historians," one longtime reenactor concedes. "They see any interpretation other than their own as heresy." Another reenactor insists that everyone—not just historians—should be able to interpret history. He says that it's "narrow minded" for scholars to believe that "we're the professional academics so we're the only ones who can speculate on this sort of stuff." Ultimately, he says, they "write their books and they don't know either."

In fact, as much as reenactors are criticized, they are also critics themselves. With very clear positions concerning the ways the American public, the academy, and the media understand and represent war, they, too, react to what they perceive to be the public state of history. And at the heart of their hobby lies their belief that history is not the privileged sanction of the elite, the professional, or the intellectual. To them, history is not a hallowed realm to be guarded in museums, copyrighted by an industry, or sold back to the public in a sleek package. And they scoff at the idea that they must hold academic credentials or professional positions in order to represent war.

Thus, when scholar Jay Anderson argues that a living history practice such as reenacting "lies outside the boundary of established academic and public history [and] thrives on independence," he is, to a certain extent, correct. Reenacting is a voluntary hobby that functions largely beyond the realm of professional institutions that are culturally sanctioned to represent war, such as the academy, the book industry, and Hollywood. In this sense, the hobby is a thoroughly grass-roots enterprise, operating largely without sanction from any official body.

In this way, reenactors are part of a larger phenomenon of people's using history to claim power over the stories of the past. Like other hobbies, such as researching family genealogies, reenacting is a way to make active and personal use of history. History, and particularly the history of war, provides reenactors with a rich terrain of human stories that both inspire and challenge them. And, for a variety of reasons, they wish to make use of that history for themselves.

Reenactors thus engage in a series of processes through which they both interpret and represent the past themselves. They consume popular and academic representations of war, evaluate historical evidence, debate the merits of sources, and challenge one another to authenticate their impressions. In doing so, they not only celebrate their autonomy to represent war, but they also extol the value of a pastime that separates them from the mainstream. The hobby, they argue, furnishes them with a way to escape the constraints and shortcomings of what they refer to as the "real world."

But at the same time, despite their celebration of autonomy, reenactors are bound by the larger social and cultural conventions of the everyday world and must respond to the very same institutions—the schools, the media—that produce the culture's official representations of war in order to determine the shape of their own. Just as history is often bitterly contested in the public sphere, so, too, is the hobby rife with bitter arguments derived from disagreements over issues of interpretation. As academics argue the merits of a particular interpretation in journals or at conferences, reenactors argue about history at events and over the Internet. From larger questions concerning, for example, a soldier's political identity to questions about war's minutiae—What color were the belts American soldiers wore in Vietnam?—reenactors endlessly debate the nature of their representation.

In this sense, the hobby is factionalized over a central question that plagues even the official, public realm of the past: Who has the right to claim authentic ownership of history? As reenactors struggle to answer to this question, they expose the contemporary nature of a hobby that at first glance seems to be concerned solely with history. Ultimately, they reveal how reenacting is as much about the present as it is concerned with the past.

In fact, the assumption that reenactors are focused only on achieving authenticity in order to "relive" history is incorrect. Their emphasis on achieving authenticity in representing war does not stem from a desire to replicate the past. While authenticity is a critical, central issue for reenactors, achieving it is not viewed as a means to time travel. Instead, as I hope to show, reenactors use the hobby in general and focus on the issue of authenticity in particular in order to cope with the real-life issues that reflect the broader culture in which they live. However much it masks its relation to the present through elaborate rituals, costumes, and props, reenacting is both a product of and a response to the very society from which it emerged.

I first heard of twentieth-century war reenacting in June 1993, when I attended a conference on World War I history hosted by the Western Front Association in Arlington, Virginia. I had been invited to give a presentation about my research on the ways the American government and media used photographs to shape a popular image of World War I, a topic that served as the focus of my master's thesis. I arrived at the hotel in the morning, armed with my slide carousel, excited about my talk, and expecting a typical academic conference. But when I walked through the hotel's meeting room doors, I did a double take: Mingling among the eighty or so attendees were a dozen men and one woman dressed in World War I uniforms: A Scottish soldier in a kilt and tam-o'-shanter; a German nurse with a Red Cross armband; an Australian private; an American officer sporting a Sam Browne belt. They looked as if they had walked right off of a movie set. I soon learned that they were members of a group called the Great War Association (GWA), a national World War I reenactment group that conducts private reenactments in Pennsylvania in April and November each year. They'd been invited to display their militaria collections and talk to the conference audience about their "kits."

My talk went well. In fact, it elicited the interest of several reenactors, who came up afterward to talk about the photographs I had shown. Over the course of the day, I got to know several of these GWA members, who would later prove central to this book: Luke Gardner, a twenty-seven-year-old graduate student in history from Philadelphia, who donned an impression of a US pilot; Ray Sherman, a thirty-something auto mechanic from Virginia, who portrayed a member of the US 369th (a unit made up of black soldiers); and the burly Perry Trent, an independent New Jersey businessman in his early forties, who portrayed a German infantry soldier of the 5th Sturmpioniere. All were more than happy to share their knowledge about World War I, but none said too much about their hobby. Late in the day, I asked Perry if I could come to a reenactment. His response was firm: "No. Our events aren't open to spectators."

Disappointed but intrigued, I stayed in contact with several GWA members after the conference. Two months later, I accepted an invitation from Luke Gardner to join him and seven other reenactors at a World War I veterans' convention in Chicago. Admittedly, I was more interested in meeting veterans than reenactors. But once there, I became fascinated by the hobby that brought this group together. Although they varied in age, background, and profession (among them were a nurse, a salesman, a video producer, a construction worker, a teacher, two policemen, and a graduate student), they were steadfast friends. From singing war songs to talking about history, war, politics, and their daily lives, they acted like brothers. And despite the hilarity of that weekend—they were quite a comical bunch—they never lost sight of their overriding goal: to interview World War I veterans.

That weekend started me on the path that would lead to the writing of this book. I established a friendship with one reenactor at the convention, Tim Reed, a thirty-two-year-old film school graduate from Boston who works as a video producer. Tim's sense of humor made me laugh and we hit it off right away. On a couple of trips that Tim made to Washington, DC, I met up with him and some of his reenacting friends, and, at my urging, he happily agreed to take me to my first reenactment: a private GWA World War I event in November 1993.

Like many in the hobby, Tim is an accomplished tailor who can create some extraordinarily authentic-looking uniforms by hand. I was grateful that he offered to make a World War I uniform for me to wear to the event, since I had no idea how to go about such a thing. He even advised me about what kind of an impression I should do, sending me various photocopies of articles about female personnel in World War I. We ended up agreeing that I should portray an American Red Cross Motor Corps driver—a female impression that had, as Tim said, never been done before. I loved the idea, since I thought that the story of these American women who volunteered to drive transports and ambulances was fascinating. The uniform was pretty spiffy, too. So what if I didn't have a truck to drive? Tim said. That didn't matter, he told me. The uniform was going to be awesome. Within a month, Tim had finished it: the gray tunic fit like a glove (it had, after all, been made to my measurements), and the little cap was perfect. Tim loaned me a pair of jodhpurs ("breeches," he called them); I managed to find some appropriate boots; and I was off to my first event. I was nervous and entirely unprepared for what I would experience (I remember getting lost as I drove around the remote and densely wooded event site, only to stumble upon three "British" soldiers who directed me to the registration building). But I was happy that Tim was at the event. Not only did he serve as my guide, taking me along during the combat scenarios, but he also introduced me to many reenactors I would come to know well over the years.

That same fall I began work on my PhD in American Studies at the University of Maryland. My research focused on the ways in which twentieth-century war has been represented and remembered in American culture. Given such an interest, it's no wonder I was so intrigued by reenacting. Here was a living, breathing example of Americans making active use of the subject of war. I quickly decided to make it the topic of my dissertation and eagerly began my research. In fact, after that first event, I was hooked. Still in the dark about why these reenactors did what they did, I was intrigued by how much I didn't understand. Unlike Civil War reenactors, twentieth-century war reenactors seemed to be grappling with issues that were far more complex, even sensational. Their portrayal of foreign soldiers (including Nazis and Soviets), their use of more modern and plentiful forms of historical evidence, and their interaction with the actual veterans of the wars they reenact made this segment of the hobby fascinating to me.

Soon after my first foray into the hobby, I attended a World War II reenactment of the Battle of the Bulge in January 1994. This event was followed by a parade in Alexandria, Virginia, in honor of George Washington's birthday, in which a couple dozen reenactors marched; and a month later, I went to a public event known as Military Through the Ages at the Jamestown Settlement, in Virginia. I was surprised at how quickly I entered the hobby and how much there was to do once I was in it. My new reenactor friends extended an endless stream of invitations for one event or another, and soon, I was going to an event every other month.

Entering this largely male and private hobby was surprisingly easy in many ways. From the beginning, I was up front about my intentions: I didn't so much want to be a reenactor as to write a book about reenacting. "I'm glad someone is looking into reenactors," one reenactor told me, and many others seemed to agree. The great majority of them enthusiastically shared their interest with me, gladly spoke with me, and fed me lots of information—newsletters, articles, and photographs. Many went out of their way to help me and make me feel accepted; one World War I unit offered me "honorary membership," and members of a World War II unit bestowed upon me their official unit patch. I quickly made many good friends in the hobby and often found myself hanging out with reenactors and talking on the phone with them, discussing reenacting and everything else as well. To be sure, my own interest in war provided a basis for these friendships, but looking back on those early days, I marvel at how warmly so many welcomed me into their midst. Many admitted that the fact that I was just as interested in "this stuff" as they were was enough to grant me a place among them. "I know you don't consider yourself a reenactor," one reenactor graciously told me, "but you should."

But there is no question that I was trespassing into a male-dominated territory. A small faction made its opposition to women quite clear. A few were blatantly cool toward me; others seemed to overcome their opposition only after I had proven myself over time; and still others admitted that they couldn't understand why any woman would want to be in the hobby. Even some reenactors who became my friends had no trouble telling me that as a rule, women did not belong.

The small number of women in the hobby was a surprise to me. Many of the women I met attended events along with their husbands or boyfriends. And, with some exceptions, including World War I reenactor Grace Hall, whom I consider to be a pretty hardcore reenactor, women were more likely to participate in public events such as air shows or encampments or in private reenactments that offered the use of barracks. Some events require participants to camp outdoors, and I found that at these events there were usually few, if any, women present.

The author in World War II uniform (photograph by Bryan Grigsby)

With so few women around, there were times when I felt the gender divide acutely, and every so often I felt uncomfortable. Whether it was listening to crass jokes and stories or feeling that I really couldn't take part in a particular conversation, I was sometimes reminded that I was an oddity among them. Given the highly charged masculine nature of their pastime, I also recognized that the hobby was a culture steeped in the stereotypical male trappings of "guy talk," teasing, and dirty jokes. For this reason, I knew that sometimes reenactors felt uncomfortable around me. But the reenactors I got to know well eventually overcame any feelings of discomfort that they might have had—I have a pretty silly sense of humor myself— and they had no problem engaging in locker-room banter right in front of me. Still, once in a while, I got in the way. "I'm sorry," was the embarrassed apology a reenactor would utter after making an overtly sexual remark. (After telling reenactors posing for his camera to "Say pussy," and then turning around to find me, one reenactor turned bright red. "Oh my God," he said before launching into a lengthy apology.)

At other times, I knew that if I didn't really feel welcome at a particular point, it was because as a woman I just didn't belong in such a culture. At an Eastern

Front event, for instance, I was relaxing in the German barracks while the unit enjoyed some after-battle downtime. A reenactor approached me to let me know that a stripper was on her way over to dance for a unit member who was getting married in a couple of weeks. His cheeks burned while he apologized. "You can stay, of course," he said. "But I just didn't want you to feel uncomfortable."

For the most part, though, I didn't feel that reenactors were against me. To the contrary, they were surprisingly welcoming and even encouraging. I often felt they were happy finally to find someone with whom they could talk openly about the hobby. And, given many of my conversations with them that had nothing to do with reenacting, and that often took place at events themselves, I also felt that they saw me as a confidante, a safe, sisterly figure with whom they could talk about personal matters, troubles in their relationships, or their feelings of stress at work. Over time, the question of gender really didn't matter once I became friends with them. And, despite some moments of mutual discomfort, I came to believe that my gender as well as my outsider status worked to my benefit.

I came to the hobby knowing nothing about it. It was like having to learn new languages—the language of reenacting and the language of American males. I had to work hard to understand why things took the shape they did or why reenactors communicated in a given way. I asked an endless stream of questions, taking nothing for granted. And I found reenactors quite forthcoming in explaining things to me—more forthcoming, I believe, than they might have been with a man. In fact, they were so generous with their explanations for everything from what happened in a given battle to why so-and-so said what he said that at first I was somewhat offended, feeling that they assumed I knew nothing. But I soon realized that their willingness to act as my guides stemmed from a perception some of them had that men simply know more than women—especially about war.

Guns. Tanks. Uniforms. The hobby's martial and masculine airs could be disconcerting. Hanging out with a bunch of men dressed as Nazis, hearing a couple of reenactors delight in denigrating women, and listening to a stream of locker-room talk could be unpleasant at times. At one particularly low moment, I watched some reenactors firing their guns madly, circling a World War II truck, yelling, falling, laughing. One of them shouted, "Man! I get a hard-on firing this gun!" My notebook bears witness to my disgust: "Who cares why they do this!" I wrote. "They're all just a bunch of warmongers anyway."

But I knew that this critical outsider's stance was a dead end. Over the years of doing my research, I became more than familiar with such negative responses. A few of my friends, especially some of my colleagues in graduate school, thought reenacting was an absurd and even frightening pastime, and some seemed truly enraged that these "bozos" were taking on such a serious subject as war. A few even expressed concern that I was slumming in the hobby. But even after I suffered my own momentary lapse in compassion, I knew that understanding reenactors could only be achieved over time through sustained interaction and listening. And listen I did.

Over the course of the seven years I spent conducting my research, I met and talked with hundreds of reenactors and conducted both casual and formal interviews over the telephone (which I tape-recorded) and in person (which I either tape-recorded or chronicled by taking notes). Since nearly half of twentieth-century war reenactors have experience reenacting both World War I and World War II, I was able to discuss both periods with most informants. I also sought reenactors who had experience reenacting the Vietnam and Korean Wars, and I tried to get a representative sample of units and individual impressions by interviewing reenactors who portrayed German, American, Russian, French, Australian, and British troops, for example.

This book draws from a nine-page written questionnaire that I developed in the first three years of my fieldwork and mailed to more than five hundred reenactors across the country in February 1997. More than three hundred responded, and the survey yielded a wealth of information, including demographic data, information on participation and experiences in the hobby, as well as the reenactors' opinions on a wide variety of issues. I also draw from a multitude of unit and personal correspondence, unit and organizational newsletters, event announcements, reenactor Web pages, recruitment flyers, sutler catalogues, and unit and individual reenactor publications; two reenactors also granted me access to their personal files, consisting of many years of accumulated reenacting-related information. Email in particular provided me with an invaluable service, and I was able to correspond with reenactors from Montana to Estonia. I also followed the often heavy traffic on several reenactor email newsgroups, including a World War II reenacting newsgroup, a World War I reenacting newsgroup, a Red Army newsgroup for Russian reenactors, a Wehrmacht newsgroup for World War II German reenactors, and the private listserv of a World War II unit, the 4th Armored.

Over the course of my research, I attended a total of forty-three events in the Mid-Atlantic states, roughly one event every other month, including seventeen private World War I and World War II reenactments and twenty-six public events such as parades, air shows, and living history encampments. I also attended five period dinners and dances and four gun and militaria shows where the reenactors I accompanied taught me about collecting militaria.

To be allowed to participate in private events, like all reenactors, I was always required to "do" period impressions, as reenactors say. For World War I events, I dressed in my Motor Corps uniform and participated as a "registered independent," since I was not a part of an established unit. For Western Front World War II events, I dressed as an American correspondent "attached" to the US 4th Armored unit. This impression made it easy for me to justify going around with my camera at events, and it was also readily accepted as an authentic female impression, since most reenactors are familiar with war correspondents such as Margaret Bourke-White. For Eastern Front World War II events, I served as a Russian soldier in the ranks of the Russian Guards unit. Since Russian women served in combat during World War II, this was also deemed an authentic impression, and it allowed me to engage in "combat."

In the course of my journey through the hobby I learned many things. Many surprised me. Some made me sad. Others made me angry. In reading what follows, readers may also be surprised, saddened, and angered. But if nothing else, I hope readers will see that the very existence of the hobby underscores how powerful war's effects are—even, and especially, for those who have never experienced it themselves.

Chapter 1

"Hazardous Activity for My Own Recreation, Enjoyment, and Pleasure"

The Battle of the Bulge, January 1994

The temperature in Washington hadn't risen above 20° for a week. The city was paralyzed by the January cold and icy mounds of snow. But warming temperatures were promised for the weekend. I set out on Friday afternoon, concerned about the weather north where I was heading, and even more concerned about attending my first World War II reenactment.

I was driving to the Battle of the Bulge reenactment held at the US Army garrison at Fort Indiantown Gap in Annville, Pennsylvania. This reenactment was the biggie. More than a thousand World War II reenactors from across the country, and even a few from around the world, would arrive there today for the weekend-long event.

Three months had passed since my first reenactment, a World War I event. Thankfully, many of the World War I reenactors whom I'd met would also be at the Bulge, including my new friend Tim Reed, who would join his World War II reenacting unit, the American 4th Armored, as a GI. In order to be allowed to attend, I had to be registered with an established unit, and I had managed to talk the 4th Armored commander, Luke Gardner, into letting me join his unit at the event.

At first Luke was reticent. Why, he asked me, would any woman ever choose to go to a reenactment? It's dangerous, he said, plus a lot of reenactors are creepy.

You don't want to put yourself in such a possibly unpleasant environment, he advised. But after I tried to convince him that I was serious about going and would do my best to be safe, he reluctantly agreed that I could attend. He told me that I should "do" a US war correspondent impression, "attached" to the 4th Armored. This, he said, was an authentic choice, since American women, he kept reminding me, were not combat soldiers in World War II. He warned me that I would not be allowed in the front lines to engage in the fighting. Thankful that I was allowed to go, I didn't argue.

Just a month before the event, Luke sent me and the forty unit members a six-page unit newsletter devoted to the upcoming battle. The newsletter included lists of required equipment, squad assignments, and even a warning about my presence: "We will have no fewer than three photo-journalists with us from various stateside publications. One is a woman, [so] behave like reasonable facsimiles of gentlemen if you know what's good for you."

Tim supplied me with an original American World War II uniform, olive drab and fit for a man: helmet, wool shirt, pants, leggings, field jacket, and parka. I packed my uniform along with the accouterments of the other role— ethnographer—I would play: notebook, tape recorder, camera, and film.

Sixteen miles east of Harrisburg, I saw the sign for Fort Indiantown Gap and drove onto the sprawling base. "FIG," as it's commonly called, is an active military post and training ground for US Army, National Guard, and Army Reserve troops. Its nineteen thousand acres are spread over flat plains and thickly wooded hills. To my surprise, no military official stopped me, and I saw no signs intended for reenactors, so I followed the directions sent out by the event host, "The Federation." Soon I reached the road lined with a couple of dozen two-story wooden barracks in which all the reenactors would be staying for the weekend. The reenactors prize these barracks, I later learned, since they're truly authentic, having been built during World War II.

When I turned down the main thoroughfare running between the barracks, I heard the song "White Cliffs of Dover" wafting into the darkening sky. A shiver ran up my spine. The street was buzzing with hurried activity. Reenactors were arriving.

They unloaded mounds of supplies stuffed in sacks, boxes, footlockers, and packs from their cars, station wagons, SUVs, and even a couple of U-Haul trucks. As they unpacked in the middle of the crowded street, a reenactor dressed as an American military policeman circled through the mess of tangled cars, blowing a whistle and trying to free up the flow of traffic. I snaked my way through the traffic, counting twelve World War II period vehicles—jeeps, half-tracks, and even a German motorcycle with a sidecar. Some reenactors, already kitted out—dressed in uniform—strolled down the road, stopping here to examine a vehicle, gathering there to gossip. I tried not to gape when I spied a trio of SS soldiers headed my way. They looked eerie; their gray uniforms presented a striking contrast to the bright white of the barracks and snow-covered ground. They wore steel helmets and black boots, and I could just make out the runes on their collars. "It's not a costume," I could hear Tim correcting me. "It's an *impression*." And yes, I thought, he's right. These Germans made a most vivid and disturbing impression—they looked as if they'd stepped out of a 1944 newsreel. As they passed, one turned and looked at me. He smiled, bowed slightly, and then disappeared into the crowd. Three British paratroopers were next to pass, singing softly, harmonizing. Next, a group of plump, middle-aged American soldiers marched in formation with deadly serious looks on their faces.

Finally, I found the registration building. Inside were two long tables, one labeled "Allied" and the other "Axis." The Allied clerk's dog tags dangled from his neck as he leaned over to page through the long lists of the names of registered participants. He found mine and asked, "You're with 4th Armored?"

"Yes," I said, relieved that he did not seem bothered that I was a woman.

"Okay, they're in Barracks 1244. You paid for meals, so make sure you bring your registration card with you to the mess hall. Sign this form and then take all your ammo over there for inspection."

The form he gave me was headed "Waiver of Liability." It began:

I, the undersigned, do hereby acknowledge that as a participant in a World War II reenactment event, I freely and voluntarily engage in a hazardous activity for my own recreation, enjoyment and pleasure. I recognize that as a part of this activity other participants and I will traverse difficult and dangerous terrain and obstacles, and transport and use various firearms and other weapons, and I freely and voluntarily assume any and all risk of injury such activity involves.

Hmmm. Sounds like fun. Hazardous, difficult, and dangerous with a seemingly high probability of injury—and all for my own personal recreation, enjoyment, and pleasure. The form went on to state that I was eighteen years old or older and would not hold responsible the United States government, the Commonwealth of Pennsylvania, the officers, employees, and officials of Fort Indiantown Gap, the event sponsors, or "all owners and operators of participating vehicles" for "any and all damages to my person and property arising out of or resulting from my direct or indirect participation in this event."

4th Armored barracks detail, the Bulge, 1994 (Photograph by the author. Unless otherwise indicated, all photographs are by the author)

owner of a 1941 American jeep that Luke uses as his command post in the field; Ted Morse, a short, stocky fellow who was working on a PhD in economics; Sid Testa, a bulky man in his early fifties who works as an airline mechanic in Pennsylvania; Hal Zane, a sheriff in Virginia; Ed Malthus, a telephone repairman, and his cousin, eighteen-year-old high school student Ben Sandler; Phil Fussel, a tall, friendly man from New Jersey who was Hal's best friend; and the Sharp brothers, Mike and Bill, two strikingly similar-looking firemen from Maryland.

The brothers bandied back and forth, while Paul Sciora, a lawyer from Atlanta, chatted in a southern drawl with Troy Carnes, Luke's best friend from grade school. I remembered many of them from the World War I reenactment I had attended a few months ago: John Loggia, the World War I British commander, had traded in his officer's status for the rank of an American private. And Perry Trent, the World War I German soldier whom I had judged to be rather gruff when I first met him, was there, too, loading his camera with film. He greeted me with a warm handshake.

The 4th Armored guys were friendly, I thought, especially given that I was an anomaly. That weekend I saw no more than ten women out of a thousand reenactors. Some were the girlfriends, wives, or daughters of male reenactors. Others were there on their own account. Together they portrayed a range of impressions: A Hitler Youth member, a Canadian nurse, a German officer, American correspondents, and even German and American "male" soldiers.

A few of the men of the 4th broached the subject of my presence and diplomatically asked what I was up to. I soon learned that explaining myself to them would occur far more often than their explaining themselves to me—despite what I thought to be the obvious need for the opposite to occur. Men dressed in fifty-year-old uniforms, wandering around with firearms—to them there was no need for an explanation. I happily complied, reciting my later formulaic rendition of why I was there: I was conducting research on reenacting. Most seemed interested. One even raised his eyebrows and laughed. "I was wondering when someone like you would show up. What's your field, psychology?"

Around eight o'clock, William Hoff, 4th Armored's vehicle coordinator, entered the barracks. His face was red and his brow was furrowed.

"What's wrong with him?" I asked Troy.

"Oh, he's just frustrated. He has to coordinate the vehicles for the battle tomorrow."

"Okay, guys listen up," William shouted over the din. "We already took care of the vehicle assignments, but we're still not sure if the Sherman's going to make it. They're working on it now."

"Did Paul Boyd show up?"

"He's here," William said loudly. "But he's pissed. They only gave him one garage. How the fuck do they expect him to squeeze three tanks in there?"

"Don't sweat it, Hoff," one reenactor said. "That's just Nat Handler's stellar planning."

"Nat Handler, my hero!" yelled another.

"Now there's a reenactor!"

"Yeah," Tim said. "He's hardcore, man. He's been reenacting World War II since 1944!"

I would later find that this kind of banter, directed at what the men of the 4th refer to as "boneheads" and "farbs," often dominated their conversations. ("Farb" is a derogatory term, long in use among reenactors, for a bad reenactor.) Such boneheads and farbs were other reenactors who, for a variety of reasons I had yet to understand, were looked upon as losers or idiots. Nat Handler, it turned out, was the hugely unpopular host of this event, and was, as one reenactor described him, president-for-life of the reenactor organization called the Federation.

When I later met Nat, I was surprised that he elicited such widespread hatred. A computer programmer from New Jersey, he seemed likable enough. But like other event hosts, Nat was demonized for various actions, such as turning away reenactors from an event because their registration forms were received after the deadline. Despite popular sentiment, reenactors paid their fees—twenty dollars (no meals) to forty-five dollars (full meals)—in order to attend the largest World War II event of the year.

Scott Friewald was smoking a cigarette outside when I went out to get some air. On the street, the haggard MP was still at it. "You!" he shouted at the driver of a red Camaro with Colorado license plates. "No POVs"—privately owned vehicles—"allowed here. You're going to have to move that!" Scott told me a little about his life in New York, where he lived with his fiancée and worked as a cell-phone salesman. "These guys are great," he said. "Some of them have been my friends for over ten years. It's a good group."

Just then Luke Gardner approached. Tall, slender, and blond, Luke looked hardened beyond his twenty-eight years. Unlike the privates and NCOs in the unit, who wore enlisted uniforms, Luke wore an officer's dress uniform—pinks and greens—complete with garrison cap, necktie, and insignia pinned to his belted tunic.

"Hey, LT," Scott said, calling Luke by his unit nickname. Luke nodded gruffly and passed into the barracks. "That's Luke," Scott shrugged. "He's totally anal. But I guess he gets the job done."

The 4th Armored was formed by Scott, Luke, Hal Zane, William Hoff, Larry Cohen, and others who met reenacting World War I and then came together to conduct small but highly exclusive Vietnam War reenactments in the early 1990s. Their ranks grew as word got out that they were developing a hardcore mechanized World War II infantry impression. Thanks to William Hoff's connection with the Military Vehicle Preservation Association (MVPA), they established relations with "vehicle people," private collectors of World War II tanks, half-tracks, and armored cars who haul their vehicles from as far away as Ohio and Florida to participate in events like the Bulge—often at great expense to them.

Later that evening I attended the Allied commanders' meeting. Harry Pindarello, a real-life major in the National Guard and a reenactor, used a large army map to instruct unit commanders where the Allies would deploy for tomorrow's tactical. Interrupted several times by a ringing cell phone, late arrivals, and simultaneous conversations, the meeting was confused. Tim Gilbert, commander of a US unit, asked Harry to clarify the initial positions the Allied units would take.

"They'll be strung out along the edge of Training Area B," Harry said. "And the Germans," he paused. "Well, we don't know where they'll be, but we're on the offensive. We'll find them."

A little while later, Luke called his own unit meeting to order. "The organizers of this event," he began dryly, standing before the men gathered around in the barracks, "have planned a typical farbfest for tomorrow. We'll go out as planned, but we'll pursue our own agenda." Laughter. "Paul Boyd's none too happy. Handler and his cohorts wanted him to let all the Allies work with his Shermans. That is not going to happen." More chuckles. "4th Armored will have the responsibility of shielding the tanks from the other boneheads who will no doubt want to be near the vehicles." Luke turned to a reenactor next to him. "What do you call tanks, Ralph?"

"Asshole magnets!" he answered, and everyone laughed.

"So," continued Luke, trying to regain order. "You'll follow the orders of your squad leaders and go into the tactical tomorrow with two tasks: keeping other guys away from the vehicles and avoiding getting killed yourself. Okay, I'm going to read out the vehicle assignments and then we'll discuss unit business."

As Luke read the assignments, Perry Trent sat down next to me.

"Silly, isn't it?" he asked quietly.

"What?"

"All this," he indicated generally with a wave of his hand. "It's just a bunch of grown men playing army."

"Is that really what you think?" I asked.

"Well, depending on who you ask, you'll get a different take. But then again, I'm not," he said, smiling, "your typical reenactor."

"No?"

"Hey, I voted for Clinton," he responded, getting up to move. Then, leaning back down, he winked and said, "But don't tell anyone."

Perry's comment remained with me as I toured around that evening. The reenactors seemed anything but typical, dressed in their uniforms. But they all looked alike. Mostly white and male, they were literally uniformed, making it hard to distinguish taste or class. They blended together, distinct only by unit designation and nationality. And they were interacting with each other intently. What were they talking about? No one discussed *reenacting* itself—why it's done. Instead, their conversations ranged from politics and their social lives to plans for an upcoming event and reflections on a previous one.

I wandered over to the flea market, which was housed in three large wooden buildings near the barracks. Inside each, long lines of tables were manned by reenactors in uniform and dealers in civilian clothes. The Federation charged fifteen dollars per table, and because space was limited, each table was crammed, stacked with gear and artifacts, surrounded by lines of uniforms hanging from portable racks. There was an endless supply of original and reproduction British, American, German, Canadian, and Italian World War II militaria: field manuals, watchbands, matches, scarves, German Y straps, boots, underwear, daggers, belt buckles, dog tags, books, stick grenades, bootlaces, goggles, insignia, magazines, prophylactics (period), photographs, paybooks, flashlights, medals, patches, socks, helmets, musette bags, bayonets, blanks, pouches, period cigarettes, foot powder, overshoes, entrenching tools, K-rations, shaving kits, blankets, tunics, trousers, canteens, gloves, raincoats, overcoats, flight jackets, and even a selection of pornographic postcards—everything a reenactor, or a World War II soldier, for that matter, could need.

As I later learned, more than half of reenactors' militaria purchases take place at event flea markets; only a tiny percentage is made from commercial sources such as militaria and antique shops. In response to a burgeoning demand, several reenactors have founded businesses over the last decade that make reproduction gear or sell period items. Craig Bass and Joe Estefan, for instance, are two reenactors who were members of the hobby before setting up shop to reproduce period militaria items such as boots and tunics. Reportedly, they've been successful: aside from selling their wares to reenactors, they both supplied reproduction militaria for use in the film *Saving Private Ryan*, and Estefan supplied reproduction tents for the film *The Thin Red Line*. Other militaria dealers across the country have also responded to the demand, selling everything from original Nazi helmets to reproduction GI boots. The sale of militaria generates large profits for such businesses, which operate primarily through mail order and at events like the Bulge.

"Barter," as one reenactor said, "makes the hobby go round." And indeed, one of the first things I noticed about reenactors was their constant talk about the sale or trade of militaria. Especially as particular items become rare and costs rise, competition surges among them as they look for the ultimate deal, seek "minty" items, and keep an eye out for dealers selling farby equipment or passing off repro items as period pieces. Some reenactors, Larry Cohen later told me, "collect everything that was ever made in World War II and they're at cutthroat competition with the next guy for the exact same thing. . . . These guys are like little old ladies with this stuff. Well, so and so did this, and he sold me that, and . . . he's an asshole, and he's bothering me about a helmet, and blah, blah, blah, blah, blah."

Perhaps that was the din I heard as reenactors crowded the aisles in the flea market, asking dealers, "What are you getting for this?" and "Can you come down a little on this?" One dealer told me the Bulge is a must-attend event for dealers, who come from as far away as California to sell their goods.

"I have a store," he said. "But you'll never get the kind of crowd you get here." And they were buying indeed, in cash, hauling away thousands of rounds of blanks, a new tunic, a spoon to replace one lost at the last event, or an entirely new impression.

Unlike Civil War reenactors, who use reproduction equipment and uniforms, many World War II and World War I reenactors use a lot of original gear. As Luke would later observe, "Reenactors use historical artifacts consumptively." For those who do American impressions, kitting out in original gear is not only easier, owing to the availability of surplus American militaria in the United States, but also less expensive. An original enlisted man's shirt, for instance, goes for about fifteen dollars. But for those who do German, items are rare and prices far higher. The German version of an enlisted man's shirt runs about fifty dollars. One dealer of German militaria was happy to explain prices when I inquired. "It used to be," he said, "that there were no World War II reproductions made—or at least very few. Guys *had* to wear original stuff or convert modern uniforms, like modern East German or Swedish stuff. A lot of guys still do that. It's cheaper, but it's not too authentic. But nowadays you've got businesses that make reproductions of almost everything—boots, uniforms—good quality repros. 'Cause let's face it, a lot of these guys are not off the racks."

I pulled out my notebook and asked what an "off the rack" was. He eyed my notebook and spoke a bit more authoritatively.

"Average sizes. Small. The average World War II soldier from any country was tiny compared to a lot of these reenactors. Thin. So there's no way a lot of these reenactors could wear originals even if they found them—they're not off the racks. So the repros are coming out, but even then you're going to pay—like this," he turned around to take down a German tunic hanging behind him. "This is an M-42, all wool, German Heer tunic, worn by your average German soldier in the field. It's got the patch pockets, scalloped fronts." He fingered the tunic delicately, pointing out its details with the language of a tailor. "Six button front. Split cuffs." He paused and looked up at me. "This is a repro," he said, waiting for my expression to register this amazing fact. "It is?" I faithfully exclaimed.

"That's right. This is a size 38. And I'm asking three hundred dollars for it. And that's a good price. But if you're bigger, like a size 50 or something, you're gonna pay even more."

"I had no idea," I said, copying down the figures.

"Oh, yeah. Doing German is expensive. You've got guys walking around here right now whose entire impressions, even repro stuff, cost them a couple thousand dollars. And they're going to go out in the field like that tomorrow and roll around in the snow." He laughed. "There's a lot of disagreement about that. Some guys will only wear original stuff because of the authenticity thing. Others feel differently, though. Why destroy an irreplaceable item simply to have fun?"

We chatted a bit more before I thanked him and continued to weave my way through the aisles, looking at the phenomenal display of militaria. I was on my way out of the flea market when I ran into a group of elderly men in civilian clothes: American World War II veterans of the Bulge. I struck up a conversation with one of them and learned that he'd been coming to the event at FIG for several years. Housed in their own barracks, the veterans spent the weekend reminiscing about their experiences in the real Battle of the Bulge and talking to reenactors. The veterans' presence came as a surprise to me. But I learned that it was not unusual for reenactors go out of their way to make contact with veterans, especially those who'd served in the units they portray. Some units even have veterans serving as their unit historians, advising members on matters ranging from proper drill to combat tactics.

The veteran I spoke with told me about the real Bulge, where he'd been captured by the Germans in 1944. When I asked him how he reacted to seeing reenactors wearing his captors' uniforms, he looked me in the eye. "I wanted to kill them." He paused. "But after that shock I guess I kind of calmed down. I don't have a problem with it. They've got to have an enemy to fight, right? These young kids are making sure we're not forgotten."

Back inside the 4th Armored barracks, a few unit members had crawled beneath army blankets and were snoring, much to the dismay of their roommates. "This happens every year," one hapless reenactor said as he applied waterproofing to his boots. "I never get any sleep at events with all these guys stuffed into the barracks. It's like a snoring symphony when the lights go off."

The lights would not go off for several hours. And despite a few sleeping reenactors, the barracks became more lively as the night wore on. Some German officers of the 12th SS were embroiled in a spirited conversation with several 4th Armored men concerning an exclusive event they'd held a few months before. I overheard one of them saying, "And when you guys came up over the ridge, Mark's like, 'Shit! Get down!' I was sure you saw us. . . ."

I'd hear many such war stories late into that night. Sitting in a loose circle, they drank beer. Some smoked cigars. Laughter boomed as the jokes became increasingly bawdy. At one point they howled as one 4th Armored member regaled them with stories about a reenactor from another unit, mocking him for everything from his girth to his "unfocused" reenacting activity that leads him to change periods incessantly. "Now he's getting into Hussar. Napoleonic Hussar. This guy's six foot four and probably weighs 260." The men laughed uproariously. "Biggest fuckin' Hussar ever. I mean a *statue* of a Hussar isn't that big, you know what I'm saying?"

I stayed awake as long as I could, sipping from a bottle of Cobalt Blue that someone gave me. But around one o'clock, I crawled into my sleeping bag, exhausted.

The Battle

When reveille sounded at 6:00 a.m., I hurriedly dressed in my uniform and joined the unit for a breakfast of eggs, pancakes, and coffee at the mess hall. Luke ordered us to form up in front of the barracks after getting ready. He was crouched down in his room amid a mess of equipment, counting out fifteen-round magazines for his M1 carbine. American soldiers, he said, were notorious for expending tons of ammunition. "I want each man armed with at least 250 rounds," he said soberly.

It took the unit members no less than one full action-packed hour to finish their intensive preparations. They dressed in their uniforms, packed rations, laced leggings or pulled on the more convenient buckle boots, slipped into thick wool overcoats or field jackets, attached their entrenching tools ("e-tools," as they call them, or folding shovels), bayonets, first aid packs, and canteens to their web gear, strung ammo clips over their shoulders, and filled their field bags with everything from period liquor flasks and modern-day cameras to Hershey bars and unfiltered cigarettes. Finally, they wrapped woolen scarves around their necks, put on their helmets, stuffed their hands into woolen olive drab gloves, and slung their rifles over their shoulders.

As we made our way to the garage to meet up with the vehicle crews, everyone seemed in good spirits—even those who'd had little more than a couple hours sleep and a lot more than a couple of drinks. I marveled at the endless number of reenactors marching or assembling in front of their barracks. The forty members of the World War II German unit Grossdeutschland (GD) stood in formation. A large German shepherd watched as the unit's commander, a tall figure wearing a belted tunic, pants stuffed into huge black boots, paced ominously before his men, speaking in German, his arms behind his back. The troops stood at parade rest, their eyes expressionless. When one 4th Armored man yelled, "Don't even think about it, ya lousy jerries!" the commander waved his hand dismissively before turning back to his men. But I noticed that several of the Germans were now smiling.

The vehicle people were still tinkering with the tanks when we arrived at the garage. The crews were buzzing about, carrying tools, wiping greasy hands on coveralls. Paul Boyd, the owner of the Sherman tanks, jumped down from where he had been perched on one of them and shook Luke's hand. He was in his mid-fifties, well tanned, and he flashed a dashing smile. He looked more like he belonged on a Florida golf course than on a gray army base in the middle of winter. His tanks were impressive, their massive forms bulked within the thin wooden structure of the garage. Painted in army green, each bore a stenciled name: "Boyd's Bad Boys" and "Battlin' Bitch."

When we finally moved out, we made quite a sight: three tanks, two half-tracks, and several jeeps ferried the 4th Armored to the battle site a few miles away. There were other period vehicles moving out, but some units took to the journey on foot, and we passed them along the way. A long line of POVs carrying troops drove on a parallel road. A van pulled up next to our column, its side door open, and I could see a German soldier videotaping our column's movement.

We arrived at the staging area, where everyone was to convene before the battle. The narrow dirt roads surrounding the vast snow-covered fields and woods where the battle would take place had been cleared by a couple of snow-plows that were parked at the edge of one road. Huge mounds of snow surrounded us as we jumped off the vehicles. For the first time, more than a thousand reenactors were gathered in one place. I was overwhelmed by the sight, a little dizzy and more than a bit giddy. Who were all these people who somehow knew to be at this remote place at this particular time, dressed like World War II soldiers? I'd never before been in the thick of such a spectacle, and I found myself feeling greedy—I wanted to talk to and photograph everyone I saw. As I stood on the icy road that morning, it was comforting to remember that I, too, was dressed in World War II garb. Even though I felt like the eager, excited, and awed novice that I was, I still somehow blended in with the crowd. My uniform, I thought, was an excellent disguise.

Some units maintained formation, but most reenactors dispersed and became entangled in the growing crowd. Hundreds of Germans wearing white camouflage, dark camouflage, and field-gray uniforms were joined by just as many Americans. A long line of airborne troops wearing Screaming Eagles patches pushed its way through the crowd. Two downed pilots in leather jackets and sunglasses inspected a German sidecar. Several Canadian machine gunners sporting magenta berets stood near a jeep, a maple leaf flag flying from its antenna. Some German *Fallschirmjaeger* troops huddled together, and I spied some veterans in the crowd, their cameras at the ready. Two signs had been erected in the midst of the chaos, one pointing in the direction of Malmedy and the other toward St Vith. In front of a small food stand, a line of reenactors waiting to buy coffee and donuts stretched out into the road.

The men of the 4th Armored also dispersed, most visiting friends from other units. I made my way through the crowd and came upon a man in a black cape, a beret perched on his head, sitting in the back of an American jeep. I stopped to talk to him.

"My son got me into this," he said cordially. "He's in an American unit, and I'm a little too old for the common soldier, so I put together this French partisan impression. It's nice," he said taking a sip from his steaming coffee. "It gives us a chance to spend some time together."

That morning it appeared that spending time together was all we were doing. Apparently, it only just so happened that we were dressed in uniform, carrying weapons, and bearing the brunt of a January winter. We were, I gathered, waiting to move out, but the members of the 4th were talking about their girlfriends, their jobs, and movies they'd seen. There appeared to be no attempt whatsoever to adopt any first-person character, and I asked one reenactor why there was no separation of enemy forces.

"Oh," he said. "There's really no way to separate before starting. At some smaller events you'll see that, but at the Bulge things just sort of get mixed up."

US reenactor reading V-mail, the Bulge, 1994

I found it odd that troops soon to fight each other were acting as if they were all on the same side. But I took this opportunity to take photographs and was surprised at the reenactors' willingness to pose for me; from SS troops to British machine gunners, they quickly adopted what I later saw as the standard serious reenactor pose. This belied, I thought, the goings on around them, where all seemed to be hilarity, confusion, and cold.

When I returned to the half-track, a German soldier was telling Tim about his newest impression. "I got some Wild West stuff," he said.

"Aw," Tim responded, shaking his head.

The German grabbed Tim's arm, "Hey, man, chicks dig that stuff!"

Tim smiled. "Yeah, I'm sure they do. These chicks aren't named Bruce, are they?"

The German laughed. "There are a lot of people doing this Wild West stuff, believe it or not. We do an event and like fifty people call up."

Tim looked out into the crowd. "Well, this is enough of fucking cowboys and Indians, anyway. At least you're dressed appropriately."

The German soldier exclaimed, "That's what I'm saying! Let's don't kid around! Let's put on the clothes, man!"

Tim now seemed distracted. "I want a big pair of California boots that look like dragoon boots."

The German soldier responded, "I got a pair of cowboy boots from the Cowboy Regimental Supply—"

"Big chaps," Tim mumbled.

The German continued, "—custom made, two hundred bucks for a custom-made pair of cowboy boots. Two inch heels, right up to here, cooper toe, made out of horsehide." He stared at Tim.

"Wow," Tim responded.

"Russet."

"Cool," Tim said.

This conversation was representative of many others that were taking place. As they talked about their clothing and accessories, the reenactors almost exemplified, I hate to say it, the stereotype of women. "Are those originals?" one asked another, pointing to his gloves. "Yeah, camo reversible to white. Minty, huh?" He extended his hand, and the other made clucking noises in admiration.

According to the Federation's event announcement mailed out beforehand, authenticity regulations were to be in effect. But I could tell by the critical assessment of the many farbs that apparently surrounded us that they hadn't been enforced.

"Jeez," Tim said to Hal Zane. "Those 29th guys need a reality check. They're wearing all postwar stuff."

"That's not as bad as their hair," Hal replied. "They look like girls. Get a fucking haircut."

Tim was laughing when I asked, as I so often would ask at events, "What's going on now?" He responded, "I don't know. I guess we're just waiting to see what happens."

Wait and see. Precisely. Especially at the Bulge event, the coordination of the battle was often complicated by bad weather, confusion, or, as some reenactors put it, "bonehead commanders." But neither Nat Handler nor any other battle commander was anywhere to be seen; no one seemed to be in charge. But the reenactors didn't seem to mind, and instead they talked and talked. Some troops sat on a mound of snow piled up near the field; several others were changing their socks, which had already been soaked through by standing on the wet ground. A couple of Germans walked by, brandishing grenade launchers, and two women stood at the side of the field dressed in Luftwaffe uniforms.

The temperature hovered around 35°, making it impossible to warm up, especially after standing outside for what was now two hours. Looking around me, I could tell from all the red noses that everyone was freezing.

Because of the snow, many were hesitant to go out in the field and take their positions. While the white covering the ground looked beautiful, it was a merciless trap for those who traversed it on foot. As some energetic troops started to make their way across the field, they were sucked into its depths—up to three feet in some areas. Using their rifles to help themselves up, or with the aid of friends, they slowly made their way across the field. The rest of us looked on.

"Call a medic!" Tim laughed. "Those guys are going have to heart attacks. Look at them struggling."

Yes, I thought, it was a worrisome sight, especially watching the more rotund reenactors weighted down with equipment. I was glad to see that, in fact, a medic could be called if need be: an ambulance was parked at the edge of the field.

As we watched the struggling soldiers, I asked Hal Zane what he thought about the delay. "I think it's a total shame," he said. "I mean, we come out here for what? One weekend to do this? And those guys, the soldiers, did it for years. Getting wet, tired, cold, going hungry. It's an insult to them and it's dishonoring their memory that we should just stand around just because a few lightweights don't want to get wet. If you don't want to get tired and cold, stay home and watch TV."

As if reading Hal's mind, the vehicle drivers decided to follow the struggling foot soldiers. We mounted up and drove slowly across the field to a copse of trees, where again we stopped. More waiting. Some of the men took photographs of the surrounding troops and tanks. The conversations continued. The wind started to blow.

Luke was the first to brave the snow. He made his way into the open field and indicated to the tank drivers, who were peering out their hatches, to follow. The tanks stuttered, charging slowly. The men followed too, gathered around Luke, resting the butts of their rifles on their thighs or holding them over their shoulders. After several minutes, they dispersed around the tanks and began to practice tactics. Luke screamed and waved his hands, trying to keep his men in formation while the tanks circled around. Every now and then, Luke would communicate to one of the drivers with a hand signal and shout to one his men. "Watch it, Harry!" "Third squad, left!" After an hour of hand signals and formations, the tanks roared back across the field. Again we mounted back on the half-tracks and drove back to the staging area.

"What happened?" I asked Sid Testa.

"Lunchtime!" he said.

The staging area was still crowded when we returned. We parked near the woods' edge, and soon the reproduction K-ration boxes were broken out. Under

US reenactors with tank, the Bulge, 1994

Luke's command, they had been copied from original models of K-ration boxes by silk-screening their copied print on cardboard salvaged from cereal boxes. The men filled them with modern equivalents of wartime rations. Tim nestled down in the snow to make a cup of cocoa on his World War II vintage Coleman stove. The Sharp brothers opened cans of peaches. The vehicle crews crawled out of their steel-rimmed holes and ate. One of them straddled a tank gun barrel as he munched on a can of beans. Everyone seemed to have followed Luke's order from the newsletter: no "non period karma blowing bullshit" was seen. But Luke was on the prowl. "Those are actually 1944 combat suspenders," he said to a reenactor who, to my eyes, looked perfectly fine. "You're going to need to get M43s. Try to pick them up at the flea market."

This correction, made in front of others, made me uncomfortable. Why not take him aside for what seemed to be a trivial violation? But that was Luke: he was hardcore. He knew, he'd always say, more about World War II tactics than anyone in the unit, and he approached each project for an event with an intensity that was scary. Aside from his silk-screening efforts, he'd worked on many of the mail call letters that would soon be handed out. Reproductions of original V-mail forms had been sent to all unit members to fill out and return with their Bulge registration forms. Luke then color-copied period stamps and even carefully drew 1944 postmarks on them. Scott Friewald then photographed each V-mail and reproduced it in a smaller size—just as real V-mail letters had been reproduced during the war.

When Scott stood on the back of the truck and shouted, "Mail call!" I was eager to see the results of their labor. We gathered around as Scott called out names and tossed V-mail and packages into outstretched hands.

The men opened their letters—sent to them by imaginary girlfriends, wives, and relatives from stateside or other parts of war-torn Europe. Many read their letters out loud, laughing uproariously at accusations that they'd gotten a woman in trouble. One 4th Armored man was mercilessly teased after having received a letter from his gay soldier-lover. Others read Dear John letters; letters demanding that outstanding bills be paid; entreaties from grandmothers to "keep their heads down." Some even received gifts, photographs, and baked goods. Luke was devouring a batch of brownies sent to him in a plain brown package.

"Tim Reed!" Scott yelled. Tim caught a small box and eagerly tore into it. Inside was a pair of silk stockings that Tim's (imaginary) soldier-brother had sent him from Italy. Along with the gift, a letter was enclosed. Tim held it up for all to see while reading it aloud. It left much up to one's imagination, since the censor had taken a knife to it and cut out all the naughty bits, leaving more holes than paper. Everyone howled at this display, which Tim later told me he had sent to himself.

I was surprised when Scott called my name. The V-mail he placed in my hands was addressed to me care of "European Postal Department 1156, US Correspondent Section, 3rd Army, France." It had cleared the censor and bore the stamp "qualified" at the top. My "publisher" in Chicago, a Mr. Niles Johnson, wrote, "Dear Jenny: Received your photos from the Huertgen Forest battle in November. Absolutely fabulous! That one shot of those muddy, cold GI's bringing in German prisoners was the best yet! I hope you are well and warm." (When I later asked Luke who had written the letter, he replied, "I don't know." The mystery remains to this day.)

The sun was faintly shining by the time mail call was finished. Other units seemed to have decided that if there was to be any combat at this event, it was now or never. They started fanning out across the field, headed toward a valley where the Germans had taken a defensive position.

We moved out as well, the troops riding in the half-tracks or crouched precariously on the hoods of the tanks. In the middle of the field, they all dismounted, stripped off their packs, hung them from the side of the half-tracks, and began to march toward the wood line, with the roaring tanks in the lead. It was slow going, but the men took advantage of the ruts left in the wake of the tanks and walked more easily now, crouching slightly, carrying rifles at the ready. Shots began ringing out, and the staccato from machine guns added to the din. The battle had begun.

Near the wood line, Luke gestured wildly, screaming at the men to hurry. They ran, stumbling, red-faced, stopping now and then to fire a few rounds, and getting up to run a few more steps. A few stopped longer and fumbled with their weapons. Their rifles had jammed. One sergeant, a ruddy-cheeked fellow, paused to wipe the sweat from his brow. Luke screamed at him and waved his arm again. The sergeant shrugged his shoulders before disappearing over the top of the hill with the men of first squad. The tanks sluggishly dipped over a slope and were consumed by the copper-tinged trees dotting the wooded valley.

All around us the sounds of the battle now raged, echoing off the snow-covered hills and then absorbed by the wide plain. I was happy to occupy such a commanding view on the half-track.

Sid Testa decided not to follow the 4th into action. "I'm too old for this," he said happily. "I've been reenacting for thirty years and I'll tell you, you stop feeling like you gotta go out there when the weather's like this." I was happy to have a companion since I would be relegated here for the duration. Sid was having a field day with his new gun, an M1A1 Thompson submachine gun. Standing on the back of the half-track, he fired at the woods where some German troops were positioned. After a while, he offered to let me shoot. "Come on!" he said gleefully, "Just try it out."

I fired the gun at some tiny figures hurrying along the tree line, their silhouettes outlined by threads of golden sunlight. *Bat-bat-bat-bat-bat.* Sid laughed maniacally. "Good! Get 'em!" he yelled over the blasts from the gun. I felt the recoil from the firing shots and heard the cling of the spent cases hit the truck's floor. It was only after I stopped that it occurred to me to ask about the danger of blanks. "Oh, yeah," Sid, now eating a Slim Jim, said. "You can't just walk up to someone and fire a blank straight at them. That would most definitely cause injury." He resumed his firing position. "About ten feet. You want to stand about ten feet away. If you're closer, just aim the gun up or to the side." He fired again. *Bat-bat-bat-bat-bat.*

Somewhere in the woods to our left, a German unit had set up a machine gun. Huddled between the thick trunks of the trees, the Germans were just barely perceptible. When two Americans tried to make their way past them, one wheeled around and fired. One American took his "hit," yelling, "Awwww!" and fell, casting his rifle off to the side. He writhed in pain for a moment and lay still. Meanwhile, his comrade dashed behind one of the trees. Video camera in hand, he managed to capture his friend's death. After a few moments, the dead soldier resurrected himself and brushed the caked snow off his trousers. With his helmet in his hand—the universal reenactor signal to indicate that one is dead, as I would later learn—he and his friend hurried past the Germans without further incident.

A little while later, three 4th Armored men appeared, leading a line of German prisoners in single file, hands above their heads. The Americans had taken their weapons from them and were carrying several German rifles apiece, each with a small white flag hanging from its muzzle. These troops had surrendered. The Germans were told to stop near the half-track. *"Papiere!"* one American shouted. He reached out and grabbed the identity book of one prisoner and then seized a pistol he had hidden underneath his tunic. The American held the gun up, admiring it. Two of the Germans glared at him. The American glared back and then snatched one of the prisoners' caps off his head. The German glared more intently. Unaffected by his prisoner's harsh demeanor, the American placed the German cap on his own head and turned toward me when I called to him. The American flashed the victory sign. The German scowled. I took a picture.

The German looked up and smiled at me. I reached into my bag and threw a piece of candy to him.

"*Danke*," he said.

"*Bitte*," I responded.

I wasn't sure if this would be interpreted as fraternizing with the enemy. I was even more unsure if I should maintain some kind of period character and hiss at these captured enemy soldiers. But when I looked at the 4th Armored men, they seemed oblivious to us; they were busy forcing the Germans into line. After enduring more harassment, the Germans were released. Armed again with their weapons, they calmly walked back into the woods.

Around three o'clock, the day's faint light had dimmed. Tiny lines moved across the snow in the distance: troops marching off the field. But the men of the 4th Armored would not return for another hour. When they began to stream back to the truck, they looked wet, tired, and worn. Small piles of snow clung to their jackets or sat on the tops of their helmets. One reenactor had a bandage wrapped around his head just above a mock injury to his eye.

When I asked who had won, one smiled and said, "I'm not sure." He peeled off his overcoat, wet and heavy from the snow. The mingling of Allied and Axis troops began again as some of the 4th men leaned over the side of the half-track to talk to some SS troops. No one seemed to know or even really care who won the battle. Instead, they joked and talked while others, looking entirely spent, rested.

"My gun jammed," one 4th man explained. "And I was totally exposed after you guys took off. I'm like yelling back, 'Cover me, I'm fucked!'" He gestured by pointing his middle finger up and holding his palm over his finger. "And Joe's like, 'Fuck you, I'm covered.'"

The others laughed and joined in, explaining what happened in the woods, each telling the story from his vantage point. There was little expression of irony here. No tongue-in-cheek rendering of what had happened in the mock battle. Instead, they spoke of their own actions, their successes and failures to perform their duties as soldiers.

"I knew you guys had been hit," Mike Sharp shook his head. "I sent a point man up ahead for recon. I had no idea the Germans had massed right in front. I heard them open up and I'm like, 'Let's get going, guys!'"

"Was that GD?" one reenactor asked, referring to the Grossdeutschland unit.

"Yeah," Mike said. "I'm pretty sure. They held us up there for a while. I was waiting for Luke. Was he down?"

"No," another said. "But he was like way over on the other side. Once we headed into that gorge, we were totally out of contact."

"Yeah. And the Sherman was flying! We were just trying to keep up. We never even saw the Germans."

I listened to them piece together what had happened and began wondering what brought them here. And what would bring them back to another event? Tramping around in the snow for what was now seven hours, firing their guns without knowing whether they'd won or lost, expending such time and energy to drive here, kit out, silk screen K-ration boxes, and make fake mail—these were investments in something whose payoff I could not readily see. Obviously they were having fun, but what seemed inexplicable was why they'd gone to such great lengths to have this particular form of fun.

In fact, so many experiences at that event defied my expectations of what reenacting would be like: their desire to be authentic, down to the stamps on a letter, and their seeming unwillingness to stay in character; their constant complaining about an event while in the same breath making plans for the next; their shared sense of purpose (no need to explain why we're here) and their often blatant animosity toward one another. But perhaps the most striking aspect of the day was learning that despite all their talk about a desire to re-create history, they did not even seem to try to replicate the Battle of the Bulge. These contradictions suggested that reenacting was more than a form of commemoration, as many reenactors say it is, but neither did it seem to be a way to relive the past. And there was little Ben Sandler, his face pale, his nose running.

"How was it?" I asked.

"Great!" he responded. "It was a lot of fun."

"Did you get killed?"

"Three times!" he exclaimed, looking to his cousin Ed.

"You got your fair share of Krauts, though," Ed said. "And this baby," he said, holding his Thompson submachine gun, "did its job. You've met your worst nightmare!" Ed now stood on the back of the half-track and yelled at no one in particular. "A Jew with a tommy gun!"

Luke was the last to return. He looked rumpled, his face wind chapped, his hands blue with cold. He was not pleased. "It was okay," he said when I asked how it went. "The typical cluster fuck, though, like all of these farby events." Luke, I soon learned, was rarely pleased after an event. "Just too many guys and no control. Farbs and idiots just running around with no sense of history. It's a shame."

Aftermath

For the next couple of hours, the men of the 4th pulled off their soaked woolen uniforms, cleaned their guns, took showers, and broke out the beer. I, too, enjoyed a hot shower all alone in the mammoth barracks bathroom, with two guards posted outside to ensure my privacy. Bing Crosby serenaded the stuffy barracks, and by six o'clock everyone had changed into dress uniforms for dinner.

The dinner was held in a large mess hall filled with long tables and folding chairs. It brought the reenactors together again for a mediocre meal of meat and potatoes, buffet style. The veterans sat at their own tables, while both Allied and Axis reenactors crouched reverently at their sides. Some bought the veterans drinks from a cash bar in the corner of the hall. At the two long tables occupied by 4th Armored, there was a great deal of complaining going on.

"I don't even know why we used the radios," one said as we ate. "The other Allied units just stopped using them. All I could hear was Tim Gilbert going, 'Where are you guys? Where the fuck are you?'"

"They were pinned down totally on the end."

"Oh yeah, by those guys from the 12th SS?"

"I think Luke had them shot. Hey, Luke, did those guys get it?"

"Which?"

"The clever fucks who held us down."

"I can't comment," Luke said wryly. "If one of my men happened to slip and pull the trigger while marching them to the rear, hey, those are the winds of war."

On and on it continued, piecing together what had happened using a curious mixture of period and present tenses. As they rehashed the event, opinions emerged about what they had to do to get ready for the unit's next event—a smaller World War II reenactment scheduled for early spring. Luke, the most dissatisfied of all, was making the grandest plans.

"You guys," he told his first squad sergeant, "have to get coordinated. You can't just go off and not maintain contact. Study those hand signals I sent out. And when you get separated, you need to reestablish contact with HQ." Luke turned to Mike Sharp. "We need to plan a unit training before the next event, especially when we're working with tanks. I don't think Paul Boyd was very pleased with our performance today."

After dinner, most of the 4th Armored decided to forgo the Christmas dance. An Andrews Sisters–type group was to perform in the mess hall, and reenactors would be forced to vie for dancing partners out of a scant number of women.

Tim suggested that we visit the Grossdeutschland unit to see their famous barracks impression.

When we entered GD's barracks, I wanted to rub my eyes in disbelief. Assembled in the long, candle-lit barracks were about forty GD members in German dress uniforms. They were hosting a Christmas party and had set up a table of food near the entryway—delicate frosted cookies with glowing sprinkles, puffy fruitcake, gingerbread cakes, dark, crusty biscuits, slabs of brown bread. A re-enactor dressed in a Santa Claus suit played Kris Kringle, handing out gifts to the unit members gathered around drinking beer from white porcelain steins labeled "GD." Standing near a lavishly decorated Christmas tree, which sported several small swastika flags, two Germans played accordions. Small wooden footlockers were tidily arranged in front of the rows of bunks, with each bed uniformly dressed in a period bedsack; their blue and white checkers imposed a sense of order on the chaos of the party. Rifles were stacked precariously in the center of the barracks.

In the dim light, I could make out flags hanging on the walls, one bearing the GD insignia and two others with huge swastikas on them. Posters on the walls declared *"Hitler ist Deutschland"* (Hitler is Germany) and *"So wie wir kämpfen Arbeite Du für den Sieg!"* (As we fight, you too must work for victory!) On one of the bunks, the German shepherd I had seen earlier rested his head and watched the proceedings from round, dark eyes.

We crowded into the barracks, greeted heartily by GD's commander, William Gregory, a fifty-year-old businessman from New Jersey. A lone Russian reenactor arrived and circled through the crowd, drinking whiskey from a period bottle. The Americans, drinking beer from plastic cups, stood respectfully to the side. Then two Germans, each puffing on massive cigars, produced their unit songbooks and began to sing songs of the fatherland. An American veteran stepped from the crowd, held up a tiny camera, and took a picture of the singing Germans. One 4th Armored man, who hours before had captured a band of Germans, now crooned, shoulder-to-shoulder, with a handsome Panzer officer. All the other Germans began singing too, holding their steins at their waists, elbows cocked, arms swinging.

I heard 4th Armored member Larry Cohen mumble, "Aw, give me a break," before he started singing his own song, known as the "Hitler Rap," a satirical song, written earlier by one of the men of the 4th, about the horrible Germans' crushing defeat at the hands of the noble Allies. Larry belted out his song, interrupting the Germans, and Tim and several other 4th men chimed in with Larry. This prompted them to march in single file around the barracks, goose-

Singing the "Hitler Rap," the Bulge, 1994

stepping madly, shouting. The Germans looked on, laughing, yelling, shaking their heads. When the noise died down and resolved itself into general laughter, a German officer walked to the head of the barracks. He peered through delicate silver eyeglasses. Casting his eyes over the crowded barracks, he removed his hat.

"Friends," he began earnestly. "We are here today to pay tribute to the soldiers who fought and died for their countries. We are not here to pass judgment, but to honor the common soldier. Today we look back on those awful days of bloodshed and only hope they will never be repeated. We come together in friendship to honor the sacrifices of those men and women who suffered so terribly and fought the worst war of the twentieth century. May they never be forgotten, and may people remember and know that all war is tragedy."

"Hear, hear!" Cups and steins were raised, and everyone drank before the noise filled the room again.

To the side of the barracks I noticed an elderly man in civilian clothes sitting at the end of a bunk, talking intently to a reenactor. I was soon told, in reverent tones, that the man was a veteran of the *real* Grossdeutschland unit—a soldier who fought on the German side nearly half a century ago. Most of these reenactors were born long after this man even became a veteran, and yet here they were, like ghosts around him, young, spirited, and authentic—right down

Chapter 2

"This Must Be Something They Do in California"

A History of War Reenacting

The Battle of the Bulge event saw the singing, drinking, and carrying on well into the small hours of the night. But it drew to a close early the next morning. According to FIG officials, the barracks had to be vacated by no later than noon on Sunday. The reenactors rose early, some reluctantly, some grumpy after only a few hours of sleep. They packed up their mounds of supplies and equipment, policed the barracks, said their goodbyes, and then, as Luke put it, "blew out of there."

I marveled at what I saw that weekend. When I returned home, I felt dizzied, confused, and tired. I was relieved, though. My worst fears about injury or harassment had been unrealized. As I looked at the normal surroundings of my apartment, I felt that I had witnessed something somehow secret, something quite extraordinary—and, as I learned when I tried to tell a few friends about the weekend, something difficult to explain. I imagined the other reenactors returning home. Did they unpack their gear and watch war movies? Did they get on the phone and talk to each other about the event? Or did they resume normal life as if nothing strange had occurred—taking a nap, playing with their kids, feeding the dog? As I tried to make the transition from the event to the pattern of my daily life, I wondered how others did the same.

I would soon learn that most reenactors return home from events exhausted, but they are able to move seamlessly from the strange world they just left back to their daily lives. Perhaps only novice reenactors, like me, find it hard to come home and go about a routine as if nothing unusual had occurred. That Sunday after I came back from the Bulge, I found that I wanted to talk with other reenactors. And so, that evening, I spent a couple of hours on the phone with Tim Reed and later with Luke Gardner, discussing all that had happened.

But the feeling of culture shock after an event became less intense the more events I attended. Soon I, too, was able to move back and forth between an event and my daily life fairly easily. Part of the reason it became easier was that the more familiar I became with the reenacting world, the more events themselves became somewhat routine. In fact, the Battle of the Bulge event, while larger than most reenactments, was fairly typical of a private reenactment, including World War I events. The schedule of events over the weekend, the blend of combat and living history activities, the unit meetings, flea market, and socializing, are all repeated in nearly every private reenactment. Whatever the particular war being reenacted, twentieth-century reenactments follow an established pattern. From year to year, as I attended subsequent Battle of the Bulge events, World War I reenactments, Eastern Front battles, and other smaller events, the more this pattern became apparent. Still, my familiarity with an event's design did not answer my initial question: Why reenact war for fun? As nearly everyone would agree, war is a horrible experience. Yet by making it into their hobby, the reenactors seem to suggest that although they admit to war's tragic proportions ("all war is tragedy," as the German officer had said in the barracks that night), it is also a source of great enjoyment. Was the whole thing a giant contradiction, I wondered, or were the reenactors being insincere?

I knew it would take me a while before I might be able to answer such a question and understand reenacting in all its apparent contradictions. So, as I began my research in earnest, I turned my attention to a simpler question: Where did the hobby come from? It turns out that the contemporary practice of reenacting past wars has its roots in America's history.

The Third Battle of Manassas

July 1961. The world was awaiting the outcome of the trial of Adolf Eichmann in Israel. President Kennedy was serving in office. *The Guns of Navarone* played in movie theaters across the country. Only two years had passed since the very last American Civil War veterans had died, and now, many Americans would commemorate the war's centennial. Along with lecture series, parades, and fairs, a modern "sham battle" would take place at the site of the Battle of First Manassas (Bull Run) in Virginia—an event not officially sanctioned by the Federal Civil

War Centennial Commission, which left planning of commemorative activities to local and state officials. Later, this battle would be heralded as the "first" of the modern war reenactments that were to multiply in subsequent years.

Over a blistering hot weekend in July, an estimated seventy thousand spectators, including the governor of Virginia and the director of the National Park Service, attended the staged Battle of First Manassas. An announcer provided commentary as more than two thousand participants dressed in uniforms, riding horses, and firing muskets and cannons re-created the July 1861 battle.

The *New York Times* disparaged the event's blatant commercialism, commenting on the "carnival of tents offer[ing] literature, exhibits, souvenirs, ice cream, frankfurters, soft drinks, flavored shaved ice and other innocent refreshments." And, although the paper judged the battle as "accurate as to sequence and detail," it had doubts about the re-creation's authenticity, since it hit only upon "the battle's highlights, displaying the broad outlines of strategy and the most interesting or critical turns." There were also more glaring moments of less-than-authentic re-creation, such as one described in the *Washington Post*: "As the artillery batteries dueled deafeningly and the cavalry charged, a field dummy representing a fallen soldier caught fire. A charging horseman dismounted quickly and trampled out the flames to the cheers of thousands—and as earnestly returned to the fearsome fray."

The ninety-minute battle ended in a re-creation of the Southern victory but closed with an act of national unity: the singing of "God Bless America." Many applauded the event as a fitting and exciting commemoration—the audience was reportedly swept to its feet cheering as the Confederates "chased the Union troops back into the woods in panic." But complaints over a host of modern battle-induced difficulties quickly emerged, such as the massive traffic jams after the event and the large number of "civilian" casualties: An estimated 175 spectators were treated at first aid tents, the great majority suffering from heat stroke, a result of the 102° temperature. Dubbed the "Third Battle of Manassas," this first centennial reenactment was followed by a string of others, including reenactments of the battles of Antietam in September 1962 and Gettysburg in July 1963. The battles were also followed by a wave of protest.

Many were quick to argue that "sham battles" were not proper. One disgruntled observer called the 1961 reenactment a "grisly pantomime." Another argued how "this silly business" glossed over the grisly effects of real war. At the reenactment, "death and suffering and the indescribable tragedy of war" were nowhere to be seen.

But it was not only the idea of reenacting war that bothered some. The civilian

The Third Battle of Manassas

1961 cartoon from the Washington *Evening Star* (© 2003,
The Washington Post. Reprinted with permission.)

participants, who had seemingly come out of the woodwork to take their battle
stations, were also the subject of derision. Although later they would be known as
reenactors, in 1961 they were called "men and boys" who "play Civil War games."
One *Washington Post* editorial described them this way: "The gaudy show at Bull
Run was a noisy piece of amateur theatrics, carried on by overgrown boys who get
a thrill out of hearing guns go off. It was play acting at about the ten year old level.
Bang you're dead." Another critic labeled them: "Civil War 'fans'—those who
consider [the war] a glorious page in our history, those who enthusiastically 'celebrate' it, those who want to perpetuate its controversies and antagonisms, those
who actually make military maneuvers their hobbies." At the next staged battle,
this critic suggested that "real ammunition" should be issued and "the United
States would thus be free of one of the sicker elements of our society."

But another less hostile critic mused, "I hope the social psychologists will get
around soon to telling us why people respond so enthusiastically to this type of
activity." And indeed, the reenactment did inspire enthusiasm. Many saw it as
a form of stark patriotism, a way to portray past sacrifices. "Be slow to criticize

the reenactment of the battle of First Manassas," one supporter argued. "For it may be that divine providence has given us the centennial years to reaffirm our faith in America."

Four years later, at the final centennial event commemorating the Appomattox surrender, the critics had won: reenactments had been barred from commemorative activities. One reporter noted their obvious absence: "The brevity and simplicity of today's observance contrasted with the massive, extravagant re-enactments that commemorated other major Civil War events over the past four years of centennials."

Despite the official rejection of reenactments, those "overgrown" boys continued to form units and expand their membership long after the Civil War centennial ended. Once the American bicentennial commemorations were underway in 1976, Revolutionary War reenacting ("Rev War," as reenactors call it) would take center stage. Around the same time, small, private World War I and World War II reenactments were already being conducted, but it was Civil War reenacting that continued to draw the public's attention.

In just two decades, Civil War reenacting would grow into a full-fledged leisure activity in the United States and Europe, and its membership would swell into the tens of thousands. By the 1980s and 1990s, thousands of Civil War reenactors were enlisted by Hollywood to serve as extras in films such as *Glory* and *Gettysburg*. By the time of its 135th anniversary in September 1997, tens of thousands of spectators witnessed the Battle of Antietam reenacted yet again by a record-breaking fifteen thousand reenactors.

As the press took notice of this burgeoning hobby, many wondered "when and how the reenactment craze began." When author Tony Horwitz suggested that it evolved out of the Civil War encampments of the early twentieth century, where Civil War veterans "occasionally performed mock versions of the heroic deeds of their youth," he was only half right. It was not only veterans who performed war and laid the foundations for a modern reenacting craze.

A Civil War Legacy

Historian George Mosse brilliantly documents what he calls the "trivialization" of the war experience. According to Mosse, especially after World War I, "the reality of the war experience came to be transformed into what one might call the Myth of the War Experience, which looked back upon the war as a meaningful and even sacred experience." Mosse suggests that in the late nineteenth and early twentieth centuries the development of mass-produced, war-related films, games, images, and novels made such mythologizing possible and encouraged people to view war not only as entertainment, but also as a "noble" enterprise. Indeed, as the American Civil War moved further into the historical distance, its popular image took on a decidedly romantic, heroic aura. As early as the 1890s, many Americans viewed the Civil War not as a divisive and bloody conflict, but as a gallant national endeavor. As Americans confronted the prospect of other wars, the soldier was held up as a figure whose positive characteristics—willingness to sacrifice, heroism, courage—should be emulated.

The Boy Scouts of America relied upon this popular sentiment toward the soldier as thousands of young members entered its fold. Playing on a young man's desire to model himself after a heroic and disciplined soldier, the Boy Scouts, along with "junior militia companies," offered boys an opportunity to play at being a kind of soldier; and some groups even offered the chance to engage in the fun of performing mock battles.

But it was not only children who delighted in playing soldier in turn-of-the-century America. In record numbers, adult males also expressed a martial spirit by joining organizations open only to male descendants of veterans. Groups such as the Sons of Confederate Veterans, founded in 1896, flourished, while the Sons of Union Veterans, founded in 1881, had branches in thirty-one states in its first year of existence. By 1901, it boasted 163,000 members.

Members of these veteran-descendant organizations promoted broad agendas related to the social costs of war and worked to help disabled veterans, as well as the widows and orphans of veterans. But by and large they viewed themselves as working to uphold a sense of patriotism and duty. Especially on martial holidays, such as "Memorial and Union Defenders Days," they expressed a desire to "keep green the memories of their fathers."

Groups such as the Sons of Veterans Guards bestowed upon their civilian members officers' titles and often conducted military training and drilling exercises, using equipment and wearing uniforms similar to those of regular soldiers. Members looked upon their appropriated military roles as connecting them with the valued ideals of their forefathers, calling themselves "the modern embodiments of age-old traditions." And often, they worked to authenticate their legacy and to school themselves in the arms and equipment of real soldiers.

At parades, encampments, reunions, and conventions, these sons came in contact with veterans. Together, veterans and their descendants took part in a type of performance to which contemporary reenacting most clearly traces its roots: the historical pageant.

Inspired by community leaders to promote awareness of local and national history, historical pageants were usually performed on holidays in outdoor settings. Drawing large crowds, the pageants were enacted by elaborately costumed amateur actors who re-created scenes from American history, such as Columbus Discovering America and the Signing of the Declaration of Independence. Pageant actors portrayed famous Americans as well as "common" individuals such as pioneers, pilgrims, Indians, and soldiers. And it was the veterans, along with their descendants, who were often cast to play soldiers in the various wars portrayed in pageants, including the American Revolution, the Indian Wars, the American Civil War, and, by the 1920s, World War I.

Like the 1961 Manassas reenactment, the historical pageant was viewed as a bridge between past and present, allowing citizens to connect with the ideals of their forebears. And having real veterans accompany the actors seemed to heighten a pageant's authenticity, allowing an audience to connect more personally with history. After all, pageants were intended to draw people together to celebrate a heroic story of the American past, and pageant advocates, including educators and progressive reformers, argued that a pageant's value lay in blending education with entertainment. While the pageants were entertaining, to be sure, they were also replete with moral and civic lessons that were seen as being especially helpful for new immigrants. In his 1914 *Handbook of American Pageantry,* pageant organizer Ralph Davol argued that despite their sometimes amateurish nature, pageants aspired to a noble purpose: "The players may not be Bernhardts or Edwin Booths; Pocahontas may enter shod in high-heeled shoes; a glimpse of blue jeans may appear beneath King Philip's blanket; slight historical anachronisms may occur; but the community pageant, as a whole, was never a complete regret, and never failed to inspire a finer fellowship."

Although a pageant audience of the time might have been less focused on whether a pageant accurately replicated history, scholars today judge the pageant's portrayal of history, particularly its representation of war, as wholly inauthentic. According to historian David Glassberg, pageants "displayed the gallantry of war without the violence." But pageant planners of the time argued that such horror was to be avoided. Ralph Davol instructed that a pageant should not portray "a stream of social sewage emptied upon the arena," and he provided an example of "questionable artistic taste." In one town's pageant, a war scene included a wounded soldier being carried on stage on a litter before he "was borne off into a cemetery which happened to adjoin immediately the pageant field."

To be sure, pageants presented an image of war that was decidedly lacking in "social sewage." Through sequential scenes, war was presented as a highly generic narrative in which soldiers marched off to war; those on the home front sacrificed and prayed; a battle was enacted; and then the soldiers heroically returned home. Such a portrayal was, however, in keeping with the ideals that the veteran-descendant groups represented as well as with American society's generally heroic vision of war. The soldier was widely viewed as a romantic figure and war as a noble endeavor. And, like many other popular war portrayals of the time, the pageants emphasized war's ultimate unifying effect on the country. Even after America's entry into World War I, pageants continued to enjoy popularity in the United States.

By World War II, however, both veteran-descendant organizations and the pageant movement largely died out in the United States. In 1943, one of the few pageant organizers still at work lamented the rise of commercial enterprises that had usurped the presentation of public history. By the time historian Carl Becker coined the term "living history" in 1931, performances of history had already been institutionalized at sites such as John D. Rockefeller's Colonial Williamsburg (founded 1926), Henry Ford's Greenfield Village (founded 1929), and later, Plimouth Plantation (founded 1947). At these sites, visitors could mingle with professional "costumed interpreters" who assumed the personalities of historic characters and demonstrated historic crafts and lifestyles.

But even as historical pageants faded from the national scene, the amateur tradition of performing history would continue. As Civil War veterans died off and veteran encampments decreased in size, collecting Civil War militaria became a profitable enterprise, and new groups began to form in the tradition of the veteran encampment. In 1933, the National Muzzle Loading Rifle Association (NMLRA) was founded as a competitive shooting group whose members used Civil War weapons. NMLRA members sponsored national and regional competitions and hosted "primitive rendezvous" where competitors dressed in Civil War clothing. Once they began to expand their focus from using historic firearms to re-creating the tactics, uniforms, and camp life of soldiers, they started forming units. They would also meet for weekend-long events to perform battle tactics while living the camp life of the Civil War soldier.

In 1950, an NMLRA member formed what would later be known as the North-South Skirmish Association (N-SSA). Drawing together other like-minded people, two Civil War units were formed, and in May 1950, in Berwyn, Maryland, they engaged in their first "period" skirmish, using original Civil War muskets. Many of these early events were staged by descendants of Civil War veterans; and, in a clear expression of their personal connection to history, they wore their ancestors' insignia on their sleeves. In May 1951, they hosted their third skirmish, this time in conjunction with the final reunion of Confederate veterans in Norfolk, Virginia. Three Civil War veterans attended the reunion, including one of the last living Civil War veterans, John Sallings, and one veteran attended the skirmish.

Known for several years as the North-South League, the group of Civil War skirmishers formed an official organization in 1956 and officially changed its name to the N-SSA. In 1958, the group was incorporated as a nonprofit corporation in Virginia. In 1963, they purchased a two-hundred-acre site near Winchester, Virginia, where biannual skirmishes continue to take place. Coming together over the course of a weekend, competitors and their families camp out, engage in shooting and period costume competitions, and enjoy cookouts and dances.

Today the association boasts 3,700 male and female members organized into two hundred Civil War units across the United States and Canada. Many are direct descendants of Civil War veterans, and some are active members of the still-extant Sons of Confederate Veterans and Sons of Union Veterans. But unlike earlier veteran-descendant organizations, membership no longer depends on one's family tree. "Becoming a part of the thrill and excitement" of the N-SSA is now "is as easy as dropping a note to the N-SSA Recruitment Officer."

This open membership policy heralded a new generation's attitude toward the soldier's role and perpetuation of his (or her) memory. One did not have to inherit the blood of a soldier to don an impression. One needed only a desire to preserve "the traditions of the Civil War" and a wish to honor "the heroism of more than 600,000 Americans who died." N-SSA members displayed these goals publicly just a decade after their group's founding. Along with other regional Civil War firearms associations from across the country, and some National Guard troops, it was mostly N-SSA members who were in fact those "overgrown boys" who gained national attention during the 1960s centennial commemorations of the American Civil War. Eventually, they would spawn the most authentic hobby of all: World War I and World War II reenacting.

The Growth of the Civil War Hobby

With little acknowledgment that they are carrying on a tradition—I have only once heard a reenactor refer to historical pageants—reenactors agree that World War I and II reenacting somehow grew out of the Civil War hobby. Many current twentieth-century war reenactors started their reenacting careers in the Civil War hobby in the 1960s and early 1970s—a tradition that continues to this day. Indeed, more than a third of current twentieth-century war reenactors took part in a Civil War reenactment as their first event.

Mark Sammons, a fifty-something carpenter from Chicago, has been reenacting for over three decades and is currently a member of an American World

War I unit and the German World War II unit Grossdeutschland. He dates his involvement in reenacting to 1962, when, at the age of thirteen, he and his father attended the Civil War centennial reenactment of the Battle of Antietam. He vividly remembers first seeing reenactors: "They wore uniforms, they marched, there was a fife and drum band," Mark says. "So I mean that was for me, I had never seen anything like that before." He was immediately hooked.

Investment banker Larry Cohen also got hooked at a young age. In 1976, at the age of fourteen, he started Civil War reenacting. "In a weird way it was kind of like the Boy Scouts," he remembers of his first event. "We dressed up in uniforms and hiked the trail to the First Manassas, and we even got First Manassas medals for doing it."

Other reenactors also draw a parallel between their youthful activities, such as being a Boy Scout, and reenacting. Lew McCarthy, also a current twentieth-century reenactor and a lawyer by profession, made the transition from the Boy Scouts to Civil War reenacting in 1979, when he was a teenager. "I thought it was wonderful," Lew says of those early days. "I have a strong interest in firearms . . . and in military history, and it kind of combined both of those along with the camping and socializing."

This blending of interests drew reenactors into a hobby whose roots had been laid earlier by groups such the N-SSA. According to Steve Meserve, N-SSA executive secretary, after the American Civil War centennial, "two schools of Civil War commemoration began drifting apart . . . over the question of authenticity." One school, made up of skirmishers, was more interested in using period firearms authentically, while the other was more concerned with the authenticity of their impressions. Many current twentieth-century reenactors entered the hobby as this drift was widening.

In those early days, events and impressions were less sophisticated than they are today. Fifty-six-year-old chemist Dave Watkins, now a longtime World War I and II reenactor, remembers first joining up with the Civil War hobby in the 1960s. He described an average Union Army impression of the time: "We just wore wool gray-blue postman's trousers, and we used to have our wives or somebody alter a sports jacket, a blazer . . . and then you could find somebody who would jerry-rig a little Union kepi. . . . It was all terribly incorrect, but from a distance it looked good and you got the ambiance of it."

Mark Sammons explains these low standards of authenticity. The early 1960s, pre–Vietnam War controversy, was a time when patriotism dictated a clean look for any martial portrayal. This ideal was challenged by a small but growing number of reenactors whose primary concern lay in authenticating their impressions.

As they began to try to mimic a soldier's real appearance and not his idealized image, they defied the spit-and-polish standard and became known as "hardcores" or "authentics." The result: they were blacklisted by other Civil War units for being too realistic-looking. Describing his own hardcore unit, Mark Sammons remembers: "We were kind of dirty, our uniforms were patched, our hair was long, and our faces were bearded, and you see, back in the early days you got your pants pressed, you shined your shoes, and you got a haircut before the event."

At first, such hyperauthenticity was largely viewed with disdain by other units, since hardcores looked, to use Sammons's word, like "hippies." Larry Cohen also remembers the growing schism between his own group of hardcores and the farbs, as inauthentic reenactors became known. "The authentics were almost looked upon the way you would look at burnouts and druggies and punk rockers nowadays," Larry says. But "we looked authentic. As authentic as you can be."

Hyperauthentic impressions would never be adopted universally among Civil War reenactors. But they did become more accepted as reenactors began researching equipment and uniforms. By the 1980s a cottage industry selling reproduction Civil War uniforms and equipment had been established, making it possible for reenactors to dispose of their inauthentic postman's trousers and blazers or to preserve their original, increasingly valuable gear. Having come a long way since its early days, the Civil War hobby now offers a host of available goods: tour any sutler's row at an event and you'll see a grand display of tents, each housing all the accouterments a soldier needs. With cash or credit card, reenactors can kit out authentically, and if unsure what to buy, they can simply purchase a Civil War reenactor handbook.

Despite the changes in authenticity standards that took place through the 1970s, the schism between the hardcores and the farbs remained. The differing interests of reenactors—the skirmishers and the authentics—began to clash, and some believed the hobby was becoming too "political" as members became factionalized. Some N-SSA members, more interested in marksmanship, moved out of reenacting altogether in favor of only participating in skirmishes. Others made the transition from the Civil War to the nascent twentieth-century war hobby. For many, it was not only disagreements among reenactors that turned them away from the Civil War.

As the Civil War hobby grew, many reenactors say that events turned into public spectacles, designed to draw large crowds and make money from spectators as well as from fee-paying reenactors. Like the veteran descendants who sought to "keep green the memories of their fathers," some disgruntled Civil War reenactors thought the hobby was becoming too commercial and that the war was being presented as entertainment. Dave Watkins began to feel that big show-case reenactments largely promoted the Civil War as being "fun." As audiences came out to enjoy the day, tour the camps, and watch an exciting battle, the re-ality of the war became lost. "People tend not to associate the Civil War with the horrors of war to some degree," he says. "They think it was a lot of fun [and] they forget how horrible it was. They think there's kind of a gallantry about it."

The portrayal of war's gallantry, coupled with reenactor politics, low au-thenticity, and large crowds, finally drove many, including Dave, Larry, Lew, and Mark, out of the Civil War hobby altogether. Over the course of a leisurely inter-view at his house in Maryland, another former hardcore Civil War reenactor, Paul Donald, recounted his fifteen years in the Civil War hobby less than lovingly.

According to Paul, Civil War event organizers were entirely uninterested in history. They didn't care about upholding standards of authenticity, but just "wanted bodies on the field." "For them to have a battle," Paul explained, "and get their names in the newspapers, they had to have masses of people out there. They had to have masses of soldiers. They would trade off authenticity for what the public would see." But Paul was equally critical of the crowds that showed up to watch their inauthentic battles. "The public didn't know any better. They didn't know if that uniform was made of polyester or wool and they didn't care. It didn't matter how they were dressed because John Q. Public didn't give a shit."

Some reenactors started looking for a new challenge. Paul and others interested in more modern wars began dreaming of reenacting other periods, and quietly, away from the public eye, they started forming twentieth-century war units. Unlike Civil War reenactments, their events would be unknown to farbs, greedy event orga-nizers, and fun-seeking spectators. They would be "reenactments for reenactors."

World War I: From Shimpstown to Newville

One story that circulates around the World War I hobby tells of two individu-als who were inspired to begin reenacting World War I after reading German veteran Ernst Jünger's famous war memoir *Storm of Steel*. Bringing together roughly thirty-five people, they hosted the first World War I reenactment in Sep-tember 1978 at Mount St. Mary's College in Emmetsburg, Maryland. A college official granted them permission to use a site on school property, and there they dug shallow trenches. Wearing original World War I uniforms, they fought each other—Germans versus Americans—in three events. In 1979, the college re-quested that they stop using the land, and the reenactors were left without a site. In 1980 they found a home on a privately owned farm in Shimpstown, Pennsyl-vania. The landowner and his son agreed to let the reenactors use their land partly because it was full of unfarmable shale, and partly because they thought reenactments were "neat." As the events grew in size, the landowners also received profits from the gate fees.

Old-hand World War I reenactors still talk reverently about a somewhat mythical place called Shimpstown. There, reenactors were free to sculpt the land. They dug an extensive network of trench lines and shell holes in no-man's-land, and they built barbed wire defenses, wooden underground bunkers, and machine gun nests. From 1980 until 1990, the original group of thirty-five grew to more than seven hundred. It also expanded its range of impressions to include British, Canadian, Australian, French, and Russian soldiers. So rapid was this growth that Paul Donald, one of the original thirty-five, dedicated himself to fulfilling the resulting demand for period uniforms; in 1982, he and a partner founded a full-time business dedicated to the sale, collection, and eventually reproduction of World War I militaria, Great War Militaria. Initially operated out of Paul's house, the business moved to a three-story warehouse in 1992 where it operates today.

Unlike the Civil War hobby, World War I reenacting took on a private cast: events were not widely advertised and no public invitations were granted. But word began to circulate within Civil War reenacting circles about these hardcore events, where reenactors portrayed foreign troops, fired machine guns, and slept in trenches. Grant Holzer had been doing Civil War for five years when he first heard about World War I reenacting in 1981. He was intrigued by the stories he heard and soon got involved himself. "It was a very atmospheric event," Grant remembers. With trenches, barbed wire, and no spectators, the events attracted only the most serious reenactors. They "were very hardcore reenactors," as Grant recalls. "Into the authenticity."

During the Shimpstown phase of the World War I hobby, precedents were set for holding events each year in April and November. Initially, these events were run by what old-hand World War I reenactors still refer to as the "Benevolent Dictators." These were the two founding members who exercised total control over the hobby. If you wished to participate, you had to send the dictators two photographs of yourself dressed in full kit (front and back) for critique. If admitted, you were put on probationary status for the first two events. The World War I hobby still operates with this probationary clause, but as membership grew, problems with the Benevolent Dictatorship began to taint the hobby with the very thing that World War I reenactors were trying to avoid: "reenacting politics." In 1990 the World War I reenactors peacefully overthrew the Benevolent Dictatorship and founded a democratic organization: the Great War Association (GWA). The GWA was incorporated in 1989; the group's by-laws

American trench line, Newville Site, World War I private event, 1997

were ratified in 1990; and the officers of the first "Gang of Seven," or "G-7," which still serves as the GWA's governing body, were elected.

In 1990, under the rule of the first GWA president, the Shimpstown site was lost when the owner suffered a stroke. His son, a lawyer, told GWA members that they could no longer lease the site, as they had done for more than a decade. If they wanted to stay, they would have to purchase the land outright. Unable to come up with the money, the GWA entered a difficult time. Without a site, the reenactors reported suffering from "troglodyte fever."

For several years, they scrambled to find another location. In the interim, events were hosted at temporary sites, such as a camp in Beaver Falls near Pittsburgh, a Boy Scout Camp near Farmington, Pennsylvania (the site of my first event), and Fort Pickett in Virginia. But because these sites lacked permanent trenches, participation dwindled dramatically, and the remaining members argued over what course of action to take.

At my first event I was privy to one of these debates as about one hundred reenactors assembled for a meeting after the combat portion of the event was over. Clearly factionalized, they separated themselves by unit in the large meeting room and argued, sometimes less than amicably, for over two hours. One faction pushed for accepting a five- to ten-year lease on a training site at Fort Pickett, where the Army Corps of Engineers had agreed to dig trenches for the reenactors;

the GWA could use it for biannual events, and in the off time, Navy SEAL and Army Ranger teams would use it for their own training. Others thought that such an agreement spelled trouble: What if the Army commander who entered into this agreement was replaced and the GWA kicked off the site? What if the trenches were dug improperly? And did the GWA really want to operate under the "command" of the real armed forces? What was needed, someone proposed, was for the GWA to purchase its own site. This prompted reenactors from midwestern and western states (some GWA members travel from as far away as Florida, Michigan, and even California to attend events in Pennsylvania) to push for a site closer to their homes and to berate East Coast reenactors for being unwilling to drive more than a few hours to an event. The site issue remained disputed at the close of the meeting, but the tension was dissolved somewhat by Tim Reed, who took to the center of the hall and performed a Russian dance.

In fact, it would take a couple of years to find resolution. In 1995, Paul Donald found a backer who agreed to bid on a piece of property near Newville, Pennsylvania. This bid forced reenactors into the public eye as they campaigned among the local township to build support. Neighbors to the site, living on large plots of land set on the rolling hills of an idyllic countryside, were actively canvassed. One reenactor went door to door, introducing residents to World War I reenacting and giving them a chance to view a videotape of an event. The GWA also spent thousands of dollars paying engineers to draw up construction plans for the site, a site development plan, and an environmental impact statement. They also had to apply for local, state, and federal permits. In the end, they beat out their competitors, an organization that wanted to turn the site into a recycling area (a "dump," reenactors said), and won the right to purchase the site. It is now known officially as the Caesar Krauss Great War Memorial Site, but commonly referred to as "Newville."

The site's owner, a grandson of Caesar Krauss (an American 79th Division veteran of World War I), then formed the Great War Historical Society, which leases the site to the GWA for its reenactments. Echoing the words of the Civil War veteran descendants, he stated, "This site is my lasting tribute to my Granddad and his comrades as well as to his allies and adversaries [and will] provide a 'living history' tribute to be used by Great War historians and enthusiasts forever."

At more than 153 acres, eighty of which constitute the battlefield proper, Newville is more than four times the size of Shimpstown. It quickly drew back many who had drifted away during the GWA's "trenchless phase." Described by reenactors as a place virtually without history, the site has not been farmed for over four decades. But the reenactors have worked to authenticate the landscape with a notion of permanence, symbolically granting it a history it could never naturally claim. Not only have they dug several lines of trenches and riveted them with wood and sandbags, but they have also carved out shell holes, built machine gun nests and lookout posts, constructed several elaborate bunkers such as that of the British command, which is complete with electricity, and strewn no-man's-land with various pieces of debris—fake body parts, rusted helmets, broken rifles. The reenactors have also begun to build a cemetery of mock gravestones inscribed with the names of their veteran relatives, and they have installed a canteen run by reenactors doing impressions of Salvation Army workers, who serve coffee and donuts at events. They have even constructed a bombed-out French "town," identified by a sign among the rubble that reads Neuville. A variety of other plans are in the works, such as building an airstrip for period aircraft to land after strafing the trenches. As one former GWA president commented, "We need not be visionaries to form a mental image of the site after toil and sweat is added to it. With revetments, bunkers, emplacements, entanglements, readouts, communication trenches, listening outposts and even perhaps an airfield, recapturing the true horror of the Great War will become the reality for which we all strive."

The first event held on the Newville site took place in April 1996. That November, GWA members performed a formal site-dedication ceremony. In front of hundreds of reenactors dressed in period uniform and standing at attention, the GWA president placed soil around a newly erected monument while others laid commemorative wreaths at its base. The soil had been taken from graves of American World War I soldiers in France. According to the editor-in-chief of the GWA's newsletter, *On the Wire,* all this effort was done "for us—not for the Publick, nor for profit. It's our hobby and we do it for the love of it."

World War II and Afterward

Parallel to the development of World War I reenacting, World War II reenacting also grew in popularity. Alain Benson, who started reenacting World War II as a teenager in 1975 and who currently works as a book editor in New York City, described the early events as "really, really primitive." But in just six short years, he "saw events go from being nothing more than thirty against thirty to a big event [which] would be like five [or] six hundred guys."

Full-scale World War II reenacting was partly spurred by the activities of World War II veterans and collectors of World War II militaria. In 1951, the Confederate Air Force was founded in Texas by several people who wanted to preserve World War II aircraft. Many of the members had served as pilots during the war, and they soon began to reenact air engagements such as the bombings of Pearl Harbor and Hiroshima. (In 2002, the group changed its name to the Commemorative Air Force.) Also in the 1950s, World War II veterans and military vehicle collectors began gathering to display their period vehicles, sometimes dressing in period uniforms and practicing combat tactics. By 1976, the Military Vehicle Collector Club had been established, linking together vehicle collectors from around the country. In January 1979, the club—now known as the Military Vehicle Preservation Association (MVPA)—hosted what was known as "the Winter War Games" at Fort Indiantown Gap (FIG), Pennsylvania. The event brought together owners of World War II tanks, jeeps, half tracks, and armored cars to conduct maneuvers. That same year, the first World War II reenacting organization was founded: the World War II Historical Reenactment Society (HRS).

Some reenactors insist that World War II reenacting had been going on long before 1978, the year that the founding members of the HRS claim to have hosted the very first World War II reenactment at the Jefferson Barracks in St. Louis, Missouri. Longtime World War II reenactor Walter Tannen, whose first encounter with reenactors took place in the 1950s when he met members of the N-SSA and who also attended the 1961 First Manassas reenactment, says he participated in small World War II reenactments as early as the late 1960s. But he agrees that it was not until the 1970s that the hobby really took off. As early as 1976, according to Tannen, three hundred reenactors, including the founding members of Grossdeutschland, convened at Fort Meade, Maryland, for a battle.

In 1979 the HRS took over sponsorship of the Winter War Games and hosted a full-scale reenactment. For the first time, reenactors were able to do a barracks impression, using the period barracks at FIG (a significant development since most reenactments of the time were primarily "field events" requiring participants to sleep outside). Also in 1979, the West Coast saw the founding of its first World War II reenacting organization, the California Historical Group (CHG). And from that point, as one reenactor remembers, "It just kept on growing."

In 1980, the HRS recorded a total of 407 members in regional chapters across the country. Just a few years later, membership topped 1,200. Now the hobby was off and running: In one year the HRS would sponsor regional World War II reenactments in Texas, Ohio, Missouri, and Pennsylvania, and a "national" battle at Camp Butner, North Carolina. The HRS continues to sponsor national battles, but in 1981, several HRS members left the organization to form their own, somewhat competing group: the National World War II Historical Reenactment Federation, known simply as the Federation. Positioning itself as an East Coast reenacting organization, the Federation began sponsoring its own events, and in response, the HRS turned its attention to reenactors in the Midwest. The breakup of the HRS signaled a splintering of the World War II hobby that would be exacerbated as numerous regionally based reenacting organizations were formed in the 1980s and 1990s. "We have many splintered groups," as one reenactor says of the World War II hobby, but "it all began with the HRS."

The majority of World War II reenactments are Western Front battles, pitting the Allies against the Germans. But World War II reenactors have at their disposal far more types of events than World War I reenacting, which is primarily limited in focus to combat on the Western Front. By the 1990s, World War II Eastern Front events (Russians versus Germans) multiplied in part because of the availability of Soviet gear after the dissolution of the USSR. Other events include Italian, North African, and even Pacific Theater events—in fact, at one event reenactors from Japan joined American reenactors to "fight" the Americans, both doing Japanese impressions.

The proliferation of different types of World War II events produced more subsets of the hobby, and some members of established units began to set their sights on reenacting even more recent wars. Both Korean and Vietnam War reenacting are still small, although both—especially Vietnam—have grown substantially since the 1990s. In part, the growth of these more modern reenacting periods has been fueled by the increasing interest in (and cost of) collecting militaria from both wars, as well as by the passage of each war's major anniversaries. Some actual veterans from both wars participate in Korean and Vietnam War events, which range from public displays to private tactical events. (Indeed, some Korean and Vietnam War units are strictly "living history" groups that only participate in public events.)

In the early 1990s, Korean War reenacting appeared on the scene. Currently, there are several active Korean War reenacting units in the United States. Most Korean War reenacting is limited to displays and public presentations at living history events, although the war's fiftieth anniversary gave rise to several tactical reenactments of significant operations.

Although some reenactors like to joke that Vietnam reenacting started in the late 1960s, it was only just a few years after the actual war was over that it truly began. In the 1980s, at a private site in Connecticut, reenactors began to convene for private Vietnam tactical events, drawing much attention to themselves among other reenactors for reenacting such a recent and controversial war. But they also drew many eager participants and eventually spawned several other groups that started hosting their own events. In the early 1990s, for example, several World War I reenactors and founding members of the 4th Armored unit

4th Armored vehicle train heading to the front, the Bulge, 1995

began to host highly exclusive Vietnam events—"doing the Nam," as they call it. Portraying grunts in the First Cavalry Division, they spent weekends at a secluded site, conducting search-and-destroy missions and engaging in combat with a handful of Vietcong reenactors.

Today, Vietnam War reenacting has become much more accepted among the greater reenacting population. It has also grown as more reenactors—usually

World War II reenactors—decide to give it a try. In the United States, Vietnam units are now established in Kentucky, Texas, Virginia, and North Carolina. Others exist in Belgium, Poland, and France.

The reenactment of these more recent wars prompts some reenactors to joke about their desire to view as history any military operation as soon as it's over. The 1990–91 Persian Gulf War, though very recent, is already the focus of a tiny percentage of reenactors who collect and display the war's militaria. But, as yet, no one reenacts it.

In the early 1980s, before the reenactment of these more modern wars—and indeed, even before the Persian Gulf War itself—stories about the newly developing branch of World War II reenacting began to circulate among reenactors, just as news of the nascent World War I hobby had filtered into other reenacting periods. Dave Watkins, now a World War II reenactor for more than ten years, described his initial negative reaction to it in the early 1980s: "When I saw these World War II reenactors, I was aghast that people were doing such a thing." Twenty-six-year-old Scott Mies, who started reenacting Civil War at the age of fifteen and is currently an avid World War I German and World War II Russian reenactor, also remembers having a less than enthusiastic response: "I first heard people talk about [World War II reenacting] in Civil War. And I first swore that I would never do World War II because I saw it as being too close. Like uncomfortably close."

The idea that people actually dressed up as "Nazis" and "Commies" initially struck some as tasteless, but others were drawn to the World War II hobby out of frustration with other periods or because of a particular interest in World War II. In fact, for some, reenacting World War II was a longtime dream. Alain Benson says he "had always fantasized about wouldn't it be great if you could dress up in American uniforms or German uniforms and get together with a bunch of people and sort of reenact a battle and then be able to really feel like you are there?" But as far as Alain knew, no one reenacted World War II. He was reluctantly planning to get involved in Revolutionary War reenacting when he attended a fateful militaria show. "I went past a table on which a dealer had some flyers . . . promoting an upcoming World War II battle," Alain recalls. "And I was like, Wow, what is this? This is exactly what I been dreaming about for the last two years. This exists?"

Richard Paoletti, a member of Grossdeutschland since 1989 and a real-life fireman from New York, would have happily joined the hobby long before he did. In the 1970s, he was a high school student in New Jersey. A friend who had moved to California told him about a fascinating thing he'd seen: "He tells us,

American reenactors in combat, Vietnam reenactment (photograph by Bryan Grigsby)

you know, you wouldn't believe this, this guy I know out here he's got a VW Thing and he painted it like a *kubelwagon* and there's another guy out here with a half-track and they go running around in the woods and it's fantastic, they play army." Although Richard wondered if people in other places might also be doing such a thing, he dismissed it, thinking, "This must be something they do in California."

Richard was right. It was something "they" did in California. But it was also being done across the country and fast taking off because so many people shared the same interests. To use one participant's phrase, reenactors are "just people who love history." They describe the hobby as "fun," "interesting," and "challenging." It's a chance to experience something different, to "learn about history," and "to accurately and respectfully represent people from another time and place who struggled and sacrificed for something they believed in and to foster among ourselves a sense of connection with the past."

Like their predecessors, the veteran descendants, reenactors overwhelmingly describe their organizations as commemorative in nature. The official credo of the HRS, *more majorum* (in the tradition before us), is echoed by other reenacting groups. "We exist," the California Historical Group proclaims, "for the sole purpose of remembering and paying tribute to the combat soldier of World War II." It didn't take me long to learn that the hobby exists for many other reasons, too.

Chapter 3

"Something a Little Strange"

Belonging to the Hobby

After the Battle of the Bulge event, I found myself immersed in the hobby. One event led to another; reenactors introduced me to other reenactors; and before I knew it, my circle was growing rapidly. I continued to get to know reenactors I'd already met, such as Ray Sherman, Luke Gardner, Perry Trent, Ed Malthus, the Sharp brothers, John Loggia, and Scott Friewald. Through Tim Reed I met several other people I would come to know well over the years: Tim's best friend, thirty-two-year-old Paul Harding, a construction worker from Atlanta, and Hank and Wilson Lyle, two brothers in their late twenties, both computer programmers, who share a spacious house in North Carolina. Luke also introduced me to some of his close friends, including Dave Watkins, a chemist who lives with his wife in Alexandria, Virginia, and twenty-nine-year-old Tom Schultz, an antique dealer from Delaware. I also met many others on my own at events. Sam Benevento, a thirty-five-year-old father of two who works for the General Accounting Office, soon became a close friend. I also got to know Fred Legum, a twenty-eight-year-old engineer who lives in Maryland and reenacts World War I with a passion. Longtime reenactor Morris Call, a fortyish social worker from California with a wife and four children, became one of my most important informants. I also got to know many of the members of Grossdeutschland, including Philip Moss, a thirty-year-old machinist who lives in Philadelphia and has been reenacting World War I and II for many years, and Patrick Hart, a thirty-one-year-old artist from Baltimore. These and many other reenactors helped me to begin understanding the hobby. Soon I would see that reenacting is about much more than authentic uniforms, powerful guns, and massive tanks. It has a meaning and structure all its own.

The Question Why

Somewhere in New York City lives a forty-year-old investment banker who divides his time between a well-lit corporate office and the field of the reenacted battle. He is Larry Cohen, a dark-haired, heavyset man whose passion has always been history. As a kid, Larry says, he was something of a nerd. Upon first hearing about reenacting in the early 1970s, he begged his parents to rent him a soldier costume and take him to an event. They declined, so Larry had to wait until he was old enough to take himself. In 1976, at the age of fifteen, he joined a Civil War reenacting unit and began collecting militaria. After college, he earned a master's degree in history while his involvement in the hobby grew. In the late 1980s, he joined the World War I hobby, and eventually he was elected president of the GWA. A few years later, he helped found the World War II unit, the 4th Armored. In 1990, Larry, Luke Gardner, and a few others began orchestrating Vietnam War reenactments and Larry also became an avid Vietnam militaria collector.

Whenever I saw Larry, I was always struck by how well-spoken and polished he appears. He is smart and extremely gracious. But once he is among his reenacting buddies, Larry can be one of crassest and bawdiest jokesters I've ever known. He especially delights in reciting the most obscene limericks I have ever heard. Perhaps because Larry felt uncomfortable with my being around while he performed, it took more than a year before we established a friendship and he seemed to accept me. Once he did, though, he became generous in talking about his experiences.

When I asked Larry what sparked his interest in reenacting modern wars (he has long since dropped out of the Civil War hobby), he launched into recounting a vivid memory. As a teenager at a Civil War event, he remembers the first time he ever saw a reenactor wearing an original World War II uniform. But it wasn't just any uniform that caught his attention: it was a German one. Immediately, he says, he "wanted to do that." He sent away for a "Learn German" record from Berlitz, thinking that he should start working on authenticating his impression. His mother sent the record back. She was concerned that Larry would offend people by running around their predominantly Jewish neighborhood shouting in German. "She was probably right," Larry says, laughing. "It's hard to explain why your son's wearing a *Pickelhaube*"—a spike-topped helmet of the sort German soldiers once wore.

Larry eventually gave himself permission to wear a *Pickelhaube*, but the problem of explaining the attraction remained. He argues that a simple love of history underlies his desire to put on a uniform, but beyond that, he agrees that it's "tough to explain the dynamics of reenacting," as another reenactor admits. "There are so many various participants. Honestly, it's often like a historical version of a *Star Trek* convention."

The convention, in their case, is an "event," a private or public event that draws them together, bonded by an interest in war and history. And in fact, almost three-quarters of reenactors cite history in general or military history in particular as their main interest in reenacting. Yet one has only to peruse *TV Guide* or visit a bookstore to see that many people have similar interests. So what compels them to take their interest, as one reenactor says, "one step further"?

Initially, I would come right out and ask reenactors why. During my first World War I event, I stood on a hillside with Tim Reed and Jack Hunter, one of the founding members of the GWA. Dressed as a Turkish soldier, Jack was proudly showing off the details of his rare impression. (He was the only Turk I would ever see at a World War I event.) All seemed in good spirits, so I asked Jack why he reenacts. He looked at me keenly, paused, and said in what I took to be a Turkish accent, "Zey pay me salary. Plus feed me well. I get uniform and boots for my feet. Very good!" We all laughed, but I was confused. What I thought was a fairly routine question was one that reenactors seemed to have a hard time answering beyond the formulaic explanation that "it's commemorative" or "it's educational." With characteristically dry humor, Luke Gardner reacted to my query: "Why does a cat have wings? Why does a dog pee on the moon? I'm interested in the American soldier. What else do I have to say about that? It's just my area of interest." "Aw," Tim Reed sighed each time I pestered him to explain. "Reenactors are a bunch of weirdoes who never grew up. We like wearing uniforms! It's cool, man!" Richard Paoletti at least tried to give me a serious answer, but after reciting the conventional reasons he admitted: "*We* don't understand, even we have trouble within ourselves."

Reenactors may have a hard time explaining themselves, but they're the first to recognize their hobby's unusual character. During a heated discussion on the World War II reenactor newsgroup concerning the best way to present themselves to outsiders, one reenactor simply asserted that the hobby "is extremely difficult to advocate" since it has the capacity to rile nearly everyone. "How can you broadcast the true meaning and character of the hobby," he asked, "without having the Jewish community offended by the Germans, the ATF offended by the weapons, the media offended by the uniforms and battles, the Poles offended by the Russians and Germans, the Irish offended by the British?"

All reenactors know that the hobby can be hard to advocate, and they characterize it as a "fairly interesting subculture" or as a bit "unusual." John Loggia, a twenty-eight-year-old World War I and II reenactor who works in a private high school, believes that the hobby is simply "politically incorrect."

Twenty-five-year-old Michael Collins was new to the World War II hobby when I first met him in 1996. He had recently graduated from George Washington University and was trying to make it as a freelance journalist while working as research assistant in a Capitol Hill office. Quick with a smile, outgoing, and very friendly, Michael was exceptionally enthusiastic about the hobby; he was always talking about upcoming events, his plans to get new items for his kit, and various aspects of World War II history. But he feels uncomfortable sharing this enthusiasm with most outsiders, particularly his colleagues at work. When I asked him why, he laughed and said, "When people ask, 'What are you doing this weekend?' and I answer, 'Oh, I'm going to sleep in the woods and shoot guns,' it does sound really weird."

Ray Sherman doesn't care if it sounds weird, even though he admits that some people he knows "think I'm crazy to come out here, get all dirty and muddy, and the money you spend to do it." But Ray is one of nearly a third of reenactors who report often discussing the hobby with outsiders. "I probably bore some of them to death with it," Ray says. "Because, you see, I'm so excited about participating in these types of events that I want to share it with everybody."

In fact, some go as far as to promote their involvement, telling everyone they encounter that they're reenactors. "I'll be the first to stand up and admit that I *love* being able to act out the fantasy of being a German squad leader," one reenactor states. "I'm not embarrassed either—I think it's cool." Others think it's so cool that they openly feature the hobby in various aspects of their lives—on their personal Web pages, at their jobs, or in their homes. When I visited many reenactors, such as the Lyle brothers and Paul Donald, I was surprised to see that their homes were full of reenactor-related decor, such as displays of photographs from events or various types of militaria. Some even have entire floors devoted to the display of hobby-related paraphernalia, and, on the more extreme end, a few even attempt to "live" in the period they reenact. Walt Mark, an avid World War I reenactor, decorates his home in period German style, from his turn-of-the-twentieth century country kitchen to his field-gray bedspread with an iron cross in its center.

These reenactors are, however, atypical. Most are not so open about their hobby, and nearly all report mentioning being reenactors only "once in a while." "I didn't tell my girlfriend I did this for a long time," Luke joked. "She thought I was just going to get a pack of cigarettes." "It's my dirty little secret," German reenactor Patrick Hart says. But he admits that in some respects, such as dating, balancing his hobby and his real life can be tough. "If a woman wants to find out after we've been dating, fine," he says. "But right up front—it's a little—I've had girlfriends act adversely to it."

Aware of the potential for adverse reactions, reenactors often try to reduce the threat they seem to pose by referring to themselves as "kids playing with army toys." They also publish disclaimers in their unit flyers and on their Web pages, trying to distance themselves from more disturbing groups: "The members of the IR63 Living History unit are not affiliated with any racist, radical or right wing political movement, especially and including, the neo-Nazi movement. We are students of military science, not political science."

Nearly all insist they're "nonpolitical," and they agree that the hobby shouldn't be "a place to sound off on one's political agenda." They also insist that in doing their impressions "there is no change of persons. They are still Americans at heart." In fact, some reenactor organizations and units deny membership not only to known neo-Nazis but also to anyone belonging to any "un-American group." The 20th Century Tactical Studies Group, for instance, bars membership to those who "advocate the overthrow of the United States Government, participate in anti-Semitic activities, [or] belong to any communist, Nazi, or hate group."

"There's no politics," as Michael Collins says. "I've never discussed any politics. Just people who love history and want to take it one step further." This is especially true, they assert, in the case of World War II German reenactors. "It's important," one German reenactor argues, "that the public realizes that reenactors are not politically motivated, especially when someone has to play the bad guys' roles." Most others agree. "Most of the guys I've met that do World War II German," one American reenactor told me, "are doing it just for the history."

Still, the "just history" argument is hard to justify when wearing the uniform of an SS officer. Wouldn't reading a good memoir satisfy a simple interest in "just history?"

Longtime reenactor Alain Benson belongs to an SS unit. During our interview, which took place in the quiet of his apartment, we talked for several hours and he openly admitted that he doesn't quite know how to explain his attraction to the German soldier of World War II. He and his unit members, he said, "always have these conversations about why. You know, why, out of all the people, are we—why do we have this deep-rooted fascination with that subject matter?

Nothing else. Not interested in American. I'm not interested in British or Russian. . . . It's only German. It's the only one that appeals to me."

Alain's tone moved between sheer delight and intense seriousness as he showed me his photographs from events, explaining how offended he is whenever people confuse his dressing up as a Nazi with his being a Nazi. "Whenever I show people some of my photographs or videos people say to me, 'Wow, you're really into this, so are you a Nazi?' And I really take offense to that because obviously that's like the worst thing you can call somebody."

Insisting that he has "no connection at all with the ideology of the Nazis," Alain believes that it's "an uneducated assumption" to "stereotype" him as a one. "I never, ever look at it from a Nazi standpoint like I'm a Nazi or I like to act like a Nazi," he said emphatically. "For me, I don't associate any of that stuff with what *I'm* doing."

Many other reenactors make this same kind of distinction between who they "really" are and what they might wear for several weekends a year. Mark Sammons, a longtime member of Grossdeutschland, readily acknowledges how "awkward" it is to reenact German. But he also says, "I'm quite aware of what I'm doing and I'm an American." Many echo this refrain, and assert, as German reenactor Philip Moss does, "That is part of the unique wonderfulness that is America. We can all do what we want!"

Still, as American citizens who've chosen to express their freedom by wearing Nazi uniforms, it's hard to rely on a generic "freedom of expression" argument to explain themselves. But German reenactors aren't alone in recognizing how hard it is to get people to understand their hobby. For this reason, nearly 10 percent of reenactors say they "never" or "almost never" discuss reenacting with outsiders. Scott Friewald explains why: "The general public [thinks] we're like these political militias you hear about, or they think we're some kind of white supremacist groups. . . . So I just keep it quiet." Luke also keeps quiet since he doesn't want people "to immediately assume that I'm some kind of nut." He says, too, that he doesn't like people to know he's a gun owner; the only time people need to know you have a gun, he often quips, is right before you have to use it.

Because most reenactors think that outsiders are quick to "jump to conclusions," they restrict public access to their private events, guaranteed by the hobby's low profile as well as by "pre-registration-required" or "invitation-only" events. Although some believe that such careful guarding is being "paranoid," others think it's essential. One reenactor confided in me that he was certain the FBI had "infiltrated" the hobby on a number of occasions, trying to identify neo-Nazis. Many more are sure their names are on some "government list" somewhere. These are just a couple reasons many oppose outsiders in their midst—including me.

In 1997, after I had mailed my reenacting questionnaire to members of several World War II units and to the entire GWA membership, I was told that one reenactor, Leonard Lord, virulently protested the fact that I had been given the GWA mailing list. This came as no surprise, since I received a note from Leonard after he received my questionnaire: "I am definitely not interested in sharing my reasons for reenacting," he wrote. At the upcoming World War I event, the GWA president asked if I would talk to Leonard. "Just to let him know that you're on the up and up," he said. We were introduced. Leonard shook my hand, but said coldly, "I don't know you; I don't know what you'll write about us, so until you prove yourself in a positive light, I have to judge you negatively."

After this encounter I felt uneasy. I was concerned that there would be a lot more reenactors like Leonard who would make research difficult. John Loggia told me not to worry about it, and others assured me that Leonard was a jerk. But I still didn't feel better. It was true after all; I didn't know what I would write about them, and I actually understood Leonard's position well. For some reenactors sharing their hobby, even to the most well-intentioned outsider, is not an option.

Alain Benson's best friend, Greg Grosshans, is considered by many to be one of the best World War II German reenactors. A handsome man with a slight, slender build, Greg makes a striking picture when he's dressed in his German officer's uniform. His unit is small, tight-knit, and viewed by other reenactors as "top notch." When I first heard several 4th Armored members talk about the unit, I decided to try to interview some of the members. But when I approached them at an event, their response could not have been less inviting. Immediately, Greg ushered me over to their "PR" man, who gave me the standard line about their unit being "educational" and "historical." They were not, he told me, interested in granting interviews.

So I devised a different strategy. Knowing that Luke was friends with them and that they had a high opinion of the 4th Armored—the two units often hook up and host small events together—I asked Luke to call Greg and vouch for me. Luke's reputation had the desired effect—"Oh! You know Luke!"—and Greg agreed that I could visit him in his Philadelphia apartment.

When I arrived, I was amazed to learn about the extent of Greg's unwillingness to share his hobby, even in his own home. The place was nicely decorated, stylish and crisp. To the casual observer it looked like an average one-bedroom apartment inhabited by a single, twenty-eight-year-old professional. "Would you like something to drink?" Greg asked, assuming the role of charming host. He was chatty, friendly, and had a good sense of humor. But then he began a tour. He showed me how he hides all his reenactor gear so his apartment bears no trace of his interest in German soldiers: a secret back closet where he stores his German uniforms; decorative pictures in frames that flip around to reveal pictures of German soldiers.

When we sat down for the interview, Greg said that most of his closest friends outside the hobby, as well as his colleagues at the accounting firm where he works, have no idea that he's a reenactor. "It's bad enough to think that I collect Nazi regalia," he said. "It would be a thousand times worse if they knew that I actually dressed up as one and went in the field with blanks and stuff and did battle with the Americans or the Russians. . . . They'd think I'm a complete loony."

I was incredulous. Clearly Greg went to great lengths to reenact and to do it well, and yet he also went to great lengths to cover it up from outsiders. "So when you put on your uniform?" I began.

"I don't put it on here!" Greg interrupted. "That's for sure. Unless I do it in my room with all the windows closed."

"And then put an overcoat on over it?"

"Oh, I never leave the apartment with it on!" he exploded. "Never!" He explained that he always waits until he arrives at the site of an event before putting on his uniform.

"Look, if I walk down the street wearing one of my uniforms," he explained. "First of all, it would probably be considered a hate crime. There would be certain lawyers in [Philadelphia] that could say that me parading through [my neighborhood], which is predominantly Jewish, me parading with that uniform, I'm committing a hate crime by upsetting older folks that remember those uniforms from Germany or whatever."

But it wasn't enough for Greg to end there with his attempt to illustrate the danger he'd encounter by setting foot outside as a Nazi officer. He continued, "If I actually walked outside in that uniform, people would look at me—first they'd look to see if I was being filmed—Okay? Then they would just shout at me, throw stones at me, call the cops. I mean, come on, you could never do that!"

Not surprisingly, a lot of German reenactors share Greg's attitude, and they, too, never appear in uniform beyond the borders of a private event. As one reenactor remarks, "Most people are naturally stupid and will jump to conclusions since they have no clue as to what reenacting is. In the Northeast, civilians find Rev War 'interesting,' [but] anyone that would wear a German uniform is a f^&*'n Nazi."

But Greg also has another reason to keep private: "I don't want the public exposure," he said, explaining why he doesn't attend the public events that most reenactors go to, such as living history encampments. "I don't want it to be [that] somehow this gets shown on 60 Minutes and then [my co-workers] happen to see me dressed up and then there goes my job." Others with jobs that might be jeopardized by the hobby—an SS reenactor who is a real officer in the US Army, for instance—also keep quiet. In fact, many report that they fear that their involvement in the hobby could impede their careers if their superiors found out about it. As Luke struggles to work his way into the academic world after graduate school, he worries that the hobby is "regarded as unprofessional" among historians and academics, and therefore, he keeps it secret.

Having a "secret" life, though, doesn't seem all bad. In fact, I often thought that reenactors enjoy the bit of intrigue that having a marginal hobby grants them. Putting on a uniform—whether the uniform of a World War I American soldier or an SS soldier—without obvious and culturally sanctioned reasons (being filmed, for example) is, after all, a kind of rebellious act. Those who do it are in some ways committing a kind of social violation by consciously choosing to do something that many people would judge as crazy, upsetting, or, at the very least, a little weird. Some reenactors even admit to being drawn by this aspect. "A lot of guys like being the 'bad boys,'" one World War II German reenactor explains. "A lot of us always liked to be the Indians whenever everybody else wanted to be cowboys. Maybe a psychotherapist could make something of that, but all in all, I suspect it's innocent rebellion."

One thirty-seven-year-old World War II reenactor I talked with has a similar sense of rebellion. After nearly two decades serving as a police officer, he says that he feels tremendous constraints and pressures in his job. But when he goes off for a weekend and assumes his role as an American World War II sergeant, he gets a kind of fulfillment in "acting out" (even if only play-acting) in a way that would never be allowed in his professional world. Greg Grosshans also claims that there is a benefit to being a secret "bad guy." "Do you feel like you're defying something when you put on that uniform?" I asked him. "Well," he answered. "There is a sort of a pleasure putting it on and knowing how shunned and despised it would be and how upset people would be by it."

Clearly reenacting provides a certain degree of pleasure. Some reenactors even enjoy venturing into a public place, such as a restaurant, dressed in uniform. A few World War II German reenactors occasionally gather at German restaurants in uniform, always calling ahead to check if it's okay. And each year, World War I reenactors in the Washington metropolitan area host a period dinner at the 94th Aero Squadron, a restaurant in Maryland with World War I decor. Whenever I attended that dinner, I felt strange when I'd notice other patrons staring at us, probably wondering what play we were performing in; but I got the sense that the other reenactors rather enjoyed causing a bit of a stir.

But aside from the pleasure they may experience occasionally, just as often, reenactors get uncomfortable. One afternoon Patrick Hart was busy repairing his *schemel* (a German footstool) when an old high school pal, Mike, dropped by unexpectedly. Mike, who is Jewish, had only a vague understanding of Patrick's hobby, and certainly did not know that Patrick reenacted as a Grossdeutschland private. So, for about an hour Mike chatted while Patrick sweated, worrying that Mike would lift the stool that lay only a few feet from him and see the small swastika painted underneath it.

The view of the hobby as bizarre, silly, or unprofessional is not held only by outsiders. "There's a lot of criticism [I] could level at myself. You know?" Mark Sammons admits of his own involvement in the hobby. "Like this is ridiculous. This fifty-year-old guy going out to play dress-up!" Greg Grosshans agrees: "I personally think there is something a little strange, maybe just a little strange, with this hobby. Okay, and maybe it's because I've been brainwashed so much by the media that I'm being forced to think this. But I think it's a little strange that I am into this, and wearing the uniform. Okay? So I don't want people to accept it. The best formula that I've found is apathy."

Others echo this desire for public apathy. As one reenactor says, "I like the fact that it is a 'private' hobby." About 7 percent of the reenactors I surveyed believe that it's "very unimportant" or "not important at all" for people to understand or learn about reenacting, and nearly 12 percent think they should always maintain strict privacy since "reenacting is a personal serious hobby and not a show."

But whether reenactors reveal their involvement or shroud it in secrecy, most believe that they're misunderstood. Many think that the public is underinformed about reenacting, while many more think that the public is *both* misinformed and underinformed. (Of the respondents to my questionnaire, fewer than 3 percent believe that the public is accurately informed about reenacting.) And most say that they think that it is important for people to understand or know about the hobby. As one reenactor says, "I think it is important to know that all reenactors are not warmongers, that reenactors are fairly 'normal' people." Ted Morse laughed as he commented, "We're not a total bunch of wackos. Maybe a little eccentric. But we're pretty harmless."

The desire for people to view them as harmless is one reason, I believe, that so many reenactors were willing to talk to me. They seemed to see me as a way to get the real story of reenacting out to the public, and perhaps even to champion their cause. As Scott Friewald says, "People don't understand [reenacting] and it's hard for them to understand. I think they see it as grown men playing dress up and going off and playing Cowboys and Indians. And they don't realize the level of our commitment to researching and understanding the times we portray, and the level of our interest and passion for history."

Reenactors may largely feel misunderstood, but they shore up their group bonds with a shared understanding: there's no need to explain why *you're* wearing a *Pickelhaube* when the ten guys you're with are wearing the same thing. "People who reenact have a certain bond," as one reenactor explains. "We're all doing something we have a huge interest in and when we get together. . . . You forget about your present-day woes." This is just one reason reenactors often say that after joining the hobby, they feel like they belong to a "family."

"The Tip of What We Do": Being a Reenactor

Even after more than two decades of expansion, members of the family of reenacting belong to a somewhat disparate enterprise. The GWA branch of World War I reenacting is often judged as the best organized, while World War II reenacting—the larger of the two periods—is splintered. Luke describes the hobby as being "led by whoever will lead it," while another reenactor thinks that it has "too many tribes and too many chiefs." Meanwhile, the reenactment of more modern wars, such as the Korean and Vietnam wars, is far less organized, made up of small units that are usually satellites of other groups, usually World War II units. Such satellites are run independently of any larger organization and thus usually host very small-scale events or living history displays.

Without any official national organization to oversee its many members, the hobby constitutes a loosely organized network of an estimated six thousand reenactors belonging to units across the country. Arguably, the East Coast is the most active reenacting region, followed by the Midwest. But the Southwest, the West, and the South all seem to be growing. Thus, the hobby takes on different regional identities, with units operating in localized areas and only coming together for large events such as the biannual GWA reenactments or the annual Battle of the Bulge. Although many dream of hosting a major national event—a kind of reenacting "Super Bowl," as one reenactor put it—they recognize that they "still have a long way to go in communication."

Communication among reenactors is indeed highly informal; it takes place in person and over the telephone. Units communicate through newsletters where lists of upcoming events, available equipment and uniforms, event and book reviews, veterans' accounts, and a host of other reenacting-related information are available. But since the mid-1990s, when the hobby entered the cyber age in earnest, the Internet has become their central means of communication. Many groups and units maintain Web pages and a variety of email subscriber newsgroups devoted to reenacting now operate. (In 1996 the first of these newsgroups, the World War II reenacting newsgroup, went online, and today it boasts more than four hundred subscribers.)

Despite their loose organization, twentieth-century reenactors share a particular identity in the reenacting world. Whether they join and quit different units or remain members of the same unit for twenty years, they move within a well-defined, highly intimate circle, mingling with many of the same people and getting to know one another well. It's not only their interest in history that unites them and intensifies their connection, but also their desire to reenact more modern wars.

Most twentieth-century war reenactors are primarily loyal to the two world wars. A majority (nearly 60 percent) reenacts only twentieth-century wars. Almost 70 percent identify themselves as World War I reenactors; 80 percent identify themselves as World War II reenactors; just over 10 percent also identify themselves as Vietnam War reenactors; and a tiny number—about 2 percent—add Korean War to the list. Most claim that their favorite reenacting period is one of the two world wars, while the Civil War hobby, most popular nationwide, ranks only third in popularity among twentieth-century war reenactors, with less than 10 percent declaring it their favorite. In fact, of those who begin reenacting in the Civil War hobby, about two-thirds cease reenacting that period altogether after joining the twentieth-century war hobby.

Although there is a lot of crossover between World War I and World War II reenacting, each period has its own reputation. World War I reenacting is seen as slightly more refined, and those who reenact it are viewed as a bit more cerebral in their interests. Meanwhile, the World War II hobby sometimes suffers from the reputation of drawing "yahoos" into it, or those who just want to fight without a true interest in history.

Still, the collective emphasis on the privacy of their tactical events separates twentieth-century war reenacting from Civil War—many call it "Silly War"—reenacting, which is mocked because of its popular appeal, low authenticity, crowd mentality, and family orientation. "Unlike World War I and World War II reenactments," Luke Gardner says of Civil War events, "a man can bring his wife along, his kids can become involved, it can become a family affair. Almost to the point of the battle aspect of it being ridiculously deemphasized." Now exclusively a World War I and II reenactor, Fred Legum unhappily "dabbled" in Rev War and Civil War before finding his home in the twentieth-century war hobby. He remembers that Civil War "began to get away from living history and more into an audience participation thing and . . . they started allowing women to fight too . . . and it just didn't sit right with me. And I'm extremely liberal, et cetera, et cetera. But something about that just bothered me."

Unlike the "spectacles" of many Civil War events, with their crowds of spectators and "camp followers" (women and children reenactors), twentieth-century war reenacting is a comparatively private and largely male hobby. Very few women and no children participate in private events. To many reenactors, that is precisely how it should be. Further, their interest in modern war not only sets them apart from Civil War reenactors but also, to some, makes their hobby better, more challenging, and more interesting. Being able to talk with veterans gives them the sense that they are more authentic in their impressions; they also have a greater wealth of sources such as films and photographs, which makes their hobby more demanding. William Gregory compares joining the Civil War hobby with joining World War II: "When you go to a Civil War event . . . you simply go to a sutler's tent and whip out the old American Express, buy your complete kit, and go right into battle. We don't have the ease of buying our equipment off the shelf."

To be sure, becoming a twentieth-century war reenactor is not always easy. Not just anyone can show up at an event and join in. Instead, a reenactor must become a member of an individual reenacting unit, since "free-lancing" (participating in an event without being part of a unit) is frowned upon, if not prohibited. Just as I did when I met GWA reenactors at the World War I history conference, a potential recruit must first make contact with reenactors and make a case for joining a given unit before becoming a reenactor. But given the hobby's low profile, finding it, never mind joining it, can be difficult.

Of the reenactors I surveyed, few said they learned about the hobby through a public format, such as seeing an event announcement or a story in the press. Some found it by attending a public event where units often recruit new members. Others found it through a related hobby, collecting militaria. But most simply discovered it by coincidence: "I saw a US Army World War II half-track driving down a road. So I followed it and asked the driver about what he was doing." Another says that he "saw a kid at school wearing a uniform jacket and talked to him."

In a fairly typical example, Luke Gardner, an avid marksman, was looking to buy an M1 Garand rifle in 1989. Through a contact at his shooting range, he first heard about a World War II reenacting unit and thought, "Aha, I bet these reenactors . . . know where to get Garand rifles inexpensively." So, as he remembers, "I called the fellow up—and now he's a very dear friend of mine—but we hit it off pretty early on and he took me to my first World War II reenactment. He was forming a new unit at that time."

Thirty-year-old Laura Paris, the mother of two small children, portrays a male soldier in a World War II German unit based in Maine. She was one of about fifteen women staying in the women's barracks during my third Bulge event. We had a chance to sit down for an hour and talk about her experiences in the hobby. She explained how tough it was to get into the hobby, even though she was aware that it existed. Eventually, she found her unit through a series of contacts: "There was a fellow who did Civil War, who also did Rev War, who knew a friend who did World War II. And he put me in touch with the World War II people back in '85. And I called them up and I've been with them ever since."

With such a complicated network to navigate, it's no surprise that more than a third join the hobby because a friend or relative is already involved; hence the preponderance of brothers, sons and fathers, coworkers, and childhood friends within units. For some, the hobby is a legacy granted by an older relative—"I was born into it. My father reenacts," as one reenactor reports—or a novel enterprise introduced by younger relatives: "My two sons were reenactors before I became one," another explains.

In the hobby's first decades, most recruits came to the twentieth-century hobby from other reenacting periods, particularly the Civil War. But recently, especially since the Internet has afforded a broader means of communication, more reenactors join the twentieth-century hobby without any previous reenacting experience. About a third of twentieth-century war reenactors received their "baptism of fire" by attending a World War II reenactment as their first event, and 14 percent attended a World War I event, the least public-oriented of all, as their first reenactment ever. This new entry trend prompted Grossdeutschland members to coin a term to describe these newcomers: "Dietz reenactors," named after Private Dietz, a character in Sam Peckinpah's World War II film *Cross of Iron*, who is a decidedly green soldier.

Although reenactors enter the hobby as young as nine or as old as sixty-three, on average, they start reenacting in their twenties. At the time I conducted my questionnaire, however, most were older than thirty, with the average age being thirty-eight. Echoing the concern of one reenactor who observes a "lack of new and young people joining the hobby," some encourage an influx of young recruits

A GI reenactor poses

into a hobby seen as getting progressively older. "Getting younger kids (17–19) involved is a good thing," one reenactor believes, "it grows the hobby, adds authenticity (fat old guys were not on the battlefields of France) and creates more opportunities for unit growth. I'm in favor of it."

But others are against opening up to all comers. "I don't want some irresponsible Generation Xer with a machine gun near me! Screw that!" Philip Moss claims. Like others, Philip believes that as the hobby expands, it shouldn't become like "Silly War." These reenactors like the fact that the hobby is private, and they argue that mechanisms for controlling membership and screening recruits should be strengthened. Luke, for instance, interviews all potential 4th Armored members, while the 1st Panzer Division reports that it accepts only a "limited number of applicants." Other units choose not to expand at all. Fred Legum, commander of a World War I British unit, explains: "We don't really actively recruit because we're more interested in having a small group of hardcore guys that are really tight knit and really into what they're doing, rather than have thirty guys bumbling about."

Members of a particular unit are often geographically dispersed. For example, most 4th Armored members live in Pennsylvania, New York, and New Jersey, but the unit also boasts members from as far away as Florida, Georgia, and California. Fred Legum's unit members reside all the way "from Indiana to Massachusetts." Still, most units are indeed bound by a tight-knit nature, and nearly all reenactors strongly identify with their units. Fourth Armored member Mark Lance refers to the unit as a "brotherhood," while Ed Malthus calls fellow 4th members his "extended family."

Units range in size from the larger, such as Grossdeutschland, which has one hundred and thirty members, to the smaller, comprising anywhere from two to twenty members. All adopt actual historical units as the models for their unit impressions, and each is founded at will, since forming a unit requires little more than declaring that one has done so. In the GWA, controlled by a band of elected officers, units must be officially admitted. But in World War II, they form without official clearance, which translates into a replication of unit impressions: There are currently five 82nd Airborne units and six 9th SS units active in the World War II hobby.

In terms of overall unit impressions—as opposed to individual impressions—there is a broad range, including Russian, German, Italian, French, British, Australian, Canadian, and American units. Korean and Vietnam War reenactors mainly portray American units, but reenactors also do North Korean and National Liberation Front (Vietcong) impressions. In both world wars, American and Allied units are the most popular, with German units coming in second.

Units are formed by a single person who has an interest in a particular impression or by a group of already connected reenactors. Scott Friewald explains that 4th Armored was formed by an "informal group" who met reenacting World War I and started hosting exclusive Vietnam events with a handful of people. This "conglomeration of friends" decided to form a World War II armored unit, and since "the 4th Armored [has] a stellar reputation in history," Scott says, "we decided to do that unit."

Units also earn their own reputations and are seen as having distinct personalities and ways of behaving. Some units earn the disreputable reputation of being farby, while many of the most respected units have been around longest, such as the World War I unit 3 Kompanie/IR (Infanterie Regiment) 63, founded in 1978, and Grossdeutschland, founded in 1976. Such units often link up with other like-minded units to host or attend events. The 4th Armored and Grossdeutschland consider themselves sister units; one British World War I unit also has a sister unit in England.

Most units are run with an established hierarchy and rank, like the real military. Most unit members serve as privates, and "newbies" are usually put on probationary status for their first few events. Usually, reenactors rise through the unit ranks and are promoted only after proving themselves. Unit officers or "commanders" are appointed or elected by unit members. (Luke, for instance, didn't start out as "LT"; his title and position as unit officer were bestowed upon him only after he helped plan what many recall as one of the best events they'd ever attended, a small Vietnam event. The other reenactors thought he'd done such a terrific job that they gave him command of 4th Armored.) Once a unit officer is appointed, he serves with a cadre of NCOs. Collectively, they're responsible for the unit at events. They also oversee other aspects of unit operations, such as planning the calendar, establishing authenticity standards, training members, collecting dues, and keeping members informed. More highly organized units have written constitutions, mission statements, and nonprofit status. They host training, drilling, and safety exercises and provide introductory packages for newbies, including unit standards, reading lists, and unit histories. And many strictly oversee initiation of new recruits. "After you sign up," one World War I unit tells potential recruits, "a sponsor will be assigned to you and he, along with unit leaders, will guide you through the processes of becoming a Great War reenactor—and a participant in a truly unique experience in a unique hobby." Other units are much less structured. While they usually have a command structure, they are less strict about procedures and sometimes allow members to grant themselves rank depending on the impressions they choose. "We just put on whatever uniform we think looks best," Greg Grosshans, *Obersturmbannfuehrer* of his SS unit, explains. "We fulfill our fantasies. If I want to wear a Knight's Cross, which is like the highest medal, the guys let me wear it. I go as the officer. Mostly because I have the uniform."

Especially for a newbie, obtaining an authentic uniform can be a challenge.

And putting together a kit is itself a rite of passage. Depending on the unit, new members are told what to buy or loaned a basic kit for their first event, and then they gradually put their own kits together. Grossdeutschland explains its process of kitting out a new member: "Our philosophy is simple: we 'guide' the new Dietz, but he has to do all the work. We support his efforts with our *'Alter Hase'* [old hand] program, in which an old hand who lives near this new person will guide him in his purchases. We suggest . . . the books [to read] so he can do his research. Now, when his kit is complete, he then will appreciate putting it together himself."

The choice of which unit a reenactor joins is not casually made. Like their predecessors, members of veteran-descendant organizations, most reenactors have familial connections with a martial past: Over 80 percent have relatives who served in the wars they reenact. A little more than 10 percent have relatives who served in the Vietnam War; 10 percent have relatives who served in the Korean War; more than 30 percent have relatives who served in World War I, a percentage topped only by those with relatives who served in World War II, at over 60 percent. Specifically, more than a third report having grandfathers who served in World War I or World War II, and just over one quarter report having fathers who served in World War II or the Korean War. Often, reenactors choose their units based on these personal connections. Peter Nathan, owner of several World War II tanks, joined 4th Armored in part to honor—but not portray—his uncle, a 4th Armored soldier who was killed in action in France in 1944. Luke, whose grandfather served in World War II, favors American impressions "because I am an American," he explains, "and I think that gives me insight. . . . I'm an Americanist."

Not all reenactors are "Americanists," however. Most of their relatives fought for the United States in both world wars, but others fought for Australia, Austria, Germany, Czechoslovakia, the Soviet Union, Hungary, France, Ireland, Poland, and Great Britain. The reason Ted Morse is most interested in doing World War I German is easy to explain: he "had three uncles that were in the German Army." Twenty-six-year-old Scott Mies's grandparents fled the Holocaust in Austria (his grandfather was one of thirty thousand Jews imprisoned in Dachau following *Kristallnacht* and was released only after agreeing to leave the country immediately). Scott's great-grandmother and great-uncle both perished at the hands of the Germans. Scott portrays a Russian soldier of "the Great Patriotic War," as he calls World War II. For World War I, he portrays a German soldier—two impressions his grandparents gave him permission to do. (Scott's personal legacy is not unmatched in the hobby. The mother and father of another reenactor, Donald Kiev, also fled the Holocaust in Europe.)

To be sure, though "not everyone reenacts to honor ancestors," as one re-enactor observes. Many reenactors choose impressions based on legacies more imagined than real. Among them are third-generation Americans, children of Greek immigrants, who portray British soldiers of World War I; fifth generation Americans of Irish ancestry who do World War II German; and first-generation Americans, whose parents emigrated from Portugal, who portray American soldiers from both world wars. Hans Gruber, a telephone company worker from New York, commands a highly respected World War II German unit. I was shocked to learn that his real name is Paul Pennetoni and his German ancestry entirely fabricated. On a similar note, although hailing from Italian American stock, John Loggia calls himself an "anglophile," "obsessed" by the subject of British participation in World War I. His obsession is most clearly expressed at events where he speaks using an "affected upper class accent" while "his men" address him by his made-up name, Captain Harlon.

Others choose impressions because their friends belong to certain units or because of their degree of difficulty. (World War I French and World War II Italian are two impressions considered challenging since items are scarce in the United States.) Others pick an impression out of pure fascination. "A lot of re-enactors do SS because it's neat, bad, scary, and they were top-notch soldiers," as one reenactor observes. Patrick Hart claims the reason he does World War II German is purely aesthetic: "All women," he explains, "love the Italians in World War II. They have the most attractive uniforms. But men love the German stuff. Visually, German impressions are the most striking. Their uniforms, equipment, all of it's the best looking."

Patrick's comment is echoed by many others: the Germans simply "looked" better and conveyed more power with their high boots, intimidating helmets, and well-cut tunics. Meanwhile, most uniforms worn by the Allies—heavy olive-drab wool uniforms, for example—were designed to be efficient, not flattering.

Many reenactors consciously avoid specific impressions—the most obvious being a World War II German impression. Ed Malthus would "never ever" do World War II German for many reasons, not least of which is because he is Jewish. And Michael Collins wouldn't do anything but an American impression since to do otherwise, especially German, would be like "spitting" on his US Marine veteran uncle's grave. Another reenactor, who describes himself as an Irish Catholic, says, "putting on a British uniform [would] never happen!" And still others say they'd never do Russian impressions since they regard Communists with a decidedly hostile perspective.

Many reenactors stick with a single impression for years and years. Others

World War I British officer impression

have what they call their "primary impressions" (those they do most often), but they also dabble in other periods and have multiple "secondary impressions." John Loggia, for instance, occasionally adopts his secondary impression as a 4th Armored World War II private and has also served in Luke's cavalry unit to "do the Nam." But John considers the British World War I unit he's been with for nearly a decade his priority and his British officer's impression his "primary impression." Luke Gardner's role as LT in 4th Armored is his primary impression, but he also does a World War I private in the US 27th Division and a private in the World War II Russian Guards, along with serving as commander of his Vietnam unit. Others have even more "secondary impressions." One such reenactor is referred to as "Mr. Impression of the Week"; another calls this behavior "flavor of the month reenacting." Paul Harding, for example, loves to "get into" different periods and impressions. Since starting out in the Civil War hobby with his brother, he gave up Civil War and joined a World War II German paratrooper unit. Next, he started doing one of the GWA's fastest-growing impressions—the French—and now makes two twelve-plus-hour drives annually to the Newville site to kit out as a *poilu*. Along with these two primary impressions, he also does World War II Italian, Spanish Civil War, and Rev War and is currently trying to form a World War II *Volksturm* unit—a German unit made up of elderly men, women, children, and former soldiers otherwise unfit for combat.

Others make less frequent transitions from units over time, sometimes even switching sides entirely. Hank and Wilson Lyle, the brothers from North Carolina, started reenacting World War II as teenagers in the early 1980s, both portraying American soldiers. In the 1990s, however, they formed the 6th Fallschirmjaeger unit with several old friends, portraying World War II German paratroopers. Tom Schultz had been reenacting Civil War many years before entering the twentieth-century hobby. For World War II he does an American correspondent impression in the 4th Armored, and for a while he served as a private in a World War I German unit. But after seeing Peter Weir's movie *Gallipoli*, he became intrigued by the Australians. In 1987, Tom formed the GWA's first Australian unit, the 5th BN AIF (ANZAC). The Aussie ranks quickly grew, but Tom, disenchanted with his role of commander, left the unit after nearly a decade, purchased a German machine gun, and went back to the other side.

Because, as reenactors explain, they're always still "themselves" even in adopting impressions and not portraying someone else, the penchant for switching sides, changing units, and doing various impressions is not viewed as shifting their fundamental identities or characters. I often saw it as a bit like being involved in athletics, where a player may choose to try another position, join a new team, or even take up an entirely new sport while still remaining an athlete. For many, the freedom and variety the hobby affords is an attractive feature, and the challenge of putting together a new impression is one that many reenactors enjoy most.

Being a reenactor is not cheap. The cost of putting together a "starter" (first) impression, which includes a basic uniform and equipment, ranges from roughly four hundred to a thousand dollars. Further, all event hosts charge gate fees ranging from five to seventy-five dollars; and units and organizations usually charge annual membership fees. Add to these costs expenditures for ammo, travel, food, and purchases of more specialized equipment or detailed items for impressions, and the cost can rise dramatically. But the money reenactors spend depends on several factors, ranging from the number of periods they reenact to their desire to "upgrade" an impression or begin a new one. The highest sum a reenactor reported having spent in one year on the hobby was $25,000; the lowest was nothing. Between these two numbers, the sums span a wide spectrum: Almost half spend less than fifty dollars a month on all hobby-related expenses, while just over 10 percent spend more than two hundred dollars each month.

Not surprisingly, the cost of being a reenactor largely depends on how many events a reenactor attends. On average, a reenactor attends four to five events a year. Among the more diehard participants, a third attends one event or more each month. For example, Luke's average annual participation includes five World War II events, two World War I events, two Vietnam events, and usually at least two public events. Despite this large number of events, Luke claims: "I don't do it as much as some people. I don't want to burn out."

Luke refers to reenactor "burnout" as PRSD (post-reenactment stress disorder), a term he coined as a play on the real combat-fatigue syndrome, PTSD (posttraumatic stress disorder). And burnout can easily occur, given the time a single event requires for preparation, attendance, and recovery. "Reenacting is really fun," as Dave Watkins says. "But it's also a tremendous strain on people in terms of money and in terms of time and commitment." For many, the commitment required involves much more than simply showing up at events. As one reenactor observes, "reenacting is only the tip of what we do." For Fred Legum, attending more than two World War I events each year would be an unwelcome burden; it takes him three months to get ready for a single event, since he makes as many as sixteen hundred (fake) grenades. When I asked him how he feels afterward, he said: "Exhausted. All my uniform and kit plopped in the collection room and it just sits there for a few weeks. . . . It's pretty draining."

Nearly 70 percent of reenactors report that they spend the same amount of time or more time on the reenacting hobby than they spend on their other hobbies. Of the top ten hobbies other than reenacting that they report, all but two (fishing and music) are related, in some fashion, to reenacting. (For the handful of bagpipers and big band musicians in the hobby, even music is a hobby related to reenacting.) Many spend time at flea markets and militaria and gun shows searching for items to add to their kits or collections, some of which are valued in the tens of thousands of dollars. ("I have about fifty firearms and thirty complete uniforms and everything that goes along with it," as Fred Legum says.

"Not blowing my own horn, but I've seen some museums that I would probably outshine.") Others focus on perfecting recipes for authentic food to serve in the field or making reproduction paybooks, identity cards, or, as Luke does, V-mail; some spend time preparing for public events, like air shows, while others attend veterans' reunions and conventions. Many GD members, for example, travel to Germany annually to visit veterans. Other reenactors study foreign languages, especially German and Russian, to authenticate their impressions. A few re-enactors, such as Morris Call and Craig Bass, run militaria businesses in addition to their "real" jobs as a social worker and a musician, respectively. And still others invest time researching their impressions. Alain Benson traveled to Germany to study period war photographs in the Bundesarchiv, or federal archive, while Tim Gilbert, a World War II reenactor and unit commander, always makes a special trip to the National Archives when on business in Washington.

Reenactors often refer to their involvement in the hobby as their "addiction." And once they get hooked, most either maintain or increase their initial level of participation, often reporting a kind of snowball effect to their hobby-related activities. "You can get addicted," one reenactor concedes. "I'm trying to cut back and get involved with something less so—like shooting heroin!"

Even with reenacting being as addictive as a drug, some find that they have to scale back their participation because of work and family. Single reenactors, who constitute about a third of all reenactors, reportedly have less trouble getting away on weekends, while those who get "married and have children," as Richard Paoletti explains, are "reduced to what we call Gappers. They only come out to the Gap once a year. That's about all they do. That's all they're allowed to do." Inevitably, after a reenactor announces a wedding, the joke is, "How much are you asking for your kit?" Paul Donald explains a typical evolution: "I remember seeing people out there eighteen, nineteen years old, gung-ho four or five years and then all of a sudden, they get married and then they disappear." And sometimes, he adds, after a divorce they reappear.

Compared to the general US population, reenactors are married at a lower than average percentage and have a slightly higher than average rate of divorce— a little over 10 percent are divorced or separated. They sometimes joke about the fact that there are so many single men in the hobby, saying that they've never grown up and are "too immature" to get married. But jokes aside, a lot of them believe that reenacting, perhaps more than other hobbies, can cause trouble in relationships. "They drive their wives crazy," Laura Paris says, "and sometimes marriages break up because of it." Even reenactors with strong marriages or relationships have trouble with partners complaining that they go away too many weekends, spend too much money on new "toys," or become too consumed by the hobby. "I think my wife's about to flip out," Dave Watkins says, describing how his house has become overrun with his reenactor gear. Patrick O'Hara admits that his wife "thinks I'm completely out of my mind" for even being a reenactor, and one reenactor once told me that he wouldn't be able to go to an event because his wife was livid over his frequent absences. Even though Fred Legum's wife "thinks it's a little weird," luckily, she doesn't object. "It makes me happy," Fred says, "and that's all that matters. She never complains if I want to get a new toy for the collection. She's even helped me make hand grenades for events, which is pretty good."

For many, having a partner who accepts the hobby is vital. At least three couples I know, husbands and wives, reenact together, but more often it is the husband or boyfriend who leaves his female partner behind to attend events. (Reenactors often joke about how their wives can't get too jealous or upset when they leave for a weekend to hang out with a bunch of other guys.)

Grossdeutschland member Richard Paoletti explains how he broached the subject of his addiction to a new girlfriend. He told her, "I like to dress up like a German soldier and go away for weekends two or three times a year." When she asked if he was a Nazi, he said no, he just liked to dress up as one. "Do you have any problem with that?" Richard asked her. "No," she responded, "I have no problem."

Richard was ecstatic. "It is so important," he says. "I enjoy it so much." But he says he knows plenty of others who aren't so lucky. "A good friend of mine hasn't been out for over a year and a half," he complains, "and it's all because of his fiancée." Like other reenactors who argue that they shouldn't be bossed around by anyone, especially when it comes to the hobby, Richard laments: "Why do you get into a relationship where you're not allowed to do what you're into doing? You know, why is it even open for discussion? . . . Why don't you put the pants on for once?"

In fact, for some reenactors, their involvement in the hobby isn't open for discussion. Greg Grosshans says that he could never date anyone who had a problem with his hobby, since it "just would never work out." Another reenactor, who remains a bachelor in his fifties, broke off a serious engagement because his fiancée expected him to quit the hobby after they married. Sadly, marriages do fall apart because of the hobby. One longtime World War I reenactor, who initially assured me that his recent divorce was not the result of reenacting, later admitted that his wife left him because he'd become entirely obsessed with reenacting "the Great War."

World War II German impression

Spending too much time (and money) on the hobby is a complaint reenactors level at themselves. "It probably is addictive behavior," Scott Friewald agrees, but he has a rationalization: "I don't drink. I don't gamble. I don't do drugs. So this is an addiction that I have [that is] harmless and there's actually good coming out of it. I think reenacting is something positive that you can be involved in, rather than something negative."

Because of the time, money, and commitment required by the hobby, many view it as more than a casual pastime. It is both a culmination and combination of interests, unparalleled by any other hobby. As one reenactor says, "No other hobbies I've tried have affected me in this way." Others describe the hobby as a "life experience," or, as one reenactor, a pastor in a Lutheran church, observes, a "religion." "I have traveled to many places all over the world due to my hobby," another asserts. "I have met many interesting and diverse people. It has helped me define my political views and my convictions to my family, church, friends, and country. It has made me think and be motivated."

Coming together voluntarily to participate in their decidedly odd and addictive hobby, the family of reenactors is bound by an unstated understanding, a strong sense of unity, and many similarities. But they also have a number of differences as well. "There are as many different motives for being a reenactor," as Dave Watkins aptly observes, "as there are reenactors."

Chapter 4

"I Lead Two Completely Separate Lives"

Membership in the Hobby

"There are many interesting, creative, and intelligent people in this hobby and I've made some good friends," one reenactor wrote, responding to my questionnaire. "There are also many crybabies and people who need to develop lives outside reenacting. Most reenactors are too conservative for my tastes, including a few right-wing nut cases. Overall, the people are pretty cool, though."

Reenactors often describe the hobby as "a big brotherhood" in which "we all have something in common." Many even champion other reenactors as "the most intelligent, talented, imaginative, and dedicated people" they've ever met. But I was surprised to find out that participation in the hobby doesn't translate into universal fraternity. In fact, reenactors often describe the vast majority of other reenactors in broad and not always complimentary terms: crybabies, right-wing nutcases.

"Losers," Greg Grosshans calls most other reenactors, while Luke often refers to reenactors as "dilettantes," or, in less generous moods, "degenerates." This penchant for referring to the group negatively—while making exceptions for oneself and one's own circle of friends, of course—took me by surprise. I thought reenactors would view themselves with a kind of one-for-all attitude. But this was only the first hint of animosity among them.

"I don't know if you've noticed this or not," Donald Kiev, a fifty-year-old cosmetic surgeon from Potomac, Maryland, said to me in an almost conspiratorial tone, "but there are some rather marginal cases in the hobby. You know, guys who like guns, like war, and they're kind of living on the edge. They're not particularly well-read or informed about history, and they look at the hobby as a good old boys' club—a chance to shoot guns, drink beer, and play army."

"Do you think all reenactors are like that?" I asked, knowing that this was one stereotype of them.

"Oh, no," Donald said. "Not at all. See, there are lots of different types in the hobby. You get all kinds. I often see it as a microcosm of human society. All different walks of life."

Indeed. I soon learned that most reenactors view the entire group of reenactors as somewhat fractured and extremely diverse. "Heroes, zeroes, and belly-full-of-beer-os," Patrick Hart said and laughed as he offered a title for this book. "Gay, straight, married, single," another reenactor repeatedly said to me, describing the range of reenactors. Many others echo this refrain. "It's impossible," as one reenactor insists, "to group all reenactors together."

As I got to know them, I found out just how many different types there were. In 4th Armored, members range from the "Clinton supporter" Perry Trent to the archconservative Ed Malthus; from PhD candidate Ted Morse to high school–educated janitor Rob Costi; from eighteen-year-old Ben Sandler to sixty-two-year-old Paul Kelly.

But as much as they reiterate the idea that there's no such thing as a typical reenactor, they also argue that in the hobby they give up, or at least mask, some of their real-world differences. It's not unusual, say, for a highly paid, high-profile lawyer to be commanded in the field by a sanitation worker or for a Wall Street broker to pal around with a small-town librarian. Even reenactors themselves sometimes seem surprised at the ways the hobby can level real-world distinctions. Perry Trent, for instance, owns a lucrative international trading business that takes him around the world making deals with millionaires and highly educated people. Once he started reenacting, he found himself becoming best friends with people he admits he'd never encounter otherwise.

For some reenactors, the differences between their real lives and the hobby are striking. Warren Grace, a nice man with a wife, two children, and a successful optometrist's practice, once turned to me during an event and said, "I was just thinking about some of my patients. Very staid, but respectable people. I sometimes sit here at events and think, God! If they could see me now, what would they think?" Ted Morse has a similar feeling as he moves between the hobby and graduate school. "It's kind of like I lead two completely separate lives."

Many reenactors acknowledge this same sensation as they divide their world into reenacting and their lives outside the hobby. This very separateness of the hobby from the so-called real world always made an impact on me. When you see reenactors gathered at an event, they all blend together. Because they're in uniform, it's hard to detect their real-world backgrounds and identities. Whenever I'd see them in civilian clothes, hanging out by their cars after an event or at occasions like militaria shows, I was always taken aback. Sometimes I wouldn't even recognize people I'd spent entire weekends with. In their normal clothes, they looked so common, so unspectacular, and often, so different from each other.

Patrick Hart, for instance, surprised me when I met him for an interview at Washington's Union Station. He emerged from the crowd not as the World War II German private I knew him to be, but as a "civilian," wearing, as he said, "late-twentieth-century street clothes." When I mentioned this phenomenon, he agreed, observing how "a lot of reenactors look better in their uniforms than they do in their civilian clothing." Patrick says he always finds it a little bit "scary" at the end of an event. "When we're taking down camp and getting ready to leave, you see everybody changed, and it's like, oh, I wish you hadn't done that." Clearly, Patrick's reaction stems from a clash in tastes. His own classic, Ralph Laurenesque style sets him far apart from the reenactor wearing acid-washed jeans and a Def Leopard T-shirt. "Their [normal] clothes don't do it for them," as Patrick says. But he describes as incredible the power of a uniform to transform even the poorest dresser into a good-looking soldier.

I never really got over the difference between what reenactors looked like at an event and what they looked like in the real world. I was always amazed knowing that their secret persona of the soldier would never be detected when they mingled in the real world, dressed in their late-twentieth-century street clothes. Walking down Connecticut Avenue with Tim Reed, heading to a local bar for a beer, I marveled at his hip and artsy look, with his usual outfit of jeans, denim shirt, and funky glasses. Who would ever imagine that his alternate wardrobe consists almost entirely of olive-drab wool? When Greg Grosshans greeted me at the door of his apartment, I nearly didn't recognize him. Having only known him as *Obersturmbannfuehrer,* and then to see him in a white polo shirt and khakis, I did a double take. He smiled and acknowledged that the tightly cropped hair style he sports to complete his World War II impression had grown out since I'd seen him. "Now," he said, running his fingers through his hair, "it's too long to do a reenactment." And certainly Luke would never be mistaken as LT— screaming on a snowy field as his men fire their rifles in the wake of a roaring tank—when he steps on the subway each morning wearing a coat and tie. It's only when they come together at a designated place and time, an "event," that they become reenactors (never mind soldiers), indistinguishable from one another, and thus seemingly disconnected from the real world.

It's not surprising, then, that most reenactors believe that the hobby unifies different types of people who'd otherwise never meet. Their demographics bear this out: in nearly all respects—income, education, and profession—they range widely. They have a broad variety of jobs, including factory assemblers, computer programmers, construction workers, lawyers, waiters, advertising copywriters, doctors, teachers, bricklayers, and bank tellers; and no single occupation or job type dominates among them. Their annual income also ranges widely, from a reported $27,000 to $400,000. And people with all levels of education, from a high school–educated office assistant to a dermatologist, participate.

In most ways, reenactors are as normal as they insist they are when compared to the general US population. But they do slightly differ from the norm in a couple of ways. Overall, they have higher than average income and education levels. And in two key areas they differ greatly: They're overwhelmingly white (97.8 percent) and male (96.8 percent). This fact, apparent to anyone at any event, is lamented by some, like Donald Kiev, who thinks it's "a shame" that there's not more ethnic diversity in the hobby. "Almost no minorities participate," another agrees. "Although we want them to!"

I did see racism rear its ugly head in the hobby on several occasions, from hearing a couple of reenactors make racist remarks to witnessing reenactors debate whether a black or Asian American reenactor should be allowed to join a unit if the real unit had been racially segregated. But according to Ray Sherman, one of a few black reenactors in the hobby, the low number of black reenactors can be explained less by discrimination and more by what he sees as a lack of interest in military history among black Americans. Ray explains: "One problem in the black population, if you talk about black history, is a lot of people are still stuck on it only consisting of the civil rights movement and slavery. That's all it is to a lot of people. And for me, I think that's not fair because you're cutting everyone else out who's ever done anything."

Most reenactors agree that certain people—women, for example—are simply uninterested in war. And in fact, women account for only 3.2 percent of reenactors, a number that, as in the case of the low percentage of nonwhite reenactors, is not necessarily the result of discrimination. Almost all units declare open-membership policies, such as this: "Membership is open to anyone

World War I American impression

with a strong interest in World War II history, and is not restricted on the basis of race, sex, religious preference or handicap." There are reenactors who view the fact that it's a "male dominant-dominated hobby" to be "problematic," and many actively encourage women to get involved. (Units such as the Russian Guards and the American Military Medical Impression are constantly on the lookout for female recruits.) Since it's all "play-acting" anyway, others just find it hypocritical to oppose women. A woman "has just as much right to pretend that she's a German soldier," Hank Lyle believes, "as the six-hundred-pound guy has the right to pretend he's a German soldier."

Laura Paris, a World War II German reenactor who serves in her unit as a "male" soldier, acknowledges a range of male attitudes toward women in the hobby. She explains the variety: "There are three types. Some people, they love to see a woman doing it, they think it's great—'I wish my wife would do this.' 'I wish my girlfriend would do this.' Some people don't care, you know, as long as you wear the gear and do your job. Some people do not like it. It's sacrilege."

Whether women reenactors do female impressions (nurses, correspondents) or try to pass as male soldiers, they are not welcome by everyone. Longtime World War I German reenactor Grace Hall reenacts as a nurse and also tends to her unit's campsite during events, doing most of the cooking. Even though there are "more and more of us all the time," she observes, "a lot of guys are still real hostile about it." Twenty-one-year-old World War I reenactor and real-life college student Laurel Moore agrees. "Most men," she told me, "are fine with my participating, even supportive." But she also says some male reenactors make "very rude comments" to her, and a few have "even attempted to stop me from participating."

In my own experience, I also ran into a range of attitudes. Most reenactors were welcoming to me. When I joined up with the World War II Russian unit, for example, I was surprised to learn that I was encouraged—even expected—to serve in combat, since Russian women fought alongside men in World War II. But some reenactors, like Perry Trent, who don't necessarily object to women participating, still ponder with real confusion: "Why would any woman *want* to do this?" Still others, like Luke Gardner, blatantly oppose women in their midst. Although Luke became a very close friend and one of my most important informants, I never felt he was pleased with my involvement in the hobby. John Loggia also became a friend and a valuable informant. But even before we met, he had objected to my joining 4th Armored. At that first Bulge event, he all but ignored me. I knew that John thought that a woman didn't belong in their stellar unit, so I made a special attempt to make friends with him. Happily, simply being nice to John won him over and we forged a great friendship. In fact, he went out of his way to help me with my research. Eventually, John told me that he still didn't like women to be in the hobby, but that I was "different."

But whether reenactors oppose or support women in the hobby, they agree that the desire to reenact stems from an interest in war, not only a historically white, masculine interest, but also a distinctly conservative one. "Liberal-minded people," Greg Grosshans explains, "are generally antimilitary to begin. They don't even like our own US Army, let alone people who reenact." And, indeed, in answer to my question, "How would you describe your political views?" nearly half responded "conservative" or "Republican."

In general, most reenactors are conservative. They are especially conservative in respect to one important issue related to the hobby: gun ownership. Many staunchly advocate the Second Amendment right to bear arms and decry any gun control laws, particularly those restricting military assault weapons, a category that encompasses the period weapons they use to reenact.

Many learned to shoot at an early age, long before entering the hobby, and among them are firearms dealers, gun collectors, recreational shooters, and several who work for the National Rifle Association (NRA). Many are well versed in legal and technical matters regarding firearms, and they often discuss gun control legislation that might affect the hobby and advise each other on issues ranging from how to apply for permits to how to convert weapons to fire blanks (also known as "blank adapting.") Luke, a lifetime NRA member and recreational marksman, explains: "There are people who are afraid of guns and there are people who are not afraid of guns. Reenactors are the latter. . . . So I would say also a lot of times [reenactors are] more conservative than other people are. Not to say that there aren't liberal-minded people there and folks who voted for Clinton, but not many."

Despite the high proportion of gun owners in the hobby, and true to their diversity, there are reenactors who purchased their first firearms only after joining the hobby, and others—although few—who actively support gun control. Only 10 percent cite firearms as one of their main interests in the hobby, and only 20 percent pinpoint gun control as a primary problem reenactors face. "I own a lot of guns," Scott Friewald says, "but the ownership of the guns isn't as important to me. I mean, I see them as the tools that soldiers used. But essential tools that they would have had and therefore I have to [have]. But the guns themselves don't mean that much to me."

While reenactors are generally conservative, "you get a mix," as Scott observes. Not only do they range from one extreme, "socialist," to another, "Christian conservative," but along with the conservative/Republican contingent, about 20 percent classify their political views as "moderate" to "liberal." Many more, however, describe their views as one reenactor characterizes his own: "eclectic." In fact, one third defy traditional political categories altogether, using altogether made-up categories to describe their politics, such as "leftist conservative" and "Patriotic Libertarian. Fiscal conservative, social progressive. Sort of old Jeffersonian democrat (small d)." Others emphasize impartiality: "very moderate, almost apolitical," "neutral—all forms of political parties have good and bad in them." Finally, many claim no political affiliation: "Been screwed by both sides."

"In terms of philosophies of life," Greg Grosshans answered when I asked him about his politics, "I'd have to say I'm pretty much conservative, but I have liberal views. Like I believe in abortion. . . . I don't have a problem with homosexuality. I believe in welfare and stuff like that." He paused and seemed to reconsider radically. "Somewhat of a socialist in a sense," he concluded. Meanwhile, German reenactor Mark Sammons describes himself as a "draft dodger and war protester" during the Vietnam War. Grant Holzer, a member of a German World War I unit, was raised in a Quaker family and is a strong opponent of the NRA. And, in the course of one interview, Patrick Hart described himself as a "Christian anarchist" and "humanist." Finally, consider how Philip Moss describes his politics: "I used to be a Republican, but George 'Pinocchio' Bush cured me of that—not that I'm a Democrat. I vote for who I want. . . . I rarely spew politics and then it's usually an anti-Clinton jab, but I get tired of the Rabid Right and the Commie Left's BS."

Like many reenactors, Philip inhabits a "gray area," as Patrick Hart calls it, a place where easily recognizable labels do little to describe people's actual identities. I often felt that reenactors were happy to occupy such a place, since it makes it tough on outsiders to fit them into neat categories.

Still, among themselves, they endlessly speculate on who they are as a group. Over the course of one year I saw no less than four different surveys circulated by individual units in an attempt to identify different reenactor types, as if in answer to one reenactor's musing: "I have always wondered what motivates people in this hobby. I'm sure we all have seen a wide range of 'characters' come and go."

But as they try to pin down their group identity, they tend to characterize their differences less by their lives outside (age, politics, profession) and more by distinctions made inside the hobby. Whether calling each other "gappers" or "cappers," they make use of what at first sound like rather odd labels to identify the many characters among them. These are labels ostensibly not rooted in the real world (for example, there is no category for a financially poor reenactor), but meaningful only in terms of the hobby itself.

Their complicated system of categorization and voracious appetite for bestowing reenactor-related labels upon each other reveal their apparent (or at least desired) escape from their lives outside. "I am not myself in everyday life," as one reenactor says of his participation in the hobby. By all accounts, reenacting is an opportunity to set aside real-world differences, to judge and be judged by a system that is removed, purportedly, from daily life. No wonder so many describe the hobby as an escape. "It's nice to get away from reality once in a while," as one reenactor says, while another finds reenacting to be "a very good break from the real world, the job, the wife." Many celebrate the opportunity to come together not in their real-life roles as parents, spouses, employees, or students, but as reenactors—uniformed, unified, and understood. "If you're in the hobby for the most part there's an understanding," Mark Sammons explains. "There's this camaraderie. It's 'Oh, you're into it?' Then you're immediately a friend."

To be sure, many are close friends outside of the hobby. They attend each other's weddings, visit each other's homes for parties, or just hang out together. "I've met some of my closest friends through this hobby, and I think we're closer to each other because of our shared interest and experiences. I wouldn't trade it for the world!" one reenactor declares. Luke, who considers some reenactors his best friends, explains the hobby's ability to draw people together: "I have met a lot of people who have become very fast friends since I've fallen into the hobby. And the reason is, you meet people who are very much like you in a lot of ways—and that's just remarkable."

Reenacting provides one common ground to build friendships: the historically masculine and traditionally conservative subject: war. Fascination with war is the reenactors' central point of shared reference. For years, before they even began reenacting, they'd been trying to understand what war was like—an experience they describe as "unfathomable," "dangerous," and "horrible," one, as Hank Lyle admits, that "we don't know much about."

"We Don't Really Know Much about War"
Nearly a third of reenactors have served some time in the military, but only a few are veterans of a war. Paul Donald, for instance, served in the US Air Force in Vietnam. When he returned home in the late 1960s, he began collecting World War I militaria, and soon after, became one of the founding members of the GWA. Glenn Master served in the infantry in the Korean War and today enjoys hanging out with the "young people" and reenacting World War I and II. Paul and Glenn are, however, a minority. The vast majority of reenactors has no combat experience, and by the time they're in the hobby, more than 90 percent are civilians.

Some reenactors recount a sincere desire to be soldiers. Patrick Hart desperately wanted to go to West Point, but low SAT scores shattered his dream. Another reenactor, Rob Schurr, also wanted to be in the military, but poor vision eclipsed his chance to become a Navy flier. A few are members of the National Guard, and others have joined the armed forces after being in the hobby. Michael Collins and Ben Sandler, for example, enlisted in the Reserves and the Marines respectively after several years of reenacting. Both seemed to believe that their reenacting experience would help them be better soldiers. But again, these reenactors are in the minority. Most reenactors don't want to be in the military; they want to be in the historically recreated military of their own making. In fact, several reenactors who have served in the military told me how very much they hated it and couldn't wait to get out. Fred Legum, a former Marine, says he has better camaraderie in his reenacting unit than he ever had in the Corps.

Thus, for most, war is an experience they'll never know firsthand. But trying to understand what it "must have been like" began at a young age. When they jokingly refer to their hobby as a "game" and to themselves as "kids playing army," they admit a certain truth. All of them have watched war movies, played war games, played with GI Joes and toy soldiers, collected militaria, or read war histories, fiction, and memoirs since they were children. For many, war was simply a part of growing up—"I was raised in the military"—or history was always their number one interest: "I've always had a passion for history, especially military history, [and] I've always been an avid history reader."

As members of a general postwar generation, broadly defined as the era following the first half the twentieth century and its two world wars, most reenactors came of age playing army—a tradition whose origins lie in industrial turn-of-the-twentieth-century society. "My best friend from second grade," Scott Friewald remembers, "all we did was play what we called 'guns.' We'd dress up in army clothes and go around the neighborhood and we'd play, get in gunfights with the other neighborhood kids." Such games were not only an established, usually male childhood predilection, but they were also reinforced by society.

Whether born at the height of the baby boom (nearly a third of reenactors); the tail end, 1957 to 1967 (nearly half); or even later, 1968–1978 (nearly 20 percent), reenactors grew up in a culture that encouraged them to experience war frequently—if only vicariously. In short, they came of age consuming war. "Our heads were filled with war stories," as one reenactor recalls of his childhood. Some of the stories reenactors remember vividly include those found in books such as Erich Maria Remarque's 1930 novel *All Quiet on the Western Front* and Charles MacDonald's classic 1947 World War II memoir *Company Commander*; comic books like *Sergeant Rock* (a DC Comic about World War II soldiers that ran from 1959 to 1988); films such as *The Dawn Patrol* (1938), starring Errol Flynn, *Battleground* (1949), starring Van Johnson, and *The Longest Day* (1962), starring

John Wayne; and TV shows like *Combat* (which aired from 1962 to 1967) and *The Rat Patrol* (which aired from 1966 to 1968). "A whole host of TV programming," as Mark Sammons remembers it, "that was very patriotic, using the American symbols and mythology and all that kind of stuff." Grant Holzer makes a further point concerning these portrayals: The good guys were always the Americans.

But even as the Vietnam War altered the popular image of war to include less than heroic portrayals of Americans, war was still on the airwaves. Despite arguments that many Americans became antiwar or at least somewhat apathetic to war as a result of Vietnam, reenactors, of all ages, tell a different story. To them, Vietnam was a "tragedy," a "mistake," a "noble cause," or, for a few, a personal experience. But whatever their opinion, it did nothing to dampen their interest in war. It even inspired some to reenact the Vietnam War just a few years after the war ended.

In tracing the source of their fascination with war, many look back on their childhood and conclude that reenacting was inevitable. "Reenacting starts at a very young age," one reenactor believes, "playing army and learning about history, visiting museums." "I mean for me," Patrick Hart says, "that's what it comes down to. I've always liked uniforms. I've always liked guns and I've always liked playing army." Alain Benson recalls, "I remember back when I was probably [in] second grade . . . drawing like war pictures, like when everyone was given a piece of paper and a crayon, I would start drawing tanks and planes and planes shooting at the tanks, exploding. So it started really, really young." Some can even trace their fascination to a single, memorable experience: "I read *All Quiet on the Western Front* when I was twelve, and that sealed my fate," one reenactor says. "I think I was in sixth grade," Ben Sandler remembers, when "my dad got me a flight simulator game. It was the Battle of Britain. That's how I first got interested in World War II."

Many others credit personal encounters with veteran relatives as sparking their interest in war. Michael Collins looks back with regret, remembering, "My great-uncle [a marine in World War II] wanted to give me a samurai sword when I was about ten years old. My mom said, 'I don't want it in the house. He'll kill somebody with it.' I was like 'Mom, put it in the bank till I turn eighteen. Put it in a safe deposit box.'"

Unfortunately for Michael, his mother failed to take his side, and the sword was lost to him forever. But this loss inspired him to savor the stories he heard as a boy from his relatives who'd served in World War II. They "would pull me aside at these family reunions and tell me stories," Michael remembers. "All my life I grew up hearing this." Brian Shore had a similar experience: "I picked my grandfather's brain to pieces when he was alive. He was in the Pacific. He was a medic. He didn't really see any action, but just to hear the stories."

Lew McCarthy also heard a lot of war stories growing up in a household of veterans: "My great-grandfather was in World War I and my grandfather . . . was a staff sergeant and a tail gunner [in World War II] and my uncle had been an infantryman first in Okinawa and then Vietnam and [all of us] lived in the same house."

Richard Paoletti's fascination with the Germans of World War II was triggered by his first contact with veterans in high school: "My best friend's grandfather was in [the SS unit] Liebstandarte Adolf Hitler; his great uncle was a Luftwaffe pilot; another guy I think was in the Navy. And you know all his relatives were just absorbed into the armed forces and talking to them and actually meeting [them], it was great, you know, it was firsthand."

Some reenactors remember that their interest in what their "foreign" relatives did was discouraged by parents who preferred that their children find another hobby. When Greg Grosshans started collecting World War II German militaria at the age of thirteen, his "parents really sort of frowned upon it, especially my mom." It was not only due to personal ties that he cultivated interest in the Germans ("I have German heritage," Greg says. "I have relatives who were in the German Army during World War II") but also because "I always thought the Germans had the spiffiest uniforms—the medals and stuff. And I think there's a bit of intrigue since they were sort of the bad guys too."

All reenactors share this sense of intrigue about what their relatives had done in wars. Some, though, became fascinated through a distant relative who had already died. Ray Sherman never knew his great-uncle, who served in the World War I unit that Ray now represents in the GWA. Many more did know their veteran relatives, but found them unwilling to tell their war stories, especially to kids. In fact, often it was a relative's—particularly a father's—unwillingness to talk that made war that much more taboo. "I always wanted my dad to talk more about it," Mark Sammons says of his World War II veteran father. "But he never would." Sam Benevento's father, a US Army Air Corps pilot, was also reluctant to talk. His silence taught Sam a lesson many other reenactors learned early on: "A lot of the veterans suppress all of this. They didn't talk about it. They haven't talked about it."

I would often recognize this dichotomy between the reenactors' ability to consume war so easily in the public realm through books and movies and their inability to learn about war from a more personal and significant source. Clearly, the experience of confronting silence in the realm of their familial relationships contributed to their near obsession with trying to find out what war was like. Somehow, war became both a personal and impersonal experience at the same time; it was the dramatic substance of movies and books, but it was also a real-life experience that had made their role models, especially their fathers, distant and inscrutable.

Whatever the initial source of their interest, their fascination with war is thus linked to the "average" people who experienced it. They universally describe war in similar terms: it is "an extraordinary thing that happened to ordinary people." "Most people think of history as something that happened to famous people years ago," as one reenactor states. "It has become clear to me that 'war' in whatever year is made up of regular people."

Thus, the reenactors' primary focus lies on portraying the "average" or "typical" soldier. "The fighting man," as one reenactor asserts, "has always been my hero." No one in the hobby, save a couple of reenactors, does an impression of a famous soldier, such as Pershing, Patton, or Rommel. Rather, they portray what they term "common" soldiers. Patrick Hart comments on this fascination with this mythic common man: "The common man, the common guy, the common foot soldier, you know? . . . That's it. Just the common foot slogger. I was reading the accounts of these guys and just how they could go through what they did, you know, full of lice and mud and dirt and filth and seeing their friends killed? You just can't imagine."

Their reverence toward the soldiers, combined with their own questioning of whether or not they themselves could have withstood the unimaginable experience of war, are two reasons that reenactors didn't give up their quest to understand war as they got older. Many argue that the hobby allows them to represent, honor, and come closer to understanding the common war experience. "What I believe to be one of the better things about reenacting," one reenactor explains, "is that it shows the common man's view of history. While TV and books will tell you about the generals who led and the battles which were fought, reenactors will tell you how the common soldier fared, what he wore and carried, what he fought with, and sometimes, sadly, how he died." Scott Friewald expresses awe in trying to imagine what the common soldier went through: "It's hard for me to fathom, at times, the idea that you can put your life and limb at risk like that, you know? Be involved in something that dangerous, that all-encompassing."

Most reenactors agree. It is hard to imagine war. And without actually experiencing a war themselves, they're left with only their fantasies. But rather than

World War I French impression

simply play war, the hobby allows them to try to satisfy their fascination in a unique way. Alain Benson summed up the way a curiosity begins "watching war movies on TV" and then "just keeps evolving" before eventually leading to the hobby. The Sharp brothers grew up glued to the TV set watching *The Rat Patrol*. And, as the youngest brother put it, "one thing led to another." They first bought a World War II jeep similar to the Rat Patrol's, discovered reenacting as adults, and found that the hobby was the only place where they could more fully pursue their interests.

Reenacting may be an outgrowth of childhood interests. "Probably most of us have been playing with soldiers since we were kids," as Patrick Hart speculates. But reenactors refrain from describing the hobby as an adult version of playing army. Reenacting is far more "sophisticated," to use Luke's word, than any neighborhood game of "guns" could ever be. To be sure, it's strictly an adult hobby. Nearly all units impose minimum age requirements, and most participants start reenacting in their mid-twenties or older. Thus, they view their game as a terribly serious enterprise that requires an investment of resources and level of maturity that most kids do not possess. And woe to the outsider who dismisses it as "playing army." "It's okay for us to call it a game," Grace Hall says. "We just don't want anyone else calling it that."

Luke, who visibly shudders when someone refers to reenacting as "playing army," thinks a lot about the difference between a childish game and an adult pastime. "You really can't get around it," he admits. "We *are* pretending to be soldiers." But for him and many others, it is their passion for history that provides a crucial distinction between a kids' game and reenacting. "I think that when you do it a hundred percent," Luke says, "and you make sure your uniform is perfect and your knowledge of the period is substantial, that you can do a good first-person impression of the character you're trying to assume, that kind of makes up for it. That dignifies it, moves it to a higher plane. Otherwise it's just a bunch of clowns, running around playing guns."

This impulse to dignify the hobby stems not only from the reenactors' desire to take their interest in war to a more mature level, but also from a nearly universal dissatisfaction with their years spent passively consuming war. Although they all came of age at a time when the media increased its scope and influence and war portrayals became increasingly "realistic," joining the hobby was partly the reenactors' response to the failure of available resources (films, books, and veteran relatives) to satisfy their interest in war. "The media," as John Loggia explains, "can promise us a lot, promise us the world, and tell us everything we need to know, yet you're not going to get the detail that you would need to get about [war] unless . . . you experience it yourself." They also argue that popular accounts of war, particularly Hollywood movies, almost always distort the common soldier's experience by vilifying, glorifying, or condemning it.

Reenactors also argue that public institutions, particularly schools, fail to educate people adequately about war. When I asked Scott Mies, a history major in college, if he thought schools succeeded in educating students about history, he quickly responded, "Oh, not at all. No. It's the rare exception when a school does a good job." Alicia Mellon, an enthusiastic World War II reenactor from Illinois, had a similar response when I asked if she'd been well educated about what women did in World War II. "I have absolutely no recollection of ever covering World War II in school," she said. "So, I don't think it was so much the education of what women did, it was the whole of World War II that kind of got skipped."

Others have more specific complaints about what was covered in school. "I think it's a shame," Ray Sherman says about the fact that he didn't receive a good education about war. In particular he laments how the contributions of the black American soldiers that he now portrays were overlooked. "In the school textbooks we had," Ray remembers, "I saw a man with his leg blown off, coming home from World War I. All the caption read was this man has just returned home from World War I. And no name, didn't tell you what unit he was in or anything. He was just some black man with his leg blown off on crutches." Ray says that it wasn't until he started doing his own research that he was able to identify the man in the photograph and unlock the history of his service. "I found out later that he was from the 369th Infantry Regiment, one of the most famous black regiments of the whole war. One hundred and ninety-one days in combat, never lost a prisoner, never lost a foot of ground."

Over and over, reenactors articulate the same belief: The real and common stories of war have been buried by inadequate educational systems, distorted by Hollywood, and silenced or lost by the veterans themselves, especially as veterans die off with their stories unheard. As a result, they believe Americans have become apathetic toward the history of war and, more important, the people who fought them. In fact, most reenactors believe that the public is better informed *about reenacting* than about history in general. Nearly 98 percent of reenactors believe that Americans are misinformed and/or underinformed about history; only about 2 percent think that the American public is accurately informed about history. "The public needs to learn about history first," one reenactor argues, "before they would have any hope of understanding why people would bother to reenact."

With a shared belief that "Americans are far too removed from their past . . . to the point where they forget the mistakes and they repeat them all over again," they echo the refrain that history's common soldiers—of all nations—have been all but forgotten. "World War I is not something that is remembered too well in this country," John Loggia believes, while another asserts, "The public has forgotten how our country got to be as great as it is: through the blood of its veterans." John Ostroski, a high school history teacher in real life, explains why: "History is something that the forward-looking people like most Americans today could not care less about. We're not traditionally oriented. We're not historically oriented. As a nation we're a people who are business- and profit-oriented, and that involves looking in a forward direction, not looking backward."

In many ways, reenactors have been looking backward all their lives. Reacting to the failures of the textbook, the movie, or the veteran relative to tell the real stories of common people involved in the world's most dangerous event, reenactors are thus left to try on their own to "fill the gaps" of history, as one reenactor puts it. Only through reenacting, they argue, can they try to understand something of the common war experience. Further, they not only view themselves as preserving history through the hobby, whether through collecting militaria or recording veterans' stories, but they also regard themselves as having a deeper appreciation than most others for what soldiers from all nations have done through history. The idea that they remember and appreciate what is forgotten by nearly everyone else is reiterated by nearly every reenactor, often with great passion and even anger: Mark Sugar, a World War I British reenactor, once proclaimed, in a moment sharply etched in my mind, "Americans are full of shit. Oh! Fifty thousand Americans died in Vietnam! Give me a break. The British lost that many in just an hour in the first day of the battle of the Somme."

Reenactors regard the failures of the public, the schools, and the media to understand history and honor the sacrifices of common soldiers in many ways. For some, they signal a general decline in society—whether due to a lack of patriotism or a liberal trend characterizing interest in things military as warmongering. For others, they expose a pervasive selfishness among Americans, whose forward-looking ways eclipse recognition of history's common people. For still others, they underscore a nation's willingness to expend its citizens in war, with little done to honor their memory in return.

No matter what reason they cite, many believe that the quality of contemporary Americans pales in the face of past generations made stronger by war. "I doubt very strongly," one thirty-something reenactor observes, "that my generation is gonna be admired and respected like the World War II vets are. The only thing we ever fought for was the Right to Party."

For my own part, I somewhat grappled with the reenactors' attitudes. Clearly, their views are in sync with the broader cultural shift in the ways that history is now represented, the move from focusing on the "great heroic individual" or grand narrative of history to documenting the experiences of average people via

World War II flyboy and ground crew member

social and oral history. And yet, reenactors still dismiss the public realm of history for failing to represent the common figure. Their argument that Americans don't care about or dislike military history also seemed illogical to me. After all, the very culture that produced the hobby in the first place is the same culture that continuously feeds the public a diet of martial substance that celebrates sacrifices made in war—commemorations, war movies, and martial rhetoric.

I soon realized, however, that their bleak assessment of the nature of public history in relation to war is essential to the ways they define their roles as reenactors beyond the hobby's borders. Thus, they argue that they can be useful to society as they try to counter the antihistorical trends they identify. They do this through performing a kind a public service that only they can perform: the staging of "public events," such as parades and living history displays at schools, museums, veterans' conventions, historical sites, and air shows. Most units schedule a variety of these events on their annual calendars, especially on holidays such as Armed Forces Day and Veterans Day (which World War I reenactors still call Armistice Day). And almost all reenactors participate in them. Even a reenactor as carefully guarded as Luke finds that "when I do a public display and a public reenactment, it's going to be top notch. It's going to be straight. And I think it only makes the hobby look good when we do a good job and we present ourselves professionally."

Gaining positive PR for the hobby is paramount since public events are a rare opportunity for outsiders to see their passion. Thus, as members of a difficult-to-advocate hobby move out of their private spaces to come face-to-face with members of the public, they try to show only their "public face." Watching reenactors march down Fifth Avenue in New York City in the annual Veterans Day parade or seeing a local TV news story featuring a mock battle are some of the few chances people have to see twentieth-century war reenactors. And when they do, they usually hear reenactors recite what I came to call their public mantra: Their mission lies in "preserving history and remembering all of those who fell in a particular conflict." And a public event is their chance "to keep alive the respect for those warriors who fought and suffered for real."

At the intersection of a private hobby and the expressly public realm of history, a public event finds reenactors presenting themselves as representatives of war, history, and reenacting to the public. Such an experience can be both gratifying and frustrating. It is also an experience, many reenactors admit, that they know more than enough about.

Chapter 5

"Dog and Pony Shows"

Public Events

Throughout the 1990s, twentieth-century war reenactors were much in demand. The clamor for their living history services noticeably increased, spurred in part by the sheer growth of the hobby as well as by major anniversaries of both world wars. The popularity of events that feature war, such as air shows, parades, and living history timelines, underscores war's enduring appeal as entertainment. Many people want to see war, and they're willing to pay good money for it.

Public events that involve reenactors are generally hosted by museums or historical sites, but larger, more influential bodies also sponsor them. The CIA, Department of Defense, US Air Force, and US Army have all used reenactors for various events. Marching in President Clinton's 1993 inaugural parade were several dozen twentieth-century war reenactors. Hollywood production companies hired reenactors as extras in films such as *12 Monkeys* (1996), *Saving Private Ryan* (1998), and *The Battle of Shaker Heights* (2003). The History Channel frequently makes use of reenactors in documentaries. And even the National Park Service, despite its official policy barring reenactments on its sites, makes use of twentieth-century war reenactors at some events, including its annual World War I and World War II living history encampments held at the Eisenhower National Historic Site in Gettysburg, Pennsylvania (also known as Eisenhower Farm.)

Event hosts usually recruit reenactors by word of mouth, email, or direct mailings. "This is a call for troops," read one invitation to reenactors for a weekend-long World War I commemoration. "Please review your calendar and consider this special remembrance ceremony." Another host asked for "knowledgeable reenactors who can tell the story of the common soldier in World War II. We are especially looking for groups that can bring military vehicles."

Using reenactors makes good business sense. After all, how else can one secure period military vehicles, most of which cost tens of thousands of dollars, without spending a fortune? Finding people who will attend a weekend-long event, set up displays of their private militaria collections, wear their own costumes, and teach history to fee-paying visitors, all for free, is a coup indeed, since using reenactors requires little or no money and often generates quite a bit of revenue. The Mid Atlantic Air Museum, a nonprofit museum in Reading, Pennsylvania, for instance, makes a quarter of its entire annual budget in just one weekend-long event: the World War II commemorative weekend. This event draws up to sixteen thousand paying visitors (at a nine-dollar adult admission fee) to see the planes, watch an air show, listen to a swing band, hobnob with veterans, watch several mock battles, and tour the period camps of more than three hundred World War II reenactors.

Hosts publicly promote their events as educational and commemorative, echoing the reenactors' public mantra. An Eisenhower Farm event is a chance "to provide a learning experience for park visitors." A World War I encampment is intended to "introduce the Great War to a larger audience." But explaining exactly who reenactors are—and what reenacting is—is usually avoided. Instead, reenactors are identified as "living history volunteers" who "recreate the look and feel of a past era." Hosts also celebrate the authenticity of the reenactor displays and presentations. At a reenactor encampment at the Marietta Mansion, a historic home in Maryland, for instance, an event brochure instructs visitors, "The encampments before you represent hundreds of hours of research and craftsmanship in an effort to bring a portion of our past to life."

Nowhere is the chance to see history come to life more dramatic than in one type of event that draws the most attention to and criticism of the hobby: the public battle. Ranging from the elaborate (a reenactment of Pearl Harbor) to the small-scale (a skirmish on an open field), public battles are performed by reenactors for "tourists," as reenactors often call members of the public—or, as Philip Moss refers to them, "touronz."

In June 1994, I traveled to Fort Story, Virginia, to take part in my first public battle: a reenactment of the 1944 D-Day invasion, this one commemorating the historic engagement's fiftieth anniversary. As the event approached, many reenactors prepared for what they hailed as "an event of a lifetime." Others, though, chose not to attend. Such a spectacle, Luke Gardner said, was sure to be a total farbfest. Farbfest or not, the D-Day event would teach me an important lesson about the public face of reenacting.

The Oxymoronic Public Battle

Three decades after the harsh criticism of mock battles during the American Civil War centennial, World War II reenactors emerged on the national stage during the fiftieth-anniversary commemorations of D-Day. In June 1994, one of the largest World War II reenactments the public had ever witnessed was staged on the shores of Fort Story in Virginia Beach.

The five-day event at Fort Story drew hundreds of reenactors from across the country, housed in wooden barracks at nearby Camp Pendleton, a small National Guard facility that is not to be confused with the Marine Corps base in California by the same name. Reenactors paid seventy-five dollars each to participate in numerous activities including: a parade of one hundred reenactor units down the main street of Virginia Beach; commemoration ceremonies; a reenactor flea market; a stage door canteen; a USO dance with an appearance by World War II film veteran Van Johnson; an invasion rehearsal, closed to the public; and finally, a public reenactment of D-Day.

A reenactment group, the Old Dominion Living History Association, joined forces with the Military Vehicle Preservation Association, the city of Virginia Beach, the Virginia Army National Guard, and the Department of Defense to host the event. French and American warships were recruited to fire blank salvos off the shores, while military aircraft were enlisted to strafe the beaches. Eight landing craft (LCUs), property of the US Navy, were secured to ferry the Allied reenactors to shore. The gentle beach of Fort Story, where the German reenactors would defend the "continent" in front of thousands of spectators seated on bleachers, had been converted into a defensive front, protected by barbed wire, obstacles, and machine-gun nests.

On the morning of the public invasion, the narrow road leading to the sandy shores where we would begin our journey to Normandy was choked by hundreds of Allied reenactors. They loafed on the grass smoking cigarettes, greeted friends, and drew their cameras out to film the impressive display. Many were giddy, others solemn, as if on the verge of a great historic undertaking. A reenactor in a chaplain's uniform gave prayer services; others listened soberly to officers' speeches. The event organizers hurried through the crowd with clipboards, distinguished by their armbands and worried expressions.

When given the signal, everyone marched to the eight US landing craft moored on a stretch of private beach at the edge of Camp Pendleton. Amid the confusion, laughter, and last-minute beseeching—"Where the hell is our commander?"—I was hastily ordered to board the one landing craft devoted to a unit of real American soldiers of the US 29th National Guard Division. These soldiers had been loaned period uniforms sporting the 29th patch, and they carried period M1 Garand rifles.

During the half-hour journey to the beach where the Germans and spectators were awaiting our surprise landing, the soldiers talked, hanging over the edge of the landing craft, and took pictures; some lay down for a nap. They understood that the reenactors sailing on the other landing craft did this kind of thing regularly, and some joked about it politely. "This is their show," one friendly soldier told me. "We're here because we were ordered to be here." But another soldier, whose grandfather had stormed the shores with the 29th fifty years before, was visibly moved. "It kind of gives me a thrill," he said as we cast our sights across the crystal waters of the Atlantic, "to know that my granddad was there. And now, in a sense, I am too."

As I surveyed the naval convoy spiriting along the sparkling blue waters, I couldn't help but be moved as well. It was impressive. As far as the eye could see, landing craft were strung out behind us. Two US warships circled and kept apace farther out, while several private vessels trailed in our wake. The only thing that appeared out of place was the modern skyline of Virginia Beach. I wondered what picnicking families would think of our passing convoy.

A few minutes before we reached the shore, the commander of our vessel, a real-life Navy officer, shouted over the din of the motor, "Remember, once the ramp is lowered, get off as quick as you can. Those designated to die, go ahead and do so. All you others watch out not to trample the dead on your way out. Okay! Go ahead and prepare your weapons."

At his cue, we readied ourselves, taking off the modern orange lifejackets we'd been ordered to wear and locking and loading our blank-adapted rifles. We lined up facing the ramp. At first there was talking and a bit of laughter, but soon the conversation died out. I stood at the back, my camera at the ready. The only sound was the steady, heavy churning of engines. My heart beat rapidly as I looked at the soldiers crouching slightly in anticipation. One turned and winked at a friend. Another glanced over his shoulder with a look of anguish. Could it be that they were actually a little scared? Even though we were not actually about to invade France, I was anxious. I waited breathlessly for the ramp to drop.

The landing craft slowed and rotated to face the shore. The engines went

Allied reenactors run to shore, D-Day event, 1994

dead. Silence. In agonizing slow motion, we drifted until the craft moored it-self on the edge of the sand and stopped abruptly. For an instant we were stat-ues, motionless in the absence of forward movement. Then the ramp flew down and hit the foaming water with a hard slap. The shrill of a whistle sounded. The fifteen soldiers at the front immediately fell on the ramp, killed by German fire. Someone was screaming, "Get going! Go! Go! Go!" But the soldiers were already on the move, shouting as they fled and jumping over the bodies as they ran to the shore. I practically slid down the steep, wet ramp and ran through inches of water to reach the shore. Hearing the Germans' fire, I flung myself to the ground. Smoke grenades and charges blew, simulating the Allied bombardment. They erupted in a dense line of smoke, obscuring my view of the beach and spectators in front of me. The wooden obstacles and barbed-wire defenses looked ghostly in the hazy outline of smoke. A deafening fire roared all around me.

Lying prone on the shore, I watched the remaining seven landing craft land, carrying the subsequent waves of reenactors. Several landing craft were unable to reach the shoreline proper and dropped their ramps in waist-high water; those on them waded madly through the water, their rifles held over their heads hori-zontally. A lone jeep drove out of one craft and promptly stalled in the water. It sat frozen, washed by the lapping surf.

Reenactors fanned out across the beach, charging meekly ahead. Ducking down or lying flat, they fired their rifles and tried to take cover. Some crouched behind obstacles; some began digging foxholes. "Oh, man!" one reenactor yelled, as he lay on his side madly firing his rifle. "Motherfucker!" he shouted with a red face. "Jesus Christ!" he finally cried before diving for cover. I looked back at the long lines of dead soldiers who now littered the paths from each landing craft.

Tank on the beach with American reenactor in foreground, D-Day event, 1994

Several planes appeared overheard, flying low and strafing the German positions. Several Allied medics, with crosses on their helmets, tended to the wounded, while others dragged the fallen to the protection of a foxhole. One wounded soldier called out to his mother. A Sherman tank roamed sluggishly along the beach.

The Allies fought to take the beach for about half an hour before a voice over a loudspeaker announced, "Go ahead Allies, make your final assault." Then, as planned, the Germans surrendered. When it was over, even the wounded and killed stood, scanning the area for the rifles or packs they'd cast off in haste and fear. We were then called to stand before the crowd. I could hear the applause, and then the colorful band of ten thousand cheering spectators came into focus.

The reenactors formed lines in front of the crowd; silence reigned, broken only by the mournful sound of Taps played in honor of "those brave Americans who fell on the shores of Omaha Beach fifty years ago." The reenactors, Germans included, bowed their heads and stood like supplicants, helmets in hand.

Then there was real chaos on the beach. Reenactors searched for friends lost in battle; they sifted through the sand to pick up spent cartridges; they wrung out wet woolen uniforms; they drank greedily from canteens. Spectators poured onto the shore and asked reenactors to pose for photographs.

"Hey, Jenny!" It was Paul Harding, who'd defended the beach with the Germans. He greeted me with a hug. "Hiya," Hank Lyle said, as he joined our growing group. The assembled band, old friends, engaged in an immediate postevent evaluation: Farbs. Disorganization. Boneheads. Yahoos. I've heard this before, I thought, listening to a string of complaints. But didn't they just succeed in recreating history in one of the largest twentieth-century war reenactments ever held for the public? They were laughing. I was confused. Why did they go to all this trouble just to be disappointed?

Before long, the Allies (and those Germans who wanted to ride in the LCUs) were ordered back on the landing craft to return to Camp Pendleton. Wet, sandy, rumpled, and tired, we trod on board. This time, I rode with a group of reenactors—Canadians, British, Americans.

"I had a total blast!" one said.

"Yeah, it was a thrill. Absolutely amazing."

"Did you think it was pretty realistic?" I asked expectantly.

"Yeah," one said reluctantly. "I mean pretty much. It was sure realistic in terms of equipment and stuff. The planes, the landing craft. I mean, it was really an incredible event."

"What about the battle?" I pressed. "Did that seem pretty authentic?"

"Oh. Well, yeah, I mean some of the guys said they got that rush, you know, that moment that seems real and everything."

But another piped up. "A realistic public battle?" he asked with a mischievous smile. "Now there's an oxymoron."

Reluctant Warriors

After the D-Day event, reenactors reported that the World War II hobby received a tremendous influx of new recruits—a "post–D-Day backlash." The spate of commemorative events across the country brought the hobby to public light and stimulated interest in World War II reenacting. It was no wonder, steeped as the nation was at the time in reliving World War II. Coverage of the D-Day anniversary was especially extensive. Immediately after the invasion, I went to a party hosted by Hank Lyle's girlfriend, Laura, and joined several German reenactors to eat tacos, drink beer, and watch the event coverage on TV. In between glimpses of the commemorative ceremonies at Normandy, CNN and other national networks broadcast clips of the invasion in Virginia Beach. Most reports praised the event's honorable goal of paying homage to the veterans and championed its success in recreating history. One reporter would later describe his delight in watching the Allies storm the Virginia shores. "History," he declared unabashedly, "had leapt from the dry pages of history books."

There were, of course, others who were not so delighted. At another D-Day reenactment in Chicago, a small group of protesters voiced its complaints that "the blanks and staged combat trivialized the terror and chaos of the invasion."

For my own part, I suffered my own personal D-Day backlash as I struggled to make sense of a shocking discovery. The reenactors largely showed disdain for the event. At the party, no one celebrated success. Instead, they complained about the exorbitant event fees. The many farbs. The event organizers who'd obviously never read a book about World War II. The idiotic behavior on the beach. And finally, the most frequent complaint: the event wasn't even close to being authentic. It didn't take me long to learn that most reenactors agree with their critics' charges concerning their public battles. Perry Trent, for instance, thinks the idea that a public battle can represent war accurately "a joke." To be well educated about war, another reenactor believes, the public is "better off reading a book."

Although most reenactors willingly perform them, they believe public battles can never succeed as a truly educational venture since they turn war into a spectacle, catering to the public's appetite for war as entertainment—a mistake too often made in "Silly War." According to John Loggia, public battles are strictly "dog and pony shows for the general public." Of the D-Day event, Alain Benson said, "I think it was more of a tourist attraction. 'Hey, honey . . . I heard they're supposed to be doing a big reenactment.' 'Well, why don't we take the kids up to see that, it'd be fun!'. . . The public, I guess, appreciates it from an entertainment standpoint."

And in fact, because a public battle is designed for an audience, it is usually "scripted," with the action orchestrated and narrated over a public address system. For example, the following is the script handed out to all participants in the D-Day reenactment in Virginia:

> 1. The first twenty men, in each landing craft, will be killed as soon as the ramp door is dropped. These men need to arrange themselves so the remaining troops can have enough deck space to run through them and assault the beach. (Sorry Guys.)
>
> 2. The second twenty man group will be killed or wounded at the 20 yard line within the first minute. WARNING: Stay clear of the ramp on the M-8 boats and LCUs! Take cover in the craters or die up on the beach. Stay away from boat ramps. (See Diagram.)
>
> 3. All remaining Allies will take cover and stay in the craters until the second wave lands. WARNING: If you are on the beach and you see that the 2nd

wave landing craft is going to land on your position, move your ass out of the way!

4. The Seal Demo team from the first wave will move to the pre-staged firing point and prepare to shoot the bangalore torpedoes (via green smoke.)

5. The Seal Demo team will insure that the area forward of the 30yd line is clear to shoot the bangalores. If Allies are out of control and not where they are supposed to be they will render the device safe.

6. Once the 2nd wave of Allies start to storm ashore, green smoke will be thrown by the demo control points near the centers of the landing lane which will start the final assault on the Germans and signal to fire the bangalore torpedo simulators.

7. As the Allies start their assault, the Germans will start dying in great numbers and/or surrender to the Allies as they reach the 25yd line. All Germans will surrender or lay flat on the ground.

8. From the 2nd wave right flank (seaward) the Sherman tank will roll off the LCU and proceed to run the length of the beach (see route) with the US flag flying high.

9. On the left flank of the beach the 2 1/2 ton truck and field gun will roll off the LCU and do a hook turn, setting the gun up to fire one round.

10. At this time, the Master of Ceremonies will accent the event with music, bringing the program to a close.

Because public battles are scripted, there are usually guarantees that all Germans will always be soundly beaten, no prisoners will be shot, and all wounded will receive medical attention—in short, war's violence will be cleaned up. Scott Friewald thinks it's "boring" to participate in such contrived spectacles. "If you're doing a scripted battle," he explains, "it's almost like you're in a play. I mean you're just kind of going from point A to point B . . . not really showing any initiative or personal involvement." Hank also says that because public battles are primarily intended to provide "a good show" for spectators, the use of a script means that the action turns into "being kind of Hollywood versions of what probably really happened."

Twentieth-century war reenactors often derisively call their own public battles "Civil War events," since they force modern warriors to fight in the open so the audience can see the action. "If the spectators know anything about history," Greg Grosshans observes, "they know World War II wasn't fought like that. Two armies would have never opposed one another on the open field like that. They would have slaughtered one another."

Hank Lyle points out one other reason that public battles are inaccurate. The presence of an audience makes reenactors "do things . . . that aren't historically correct. That's the problem I had with D-Day. I mean here we are ten feet from the ocean, dug in, in the sand . . . and what I thought was hysterical was they started shelling [and] we're all with our heads up, looking at the kaleidoscope effect, whereas any soldier worth his salt would have tried to get down underneath the sand." "It borders on the absurd eventually," Scott Friewald agrees. "You've got guys charging machine guns from twenty yards away standing full upright. That kind of thing would never happen. It doesn't represent at all what it must have been like."

But all this begs the question: why do they perform them?

To be fair, some simply enjoy them; some even recount moments in public battles when, regardless of the overall spectacle, they are able to ignore the crowd and have an "authentic" experience. Others see them as potentially stimulating people's interest in history. But many more acknowledge that because the public likes and expects them, they're part of their "public duty." "I don't worry so much about making public battles 'less hokey,'" Wilson Lyle reflects. "It's just a fact of life, given the parameters we have to work within."

Being told when to arrive, when to leave, and when to die are just a few of these parameters. ("When the Allies clear the mine field signs," the D-Day event rules implored, "all Germans will die or surrender. Don't prolong this event by being a die hard and making an ass out of yourself. Follow the script!") Some believe that conforming to such demands is an act of submission—those who bend too much are known as "mercenary" reenactors—but others see it differently. "The whole point of a public event," one reenactor asserts, "is to entertain, educate, and impress the spectators."

But there is another kind of presentation reenactors also do strictly for the public: a "static display." Reenactors use this form of presentation in their living history events by setting up camps, displaying equipment, and allowing visitors a chance to handle period artifacts, watch demonstrations, and listen to reenactors "explain the display to the curious public." When given the choice between "living history [or public] combat," most reenactors agree that "we can do the former far more realistically than the latter."

The Static Display

Welcome to the Jamestown Settlement's 15th annual Military Through the Ages. As citizens and professional soldiers, men and sometimes women have participated in military actions throughout history. Military Through the Ages examines the military experience, providing a unique opportunity to observe first-hand the evolution of military power from the 1st century B.C. to 1998. The warriors, skills, tactics, and weapons have changed, but their role in history continues.

I always loved the public event known as Military Through the Ages (MTA). Each year over a weekend in late March, reenactors of all different periods—from Vikings to Vietnam soldiers—are invited to the Jamestown Settlement near Williamsburg, Virginia. There they set up their static displays and camps on the grounds surrounding the museum, demonstrate drills, and serve as public historians for visitors.

For several years in a row, I drove down from Washington, dressed in my late-twentieth-century street clothes, eager to tour the displays and hang out with the reenactors. MTA always drew quite a few of my reenacting friends, including the Lyle brothers, Bill Lauter, Tim Reed, Paul Harding, Grace and Max Hall, and Scott Mies. The event was very much like a happy and casual reunion, with plenty of time to catch up, take photographs, and enjoy what was usually one of the first springlike weekends of the year.

On my 1998 MTA visit, I walked onto the site reading the event flyer, struck by the fact that it does little to explain that the people dressed as soldiers, milling about with weapons on the museum grounds, and instructing people about history are, in fact, reenactors. Instead, like most public events, MTA offers visitors a rather heady, generalized promise: by "observing first hand the evolution of military power," they'll find the means to "time travel." Such a promise is echoed by numerous historic sites that invite visitors to "experience three centuries of history in just one day!" or "Beat a Path to the Past!"

For those visiting the Jamestown site during the annual MTA, the "trip through time" begins at the admission counter. Museum employees gladly take your money ($9.75 adults, $6.25 children, credit cards accepted), provide you with a flyer listing the day's activities, tell you that you're free to tour the displays inside the museum, and remind you to visit the gift shop.

Once visitors exit through the double glass doors of the museum, step out of the air-regulated environment, and onto the outdoor encampment site, the world of living history unfolds. It is here that the time trip really begins. But there is no magic. There's not even a tour guide to help you start your journey. Instead, visitors may choose to turn left and venture into the wooded area where campsites of the early periods are set up (Roman Legions, Vikings, Civil War soldiers), or turn right and tour the twentieth-century war encampments.

Toby, the Russian antitank dog, World War II Eastern Front private event, 1997

The reenactors' encampments are arranged chronologically in a semicircle on an open field. First, visitors find themselves still in the present, greeted by real soldiers of the 29th National Guard who stand near a display of modern equipment and weapons in a clear effort at recruitment. Just a few feet to the right lies a Vietnam War camp, marked by a sign plunged into the dirt: "Vietnam 1969." The camp is manned by several reenactors in jungle fatigues who stand in front of a large olive-drab tent full of period objects belonging to the average American soldier in Vietnam.

Stepping farther back in time, visitors find two large tents that house a unit of World War II pilots, or "flyboys." Inside one, marked by a sign reading "414th Bomb Squadron," folding chairs provide a place to sit while visitors listen to reenactors discuss the hazards of bombing runs. In the other tent, two pilots lie on their cots surrounded by various personal and government-issued items, including two footlockers, a mainstay presentation device of the static display. Both are packed with the gear of a common flyboy: cigarettes, shaving kits, Juicy Fruit gum, *Life* magazines, pinups, and a dog-eared copy of the World War I novel *Wings*.

Next to the flyboys, members of the World War II Russian Guards unit have made their temporary home. A large tent covers a straw bedding area, and on a wooden table lie various objects, including a hunk of black bread, a soldier's paybook, a bottle of vodka, and a field telephone. Lying on a blanket is the Russian unit commander's dog, Toby. A well-loved, old-hand reenactor (he usually does an "antitank dog" impression), Toby sits quietly as Scott Mies, dressed in his Russian kit, talks with a visitor about the siege of Stalingrad.

Next to the Russians lies Grossdeutschland's camp. William Gregory leads his men in a rousing version of "Lili Marlene" while Richard Paoletti prepares supper on an original German field kitchen. Richard wipes his hands on a smudged apron and smiles. "We've had a great response this weekend. People love this. They stop here, taste our homemade gingerbread, listen to William play the accordion, watch the guys drill, handle the mortars. It's great. I love it." As Richard cooks, a visitor can ask him questions about his field recipes or Grossdeutschland's order of battle. This instruction may be followed by an opportunity to sample the artifact's product: cabbage soup.

In the next camp, several Spanish Civil War volunteers, Tim Reed and Patrick Hart among them, are singing the "Internationale." Dressed in full kit, complete with red kerchiefs tied jauntily around their necks, they offer visitors a chance to ask questions, pose for photographs, or peruse the works of Leon Trotsky. (No one actually reenacts the Spanish Civil War; it is strictly a public impression, since public events offer reenactors a chance to put together impressions and displays for performance value only.)

Next, Grace Hall handily commands her unit of World War I American Salvation Army "Donut Dollies." She stands in front of an elaborate period cooking operation, handing out free donuts to an appreciative crowd. In the center of the field, her husband, Max Hall, commands his World War I German unit, shouting instructions in German to the men, who march in step, rifles at their shoulders.

After arriving to set up their camps on Friday afternoon, the roughly one hundred twentieth-century war reenactors will be busy. For two days, from nine to five, they'll interpret war for the public, left on their own to fulfill the promises the event hosts make. They'll also compete with each other in a museum-hosted competition, with awards given for "Best Display" and "Public's Favorite."

In preparing for this event, they've had anything but a time trip on their minds. They've been living in the real world planning the logistics: getting a day off from work, promising wives or girlfriends they'll be home next weekend, packing supplies, coordinating unit members. Fred Legum describes the flurry of activity before an event: "There's a lot of phone time before an event. People start getting excited, and they call just to chitchat or to make sure things are ready, make sure everybody has everything they need, trying to see who's going to be there, who's not going to be there." Having spent hours preparing, they head to Jamestown. Some, like Grace and Max Hall, drive more than twelve hours to attend this reenactor favorite.

Although the event may make the grand promise of a trip through time, many reenactors argue that when their public face is put forth professionally they can "get the public interested in history." And they look upon a static display as "a wonderful tool for teaching . . . about the tragedies and sacrifices throughout history." They often refer to their displays as "tributes," dedicated to the common soldiers of the past. "Back then when the war broke out," as Ben Sandler nostalgically observes, "the high schools emptied, the colleges emptied, almost all the young men enlisted. Nowadays if a war broke out hardly anyone would join. Everyone was more patriotic back then."

In many ways, reenactors do attempt to inspire patriotism. "We teach the public about the sacrifices and accomplishments of American medical personnel during World War II," one unit explains. But they also say they don't want to present war as something positive. "We do not glorify war," one reenactor says, "but we do respect the warrior."

Sometimes, I felt reenactors were effective in achieving such a balance. But at other times, I couldn't help noticing how fine the line is between respecting the warrior and respecting war itself. After all, the experience of eating an ice cream cone while listening to a reenactor talk about a soldier's bread bag is certainly not akin to walking through Arlington National Cemetery or watching a newsreel of Nazi atrocities. In the golden sunlight of a Saturday in late March, with the buds blooming and the Virginia sky bright and blue overhead, I often felt there was something more to their public mantra that I hadn't yet understood.

I soon learned that reenactors make a sharp distinction between their public and private events. In fact, in performing for the public, they do not "reenact" at all, reserving the term for private events. (Even a public battle is not seen as "reenacting" as much as "performing" for the public.) They also tend to downplay the recreational aspect of their hobby, and many even entirely avoid mentioning that they're reenactors. William Gregory prefers to call himself a "living historian" in public since "it's very tough to explain yourself as a reenactor." They also banish some elements present at their private events: truly controversial symbols, such as the swastika, are usually nowhere to be seen in a static display.

By and large, reenactors present themselves as historical interpreters as they perform living history activities such as drilling, conducting inspection or guard duty, playing period games, cooking, or singing. Many also engage in small-scale dramas set within their displays. One reenacting unit, the American Military

Medical Impression, sets up elaborate field hospitals from World War II, the Korean War, and the Vietnam War and performs for the public as nurse and doctor reenactors tend to wounded soldiers. With the idea that "people will learn history more quickly by visually seeing it rather than just reading about it," many units carefully orchestrate visitor interaction with their displays. "For a public display," one reenactor explains, "it is imperative that you script things as heavily as a stage play or a Civil War event. For the interests of safety and spectator enjoyment, the 'encounters' should be staged in such a way as to be photogenic." Reenactors guide visitors through their camps, where the visual intricacy proves irresistible. Visitors pull out cameras and video recorders, documenting this or that martial extravagance. At one MTA, a group of Pacific Theater reenactors willingly agreed to pose for me. "What would you like us to do?" one asked. "How about a combat shot?" Without a word, they positioned themselves; one American manned a machine gun and the other brandished his pistol while a "Japanese" soldier lunged at them with fixed bayonet. They held their positions, waited for me to capture the moment, and then resumed their field duties.

Other reenactors highlight their capacity to engage the crowds by offering brief lectures or telling stories. In telling these stories, however, most do not talk at length about war's social, economic, and political causes and effects. Rather, they focus on the minutiae: what the common soldier ate, carried, wore, and fired. "A personal story behind a uniform," as one reenactor advises, "makes it most interesting for the average viewer."

Because the public already knows war is horrible, they say, they try to instruct people about other aspects of the war experience. Usually, their stories take how-to form, as if a military manual on small arms was brought to life. A reenactor will explain, for instance, the production history of a gun model or show how to use a field phone in combat. Woven through are more general tales, concerning how many troops were killed in a certain battle, where a unit was mobilized, a soldier's training history.

Some reenactors promote their presentations as "the only accurate interpretation of historical events that [the public is] likely to be exposed to." And they constantly remind the public that their displays are high-quality. "Most of the equipment you will see is original and very rare," one unit instructs visitors, and others sound a similar note. In fact, Grossdeutschland is so committed to the authenticity of its campsite display that one member makes "period" World War II trash—candy bar wrappers, newspapers—with which to litter the ground. Because they take these presentations so seriously, they encourage each other to "bring all your best gear to spectator battles/public displays," catering, in part, to the inevitable scrutiny of veterans—who show up at public events in surprisingly large numbers (some dressed in their own uniforms as well). As one reenactor reports: "We have consciously set a standard for equipment designed so that every man can appear on parade and in the field with a degree of accuracy such that a veteran won't find any obvious fault."

Reenactors also seem to embody the subjects of the stories they tell, since, of course, they perform their public duties while dressed in period uniforms. Perhaps no other aspect is more important to them than their impressions. "Let's face it," observes one reenactor. "What we physically look like . . . is the cornerstone of the hobby and separates us from . . . other hobbies." But to do an impression is not just to dress up. Instead, it means authentically appearing like an actual soldier from a past war would have appeared.

Despite their emphasis on authenticity, however, reenactors don't attempt to convince themselves or others that they really are the soldiers they represent. First-person interpretation, acting and talking as if you really were the soldier you represent, is acceptable at a private event, but most regard its public use as detrimental. Presenting themselves as real soldiers would be problematic and even embarrassing since so many veterans tour their camps. But, more important, they think it alienates people.

"I'm very uncomfortable with it as a visitor to a historic site," Grace Hall says, whose real-life job is in the field of historic preservation. "Sometimes it's fun to play along with [first person interpreters] but sometimes it just makes you really uncomfortable." "It turns people off," Dave Watkins agrees. "I feel uncomfortable with doing it with spectators. . . . I would rather stay in whatever day it really is and say, well, this is a German gas mask. Because if you don't do that people will be hesitant to ask you questions."

Most reenactors stay in whatever day it really is and maintain their real-life identities; only a few adopt first-person characters in public. One such reenactor, known by his fake name, "Biff," is a freelancer who haunts various events. In public, he appears not as the real-life nurse that he is, but as a World War II flyboy. At a period 1940s Flag Day dance I attended at Gadsby's Tavern in Alexandria, Virginia, Biff was in his glory. Despite the fact that most people there were not reenactors, Biff, dressed in uniform, spoke to everyone as if it really were 1943. At one point, another reenactor approached Biff to tell him he was leaving, and Biff responded seriously. He lowered his voice and asked, "Did you get your orders?" At another point, he addressed the crowd and invited everyone to visit a nearby supper club where Miss Dinah Shore was currently performing in a limited engagement. When people looked at him quizzically, he responded to their apparent confusion: "There's no cover charge," he assured them, "to men in uniform."

At public displays, one may spy Biff sitting in his elaborate camp, sipping a Coke from a 1940s bottle. He sometimes smiles but is usually unwilling to communicate in present-day terms. "He's not very publicly friendly," explains his friend, Patrick Hart. "A lot of times I have to explain what he's doing." To most reenactors, such an immersion in character is destructive. "To tell you the truth," Patrick says, it "makes a lot of tourists uncomfortable. They don't know how to deal with it. They can't deal with you period and when you start doing that they're like, oh, he's fooling with us. They just don't get it [and] a lot of the guys who do it, they don't know when to turn it off." Patrick laughed and identified what he calls Biff's "sickness." "Some people do drugs, some people drink," he says, "Biff reenacts."

As reenactors attempt to present themselves as normal people with a commendable desire to educate, many of them express a sense of accomplishment. "It's nice to receive recognition occasionally for the time, money, and effort put into this hobby," one reenactor says. High school student Ben Sandler loves public events since "you get to talk to the public and stuff. That's a whole lot of fun. . . . I've actually had kids ask for my autograph." Ben is not alone in feeling like a celebrity. Richard Paoletti describes one unit member who "really shines": "If you're at the air shows sometimes you'll see a flock of people around him and he'll be explaining all sorts of stuff like the *panzerfaust*, the grenades and such, and people are really fascinated."

To be fair, most people who attend public events are probably already interested in martial displays. But even in the case of displays of Nazi equipment, reenactors often get enthusiastic responses. I once watched several World War II German reenactors perform rifle drill in front of their MTA camp as their commander barked out orders in German. I asked a friendly-looking couple in their thirties what they thought of them. "Very good," the man said, nodding and smiling. "Yes," the woman agreed. I was shocked to hear their accents: they were German. "Of course," the woman laughed, "they could never do that in Germany!"

But in America, reenactors report, the general response is pretty positive. "Whenever I'm involved in living history, portraying a German soldier," Grossdeutschland commander William Gregory says, "there is always a good deal of genuine spectator interest and questioning, just about all of which has been positive." William described an event where his unit was "criticized while we waited in formation for our cue to go out and die for the crowd like a bunch of 'good krauts.'" The criticism came from an elderly lady, her complaint, "You don't sing enough." After dying in the public battle, the unit marched through the air show singing "Westerwald." "The same American public that had wanted to see a bunch of krauts die," William recalls, "were now applauding us."

It's not only applause they receive. "The public really appreciates what we do," William continues, "and they filled our donation box to the top." The small wooden padlocked box the unit erects in its camp was filled with three hundred dollars at the end of a single day at the Reading air show in response to their plea, "Through your generous donations we are able to present the regular German soldier of World War II with greater accuracy." (The unit uses donations to defray the cost of their extensive display or to purchase something for the unit, such as the field kitchen.)

Donations, thanks, or genuine interest are evidence that a public display touches something in their audience. "I don't mean just the kids who wet their pants to see guns go off and airplanes buzzing around," one reenactor says, "but the people who lived through that era. Both the service men and the folks on the home front."

For some reenactors, making veterans happy is deeply satisfying. And time and again at public events, I heard veterans—German, Russian, American—express gratitude for seeing young people make sure they're not forgotten. One World War II German veteran told Dave Watkins "that he was really happy to see people doing what we were doing because, he said, it had to be told. People had to be exposed to it and he really was enthusiastic." Some veterans become so enthusiastic that they talk the ears off reenactors. At one MTA, an American World War II veteran, dressed in his own World War II uniform, chatted happily with Paul Harding and Wilson Lyle, who were dressed as German paratroopers. The odd triumvirate clearly enjoyed each other's company and exchanged war stories for a solid hour. At other times, veterans become so enthusiastic that they're prompted to conduct their own living history lessons. "We would never march with our rifles pointed down," one German veteran instructed members of Grossdeutschland, as he took up a rifle to demonstrate. "Even in the rain."

Seeing some of these veterans—particularly German veterans—come out and wax nostalgic about old times can be disturbing. I once saw a World War II German veteran talking with German reenactors away from the public eye. With a great big smile on his face, he told them how thankful he was to see them since, he said in a hushed voice, so many people vilify the German soldiers of World War II and don't really appreciate what they had done.

Grossdeutschland's camp, Reading Air Show, 1998

I was chilled to hear this man express gratitude for having his memory cleaned up and presented in a positive light. But I also knew that even some American veterans enjoy seeing Germans portrayed. An SS reenactor was at a public display when a group of American veterans from the famous World War II unit, the 101st Airborne, showed up. "They loved the SS and German impressions," the reenactor reported. "They would stand around and just stare at us and tell us over and over how great it was. And they just were fascinated with the SS with comments like, 'Damn, I get goose bumps just lookin' at this guy.'"

But not all veterans are happy to see their former enemies portrayed. "Some vets get ticked," the SS reenactor admitted, "when they see us." And indeed, seeing reenactors, even at events notable for their military theme, can incite unfavorable reactions from veterans and civilians alike: reenactors are reliving a past that's better forgotten; they're distorting history; they're crazy, call the police.

When Laura Paris took a break from a public event near a highway rest area dressed in her World War II German uniform, she found herself confronted by a policeman. He was responding to a complaint that there was "a nut with a Nazi helmet and a rifle at the rest area." When John Loggia showed up at a Celtic festival in Pennsylvania dressed in his World War I British officer's kit, he was accosted by "big guy with tattoos." It turns out that the man was a member of the Bethlehem branch of the IRA and was "not too happy to see" him. The Irish Guards report similar incidents, the most dramatic of which was when some Irish Americans threw bottles at them.

Sometimes, public reactions even shock reenactors. In one case, an elderly lady with a cane began yelling at a group of British, SS, and Russian reenactors at a public event. As she came closer, the SS reenactors braced themselves, preparing themselves to be chastised. But she only pushed them aside and proceeded to berate a reenactor standing behind the Germans, who was dressed as a Russian commissar.

But there's no doubt that the World War II German impression stirs up the most hatred. One German reenactor remembered a hostile encounter at a West Point display. A spectator, he reported, "could not comprehend my interest in the German military. So, my impression was perceived as an expression of prejudice." The spectator was furious in fact. The "blood of children" is on your uniform, he told the reenactor. He departed saying that he intended to write a letter of complaint to West Point.

This spectator's reaction is certainly understandable. But no matter how hard reenactors say they try to stick to their mission of public education and not blame people for their hostile responses, I noticed that certain reenactors sometimes appear less than friendly in public. I witnessed this on several occasions when I approached a display, only to be met with a quick, cursory glance by the reenactors. No word of welcome. No smile. Feeling like a trespasser, I would ask, "Do you mind if I look around?" "Feel free," was the cool response. At other times I watched reenactors joke and talk among themselves, ignoring the visitors who approached to stand hesitantly at the sidelines of their camp. The reenactors paid them no mind, but continued a non-period discussion. Meanwhile, the visitors probably wondered why they were hearing a story about a reenactor's 1996 Ford Taurus and not about the soldier's role in World War II.

In light of their desire to portray themselves professionally, the cold shoulder routine seems counterproductive. But it's only after the public goes home, the event hosts take their leave, and the cool of a remaining winter blows through their camps that I begin to glimpse some of what lies behind their public mantra.

The Jamestown Settlement is now closed. The first day of MTA is over. After a barbecued chicken dinner, reenactors enjoy some down time, sitting in their camps, gathered around campfires, drinking beer, swapping stories. By the time darkness completely envelops the wooded site only the glow of fires provides light.

At a World War II German camp, I join Paul Harding, Bill Lauter, and Hank and Wilson Lyle to share the warmth of a blazing fire. Amid the sound of crickets and muffled voices, they begin to assess other reenactors, employing their handy labels to distinguish the many different types among them.

The group first turns its attention to a unit of bonehead flyboys. Not only were their impressions bad, they say, but they also misquoted facts, treated the public with contempt, and in general acted like idiots. Later, another unit is subject to critique: A World War II Japanese unit made up of large—in some cases, mammoth—white guys.

"Jeez, Louise," one reenactor howls, "I thought I was gonna wet my pants watching them."

"Did you ever see such a lot of fat in one place?! That one Jap was on the verge of losing his pants all day."

"I tell you, if the Japs really were that big, they'd have won the war!"

It was a truth I quickly learned. Despite promoting themselves publicly as "sincere historians" who are "well versed in the time period they portray," privately they agree that not all reenactors are suited to the role of public educator. "There's powder burners and then there's the living history people," John Loggia observes, making a distinction between reenactors who just want to "burn powder," or fire guns, and those who are serious about history. "Learning to credibly portray the army we claim to belong to is hard," Phillip Moss comments, and "not everyone has the knack." Perry Trent smiled when he said that he thinks most reenactors are "not too bright," but others bear clear resentment. "Those of use who have done hours and hours of research to perfect our impression," one reenactor laments, "resent the yahoos in our vocation."

When I asked Luke for his opinion, he responded by saying that he thinks most reenactors look at a public event as nothing more than a chance to show off. It has "a certain amount of vanity to it," he says. "I think [reenactors] like to have their pictures taken, kind of like to ham it up a little bit." Hank Lyle agrees, criticizing reenactors for acting like "peacocks strutting around a barn yard . . . all [wanting] to have the prettiest feathers." And Michael Collins gripes that a public event often turns into "a fashion show." Too many reenactors, he thinks, just "love to wear all these pretty costumes, but they have no appreciation of the history."

Such evaluations are certainly not meant to be heard by outsiders; they belong in the backstage region of a public event. And it's usually only in private that reenactors reveal an often bitter animosity toward one another. "There are mostly Americans under those helmets," as John Loggia observes. But because of their deep divisions, John finds it amusing that in some ways reenactors seem as divided as they would be if they truly were from the warring nations they represent. "God," he laughs, "you'd think they were really from those countries."

I listen to some soldiers singing in harmony. Hank and Bill are cracking up about a small tent nearby that two oversized reenactors are going to share. "I think there's going to be a little spooning going on in there," Hank says, his face red from laughing. "That's fine," the reenactor getting teased responds. "As long as there's no forking." At this, Bill and Hank double over laughing. Wilson looks at me and shakes his head.

I sit at the campfire and wonder what people would say if they saw all this. Not only do reenactors reveal themselves to be at odds with each other in performing their public duty, but their own behavior also fails to affirm the stereotype of reenactors dutifully trying to relive the past. They talk about events that occurred last month, last weekend, or earlier in the afternoon. Leaning back against a cooler, smoking a cigarette, drinking a Coke, they joke and laugh and talk with each other. It only just so happens—it would appear—that they're dressed in period uniforms.

One reenactor emerges from his tent with his pants off and his shirttails hanging in front of him. "I can't find my jeans," he says.

"Oh, man," Paul says.

"There's a lady present, you know," Wilson, ever the gentleman, tells him. But others are already giving him shit.

"It looks like a penis," the wiseacre Bill Lauter laughs, "only smaller."

And on it goes. It's nearly midnight. One reenactor calls his wife on a cell phone; another returns from a run to the store with beer and pretzels. A few crawl into their pup tents to get some sleep. Others retire to nearby motels before getting up early the next morning to start their education efforts again. This, I think, as Hank, Wilson, Paul, Bill, and I head off to Bill's nearby house, is an experience of the present, and not the past.

Chapter 6

"We Must Police Ourselves Constantly"

Behind the Public Mantra

As much as reenactors squabble among themselves privately, in public they tend to lay their conflicts aside. To the outside world they want to present a unified front since, as John Loggia sees it, "a couple of bad apples can make everyone else look like total morons, and all the people think we are idiots." Thus, whatever their opinions are about each other's attitudes, vanity, or farbiness, they continuously remind each other to "work together." "Together! United!" one reenactor declares, "Or we all fall together, united or not!"

Many reenactors agree that the need to unite is urgent, especially in light of opposition to the hobby. One alerted others to the dangers the outside world can present when he reported a sudden cancellation of a public event in an Illinois town. Initially, the town had agreed to sponsor a World War II battle demonstration and display. But, reportedly, town officials, including the chief of police, were "aghast" to learn that the reenactors would be "running around their village armed," and they summarily canceled the event. "It is doubly disappointing when an event is canceled because ignorance has triumphed over reason and common sense," the reenactor wrote. He lamented how "the historical significance of the proposed event has been lost amid voiced fears concerning guns," and he closed with an ominous assessment: "perhaps we are not perceived as historical saviors by the public at large."

The idea that the public at large may not view them as historical saviors doesn't really surprise most reenactors. Many even feel that they're "tried, convicted, and condemned before the fact." And condemning them takes many forms.

Critics often judge reenactors (or volunteer living historians) to be "amateurs in the strictest sense." They are, after all, just average people whose memory of history, as historian Michael Kammen, reminds us, "tends to be people-oriented, impressionistic, and imprecise." Scholar Jim Cullen concedes that reenacting may be a "sincere and meaningful cultural act" that has some "legitimacy." But he also has reservations about it. In particular, he criticizes reenactors for having "little knowledge of political, cultural, and social movements before, during, and after the war."

Critics also wonder about the value of living history in general. Scholars Richard Handler and William Saxton argue that living history is often used as an attempt "to replicate rather than interpret the past." In doing so, interpreters "overlook the present-day cultural routines that underpin the production of particular simulations." Further, because it is ultimately impossible to "replicate" history, living historians are "almost pathologically doomed to failure in [their] enterprise."

Much of the criticism of living history is focused on tourist attractions whose employees are hired to perform as historic figures such as George and Martha Washington or to enact more controversial histories such as slave auctions. These living histories are connected to respected institutions that base their reputations on their research. War reenactors, however, fly solo. They don't have a Williamsburg or Mount Vernon to back them up. As they undertake the task of representing the sensitive subject of modern war, they are often viewed as untrained or unprofessional interlopers. Who's given these history buffs the authority to educate the public? At an oral history conference in New Orleans, I met a National Park Service guide from a small historic site. He was vehement in his belief that reenactors are "not capable of accurately educating the public." Further, he said, they pose a "danger" to an unwary audience since no one is "checking the accuracy" of their portrayals.

Some even view reenactors as marginal or suspect characters. Especially throughout the 1990s, when national attention was so focused on the issues of gun control and militias, war reenactors were charged with being "gun lovers" or "paramilitary." As one journalist put it, "it's hard to tell the difference between hardcores [reenactors] and skinheads."

Reenactors are also accused of possessing some kind of innate character flaw or leading less than satisfying real lives. A well-known English professor dismisses reenactors as having "the moral dimensions of twelve-year-olds." Scholar James William Gibson believes that the "development of mock-combat war games in the United States a few short years after the Vietnam War is not in itself surprising." Not surprising, according to Gibson, since such games arose out of a male identity crisis. Gibson asserts that in the wake of the civil rights movement, women's rights movement, and the US defeat in Vietnam, some men "began to dream, to fantasize about the powers and features of another kind of man who could retake and reorder the world." And these men sought to reorder the world through highly masculine pastimes such as target shooting and war games.

People are also uneasy with reenactors assuming the roles of real soldiers. Wearing medals not earned. Telling war stories. Showing off war trophies. Even a non-reenactor friend of Luke's from graduate school confided in me that although he liked Luke and the others, he found something innately "sacrilegious" in their wearing uniforms they hadn't earned themselves.

But most often, people are bothered by the idea that reenactors do nothing to convey war's real horror. Watching kids smile as reenactors let them handle a mortar at a public display or seeing a crowd cheer at a mock battle riles those who feel that these wannabes are turning war into entertainment.

For their own part, some reenactors dismiss their critics: "I did not get involved in this hobby to please the public and I'm not really interested in their opinion," as one reenactor says. But many more simply acknowledge how hard it can be for people to accept them. With the idea that they're being judged "too quickly," as Ray Sherman believes, and that "reenacting's misconstrued," as Scott Friewald says, some believe that they can effectively reason with their critics.

Nat Handler reported an instance when he was able to turn one critic into a supporter. At a public event at Fort Myers, Virginia, an "irate lady" was so upset at seeing World War II German reenactors that she yelled at the MPs and the post commander to "have them removed." When Nat approached her to try to calm her down, he learned that "she was a young girl in Europe during the war [and] watched the Germans kill both her parents." Nat says he talked with her for half an hour, explaining that they were trying to educate people about war, not glorify it. Surprisingly, Nat reported that after hearing this, "she did a 180, posed for pictures with all of us, and wished us good luck."

Although Nat did not explain precisely how this woman turned around, he concluded that even in the worst confrontation, they can win over their opposition: "It just takes believing in what we do," Nat concludes, "and a lot of honesty." But others acknowledge how hard such a feat can be, since "people are still suffering emotionally from [war]," as Scott Mies says. "We have to respect that," Scott believes, "because these people went through something that none of us have ever even begun to understand."

Many reenactors find it impossible to reason with someone whose family was killed at the hands of a soldier they represent. "I guess I'm of the mind that we all reenact for the fun of it (if I were to give a completely honest answer)," one reenactor says. But "that in itself wouldn't be a great line of reasoning with an angry war survivor, to be sure!"

Encountering angry war survivors is just one reason some reenactors feel uncomfortable in public. "I myself do not like public events much," one reenactor admits. "I feel a little self-conscious." Patrick Hart concurs. He doesn't give a second thought to dressing like a Nazi for a private reenactment, but, he says, "I really have a problem with doing it in public."

In admitting to having a problem with doing it, reenactors also express a great deal of frustration. Despite their willingness to perform "discount, low budget or freebie work" in a variety of public settings, they believe that too often they're treated poorly, unprofessionally, or viewed with suspicion.

Just three days after the Oklahoma City bombing, Alicia Mellon went to a public event dressed in her World War II American uniform. "I will never forget how many people came up to me," she recalls, "and ask[ed] me about my political beliefs." Alicia thinks people "were all looking for someone to hang," and she was annoyed. "Just because we happened to come out with a fifty-caliber machine gun, I mean, and we were just like, you are so missing the point of why we're here."

To be sure, since the hobby involves the ownership and recreational use of guns, reenactors are highly attuned to any accusation that they are amassing weapons for some kind of subversive purpose. "Anybody who possesses a weapon is under suspicion," as Dave Watkins believes. "And now with this militia thing and Waco thing, and now the Freeman thing, they tend to put us all in a lump." Quite a few reenactors work in law enforcement, including one reenactor I know who works for the ATF, and others, such as those who work for the NRA or run gun shows, steadily work against the image that they are irresponsible with guns, or worse, political. In this one respect especially, reenactors believe the public is woefully uninformed. "I'm not even sure people understand we're using blanks," Luke observes.

As they try to reason with critics or separate themselves from truly extreme groups, many reenactors report that they feel "that doing things for the public is

Demonstrating a bazooka, Virginia Museum of Military Vehicles, public event, 1995

sometimes tedious, unappreciated," as Mark Sammons says. "It seems like work." Wilson Lyle put it more bluntly: "The vast majority of public events are a real hassle."

And indeed, as much as reenactors are critical of each other, they're even more critical of the very body they serve: the public. As they privately assess the people who file their way through their displays and campsites, fingering their collections, thanking them for doing a terrific job, or questioning their motives, they cast aside their public face entirely to evaluate their experiences honestly. What to one reenactor is a day dedicated to education is to another reenactor an exercise in futility; as one reenactor said, paraphrasing H. L. Mencken, "You will never be wrong in underestimating the ignorance of the American public."

"The vast majority of the public doesn't want to be educated," Wilson Lyle declares. "I for one," Philip Moss states, "rarely want to be around touronz, especially in World War II garb. I find them inane and highly irritating. Once or twice a year is okay, but more than that, it isn't fun." Others assess touronz in similarly less than admirable terms: "The general public either derides us for spending a small fortune on something they don't want to understand, or they bring their children out to gape at us like animals."

Their criticism does not end with their public, however. They also counter their academic critics. Michael Collins laughed when he said judging others is easy when you "sit on your butt in your ivory tower." Another reenactor dismissed academics as being all "friggin' wet." Meanwhile, Perry Trent railed against Tony Horwitz's "derogatory" portrayal of reenactors as a bunch of time-traveling nuts in his book *Confederates in the Attic.* He made "a fool out of us," Perry fumed. But to him, Horwitz was only typical of those "intellectuals" who "look down their noses at us and think that we're idiots."

Alain Benson locates negative public attitudes toward reenactors in more general social trends. "I thought the way things were going this last couple of years," he explains, "especially after the Oklahoma City bombing and the banning of assault weapons, that slowly but surely reenacting would become sort of like politically incorrect." He went on to illustrate what he considers the general attitude of their critics: "It's sort of like why would you want to own a machine gun? Why would you want to dress up like an army guy and run around the woods and go bang-bang? War is bad. Haven't we learned our lesson by now? You losers are keeping this alive. We want to put all this stuff behind us and move on. So go away." According to Alain, "the way to make us go away is to slowly cut off our freedoms of owning historical weapons and places to reenact."

The idea that their freedoms—whether to own guns or interpret history—are threatened is widely shared among reenactors. In the aftermath of September 11, 2001, concern about the hobby's future was especially intense. In October 2001, an HRS World War II event that was to be held at a US military facility was cancelled because all federal posts were on heightened alert and closed to "non-mission" oriented activity. Several units pulled out of other events voluntarily, since it was considered a bad time to cross state lines with military equipment and weapons, especially given that one of the fall's major events was being held in New York State. Further, "in view of recent current events," as one reenactor commented, "it was also thought that it would be in bad taste to run around playing war games." Given the tremendous violence the United States had just experienced, reenactors worried they would undergo even more hostile critique and intensive scrutiny. One reenactor even went as far as asking if they should continue reenacting at all.

But as the events of September 11 grew more distant and reenactors, like the rest of the country, mourned the losses and sought to move on, reenactors again shored up their defenses. Whatever opinion they have of touronz, intellectuals, and even each other, the feeling that they're under attack serves a constructive purpose: it unites them and compels them to defend themselves. Even those reenactors who argue that "the public's lack of understanding [and] knowledge is their loss, not mine, so it's no concern of mine" are careful to add an amendment: "But only up to the point where [the public's lack of understanding] creates restrictions or other problems to *my* enjoyment."

Because fear and ignorance can restrict their enjoyment, most know that they can't just ignore their critics. "If we get tagged as 'militias' or such similar groups," one reenactor warns, "we're done." Thus, many agree that "we must police ourselves constantly," as one reenactor advises. As they attempt to work together, they try to shore up their image as public servants. And among themselves, they engage in a media-savvy assessment of the best way to project their public face.

Public Relations

"I do feel strongly," World War II reenactor Tim Gilbert argues, "that we can improve our public image by participating in public displays that do not involve reenactments." Educational displays at veteran conventions, schools, and military ceremonies that emphasize public service over entertainment, he argues, can bolster the hobby's image.

Others believe that managing their image in the media is the best way to gain credibility. "Obviously, we can and should take time to educate the public as to the history behind what we're doing. That's the whole idea behind living history events/displays," Wilson Lyle states. "But let's focus on the press/news media, who, for all intents and purposes, are a completely different animal."

Compared to the Civil War hobby—which has far more name recognition—twentieth-century war reenactors receive limited coverage on TV and in newspapers. Most is local, and according to reenactors, mixed in presentation. Nearly half of reenactors think the media portrays them and the hobby in both positive and negative ways.

Although "the media hasn't done anything yet," as one reenactor observes, "we need to anticipate such an attack and eliminate as many possible problems as possible." Many reenactors concur, often trying to take charge of the media's coverage of the hobby. One reenactor instructed others that: "because [an upcoming event] will be covered by Maryland Public TV's *On Location,* as well as the major network TV affiliates, we all have the opportunity to promote the positive nature of World War II reenacting; let's take it!" Some even court press attention. Perry Trent invited a local reporter to his home to do a story on his military vehicle collection, in part to ease any fears his neighbors might have in seeing a fleet of tank destroyers massed on his property. Another reenactor who runs gun shows for a living was a guest on C-SPAN's *Washington Journal* in 1999, when the network broadcast live from his show. Although he did not identify himself as a reenactor, he clearly tried to dispel the image of gun owners as reckless or subversive. Others assume their real life roles as members of the press themselves. One reenactor has published several stories in newspapers such as the *Washington Times,* where he has covered reenacting from a decidedly commemorative angle.

But others believe that they will never get a fair shake from the media. "Regardless of what uniform we wear," one reenactor believes, "the media will find something to exploit." Another agrees: "Reasoning with them is like arguing with a drunk who has a bottle of whiskey in one hand and a gun in the other. Staying away is the only solution." The threat of being exploited is manifest most clearly in events where the media is present. At various events I've seen reporters thrust cameras or microphones into reenactors' faces, asking questions ranging from "What happened in World War I?" to "Why are you dressed as a German soldier?" Usually, reenactors respond by faithfully repeating their public mantra. An event is about "honor and preserving that honor," Larry Cohen said in a voiceover for a local TV news story featuring reenactors; his sentiment was followed by another reenactor who explained their desire "to maintain the memory of what those soldiers did."

But with so many different characters in the hobby responses to media queries cannot always be monitored. "There can be a hundred well dressed, polite, knowledgeable people that the press could talk to," one reenactor states, "but they will always find [some] kind of stooge and put him on the six o'clock news." Wilson Lyle calls all events with the media present "potential disasters." "More often than not," he observes, "reporters singled out our most bone-headed members to talk to. . . . I've seen reporters run past two large groups of Brit and US airborne [reenactors] just to get to the German reenactor and proceed to ask him a lot of pointed questions. And every time, I hold my breath and hope the poor guy doesn't put his foot in his mouth."

To control interaction with the media, some reenactors hand out press packets and promotional videos or appoint reenactor "press liaisons" to serve as front men for their units. "Make the calmest, most laid back, most thoughtful person in your group the official press liaison," one reenactor advises. "Have everyone else smile politely at the reporters, claim they don't know the answer to whatever question was asked, and send them to that guy."

Even in the case of World War II German impressions, many believe they can project a positive image. "Just remember," one German reenactor states, "we have nothing to be ashamed of as German reenactors, but bear in mind that we portray the military might of one of the most evil empires in history. Be sensitive to this and nothing bad will happen to you in terms of PR." But not all German reenactors will have such an easy time. "If you are in an SS unit," he added, "you're fucked!"

To be sure, "the pall of Nazism," as Luke proclaims, "hangs over World War II reenacting." And there's no question that the sharpest thorn in the hobby's side is the Waffen SS impression. Even the most well-mannered press liaison will have a hard time presenting an unthreatening image wearing SS runes and death's-head insignia. Although reenactors insist that they are not "political," privately they agree that some reenactors, particularly those who do World War II German, are "one brick shy of a full load." Aesthetic or historical interests aside, "I don't think that's all that motivates some of these people," one reenactor observes. "It is the more sinister motives that make the SS impression problematic, not only for all reenactors, but for those who do it for a little innocent fun." "You can't do it without an enemy," Luke agrees, "and that attracts a sometimes unseemly character into the hobby—not a pure historian, not a pure collector, but an ideologue."

By all accounts, some reenactors are sinister. I've heard several stories about some reenactors who were identified as being radically extreme in their politics. Grant Holzer told me of a couple of encounters with World War II German reenactors that made him wonder "if I wasn't dealing with neo-Nazis." Paul Harding affirmed this when I asked if he knew any in the hobby. "Sure," he said firmly. "How many?" I asked. "Well, I know of two for sure," he responded. "They're really neo-Nazis?" I pressed. "Well, I don't know if they actually are, but they do love that German thing a little too much. They really get into it. And it kind of makes you wonder."

In my own interactions, I ran into a few ideologues myself. At one MTA, Paul Harding, Hank Lyle, and I were relaxing at camp when we were joined by three World War II German reenactors we'd never met before. When their conversation suddenly became extremely offensive as they made racist and anti-Semitic remarks, we hightailed it out of there, even though Hank wanted to confront them. At another event, I spied a World War II German reenactor who does a vague impression of Adolf Hitler. Small of stature and sporting the telltale mustache, he often wanders about by himself at private events. I was told that he was a real soldier in the US National Guard! I was also told in no uncertain terms that he is largely shunned by others; one unit once ejected him from their barracks, and once he was kicked out of an event.

Although these extreme types exist in the hobby, they are not the majority. Still, their presence serves as a constant worry. Many argue that "a high level of authenticity will normally weed out the political nutzos that are inevitably drawn to the hobby, especially on the German side," as one reenactor believes. "I have found that most persons who are drawn to the hobby for political reasons will leave because they are not interested in wearing the 'correct' equipment, etc. They just want to have a reason to wear a swastika." But others advocate taking an aggressive stance. "If this hobby is to have a future, the historical minded among us must attempt to correct those who transgress . . . and exclude those who are beyond hope."

Not only do reenactors sometimes exclude those deemed beyond hope through membership restrictions, but they also censure those who behave unprofessionally. When one hapless reenactor was arrested at Chicago's O'Hare Airport wearing a World War II German uniform, he created a small flurry of media attention, including coverage by the *Chicago Tribune*. The police took him into custody not because he was sporting a Nazi uniform, but because he was illegally transporting a weapon on his way to a public event. As a result of his mistake, he was forced to resign from the Historical Reenactment Society.

Reenactors also exercise control in their private dealings. When Philip Moss argued against participating in an Eisenhower Farm public display, since German reenactors would spend most of their time in an "enclosure" as POWs, he complained to the World War II newsgroup: "I would sooner eat dog shit than go to that murdering bastard's farm"—a comment for which he was soundly rebuked. "For a 'German' reenactor to refer to [Eisenhower] as a 'murdering bastard' is A hypocritical in the highest, and B in extremely poor taste," one reenactor wrote. "It is difficult enough to remove the politics from the first half of our century from our attempt to honor the soldiers who fought and died for their countries without making profane attacks upon a leader of the 'Good Guys.'" He concluded with one final thought for Philip: "Reenacting German soldiers is so fraught with political subtext that others can read into it . . . that I suggest a more restrained, and less obscene response in the future."

As reenactors try to restrain those who put the hobby in danger, some even go as far as arguing that in order to assure the hobby's future: "the eventual elimination of the SS impression needs to be seriously examined." Doing SS, one reenactor insists, "is a lightning rod for nothing but trouble [and] no argument to the contrary has ever convinced me that the minimal variety the impression adds . . . in any way offsets the potential dangers and liabilities the SS impression imposes on reenacting." But another reenactor who does SS disagrees: "To eliminate Waffen SS units from the hobby completely because of the unsavory perception of a largely uninformed public has of them would be revisionism."

Soon a British reenactor chimed in: "We need to stand our ground as a living history organization. . . . We can't turn on one segment of our hobby because when they are gone, it will be another. Then we will all be looking at uniforms in closets."

To be sure, not all reenactors think taking drastic measures to control their image is key to their livelihood. To them, any concessions only cater to their "PC" opponents. One reenactor satirized attempts to make reenacting "publicly friendly." "Early horsehair backpacks are banned," he jokingly ordered. "All other gear must be certified to have been made without the use of animal testing." His final order: the German belt buckle must be changed: "replace 'Gott Mit Uns' with 'We are the World.'" (*Gott Mit Uns,* a German military motto used in both world wars, means "God is with us.")

Such jokes may be funny in private, but in public, they're risky. "I've seen some things done in very poor taste," Hank Lyle told me, giving an example of a PR faux pas: At a Korean War public battle, a reenactor "captured some guy doing North Korean and executed him." Although Hank thought such an action was authentic since in war "everybody slaughters everybody on both sides," it was, he said, entirely inappropriate for a public event. Another reported a similar transgression at a World War I event: "There were two battle reenactments during the course of the weekend. The public enjoyed both battles with the exception of a doughboy sergeant committing atrocities against wounded German soldiers."

Although this reenactor argued that the act successfully "illustrated the high casualty rate of the First World War," others find that "tasteless antics are ill-afforded." And most know that committing atrocities in public is taboo. "Executions do not play well, especially if they happen to be witnessed by the public," one reenactor said, sharing his experience at an event hosted by the US military: "A stunt by the Germans and the GIs just having fun almost cost us an excellent battle site as the post commander happened to witness the event. He was livid. Also, in the zeal, one of the Germans committed a nasty safety violation by finishing the GIs off with his pistol. He was sort of close. Mock courts martial and firing squads are not a good idea either. Sometimes we can get carried away."

Aware of their capacity to get carried away, and ever mindful of some reenactors' transgressions, reenactors rise to the occasion of the public event, gauge their image for public consumption, and try to control those "unserious yahoos who give reenactors a bad image."

After viewing this private side of the hobby, the internal strategizing, and efforts to mask tasteless antics, I saw how their desire to present a professional public face stems partly from the pressure they feel from their opposition. Accusations of being political, ignorant, or pro-war not only threaten the very existence of the hobby, but perhaps more important, they also cause reenactors to defend their right to represent history.

"There is, after all, no such thing as 'the past,'" historian Mike Wallace observes. "All history is a production—a deliberate selection, ordering, and evaluation of past events, experiences, and processes." The reenactors' public displays are, to be sure, their own productions. Although it took me a while, ultimately I found another more contemporary lesson in their public war presentations that is initially hard to perceive. But this lesson goes a long way to explain why reenactors choose to move such a carefully guarded hobby into the public spotlight in the first place.

Losses Not Quickly Restored

Tim Gilbert returned home after a Memorial Day public event in North Carolina brimming with enthusiasm. His World War II American unit's display had been a success. In a newsletter report, he celebrated the unit's "impressive amount of display material" and saw fit to provide a lengthy, detailed account: Aside from three vehicles on display, unit members erected "a command tent [with] a cot, field desk, and a map table." They also had a kitchen display "which included a small detachment field stove, an immersion heater, a M21941 mermite can, a M1942 single burner stove, a mountain cook set, and repro K ration boxes." A reenactor in the mess tent played host and "graciously explained the equipment to the crowd." Near the kitchen were two pup tents—"an early war open ended style and the later war closed end style." There was also a heavy weapons display, which was reportedly "a very popular area." On display were: two bazookas (an M1 and a M9A1), a Thompson, a M3 grease gun, a M1918A1 BAR, a M1919A4 and M1917A1 Browning machine gun, a 60mm mortar, a Garand with a grenade launcher," and "a mine detector and a land mine." As if all this equipment were not enough, there was also "a display of packs, which included a M1928 Haversack, M1936 Field Bag, a Mountain Rucksack, M1943 Jungle Pack, M1944 Field Pack, M1945 Field Pack, and early and late war packboards."

To the untrained eye, the mind-boggling details of a static display are inscrutable. How many people care about the difference between late war and early war tent styles? What does an authentic M1945 field pack mean in terms of understanding World War II? But in many ways, the answer is simple: such a production is not intended as a complex treatise on war's meaning.

Instead, a static display is often a distracting preface to a more general message reenactors hope to convey. "Since it was Memorial Day," the above report continued, "we stuck a Garand in the ground with a helmet on top and placed a sign next to it which mentioned the number of US service personnel that died in all the wars from the Revolution to the Gulf and asked them to take a moment to remember them." Asking visitors to remember fallen heroes, reenactors evoke a heroic vision of the past. But they also try to teach what they consider to be harsh lessons about the realities of war. Such lessons are most clearly evident in their "dramatic recreations" or living history vignettes. Unlike public battles, these mini-dramas are designed to give the public a more accurate view of the soldier's plight.

At an Armed Forces Day public event, 4th Armored staged a short "combat vignette" designed to "demonstrate," as Luke explained to the crowd, "World War II tactics and weaponry as they would have been used on the battlefields of Europe." After describing each soldier's role in a "typical combat patrol," Luke prompted the audience to embrace the reality of the solder's experience. "The theory [of combat] was sound," he said, "but in practice the Americans found that they could rarely establish the critically important fire superiority they needed to have freedom of movement." As he spoke, unit members demonstrated on the field, their actions illustrating the unraveling of the theory. Luke continued: "Another problem that faced the United States Army in Europe was the frequently inadequate supply of infantry replacements. . . . The divisions involved in the hedgerow fighting in Normandy suffered 85 percent casualties among riflemen and those losses were not quickly restored."

"Losses were not quickly restored"—although stated in the passive voice, there is no idea reenactors embrace with greater compassion. I've heard them articulate such a sentiment in a thousand different ways. The common soldier suffered not only at the hands of the enemy, but also at the hands of the very nation he represented. Poor supply lines, inadequate replacements, lousy theories, deathly tactics. These are the real difficulties soldiers faced. But the losses such difficulties engendered, reenactors believe, have never been restored, since even after the war soldiers continued to suffer as their experience was distorted or ignored, especially by those who oppose war.

"They went over there and fought on a foreign soil and came back and didn't get the recognition," Paul Donald says of American soldiers in World War I. Ray Sherman comments on the black American soldier in particular who went "to fight for this country while he had to sit on the back of the bus here in the United States." Ray laments how "these men thought they were going to come home to equality, and they didn't get it."

Although the vast majority of reenactors in the United States are American citizens, regardless of the nationalities they portray they have a shared lesson to convey: all soldiers deserve recognition. "I don't think it's fair," argues Scott Mies, who favors a World War II Russian impression, "the way Americans have bashed the Soviets during the Cold War and not given them any respect for World War II." Alicia Mellon says of her portrayal of American women in World War II: "I love teaching young girls and women that the feminist movement didn't begin in the 1970s. Most people under fifty don't even realize that women were in the military during World War II." Ray Sherman believes that "the black man in uniform needs his equal amount of honor from everybody. Not just the other races, but his own race too." And finally, in perhaps the most controversial statement regarding the need to understand the common soldier, Philip Moss argues that even German soldiers deserve recognition: "the German Army uniform has had quite enough dishonor heaped on it over the last fifty years."

With this shared message of restoring honor and respect to the soldier, reenactors present themselves at a public event in a uniform manner. To talk to a British reenactor is essentially equivalent to talking to an American reenactor. What a visitor is likely to hear are explanations of soldiers' equipment, life in the field, and combat experience—not descriptions of political ideologies. Thus, they present soldiers as generic figures of relatively equal value who are meaningful not because of nationality, religion, political affiliation, or even individual historical experience, but because of their shared experience on the battlefield during the world's most momentous event—war. "Reenacting pays homage to those men who do proud their uniform," one reenactor declares, "regardless of what uniform they wear. . . . The soldiers who fight well, hard and honorably are the ones whom I believe reenactors choose to emulate."

If their collective view of history must be categorized, it belongs somewhere in a gray area of interpretation. They favor a view of history that seems progressive, that is, rooted in understanding the experiences of ordinary people. But they also believe "there is too much rewriting of history" and that "the public [should] learn the truth and not the politically correct version." And many argue that in public they must try "to debunk a lot of mythical and inaccurate nonsense actually taught in our public schools."

Thus, in confronting the public with various offensive symbols, reenactors plead education. They argue that they are trying to force people to face their own biases and see beyond a narrow view offered by the media. "My main reason for doing living history," William Gregory explains, "is to get a chance to speak to the public and try to rid them of the Hollywood hype." This means combating

World War II US reenactor's tent, Military Through the Ages, 1998

an image of war that glorifies or vilifies the common soldier. Most reenactors believe that people view history from a black-and-white perspective and hold a simplistic view of war as being fought "between the good guys . . . and the bad guys." Paul Harding calls this the "Smurf" vision of reality. Luke calls it "naive."

So, while they celebrate sacrifice, they also argue that all aspects of the war experience must be confronted. "The bad incidents are the tragedies that come with war," one reenactor observes. "They should be acknowledged but not glorified." "History is history," another agrees, "not a movie you can rewrite . . . to avoid offending people." Thus, they strive to represent history through the eyes of the common soldier—arguing that such a presentation is ultimately more realistic, humane, and even more "American."

And in fact, even though I consider most reenactors to be pretty patriotic, many of them are quick to admit that even Americans were not necessarily governed by saintly ideals. "It certainly wasn't the good war some would like to believe," one US reenactor says about World War II. Another agrees: "There is a tendency to see ourselves on the moral high ground when in fact . . . the US had policies (albeit unwritten many times) that were as unfair to segments of our population as the Nazis were to the Jews."

Reenactors largely reject the idea that soldiers should be judged on the basis of their position on a moral landscape. "People have got to get beyond . . . the vilification of the enemy," Patrick Hart states firmly. Hank Lyle agrees: "On both sides," he says, "it was preached that the other side was the anti-Christ." When I asked Luke about his view on this subject, he responded with typical nonchalance: "I think the whole history of the world is one of conflict and war, coming to blows about things that couldn't be worked out in other ways. What else is new?" Like other reenactors, Luke doesn't think that any given nation is inherently more or less warlike than another. "Why would your society be any different than the society that's existed since the beginning of man?" he asked. "I've always found that kind of thing peculiar. I don't know why people tend to like to think that they're exceptionally unique in some ways."

With this perspective, reenactors present a version of history that refrains from making moral judgments. And they often condemn each other for doing the same. During a discussion on the World War II newsgroup about wars that erupted from religious differences, one reenactor commented: "[It's] amazing what civilized people will do in the name of Christianity." But another reminded him, "Your religion alone doesn't make you civilized. The Christian Knight who hacks down Moor children in a crusade, the Catholic Spanish Inquisitor who tortures 'heretics,' the Muslim suicide bomber who destroys a busload of tourists, the Jewish settler who opens up auto fire on a group of unarmed Arab demonstrators, the Hindu who smashes mosques in Kashmir. . . . The list goes on, my friends."

The view of the moral duality of all soldiers reflects their understanding of history, and distinguishes their perspective from what they perceive to be the general public's. "Unlike some narrow imbeciles," Philip Moss argues, "I can see both sides. If all Germans in the Wehrmacht were 'evil' because of Hitler and the

Nazis, does that mean that all Americans that served in Vietnam were bad because of William Calley and My Lai?" "Judging years after the fact by today's standards is pointless," another argues. "It was war," another agrees. "Politicians started it, soldiers fought it, and the world's people paid for it. To fault a soldier for the ideal[s] of the government he serves is the same as blaming a hammer for driving a crooked nail."

To be sure, reenactors often debate issues related to soldiers' political identities privately. But in public they go to great lengths "to keep the sacrifices of *all* soldiers . . . out of politics." Emphasizing the soldier's essential "neutrality," they convey an image of the soldier as himself an inhabitant of a gray area: part hero and part "poor slob." Fred Legum describes his unit as "just your common straight leg unit" that "didn't have any glorious moments." Thus, they present the common soldier as an average individual doing his job; he is a hero for his endurance and sacrifice. But he is also a pawn. "People had no control over what their government did to them," Scott Mies says, while Patrick Hart argues, "You can always incite the rabble to fight for you." To use their terms, soldiers were "just blindly obedient," "cannon fodder," or, as Luke describes American soldiers in Europe in World War II, "somewhat indifferent perhaps to the whole affair. . . . Because who wants to die for France?"

Reenactors often underscore the commonalty of all soldiers throughout history with great emotion. Paul Donald almost brought himself to tears when I asked him about his view of the common soldier. "I've studied a lot of wars," he said, shaking his head, "and it really scares you when you start looking at all the Civil War tintypes and daguerreotypes and then you flip open a World War I book and you see the same faces, and then you flip open a bunch of German photo albums, there's the same faces. The only difference is the uniform they've got on." Paul continued. "Under that uniform . . . they're all the same. They're all scared. They're all dying. They're all worried. They're all wanting to go home, you know? . . . It don't make a damn bit of difference what uniform you got on. Underneath they're all human beings."

Knowing that this compassion for all soldiers came from a man who himself was a Vietnam veteran, I wondered if Paul included himself in his description of all soldiers as "scared" and "wanting to go home." But even reenactors without military experience get emotional when they echo this notion of a soldier's ultimate humanity: "People were people no matter what the time period," Patrick Hart said solemnly.

With this insight into the ways reenactors view soldiers, I was able to see why their public presentations take the shape they do. To them, war is not a story of grand perspective, scripted battles, political ideologies, or Hollywood movies. As Alain Benson put it, the "whole story itself" is that of the minutiae, what the common soldier carried, wore, and fired. It is a story capable of being told without benefit of a larger context, and one that can only be understood in the absence of such a context. War, the most unfathomable event in human history, can be imagined once it is reduced to its details, its common, individual level. Patrick Hart explains this minimalist approach: "It doesn't come down to your flag or your country or your politics. It's the men in your platoon. The men in your company. That's who you're fighting for. You're not fighting for any glorious cause or whatever. What it comes down to is you're fighting for the twelve guys that you happen to be in combat with."

The reenactors' own penchant for grouping together in units replicates this image of camaraderie, or *Kameradschaft,* as German reenactors call it. Through such a unified stance, they reveal another lesson not explicit in their public mantra: people need to learn about another misunderstood, underappreciated group of common people who also sacrifice their time and effort with little recognition: reenactors.

Nowhere is this underlying lesson more apparent than in the ways they conflate an understanding of the common soldier with an understanding of the "common reenactor." "Everyone should know about their history and why we reenact," one reenactor declares in no uncertain terms. Another believes: "It is important that the American public know its history and that we are trying to preserve it through living history." Some even argue that the public's capacity to understand history relies on its willingness to overcome stereotypes of reenactors. "Being properly informed about the hobby," one reenactor says, helps the public better "understand the period of World War I."

By presenting war as a universal experience, reenactors define not only the common soldier, but also themselves. After all, why shouldn't they be capable of identifying with the soldier's plight when their descriptions of soldiers are identical to those they use to describe themselves? If the soldier is accepted as an apolitical figure, then, their reasoning suggests, so should they be seen as apolitical. And they imply that their own mission as public servants runs parallel to those of other people who sacrificed through history. Thus, their goals related to educating people about the common soldier are the very same goals they hope to achieve for themselves: to overcome stereotypes, deflect moral judgments, and recognize sacrifice.

By literally embodying the image of the common soldier, reenactors underscore the ways they identify with history's heroes and pawns. Dedicated to the mission of public education. Gaped at like animals. Actual soldiers may have fought on battlefields, but reenactors fight in the public realm. But as public servants, they do more than commemorate the sacrifices of others. They also seek to restore their own losses by gaining public credibility, respect, and pleasure.

One way they gain status is by "authenticating" their right to represent history by portraying themselves as its literal owners. They own the artifacts they display, but in telling their stories, they also possess a rarefied knowledge that most people lack. ("This is a M1942 field knife and here's how it would have been used on the Eastern Front by a soldier of the Russian Guards in the winter of 1943.")

"I love to teach and I love to have people come up and ask questions," Richard Paoletti says, describing the value of such expertise. "It's like you go to a book and you say, Okay, that's a uniform. But now you can come up and you can touch it. I'll show you everything about it because . . . I've been wearing it [and] I can show you what these buttons are for and what this is for, and what that's for, and you would never learn something that deep if it wasn't from firsthand." Ray Sherman agrees. In fact, he even argues that: "the only difference between us and the real veterans is that we don't stay in the rain as long as they did or in the cold or run out of food or try to dodge real, live bullets."

Most are careful to argue that this difference is indeed vast. But they also believe their own knowledge can surpass even that of a veteran. Richard Paoletti was once doing a German impression when an American World War II veteran approached to ask a question he'd wondered about for decades. "We'd always seen the Germans with these cans strapped around their backs," the veteran recalled. "What are they?" Happy to be able solve the mystery for the veteran, Richard opened up the can and told him, "'Well, it's a gas mask.' And he was like, 'Oh my god, it's a gas mask.'"

Through such encounters, reenactors gain credibility, since despite any public outrage, ultimate affirmation comes from history's true actors: veterans. When John Loggia and others traveled to Belgium for the seventy-fifth anniversary of the battle of Ypres, some civilians objected to their wearing British kits. "One of the veterans was asked, do we offend you that we're dressed this way?" John recounts. "And the response was, 'No, you remind us of our friends who didn't make it.' And they weren't offended, although other people who were not in the war [were]."

When uncomfortable encounters understandably occur, reenactors often dismiss them as a result of the public's inability to understand reenactors. One reenactor responded to a spectator's anger at seeing him in a World War II German

World War II reenactors pose for photographs

uniform, stating, "That individual could not accept that I have a genuine view that all soldiers are basically the same." Such a misreading of their perspective may frustrate them, but it also provides further evidence to warrant their identification with the common soldier. Like soldiers, they too are often wrongly stereotyped or politicized. "I've been called a 'sicko,' a 'gun nut,' a 'warmonger,'" one reenactor complains, "and worst of all, a neo-Nazi for doing World War I!" Michael Collins laughed as he remembered marching in a parade wearing his GI uniform: "I really thought I was making it so obvious. I had Lucky Strikes in my hand and I'm walking around going, 'Victory in '43! Win the War in '44!' And people are stopping me and saying, 'Oh, you're a Civil War soldier?' And I'm, like, you've got to be shitting me. And I'm saying, 'Home alive in '45!' and one guy says, 'Is that from the Spanish American War?'"

Such responses confirm their belief that "Americans are ignorant," as Michael concludes. "I would say ninety-five percent of the people that come to our events have no clue," Alicia Mellon concurs. But confronting public ignorance fuels their sense of having an important mission: "So maybe you don't like uneducated 'touronz' in your face," one reenactor argued to another, "but face it; it is those masses that need your expertise." Encountering ignorant people not only serves to "inspire us" as Michael Collins says, but also affirms the fact that reenactors have a greater appreciation for and understanding of history than the general public. "They live boring, stuck-in-a-rut lives," as one reenactor says of their audience, "and, sadly, like it that way."

Privately, reenactors not only delight in encountering "stupid" people, but they also secretly love to mock public gaffes, especially the dumb questions people inevitably ask, such as "Do you get wet if it rains?" "Is that a real gun?" and "Is that uniform hot?" Many also admit they take pleasure in causing outrage and confusion. "Messing with people," as Perry Trent put it, can be "enjoyable." "It's fun to freak people," Laura Paris agrees.

Others find pleasure in rising to the challenge of reasoning with an accusatory audience, and trying to control reactions becomes a kind of art form. A member of the Irish Guards reports: "We get asked questions at every public event about the troubles in Northern Ireland." But, he continues, "I refuse to make any comments one way or another . . . while trying to portray a non-political view of history to the public."

Dave Watkins was dressed as an SS soldier at an air show at Camp Edwards, Massachusetts. He recalls, "People were absolutely fascinated by what we had on display. Whole families came. Some people came back three times to look at our stuff, asked us a lot of questions." Throughout the entire day, only one person asked Dave if he thought they might be offending people. Dave's response was direct: "I said, look, this is just a historical representation. We're not political. We're not confrontational and our feeling is that if you don't like it, you can walk away. If you do like it and you have questions we'd be happy to deal with you."

With the attitude that "if you don't like it, you can walk away," most reenactors believe that people too often make uninformed judgments, quick to condemn them as the actual soldiers they portray, and they're only happy to deal with those willing to view their presentations in the ways they intend. Scott Mies recalls a time when an American veteran of the Battle of the Bulge confided in him that it really bothered him to see the German reenactors. Scott said he was able to "fully sympathize with him, given the bitterness of my own relatives, my own family." But at the same time, Scott didn't "want to give reenactors . . . crap for doing German because I know they put up with it a lot as it is."

For Scott, overcoming his personal history as a grandchild of Holocaust survivors in favor of defending German reenactors means that working together takes priority in public. Not wanting to give other reenactors crap is the ultimate act of group loyalty, an example of the bonds of *Kameradschaft*.

Spending the day bearing the scrutiny of a gaping, ignorant, apathetic, or hostile public does come with its benefits. A member of the Irish Guards championed his comrades' "endurance" in conducting public guard duty and commended them for their "splendid performance shown in the face of great hardship." Along with "braving the heat and sun of a hot day, they braved most of all the bees crawling up the backs of their shorts, the kids laughing in their face, the women watching them from behind (not much of a hardship there is it?) and worst of all the Yank reenactors trying to get them to laugh or move. Well Done!"

Having sacrificed in the line of public duty, the Irish Guards spent the evening not imagining themselves to be real soldiers, but engaged in pure contemporary recreation. "The next morning," continued the report, "brought the after-effects of mixing hard alcohol and ale. The Irish Guards decided that public duties and drill were not necessary this day and L/Sgt O'Hara decided that large amounts of movement were not recommended until well around noon."

Reenactors also reward themselves with rather ridiculous and wholly inaccurate historical play—but only after the public disappears. At an historical timeline that included displays from Rev War through World War II, reenactors planned "a bonus battle (Union Army vs. [German World War II] 2nd Panzer) after the crowds go home." According to a reenactor at the event, the Union Army reenactors did attack the Germans; "They wanted our keg!" He described the hilarity that ensued after Rev War, World War I, World War II, and Confederate reenactors joined in the battle. "We all joined afterwards and had the best party of the year. . . . A true meeting of the reenacting world."

Such hijinks are necessary after performing what Luke calls "a full day's work" by assisting "in the operation of the [event] by parking cars, keeping children off the vehicles, [and] answering questions for the public." But many recognize that such well-performed work has many benefits. These benefits include raising money, enlisting new recruits, and making contacts with site owners. Even the GWA, for many years one of the most private-minded reenacting groups of all, considered allowing spectators onto the strictly guarded Newville site for a public event. Such an event would certainly "inform the public about World War I," but it would also "establish the GWA's reputation as a living history organization; build good relations with the local citizens; allow GWA members to utilize their knowledge and collections; [and generate] additional revenues." With the benefits of performing public duty clearly outweighing the liabilities, in 2002 the GWA opened the gates of the Newville site to members of the public for the very first time.

But perhaps the most valued benefit of public service is to battle the assault on their freedoms. "When handled tastefully and tactfully," Wilson Lyle believes, "public displays do a lot to 'legitimize' our cause." Luke agrees. He says a public event "increases public awareness [and] public appreciation, and then they don't look at you as a bunch of nuts with guns." And in fact, when a local California politician reportedly "tried to ban Civil War reenacting or public displays as 'encouraging the cycle of violence' or some sort of liberal psychobabble like that," as one reenactor reported, she was obstructed, since "the amount of money generated by spectators and parking fees to get in to see the event was more money than the county was willing to kiss goodbye." With his characteristically harsh attitude toward critics of the hobby, Luke underscores the impact positive public reception has on the hobby's livelihood: "If the public likes a living history display, they're going to say, Hey wait a second—like this bitch in California who wants to ban all reenacting from government property—they're going to say, Hey wait a second, these guys do a nice job."

Although this kind of benefit is never explained to outsiders, it reveals how reenactors' private and public missions feed upon each other. They attempt to teach people about the common soldier as well as the common reenactor. They pursue a mission of public education while trying to advance their own hobby. They wish to share history with a wider public, but they also desire to represent themselves as the owners of that same history. All of this reveals how their own historical productions are designed to achieve far more than a recreation of history. Yet most outsiders never acknowledge these more contemporary goals. Instead, they are satisfied to conclude that these time travelers are either dedicated historians or misguided amateurs.

Ultimately, I came to see how much reenactors' lives are enriched by their work within the hobby. How many of us, I would wonder as I watched a reenactor instruct an interested group, feel that our voluntary efforts are both needed and appreciated? That what we do on our own time, away from our daily lives, makes us feel like experts or heroes? And how many reenactors, I would come to ask, seek a kind of pleasure in the hobby that is unavailable in their real lives?

The answer to this last question lay in the reenactors' private events, which are wholly different from their dog and pony shows. As one reenactor observes: "A different set of hows and whys confront reenactors when they are being scrutinized by the public versus [when they are] sitting alone in a trench." In fact, what outsiders see at a public event is not representative of the hobby as a whole. "I personally enjoy both public and private World War II events," one reenactor states, "but they are very different." Not only do different standards govern them, but because "the public will never be invited" to a private event, their presentation of war also takes a different shape.

Everyone, reenactors say, has "a much more enjoyable event when they can concentrate on the weekend without the hassle of public intervention." And it's only in private, free from the touronz and the media's gaze, that they may "create an illusion for ourselves," as John Loggia puts it. The rallying cry, "Work together!" still resounds in their private settings, but the task of representing war by themselves and for themselves poses a new set of hows and whys.

Chapter 7

"It's Not on the Page Anymore"

The Private Face of Reenacting

Western Front, Pennsylvania. A bitterly cold day in November. I'm standing somewhere in the middle of dense woods on the Heritage Boy Scout Reservation, the site of a private World War I reenactment. It's midday, just after a lunch eaten in the field by the nearly one hundred reenactors who've shown up to attend this weekend-long event. Tim Reed, commanding his small unit of Russians, leads me to the top of a hill. Before running off for the next combat scenario, he assures me that I'll be able to watch some of the impending action from here. I stand near a picnic shelter as a unit of British reenactors assembles at the top of a steep ridge nearby. It's not long before I hear the sound of firing guns from the valley below. The British troops begin their defense, firing rifles into the thick woods below them. The thin line of soldiers hugs the slope of brown dirt; the men shoot round after round and lob grenades onto the heads of the approaching enemy with sweeping arcs of their arms. The charges in the grenades exude small explosions, making sharp sounds, "Crack!" An acrid smell of smoke drifts past me. Their commander implores, "Hold steady, lads!" before ducking down to avoid return fire.

I watch with a mixture of awe and fear. Each time their rifles crack, I flinch. Wondering what to do if the action comes any closer, I spy two gray shapes in the bushes. Two Germans have infiltrated the area, but they pay me no mind as they sneak up on the British troops. Once they're spotted, all hell breaks loose. The British, still defending against the uphill invaders, now fire in two directions—in front and behind them. Tom Schultz suddenly sprints from the woods followed by several Australians. He runs madly, chased by a couple of Germans. He takes a hit and falls just several feet in front of me. Now the Americans are on the scene, mixing it up with the fifty Germans who swarm the area. *"Hände hoch!"* they shout.

The hell of battle quickly dissipates once all the reenactors come out of the woods to create an impressive, colorful crowd: Scottish soldiers in kilts, Americans with their telltale round steel helmets, the French in their pale blue uniforms. Tim rushes up to me, "Are you okay?" he asks.

"Yes," I respond. "I'm fine." Tim adjusts the collar of my motor corps tunic, admiring his handiwork. "Yeah," he says absentmindedly. "We didn't even have time to deploy. Some of my men surrendered immediately and the rest defected."

"This is the best Civil War event I've ever been to!" Hal Zane says as he approaches, looking menacing in his German uniform.

"Civil War?" I ask.

"Without the trenches World War I just isn't World War I. It's Civil War."

"Fucking bastards," says Larry Cohen as he joins our group. "Fucking Germans just walked here. Some Allied defenses. Shit. This is a fuckin' farbfest." He drinks from his canteen, and then says, "Tim, I'm telling you man, I've got to get those ammo pouches from you."

"Aw," says Tim pulling his overcoat closer around him. "You'll get 'em. But what are you willing to give me for them?"

"You can have sex with John Loggia at the next Bulge event."

Tim looks nonplused as he considers this ridiculous offer. "No, I don't want him. He's damaged goods."

"Everyone and his brother has had a chance at him," Hal says with a wink.

The raunchy banter continues until Tim directs our attention to some action unfolding before us. Despite the erosion of the battlefront, the scenario is continuing on a smaller thread as a German officer takes two French prisoners, ties them to wooden posts, and orders his men to form a line facing them. The commander steps up to one of the hapless prisoners, who shouts in protest, *"Vive la France!"* The commander lights a cigarette and puts it in the defiant prisoner's mouth. He promptly spits it out and coughs. The commander grinds out the butt with the toe of a mud-caked boot and surveys his captives with a menacing eye.

Turning sharply on his heel, he struts to the side of his men. "Ready!" The German soldiers raise their rifles, (pointing them above the heads of the two

World War I German firing squad, private event, 1993

prisoners). "Aim!" he shouts deliberately. "Fire!" In unison the soldiers shoot their blanks into the gray sky, executing the two Frenchmen, who respond to the fired blanks by slumping at their wooden posts, feigning death.

Although no spectators are present at this private event, this little play does have an audience: the other reenactors who've gathered behind the firing squad to watch the performance. Once the two prisoners are dead, the scenario draws to a clear end, and everyone becomes absorbed in conviviality, posing for photographs, rehashing the scenario, or carrying on non-period conversations. Larry Cohen is truly at his best now, telling racy jokes despite the mild-mannered Joe Nelson's pleading, "Hey, there's a lady present." Tim and Hal discuss the ankle boots Perry Trent promised to get for the 4th Armored, while Ray Sherman tells me about the exploits of the "Bloody Hand" Division in World War I. I listen to Ray while keeping an eye on the activity around me. I stamp my feet to warm them. As if in answer to my silent lamenting, the sky opens up, and thin, wet drops of snow begin falling. The ground, already quite muddy, becomes slippery, coated with a light film of white.

As I watched the execution, an episode in what was my very first private reenactment, I was admittedly stunned by the cavalier manner in which the reenactors chose to enact an atrocity, and even more surprised by the way others so casually and even gleefully witnessed it. I marveled at how comfortable they seemed simultaneously engaging in two activities: re-creating the horror of war and enjoying each other's company. If they had been dressed in civilian clothes instead of uniforms and holding cocktails instead of weapons, and if cheery music swirled around instead of snowflakes, they could have been guests at a party and not participants in a private tactical event.

After the close of the grisly scenario, the Allied combat commander, John Loggia, directed us back down the hill. We began a slow march to level ground where the units would form up again for the next scenario. "Let it snow, let it snow, let it snow," two Marines march past singing. "It just isn't World War I without a little misery," says a sturdy German with tiny spectacles perched on his nose.

As we move away from the site of the execution, treading on the slippery mess of cracking leaves and slick patches of icy mud, the snow falls with more certainty, coating woolen tunics and metal helmets with a frosty hue. We move past the edge of a parking area where the reenactors have parked their cars. I notice a bit of graffiti that some reenactor has traced in the snow covering a car's rear window: "WWI Sucks." After standing outside in the freezing cold all morning, tramping through the woods, and witnessing a summary execution, I find that I agree with this sentiment. But I'm not sure whether the author was referring to the actual war or today's reenactment of it.

Wholesale hilarity as much as the representation of atrocious violence are aspects of the hobby that may only be barely concealed in public. But in a private event, they rise to the surface in a most amazing way. Many people, no doubt, would find themselves uncomfortable in this world. From the ubiquity of firearms to the bawdy humor—especially what reenactors jokingly refer to as their "homoerotic" sense of humor (as we stood outside that day, one reenactor jokingly "mounted" Phil Fussel, who dryly responded: "I'll give you twenty minutes to stop doing that")—this is a world that is unquestionably and overtly masculine. It is also a place where, according to one reenactor, "we have the most fun."

But their fun in difficult to explain easily. As I look back at that first event, I marvel at my naiveté, having initially suspected that reenacting would be simple to understand. They just put on their uniforms and run around and fight, right? But the private face of the hobby does not reveal itself so easily. Over time, I would come to learn that there are both written and unwritten rules that govern the private event. Its form is highly structured, developed over years of trial and error. I would also come to see that far more than meets the eye is going on in the most seemingly trivial or petty exchanges between reenactors, or even in the cruelest execution in the field. But this structure and meaning are not apparent to the novice who finds herself extremely confused at her first event, pondering simple questions such as, How do they know when to die?

For their own part, reenactors don't seem very interested in explaining the private event. It is, after all, viewed as something that is "strictly for us." "When I'm at a private reenactment," Luke says, "I'm there for myself." "I don't want to see crowds," Fred Legum agrees. "I want get immersed in what I'm doing."

What reenactors will say is that a private event is a "chance to do . . . something extraordinary." It's an opportunity to "feel as though you are in another time" and to come as close as possible to experiencing what actual soldiers experienced. After all, how many times in your life could you "go over the top at the Somme, move through the hedgerows of Normandy against the Waffen SS, or drive across the steppes of Russia against the Soviet Army?" one unit asks. "Well, here is your chance to find out!"

Having grown up wondering how it felt to experience war, reenactors argue that a private event is the only way to go beyond passive interaction with history, and, as one reenactor put it, "fill the gaps left after reading about history." "The History Channel is great," proclaims one unit, "and publications on the war are a wealth of information, but once you put on sixty pounds of equipment, stand knee deep in muck, and enjoy bully beef out of the tin on a damp chilly morning, the pictures on TV and the text from a book don't carry the weight they used to." As a way to move beyond the limits of other war representations such as those in books and movies, reenacting allows reenactors to create a three-dimensional war experience. "It's not," as Michael Collins says, "on the page anymore." Acting autonomously, away from the institutions of the media, free from the judgments of the ivory tower, and hidden from public scrutiny, they are, they say, able to "find out for themselves."

"You're recreating a little slice of history and you're doing it in a way that you can't normally do," Luke explains. "You can watch a war movie on TV—and it'll be terrible probably—or you can read about it in a book. But it's another thing to be standing there in the snow, behind the machine gun, watching a German patrol creep up." Luke pauses. He looks away. He seems lost in some other place. "Hearing the sounds of their equipment jingling back and forth, moving up through the cool air, the cold air. It's kind of quiet at first and gradually getting louder." He pauses again, shakes his head, and looks back at me. "It's just a very interesting experience," he says with a shrug.

As I would come to find, Luke's description was apt; the private event does indeed create many interesting experiences. And soon, I would have some of my own.

A Drive-By Shooting

Kitted out in my World War II correspondent's uniform and seated uncomfortably in the back of a deuce-and-a-half (a period truck), I've spent a chilly morning getting to know my reenacting companions at this private World War II reenactment: Tilden Scott, a thirty-something high school history teacher from Virginia; Brian Shore, a mechanic from Pennsylvania; and Sam Adler, a friendly New Yorker in his early forties. They have warmly welcomed me, and we have been spending the morning chatting as we move through the site, bringing up the end of the long train of 4th Armored vehicles on its way to battle. We are in charge of the radios linking together the Allied units. After our group has mastered the code names for each US unit commander linked to the network and schooled ourselves on authentic radio protocol, our conversation turns to contemporary matters.

"So what field are you in, Jenny?" Tilden asks as the truck bounces over the rough, narrow road.

"American Studies," I respond.

They're curious about my project and want to know more. I explain that I am studying reenacting in order to understand it from a cultural perspective. They nod encouragingly.

"I'll tell you what my wife says about the reenactors' perspective," Sam says, resting his rifle against his knee. "We're fuckin' nuts."

"It is a little strange," I say delicately. "But I think it's pretty interesting."

Russian reenactors advance, World War II Eastern Front private
event, 1997

"My wife's what I call a feminazi," Sam continues. "You know, hates guns,
thinks war is bad. She thinks I'm crazy for doing this. She thinks it's sick and
testosterone and all that. But look," he says suddenly. "Look at this." He pulls the
truck's canvas flap aside to reveal the mass of reenactors streaming across the
field. "This is absolutely amazing. You can read, you can watch movies, but try
to put yourself in it, you can't. Not unless you reenact."

Several minutes later our truck comes to a lurching halt. We get out to find
that all the other vehicles have stopped. "Waiting around. That's pretty realistic," Brian says.

Up the road, Luke is conspiring with his sergeants, pointing in various directions. Several 4th Armored men appear to have been ordered on a reconnaissance patrol, and they move along the road, sliding every few feet on the
sheet of ice covering its surface.

"Let's wait in the truck," Sam says. "I don't want to freeze my ass off."

We pile back into the truck and continue talking. A few minutes later we hear
a loud churning sound coming down the road. "Jeez, Louise," Sam says, scrambling

madly to load a clip in his rifle. "That's them! That's the fucking Germans!" Tilden and Brian unlock their safeties and are on their feet, crouching in the back of the truck. Seconds later, a German truck approaches; two Germans manning a machine gun perched in the truck's bed begin firing at us, shouting wildly as they speed past.

"Shit!" Sam yells as he flings his heavy body up at least half a foot before falling like a mound of dead weight on top of me.

"Awwww!" Sam groans as if really injured. I lie there, listening to Sam's heavy breathing. The only other sound is that of the German truck's churning motor growing fainter as it speeds away. What seems to be an eternity passes before Tilden, Brian, and, thankfully, Sam rouse themselves, all having been killed in what reenactors jokingly refer to as a "drive-by."

"They wiped us out!" Brian exclaims.

"Man!" Tilden says. "That actually scared me. It took me totally by surprise."

"We couldn't do anything," Sam declares in excitement. "We were totally defenseless. The Germans just opened fire," he says, describing what just happened as if he had been the only witness.

I dust off the back of my pants, feeling a little embarrassed. But they're engrossed in recounting the moment. Soon they lapse into a discussion of history.

"That really happened," Sam urges.

"Sure," Tilden responds. "The Germans wiped out GIs sitting in a truck just like this. I can't remember the unit, but another unit came by later and all they found were the bodies."

"Oh yeah, that happened a lot," Sam says shaking his head. "Guys just parked at the side of the road. The Germans picked them off, didn't matter if they were defenseless, didn't matter if they couldn't fight back. Supply trains, medical trucks, you name it. It was fair game to the Germans."

A pair of eyes peers into the back of the truck. "You guys okay?" asks our driver.

"Yeah, we're okay," Tilden says breathlessly. "We were all killed, were you?"

"Nabbed me right on the side of the head. I fell right over the gearshift."

"Shit!" Sam says with a level of bitterness appropriate to the real passing of friends. "You know," he repeats to us again, "that really happened." He sits dumbly, his rifle cradled in his thick arms. He is speechless.

The Private Event

"When it's really real?" Ben Sandler said when I asked him to describe a realistic reenacting experience. He cast his eyes away and seemed to picture something in his mind: "I mean everything's going according to plan, sometimes there's confusion which happened a lot; people are taking hits and everything. There are actually wounded people like screaming, like actually shot. I mean, it really gets you into it. . . . The first time [I was in a reenactment] my adrenaline was pumped up and I was actually scared a little. The confusion and all the shooting and stuff."

The inevitable chaos of combat in a private reenactment is judged as realistic because it replicates the confused reality of actual war. "Any time there's confusion," John Loggia observes, "that's like World War I. Where confusion reigns." Indeed, my truck companions seemed truly flabbergasted by what happened. They kept repeating, "That really happened!"

Many view such moments as the best. During a World War I event, Paul Harding was trying to make his way across no-man's-land after the Germans had launched a gas grenade: "We put on our gas masks and guys were falling over each other, over the wire, getting caught in it, stumbling around in no-man's-land. I couldn't see anything with my gas mask on. I didn't know if guys were shot or just falling 'cause they couldn't see. It was excellent."

But for some, the real confusion and even fear they can feel during an event doesn't seem fun at all. At one event, I rode in a jeep with a pair of reenactors. One of them became so worked up during dramatic moments in the battle that he thought he was having a heart attack. "Can you take my pulse?" he asked me several times, without the slightest bit of humor in his plea.

Within a private setting in which reenactors are ostensibly pursuing the same goal—to recreate war authentically—tempers, emotions, and blood pressure can run high. And, for many, it is this intensity that makes reenacting worthwhile. Going off to experience war, they show up at a private event to escape from the daily grind and lose themselves in the past.

Nothing impressed me more than arriving at some remote location only to come upon a sea of cars, station wagons, and trucks. The parking lot seemed to symbolize a point of departure, the last connection with life outside the hobby. As if the reenactors themselves are aware of the transformation from the real world to history, they often mark the edges of this boundary with literal signs. At the head of the path leading to the Newville trenches, for instance, an elaborate wooden cross reads: "War is very uncomfortable business. You should avoid it if at all possible." I once overheard a reenactor say to another, "That's perfect. If anyone comes through here they'll see that and they won't get the wrong idea." As a buffer against the world of outsiders, of criticism and praise, of daily jobs and real-world roles, an event's boundaries seem to promise participants that by entering the site, they may abandon their real lives and immerse themselves in history.

But neither chaos nor immersion comes automatically. In order to have a successful event, they must be vigilant in making sure that there is discipline, organization, and unity. They must "play fair," "honor" the real soldiers, and "make it look as real as possible." And, if there is such a thing as the reenactors' private mantra, it's the repetition of a single word: Authenticity. Virtually all reenactors agree that it is vitally important or very important to be concerned with "achieving the complete authenticity of an event and its participants." But they also admit that achieving authenticity is "not easy."

For the reenactor groups or units that host private events, preparation includes securing the event site, taking out an insurance policy, and arranging for amenities such as portable toilets, food services, and an ambulance. They also have to send out event announcements and registration materials. For participants, preparation includes making travel arrangements, assembling uniforms and gear, organizing unit members, paying event fees, registering the transfer of automatic weapons, buying blanks, and often getting a day or two off from work. Some units prepare by hosting training events, others by studying history or working on their period vehicles. Others spend time loading blanks, making uniforms, testing weapons, or writing mail call letters. Some GWA reenactors host "trench parties" throughout the year when units come to Newville to work on their bunkers or trenches and clear away all of the brush and weeds before each event. Sam Morse, Allied Trench Master, uses his privately purchased backhoe to remove debris and dig new trenches; John Loggia once chartered a private plane to fly over the trenches to take aerial photographs to use as intelligence; and Ralph Pace spends more than a few evenings carefully reproducing period cigarette packages, matchbooks, and other paper goods. All of these hours of preparation lead to the time when reenactors arrive at an event site, seeking, among other things, to experience chaos.

Most private events take place over the course of an entire weekend. They can involve well over a thousand reenactors, or they can be more exclusive, involving anywhere from fifteen to one hundred reenactors. Events are either "field events," with outdoor camping, or "barracks events," which afford the luxuries of bunks and showers. But no matter an event's size or amenities, each one is highly ritualized. Like a meeting of lodge members, each event follows roughly the same schedule. Fridays are spent setting up camps or barracks, registering, socializing, bartering at the flea market, and sometimes night fighting. Saturdays are devoted to the "tactical" or the battle itself. On Saturday night, if there's no night combat planned, reenactors eat, drink, and socialize more. Sundays are sometimes spent fighting a bit more, but usually they're limited to cleaning-up, saying goodbye, and traveling home.

Most reenactors prefer these weekend-long events. But rarely, I was surprised to find, do they spend the whole time re-creating history. "We spend as much time discussing our home, jobs, families and plans," one reenactor admits, "as we do anything else." Even events promoted as hardcore, with a stress on twenty-four-hour first-person interpretation, usually fail to live up to such an extreme. Not only is total immersion hard to maintain, but reenactors span a wide spectrum of period behavior. They either continue being themselves through the course of an event, as my truck companions did, or try to limit nonperiod behavior to downtime. At many events, I simply wondered what was going on much of the time. No one seemed to be following any strict timetable, and no one appeared to be definitively in charge, and so we spent a lot of time waiting, sitting around, or just hanging out together.

Despite their emphasis on authenticity and seriousness, most reenactors look upon a private event as an enjoyable time. As Mark Sammons observes, a private event is really "more than just fighting a battle." Even though they often complain about the amount of preparation required to attend, once there, they clearly love being with others who share their interests. They also love spending time with old friends or meeting new ones.

For my own part, I usually truly enjoyed myself at events. As I got to know more reenactors, I looked forward to events not only because I liked my research and was fascinated by seeing the hobby in action, but also because I loved hanging out with them, talking, and laughing. I must admit that at times I felt like the reenactors were a lot more fun than many other people I knew. I also recognized just how rare this kind of intensive and communal experience is in the real world.

So it's no wonder that reenactors spend so much of their time during a private event just enjoying each other's company. So many of them are simply hilarious—and even more so once they're all together—and in all events and within all units, there is much silliness. Even members of units that promote themselves as hardcore authentic, such as 4th Armored, invariably "laugh so hard they split a gut," inspired by antics such as Bill Sharp's fashioning of a small red wax phallus that he attached to his helmet and then strolled around commending the "Big Red One," or Scott Friewald's donning of his wife's underwear to flash unit members. Such hijinks are sometimes aided by the alcohol many consume during downtime, inspiring Patrick Hart jokingly to refer to private events as "ATF weekends," a satirical reference to the reenactors' use of alcohol, tobacco, and firearms.

Beyond the general agreement that events are fun and that all should strive for authenticity, reenactors differ in the ways they prefer to spend time at events. Some favor socializing. Others like to devote themselves to "plenty of shoot 'em up!" Others are focused on devising and implementing tactical strategies, while others, like the members of Grace Hall's unit, "prefer to do living history rather than battles." Especially after years in the hobby, others show up just to go to the flea market and catch up with friends. Some even attend to show off a new impression, like the Turkish soldier I met at my first event.

Some reenactors even find combat to be an event's least interesting feature. "I don't even really particularly shoot at individuals anymore," Fred Legum says after nearly a decade reenacting World War I. "Been there, done that." Hank Lyle agrees. At one World War I event, Hank showed up in his civilian clothes just to catch up with his buddies. I was pleased since we were able to sit and chat for a while. I asked him how his interests had evolved over his many years reenacting. He explained that a new reenactor finds that "all events are good, because you have nothing to compare them to." But after about five events, he said, "things get to be the same." And now, he said "there's hardly anything to do at a reenactment that I already haven't done. You know, you can only sneak up behind the bad guys or good guys, whatever you want to call them, and shoot 'em all down so many times before it's not even worth it to me putting blanks in the gun."

Hank's attitude is shared by a lot of veteran reenactors. But that's not to say there aren't plenty of reenactors who love the combat. Firing weapons, they say, is exciting. When Luke shot another reenactor at his very first event, he was "thrilled."

And to be sure, the battle is always the weekend's main focus. Once units assemble to begin fighting, the immersion in history can begin. In World War II events, action is far ranging. Units and vehicles, if present, are deployed in fields or wooded areas. In World War I events, units take position in their designated trench sectors. In both types of events, combat consists of small-scale engagements conducted by individual units or perhaps only several reenactors. In both, reenactors face the impending action knowing little if anything about what will happen.

During a World War I event, I stole into the French trench sector at nighttime. Flares illuminated no-man's-land, and I watched in awe as reenactors hurried to and fro, walking ghostlike through black trenches. When the French commander saw me, he kneeled down and whispered: "Just be careful." After a dramatic pause, he warned, "You never know what will happen."

Indeed. I was quite surprised to learn that reenactors don't attempt to replicate actual historic battles in their private events. Unlike a scripted public battle, a private battle is "open-ended" or "free-flowing." This means that soldiers who were historically vanquished in a war, such as the Germans, or those who lost a particular engagement are not always defeated in a reenactment. "Can the Allies force the German Army out of Italy, or will reinforcements reach Kesselring in time to blunt the Allied Advance?" one event announcement asks. "Join us for the Italian Campaign 1998 and find out for yourself!"

Although reenactors talk about recreating history, their battles are designed so that anything essentially can happen. And even though events are given specific historic titles such as "Duel on a Dutch Levee" (based on Operation Market Garden) and "Elbe River" (Eastern Front), they're set only within general time frames and locations. "The historical time frame for this event," read one event announcement, "is September–October of 1944. The area is eastern France, Belgium, or Holland."

These basic time frames and places give reenactors a chance to enact what they call "scenarios"—small- or large-scale dramatic sequences within an overall event itself. "We're talking about night attacks, individual raids where two or three guys can go out and try and get in the enemy lines," Paul Donald says, describing some of the likely scenarios in a World War I event. "We're talking about firing machine guns and mortars. . . . If there's an attack at the right-hand line they can call for reinforcements from the left-hand line. You can actually go out and set up a scenario where you fake an attack on this end, the enemy draws their reinforcements down there and then you get them at the other end." Like others, Paul stresses the variety of opportunities reenactors have to take action.

"We are bound," as one GWA member says, "only by our creativity and knowledge of World War I in the creation of our scenarios." Using a combination of creativity and knowledge, reenactors are free to act regardless of history's actual outcome. And what they choose to do in an event is shaped more by their sense of what could have happened rather than what actually happened in a given time and place.

Reenactors prefer open-ended battles with only the slightest script used to frame their action, since attempting to replicate historical events is largely viewed as "counterproductive." Ironically, it is only in the absence of a predetermined historical script that they believe they can achieve any degree of authenticity. "Scripted scenarios are okay (if not required) for public events," one reenactor believes, "but they are the kiss of death for a tactical event." For instance, during the D-Day reenactment in Virginia Beach, there was no question that the Germans would lose. And even though private battles may be partially "choreographed," to use Luke's description of how he plans a Vietnam patrol, they never script the action. In Luke's case, his choreography takes the form of spending hours before the tactical mapping out and timing the route his American patrol will take. He works with the Vietcong commander to stage ambushes, but none of the other reenactors involved know anything about the plan and are thus free to take action as they see fit.

Since reenactments are limited in scope, trying to recreate an actual battle would "cheapen the actual event by presenting a lame-o parody." Thus they design events according to their own capabilities. For example, World War I events lack an important element of real combat of the Western Front: artillery. "Big battles of World War I of course are hundreds and hundreds and hundreds of guns and masses of infantry," John Loggia explains, admitting that reenactors lack those essential components of combat. But John rationalizes such a discrepancy, saying, "The kind of sector that we're portraying is maybe a semi-active one away from where a big battle would be going on."

Whatever action reenactors decide to take during an event depends less on what happened in history and more on the fact that "sometimes they might want to stir things up and sometimes they don't," as John Loggia says of his own unit members. The freedom to decide whether to "stir things up" is vital. Commanders may plan an attack or a certain scenario in advance—at one GWA event, the Germans planned a twilight surprise surrender to the Allies en masse—but they don't inform the enemy of their intent. "I don't believe in letting the Allies know when we will attack," one reenactor says. "This way neither side knows what to expect and it will be more realistic." "I like that aspect of not knowing what the hell is going on," Fred Legum agrees.

As much as an event is open-ended, however, reenactors are not supposed to "run around" without a purpose. "You can't do something and not have any knowledge about it, if you want to do it correctly," Fred Legum explains. "You can't just go out there and flub about." Thus, they are expected to "implement the appropriate period tactics for a given situation." In short, they try to fight using tactics that are historically authentic, such as ambushes, trench raids, gas attacks, or tank battles. A lot of reenactors find that having a tactical mission or a plan for a scenario makes the action more interesting. Greg Grosshans says this helps them avoid "mindless running around in the woods shooting at one another." Unit members are also expected to follow orders and pursue assigned objectives. "Being given realistic goals for units of similar size that were actually given to historical units is good," one reenactor says. "No one should be out there without orders, but leave the scripts to people on a stage."

Aside from performing tactically in period fashion, reenactors are also expected to behave with "some degree of control." From being told by event hosts where to park to what to wear, event rules and guidelines are profuse, beginning with the inevitable safety inspection. "Remember," one event announcement instructs. "No pop-up flares, no military grenade or artillery simulators, no shotguns, no weapons with inoperative safeties, no affixed bayonets, no red flares, and *no live ammo*!"

Next come the rules of engagement: "Do not aim and fire directly at individuals within twenty yards of you. Blanks can be dangerous at close range. If in doubt, aim and fire your weapon straight up, or when in close combat inside the trenches, just yell, Bang!" Unit commanders also issue orders regarding period behavior in the field: "Don't start talking about your '94 Honda to your fire team buddies. Don't talk about anything anachronistic unless it's absolutely necessary! (i.e. someone is having a heart attack)."

Even when not in combat, behavior is subject to restrictions: "Please do not stand on the battlefield and become spectators and/or take pictures of your fellow reenactors. [This] distorts what we are trying to accomplish." Finally, they are instructed about more personal conduct: "No use of controlled substances. No disorderly conduct. No drunkenness."

Some reenactors, such as Grace Hall, complain that they issue "so many rules that they're going to regulate themselves out of existence." But, especially given the potential for real injury, most regard rules as necessary. Reenacting may not be real war, but it's "a dangerous hobby," Luke says grimly. "It's fraught with peril. You can shoot yourself in the foot, you can stab yourself accidentally, you can fall off a vehicle, you can break your leg running through the woods." A couple of reenactors have suffered heart attacks in the field, and a few have been injured by blanks, but most injuries aren't serious—heat stroke, twisted ankles, bruises, and cuts. Still, they often recount the danger they encounter in the field: "I lost my hearing for three days once due to a jerk sticking a Mauser in a concrete bunker and firing," one reenactor reported. Another suffered a "broken femur, broken pelvis, crushed ribcage, [and] punctured lungs" after being run "over twice and nearly killed by a US White Scout Car . . . which was being operated very recklessly in high grass, with no ground guard."

To hear a reenactor yell "Corpsman!" at a World War I event, for instance, is to hear the code word for a real injury. All action must cease as ambulances or emergency medical technicians make their way to the scene. Unfortunately, hearing the word is not a rarity. At the 1996 Fall GWA event, it was called six times.

Fortunately, the injuries turned out to be minor, but many reenactors were furious since "the injuries were entirely *preventable* if the people involved had either exercised some common sense or played the game with respect for the rules."

Reenactors are expected to conform to safety guidelines, and any serious violations are grounds for ejection. They also tend to agree that they should avoid representing what they consider to be war's "exceptional" aspects. Luke's timeless order to his men that "John Wayne stuff has no place here" underscores their aversion to rendering war à la the "Hollywood mentality." Surviving a battle or performing a feat of heroism is generally frowned upon. "The idea is not so much to kill Germans," Luke always says, "but to avoid being killed yourself." Hiding from the enemy, often more than attacking, consumes a great majority of their time. "We try to put ourselves in the most horrific situation we can and it's usually trying not to get shot or get spotted, which is what I think a lot of it was," Fred Legum says. "During war you tried to stay clear and stay hid as much as you can because . . . you don't want to be where it's really hot all the time."

To be sure, real soldiers try to avoid being killed. But most reenactors think they must suffer and inflict large numbers of casualties—for authenticity's sake. In the words of a GWA officer, "Everybody dies!" Unlike their attempts to control violence in public, in private they are willingly and mercilessly violent. Not only do they freely and repeatedly kill each other as well as die themselves many times in a single event, but they also inevitably enact a variety of war crimes and executions. "I'm like a wanted man among certain units," Luke says of his penchant for executing unarmed prisoners. Greg Grosshans, who's been executed several times by Luke, wryly concedes that Luke "always shoots us out of hand," adding, "I think we commit atrocities much more than real troops did in real battle."

Trigger time—or combat—lasts until one side or another (or both) is overrun. This might take three hours or it might take twenty minutes. They then retreat, regroup, and either break for a meal or begin another scenario. Interspersed within combat scenarios, they spend a good deal of time performing rather unglamorous activities, such as standing in formation, marching, drilling, assembling equipment, digging foxholes, fortifying trenches, and inevitably, waiting around. ("The life of an infantryman was 99 percent boredom," as Tim Gilbert observes, "and 1 percent being scared out of your wits.") They also conduct noncombat scenarios such as patrols, wire cutting parties, intelligence missions, and guard duty. They capture prisoners and interrogate them. They write up commanders' orders. They study maps and captured intelligence. They string out phone lines and operate radio systems. They sit in their camps, bunkers, and trenches. They open lonely soldier packages. They eat, talk, write letters, conduct mail call, and, especially at World War I events, they sing. (Many times I heard reenactors' voices rising from the trenches in mournful harmony: "There's a long, long trail a-winding . . .") Women reenactors either fight as soldiers or serve alongside units as correspondents. They also serve as nurses and Red Cross and Salvation Army personnel, tending to the wounded, cooking, or knitting. And all reenactors engage in variety of other activities, such as posing for photographs, bartering at the flea market, and talking with each other about contemporary subjects.

In all types of private events, the same kind of common scenarios are replicated over and over. But a reenactment is never complete. No one ever decides, "Well, we successfully recreated the Battle of the Bulge, let's call it quits." Instead, an event's open-ended structure allows for a kind of reenactment of reenactments ad infinitum. One reason for an event's repetition lies in the fact that they do not enact any specific historical narrative. "We don't reenact any particular thing," Paul Donald says. "But we do re-create a time period and live in it." In fact, reenactors universally describe their events as portraying certain "periods," such as "the World War I period," rather than as portraying specific battles. Hank Lyle explains, "We're not necessarily trying to recreate a significant action because if that was the case then I think we'd [say], okay, we're going to recreate Sunday afternoon on July 3rd where my uncle's platoon was wiped out and you guys will do this—cause that's all choreographed." When I asked him why they don't want to replicate historical battles, Hank said, "I think it gives us a chance [to say], okay, this could be anywhere in France, and given the same tools that they had we're given a chance to explore those bits of history, those time frames, those years."

Reenactors explore those bits of history using period tools that provide a tangible link to the past. In doing so, they try "to experience the life of a soldier," as Richard Paoletti says, "just an average soldier." Despite a few elite impressions and officers, most reenactors portray privates. Often, they do first-person impressions and interact with each other in period fashion, using period jargon and slang or engaging in discussions of the war, their home life, or their units as if they were soldiers. Within varying degrees, they also adopt historical attributes. Many use period names, speak in accents, or create historical personas. "I try to take on the personality of a soldier," Fred Legum says. "I speak in a Scottish accent. My basic history is [born] in Scotland, ran away from home at sixteen, moved to London, starved for two years, joined the army. That's my basic history." But no one—save a couple freelancers—portrays an actual historical individual.

Marching captured Germans, World War I private event, 1993

In fact, no matter the extent of their personas, reenactors still see themselves as themselves throughout the course of an event. "We're being ourselves," John Loggia urges. "We're not being Australians or Germans." British reenactor, Craig Bass, put it this way: "I think of myself not as someone else, but rather me, but it's 1944. My family and wife are all the same, but it's fifty-four years earlier."

By adopting basic characters and living a common soldier's common war experience, reenactors seem transfixed in a generic war setting, their scope limited to the narrow context of life within the period of the war itself. For instance, there is no scenario of a soldier going on leave or a celebration at the end of a war. Instead, their portrayal seems very claustrophobic. But for the reenactors, this seems appropriate, since "war is not glamorous," as one reenactor explains, "or fun like it is in the movies. It's sitting alone in the mud, seeing your friends die. It is an experience."

I often thought that reenactors enjoy the tedium and routine of an event. After spending hours at a secluded site, I found that it was impossible not to lose myself in an event's rhythm. And in fact, many reenactors argue that it is only by existing within such a setting for an extended period that they can come closer to understanding what war must have been like. "It's one thing to sit in a classroom and speculate about [war]," Luke explains. "Well, sit in a foxhole in the woods and see what you can see. You can't see anything . . . in front of you. Sit there and see if you feel lonely and isolated and by yourself, and see how comfortable you feel sitting there." Like others, Luke finds that experiencing isolation and discomfort adds a dimension to his understanding that a book or movie could never provide. "You think that it's no big deal to march and to maneuver armies—you read about moving armies," Luke says. "Well, actually get out there and try to march, try to carry a .30 caliber machine gun and boxes of ammo and grenades and rifle, and march through the snow, and see what that experience is about. It's not a bunch of map figures that you move around. Wars are fought by people."

For most reenactors, gaining insight into what war was like does not involve grappling with history's higher meaning. John Loggia says he wants only to understand "what the ant is thinking on the ground" since, he reasons, even if he had actually "been there," he wouldn't have had any larger perspective. "It's too vast for me to comprehend," he concludes. Many others agree, describing their most meaningful reenacting experiences as feeling lost in the moment. "It's easy to get lost when you're sitting in a ditch," Terrence Scott explains. "You're living in a hole and you look above you over the trench and you see nothing but barbed wire, pieces of rifles and old helmets and such, and then at night you're sitting in the trench and this flare goes off and a machine gun cracks in the distance and you hear these little whistles, 'beeeeer,' guys running, and rifles starting to fire and grenades launched in the trench." Such an experience, Terrence concludes, "just gets very realistic."

In fact, according to Luke, there must be an absence of any historical thinking in order to achieve realism. During an event, Luke says, a reenactor doesn't ponder "the greater implications of American involvement in Europe" or "the wonder and beauty of shaking the yoke of fascism off of the subjugated people." (Nor, Luke adds, would an actual soldier be thinking about such highfalutin issues.) Instead, a reenactor should be thinking "about where the enemy machine gun position is and how you can put enough fire on it so that it can be suppressed while you can move men up on the flank to take the position out." When it's over, Luke says, "you're just thinking about finally I got a chance to stop and boy does it feel good just to not walk on feet that are sore and just to get a rest for a second and to take my pack off and to eat a meal—to have a meal, even if it's cold."

Whether emphasizing the hardship or simple pleasures of a common soldier's plight, reenactors seem largely focused on the here and now of a war itself. But in various ways, they reveal their perspective on the civilian world lying beyond the war's narrow boundaries; it is not only a place where the common soldier is misunderstood and unappreciated, but in many ways it is a world even more hostile to them than the war itself. Such an implication is revealed in the mail call letters they write to each other and read in the field. Grace Hall describes their typical content of bad news: "One guy just won the lottery except that he had to claim his prize by a date that was six months earlier. And somebody else is getting his farm foreclosed on. And somebody else's wife writes to say she's pregnant and he counts and sees how long it's been since he's been on leave." In his own mail call instructions, Luke asks: "Who will yours be from? Angry creditors, a cheating wife, the French farm girl carrying your child?"

Sending such missives to themselves underscores the ways they both perceive and identify with the common soldier. He is a pawn, discharged to fight and wait and die. At the same time, he is a hero, capable of enduring, sacrificing, and suffering. He is also exceedingly masculine. During one event, Private Bill Sharp received notice from HQ that he was being charged by "four (4) females in previously occupied areas"—who had named him as the father of their children.

As they seek to explore history for themselves, reenactors ironically seem to find meaning in the meaninglessness of war. Some even think suffering is the most authentic way to gain insight into a soldier's experience. "It rained on our original *zeltbahn* tent all night at this event," one German reenactor recounts, describing a particularly memorable experience. "After the water table rose from the ground and soaked us in our blankets, we evacuated the tent and made for a wooden shed about three hundred yards away. We started a small fire and spent the rest of this miserable, rainy night trying to get dry and warm. Sleep was an afterthought." Although miserable—"At the time it really sucked," he recalls— this reenactor judged his discomfort as terrifically realistic. "That rainy night

Keeping warm, the Bulge, 1995

gave me a feel for what it must have been like during the war." And he was left to wonder "how many times a similar story was repeated during the war."

In my own experiences at events, there were many times when I found myself freezing cold, exhausted, or sweltering in the summer heat. Although I wasn't too keen on being out in the elements for extended periods and found it unpleasant to sit for hours in a trench or the woods, I marveled not only at the stamina of some reenactors, but also at the way some of them seemed to take pleasure in suffering. And for many, those times when they find themselves miserable, lonely, and isolated serve as tests of their endurance. "On a personal level, I have quite a few of [those moments] when I'm tired or I don't feel well and I think well maybe I'll go back to the tent and sit down," Fred Legum says. "And you don't do it because they couldn't. You know, if you were sick or wounded, you had to carry on."

Whether suffering, carrying on, or having fun, reenactors are unconcerned with issues beyond this narrow scope, including victory or defeat. According to my questionnaire, most reenactors—more than 70 percent—look upon winning in an event as either somewhat unimportant or not important at all. Many find winning irrelevant, since their highest standard is not victory but authenticity. "Who cares who wins?" one reenactor asks. "Reliving history should be our number one concern; otherwise we are just expensively dressed paintballers." Others admit how hard it is to tell who wins a given scenario, since so many die and it's often so confused. "In every reenactment everyone ends up dying, so to say that one side won a battle and the other side lost is very difficult," Greg Grosshans explains. "The end of a reenactment is usually just spent recounting different instances in the scenario where one guy shot another guy or you were able to sneak up on someone or, you know, little surprise things."

And indeed, little surprise things constitute an event's substance. And no detail is too trivial. John Loggia was at a World War II event when Luke led the unit into a clearing for mess. As everyone broke out K-rations, Luke pulled a china plate out of his rucksack and ate his meal off it without a word. For John, this detail fleshed out the moment's authenticity. "That was actually something that could have happened. Like all these GIs looting the deserted homes of French peasants. And Luke did it just to do it. To make it real. I really thought that was great."

Chaos and organization, fun and misery, horror and conviviality exist peacefully side by side in a private event. As reenactors try to fill in the gaps of history, they shape their events through specific, though somewhat contradictory, choices. They attempt to re-create war but are unconcerned with replicating specific historical events. They try to immerse themselves in history and yet are free to act autonomously, governed by their knowledge of what could have happened more than what actually did happen. They seek insight into the common soldier's experience, but through enacting their own repetitive scenarios, they seem to know already what that experience entails. But perhaps the most striking contradiction lies in the fact that despite their endless promotion of authenticity and the great deal of energy they expend to achieve it, they willingly concede that they cannot replicate war authentically.

John Ostroski was quick to admit that reenacting comically pales in comparison to the real thing, since reenactors have so much fun and even smile and laugh in combat. "If you haven't spent an extended amount of time, not a couple of days, in the mud and muck with someone actively trying to kill you," another agrees, "you will never have a 100 percent accurate re-creation." Of course, it is only the absence of any real danger that makes reenacting possible or desirable. "To do it for real," Luke says, "you'd get killed. It's not like playing tennis, you know. You can play tennis for real and not get hurt. But if you want to try to get a sample of what war was like without getting killed, this is about as close as you're going to be able to do it."

These sentiments underscore an important fact: reenactors do not want to experience real war. "I would never begin to think my experiences come anywhere close to what the average World War II soldier experienced," one reenactor states. "We haven't come close to experiencing what a . . . soldier experienced. I hope to God we never do." Hank Lyle thinks their interest in war may have something to do with a "fascination with death," but most readily claim they do not want to experience war's true terror. "Really all reenacting does," Ted Morse explains, is "give you just a tiny little taste of what they had to put up with. Without having real bullets flying by your head, it's as close as I would like to get to that period." In fact, whenever reenactors experienced the actual deaths of their own friends or relatives, they became hesitant to reenact or avoided it altogether. "I'm not sure how I feel about going to events," Paul Harding said after attending a funeral of a fellow reenactor, while another reenactor whose close relative passed away said he tried to go to events but couldn't. It took both a while before getting back into the hobby.

The reenactors' attempt to represent war authentically while thankful that "reenacting cannot compare to the horrors of true war" is the hobby's central paradox, and one never really examined by those outside the hobby—or inside it, for that matter. Sitting in a ditch, listening to the sound of gunfire, knowing little about what might happen next, a reenactor might feel that history has indeed come alive. But at such a moment, history does more than come alive. History becomes part of one's own life.

Chapter 8

"Look! I'm a Stamp!"

The Ownership of History

The thick Maryland woods are spread over steep hills, providing a challenging setting for what today serves as the Eastern Front of World War II. This is my first time reenacting as a private in the Russian Guards. This weekend-long, invitation-only event is being hosted by the Grossdeutschland unit. About fifty reenactors are here at a state-owned camp in Maryland, which GD rented for the weekend, promising complete privacy. Everyone arrived last night and will sleep again tonight in wooden barracks on the site (segregated by nationality.) Six other women reenactors are here, a number that can be attributed to the fact that women portraying Russian soldiers are quite welcome at Eastern Front events, since women served as soldiers in the Soviet Army during World War II.

As we head out Saturday morning to begin the first combat scenario, I am accompanied by Dave Watkins, John Ostroski, and Luke Gardner, all portraying Russian privates. We're moving out into the woods to take positions and hide from the Germans, who have deployed somewhere secretly earlier in the morning. Our commander leads our group of Russians, about twenty in all, with little comment as we make our way down a path lying at the base of a narrow valley. Our group stretches up a steep hill, climbing steadily, silent, rifles in bare hands. Several lag behind. By the time I reach the top, I find myself alone. Where are Dave and Luke? I continue walking on to a flat plateau where the woods begin to thicken. I see John up ahead, crouched behind a fallen tree, peering intently into the woods. Now what?

Someone is calling my name. Luke and Dave must be close by. Their brown tunics must blend into this brown earth, hidden by the leaves. I hesitate to call back when I hear my name again. What if the Germans are nearby? A burst of gunfire ricochets off the side of the hill below. Our commander had told us to stay together, warning, "We know the SS likes to come over that ridge." He remarked that by 10 a.m. we should have some trigger time once the Germans locate our positions.

John turns around and indicates that I should take cover. I kneel down where I can keep an eye on him. For what seems like an eternity, I wait, crouching in silence. I see nothing but leaves. I hear nothing but an occasional rustle as John shifts his weight. He seems determined to defend this position. From what? I ask myself. But there's John, holding his silent vigil, staring in front of him, his rifle at his side.

I resolve myself to eternal waiting and sit down, trying at least to get a little more comfortable. More than forty-five minutes pass, each one finding me increasingly uncomfortable in my itchy uniform: woolen shirt, skirt, and high black boots. I find myself growing exasperated. What am I doing here? I feel tired and begin to long for my nice soft bed at home. I could be home reading, I think. Or relaxing. Or shopping. After a while though, I begin to settle down, letting my mind drift as I sit in my little clearing, still keeping an eye on John. I'm in the midst of contemplating the lesson plan for my Monday morning class, when I hear: Crunch. Crunch. Crunch. The sound of a slow step from the woods.

I sit up quickly and peer ahead. My heart leaps as the leaves give way to a single German soldier headed in our direction. He walks in slow motion, holding his rifle at the ready, turning his head cautiously from side to side, scanning the woods. John glances back to me, nods his head to acknowledge that he sees him, and then gingerly shifts his weight, moving noiselessly into firing position.

I am now paralyzed by a sense of fear; my heart is thumping in my chest and the blood racing through my veins. What next? My thoughts race as I realize that I'm entirely overwhelmed by a sense of vulnerability. After all, I hardly know these guys. What am I doing in the woods with them? Before I can answer that question, John brings his rifle to aim, pulls the trigger and—"Crack!"—he fires in the German's direction. John pulls the bolt, expends the shell, and fires again, "Crack!" I barely see the German take his hit and fall before John is on his feet, signaling me to run. Without any hesitation, I race through the woods alongside him, fleeing, I surmise, the multitude of Germans signaled by the appearance of that single soldier.

A few minutes later, we stop near several towering trees. John whispers, "There are some Germans to my right." My eyes adjust to the leaves, and I shiver when I realize that there are several other Germans about thirty feet to the left. Surrounded by the dense woods, they're sitting on the ground eating lunch. They talk quietly; a big German shepherd sits near its master. (I had not seen these particular reenactors before.) "There are Germans over here too," I tell John. "Okay," he whispers, "I'm going to kill these guys." He indicates the Germans to his right. "Then let's surrender to them." He points to the lunching soldiers. "It's fun," he says, "to be captured."

As John fires to the right, I watch the members of the lunch party. Upon hearing gunfire, they spring to their feet and grab their rifles. John turns to me with a look of glee, and we move out from behind the tree. I now face three Germans walking toward us, dog in tow, their rifles high against their cheeks, muzzles pointing directly at us. They yell at us fiercely in German with a note of panic in their voices. Hands in the air, we walk toward them. As we close ranks, one indicates for us to kneel. They surround us. The officer stands at the helm, his dog panting at his side, while the two privates begin to search us. One soldier rifles through my pockets and bread bag. I'm worried that he'll get mad when he finds the nonperiod items in my bag—rolls of film, a bottle of apple juice. But he ignores them and instead concentrates on my camera. He points to it and says knowingly that I'm a spy: *"Spion!"* He glares at me, squinting. I hesitate to respond since I can't speak Russian, so I only glare back, trying to look bitter and defiant. When he notices my pistol his face lights up. He takes it from me, examines it, and tucks it in his belt, smiling.

Meanwhile, John is performing much more authentically than I am, shouting in Russian what I take to be unfavorable evaluations of the German army. When one of the soldiers takes John's rifle from him, John tries to explain something that seems not to be part of the game. In a combination of hand gestures and Russian, he tries to tell the German to release the bolt for safety purposes. The German holds the rifle, looking at him quizzically. He doesn't understand. Finally, John gives up and asks in English, "Would you release the bolt?"

The German nods. He fumbles around but apparently doesn't know how. He gives up and hands the rifle back to John who quickly releases it, sets the safety on, and then hands it back to his captor. After watching this exchange, the officer reprimands his private and says, also in English, "Never give a weapon back to a prisoner!" All of us try to muffle our laughter at this comical breach in authenticity.

"*Tot?*"—Dead?—one soldier asks the officer after the search and interrogation are complete. "*Ja,*" he responds, barely looking up. The soldier walks slowly around us and stands behind our kneeling figures. I see him from the corner of my eye as he raises his gun and rapidly fires several rounds over our heads; for a split second, I'm not sure if he has killed me, but deciding he probably has, I drop to the ground at the same time as John. I keep my eyes closed, wanting to appear dead. There's no more talking, only a steady crunch, crunch, crunch as the Germans and their dog walk away into the woods. My ears buzz from the rapidly fired blanks.

When I open my eyes I see that my pistol has been returned and is lying on the ground in front of me. John stirs and asks if I'm okay. "Yes," I say weakly.

"That was fun," John says, picking up his own weapon lying in front of him. He runs his hand through his hair and rests an arm on his knee.

"Yeah," I respond, feeling incapable of any deep conversation. Suddenly, the German soldier, our executioner, reappears. He is smiling. With an extended hand, he congratulates us for doing such a good job. "Thanks a lot!" he says amicably. "That was really great!" We all shake hands, and John says, "Hey, you know, you guys could have roughed us up more than you did." The German laughs. His face is ruddy with cold. His eyes are shining. "Maybe next time," he says. With a quick nod, he disappears once more into the woods.

John says that we now must make our way back to the Russians. To indicate that we're dead, we take off our helmets and begin our journey back. When we reach a nearby clearing, we find a dozen Germans on patrol. John hesitates when he sees them and says, "I don't want to ruin their karma." But a large German soldier, standing near a tree smoking a cigarette, sees us, helmets in hand; he indicates that we can pass through.

"We're Here, We're There, This Is It": The Authentic Illusion

During that little scenario in the woods, I was surprised at the way the participants conducted themselves. Each of us behaved as if following an unwritten script with a vague storyline: What would happen if some German soldiers captured some Russian soldiers in the woods during World War II? The result, from the Russians' perspective, was not very good of course, but from the reenactors' perspective, it was a success. Although our execution was enacted in a rather offhanded way, as though unbridled cruelty (never mind a war crime) was perfectly acceptable as well as authentic, it was performed within a larger context of teamwork and even friendship. One minute killed and the next congratulated by our executioner, we were clearly acting. But we were also our own audience, able to break character and evaluate the quality of our play. And there was something very playful, however macabre, about the scenario. But nowhere was there any evidence that we were truly convinced we were reliving World War II. Something else seemed to keep our behavior in check. Certain ideas about history as much as the rules and boundaries of reenacting itself seemed to exercise more control over our actions than any effort to lose ourselves in a time-travel fantasy. In fact, both the bolt incident and the eventual return of our weapons suggested that real-world considerations (safety and property rights) were not to be ignored even in the most authentic of scenarios.

"We had become actors in a historical play," Luke said describing a reenacting experience that he judged to be a success, "that we were all benefiting from. We were all enjoying the play, we were acting in it, but we were also watching it. So it was very intriguing. That's really what the hobby can be at its best."

Luke's description of what it is like to experience a scenario when things seem real describes my feeling as I watched those Germans approach us in the woods. As they walked toward us with their rifles raised, the dog panting, the trees swaying in the breeze, I was captivated. I remember thinking, "Gee, this looks really real." For a second I was disoriented as I waited breathlessly to find out what would happen next. As I watched the incredible spectacle unfolding before me, it was hard to remember that I was also part of it. I had to remind myself that I too had a role in this drama and whether I liked it or not, the others expected me to perform. It was both thrilling and scary. After all, it isn't every day that one finds oneself dressed as a Russian solider in an isolated wood in the heart of the Maryland, confronting strangers dressed in Nazi uniforms and carrying guns. Anything, I thought, could happen.

I was later able to understand my experience in terms of the larger context of reenacting. My experience was, to use the reenactor term, "a magic moment." All reenactors have their own stories of achieving a magic moment, a time when suddenly everything comes together and they achieve their goal: they have created an authentic war experience so pure that, always only for a moment, they feel as though they are "there." "We all talk about that magic moment," Scott Friewald says, "when you feel like you're back in the period you're recreating. I mean, it's easy at that point to almost forget you're in [the present]."

I imagine that the feeling of experiencing a magic moment is akin to similar feelings described in other contexts: being in the zone, achieving flow, or getting a rush or high when engaged intently in an activity. But those sensations are usually experienced when one is alone. What is unusual about a reenactor's magic moment—and what definitely intensifies it—is that it is usually shared with others, and many times those others are strangers, which surely adds to the drama of the moment.

Although a magic moment is "usually a very occasional thing to experience," as one reenactor says, it is often described as the apex of the hobby. A magic moment is "fantastic," one reenactor says simply. Another insists that it "border[s] on something spiritual." And another calls it "Nirvana." Alain Benson struggled as he tried to give words to the sensation: "It's sort of—is the word euphoric? You feel sort of—it sort of makes you feel like really great because you—it's the closest you can come to being there without really having to live through all that stuff."

I knew not having to live through all that stuff while still achieving authenticity was the central, if contradictory, goal of a private event. And the more I noticed how action easily went in and out of certain boundaries, from period behavior (fighting, executions) to nonperiod commentary (socializing, congratulating), the more I came to believe that the terms re-creation or reenactment do not, as some reenactors themselves argue, accurately describe what goes on in a private event. In fact, many reenactors think the term "reenactment" is a misnomer, even though they usually use it themselves. One reenactor explains that many reenactors "prefer to use the term 'living history' to describe the events which are not exact 'reenactments' of historical events." Another agrees: "I prefer the term 'living historian,' and for the hobby 'living history,' since I usually do not reenact a specific event."

Not only is a private event structured by rules (helmets off to indicate that one is dead) but there are also certain limits to authenticity, times when it is acceptable to be oneself and times when it's not. Why else would a reenactor conclude an execution scenario by shaking his victim's hand? Or talk about being killed while still, ostensibly, dead? Even if some speak of achieving authenticity in terms of "feeling that you're back in the period you're recreating," I suspected this only came close to describing something hard to explain. Only after I listened to reenactors describing their magic moments and experienced my own, did I understand precisely what they were trying to achieve.

"There have been quite a few times when I've felt like I was actually there," Scott Mies answered when I asked if he had ever experienced a magic moment. He recalled a Russian event when he went on patrol with several other reenactors in the rain. "I was thinking to myself about actually seeing this as a real experience before my eyes," Scott remembers. As they moved cautiously through a field, single file, he was suddenly reminded of "film footage of Soviet troops, moving among this swamp area in some of the Russian back woods, and you know, a couple guys were ahead of me and even though—I mean"—Scott stumbled. "Moments like that make you seem like you're actually looking at something that could be incorporated as an actual, you know, historical scene."

Such a description, however confused, reveals that reenactors do not judge the authenticity of their experiences by their success at transporting them in time or re-creating actual war. Instead, they judge a moment's authenticity by its success at resembling authentic *representations* of war—in Scott's case, film footage. What they strive to achieve, therefore, is not a pure re-creation of history. Rather, they try to create authentic-looking moments that are judged authentic because they resemble other representations that document history, or, more precisely, what history looks like. The creation of an authentic war experience, therefore, does not rely on replicating history, but on duplicating elements from its authentic representations. In this way, reenactors create their own war representation—an "illusion for ourselves," as John Loggia describes it—that appears authentic-looking. Understanding the concept of a successful illusion is, in essence, the missing link to understanding reenacting. It is usually assumed that reenactors simply try to "re-create" history. But for me at least, the steps between the past and its re-creation are the central, if often overlooked, elements in any enterprise that ostensibly seeks to bring history to life.

Acting within their generic, open-ended scenarios, reenactors try neither to relive history nor to transport themselves in time. Instead, they produce and simultaneously consume their own illusions—"watching it while acting in it." No longer are they passive viewers in a movie theater or comfortable readers lounging on a sofa. Rather, they have assumed the powerful, dual roles of creator of and participant in a war experience.

Once I understood this essential aspect, I understood why they don't assume identities of actual historical individuals, which surprised me at first. For, in order fully to experience the phenomenon of an illusion, they must remain themselves. Like actors, they must have an ever-present consciousness that what they are experiencing is not historically real, but only looks as if it were. Their own descriptions of magic moments universally acknowledge this near reality. "I was really wrapped up in the intensity of it," Luke says, recalling an incredible reenacting experience. "Only because it was so real, realistic seeming." John Loggia describes another realistic-seeming experience when he led a night attack across no-man's-land: "[We were] moving up to the Allied lines, there was smoke everywhere and there were people who were feigning death and they looked like they were really dead. There was a guy very stiff with his arm up and that was like being there. . . . My heart was beating because I kept thinking when are the Germans going to get us? When are they going to open up on us?"

Photographing the photographer, the Bulge, 1994

Keenly aware that others were only feigning death, but looked like they were dead, John underscores how the experience of an illusion doesn't involve believing oneself to be in the past. Instead, it relies on knowing one is not. They admire one another's performances, and, aware of their own roles, they marvel at the illusion they are creating. Only then, unsure of what will happen next, do they experience the real emotions that add further authenticity to their experiences: John's heart beating, Luke getting "really wrapped up in the intensity," or my truck companions' fear at experiencing a "drive-by."

Reenactors argue that it is only through experiencing a magic moment that they gain a deep and personal perspective on history. For John Loggia, such a perspective came during that scary nighttime raid; Luke says he gained perspective during a particularly memorable Vietnam patrol. Just moments before an ambush, Luke says, all seemed to become intensely real as he and his unit moved cautiously through a field of high grass. Luke crouched slightly, his breath slowed, and he could hear his heart thumping in his chest. He slowly turned his head, and saw his men walking steadily, strung out through the field, their rifles at the ready, sweat pouring down their faces, their eyes scanning the woods for the enemy. Just seconds later, the ambush began. To this day, Luke describes this moment as the single best reenacting experience he has ever had. "It's amazing," he recalls. "It still sticks in my mind."

For Fred Legum, insight came during a twilight raid in the World War I trenches. It was dusk when the Germans launched a smoke grenade in no-man's-land. Fred was in his trench sector, along with his British mates. Soon, Fred recalls, they could see the Germans going over the top, making their way toward them. Fred remembers watching them "coming in through the smoke with their helmets on. I was right next to the machine gun, the machine gun was flashing, and you could see them illuminated in the flash of the machine gun." So vivid and eerie was the experience that after it was over and the Germans were pushed back, "Frank, the guy who was operating the machine gun, and like three of us just sat there and we were real quiet and I don't know who said it, but one of them, somebody said, 'Can you imagine what that must have been like when it actually happened?' . . . I know that's what we were all thinking. It was an extremely real moment for us. You know, it makes you think what those poor slobs went through."

Alain Benson also recalls a moment that he will not soon forget. Before a combat scenario, he and the other members of his German unit were standing in the frozen January woods dressed in uniform. He remembers that all of a sudden he glanced over at Greg Grosshans, who was standing with another unit member. Alain was overwhelmed by looking at them. "It trips you out," Alain says. "You really think you're there because everything that they're wearing is real. It's exactly what they wore—it's all real. It's real equipment and uniforms and the other part is it's all used and dirty. It's exactly how the guy would have looked who had worn it probably the day when it was taken away from him." But rather than thinking that he had literally been transported back to 1942, Alain says he found himself able to imagine history by looking at the scene from the perspective of a 1942 movie camera. "It's always just a few seconds—where you just sort of—you can imagine the films that you see, the documentaries of the German soldier smoking a cigarette with a bunch of other guys at the side of a road, with the tanks driving by. It's black and white. For a few seconds you can just sort of imagine that from his perspective, taking a drag from the cigarette, that's what it looked like from his perspective, in color."

It's always only for an instant that they can see what history looked like. And of course, it's only possible, as Alain says, "when you have nothing else to remind you that you're in [the present]." Such experiences may give them a deeper appreciation for other common men and women in history, but by creating their own images of the past, they actually do see war from an unusual point of view—

their own. Describing the awe he and his friends felt at that moment, Alain remembers: "We even like stopped. We just stopped and said, 'Check it out. Check out the mist and the snow and doesn't it remind you of the photographs and the films we've always seen so much of? We're here, we're there, this is it.'"

Such a point of view, confusing in its own right (being here, being there) is one that seems unconcerned with history's big picture; it doesn't require one to consider, as Luke put it, "the greater implications of American involvement in Europe." Instead, revelations are far more personal. One reenactor felt closer to history by walking through a trench at dawn, the fog clinging to its rough sides. But he was not, by his own account, imagining he was a soldier. Instead, he was enraptured by the illusion. What he saw and had a part in creating, he said, looked as if it were a replication of the trench-life descriptions he had read in Paul Fussell's book *The Great War and Modern Memory*. Others forge a connection by getting killed in the back of a truck and then discussing how their experience resembled an event they had read about. Others marvel at their illusion's capacity to let them "imagine what that must have been like when it actually happened."

Guided by their knowledge of what could have happened and what history looked like, reenactors are thus unencumbered by having to relive particular historical experiences. Instead, they step into the boots of common soldiers and walk around in them for themselves. "We're not reliving the experience," as Hank Lyle explains. "We're living it for ourselves."

A War Story

By two-thirty in the afternoon the fighting at this World War II private event is in full swing. I lounge on the front seat of a World War II truck next to Brian Shore, who's happily devouring a chocolate bar. I watch the Allied reenactors advance across the rough terrain of a wide-open valley. Vehicles loaded with troops, jeeps, a few tanks, and hundreds of reenactors on foot converge on a wooded area where the Germans are making a defense. Suddenly, I notice Craig Jones, a reenactor I've known for a few years, and another fellow I don't know, standing next to the truck, dressed in GI uniforms, carrying rifles.

"Hi, Craig!"

"Hi," Craig responds nervously—a strange reaction from someone who's usually extremely gregarious. "Uh," he begins, his eyes surveying the truck.

"What's going on?"

"I'm afraid I'm going to have to ask you to get out of the truck." He smiles weakly. Craig's companion walks around the truck to confront Brian, who seems just as confused as I am. I turn to Craig.

"I'm going to have to ask you to get in the back." He holds his rifle at an angle in front of him. "We're taking this truck."

"Oh," I say as I realize what's happening. I spy a hint of a steel blue shirt collar peeking out from underneath Craig's olive drab field jacket. Craig and his companion are Germans in disguise.

Guided by Craig's rifle, I climb into the back of the truck. I was surprised, of course, but this was not the first time I had encountered spies in enemy clothing. The attempt to fool an opponent by passing oneself off as an ally is somewhat common, but reenactors disagree over its propriety, since, lacking authentic language differences, it is easy to be fooled by such a ruse.

Craig climbs in after me. "We're hijacking this truck and heading for the German lines," he says. Now he seems more relaxed. "We had to make our way over here and find a way back. We're on a mission from Axis HQ."

The other German is back. "Okay," he tells Craig. "I tied him up. When we're ready we'll have him drive us across to HQ."

"No way," Craig says emphatically. "You gotta drive. Just leave him tied up. We don't want any problems."

The small German pulls out a cigarette and lights it before responding. "It's like a double clutch. I don't know how to drive one of those."

"Shit," Craig sighs. "Okay, make him drive, but do it now."

He ignores Craig as he notices our radio system in the back of the truck. He grins mischievously. "Hey!" he declares, picking up one of the handie-talkies and flipping on the switch. He holds it close to his mouth. "Come in. Come in." He smiles as he waits for a response. The radio crackles, and I can hear an echo of gunfire over it.

"This is Red Dog Two," a voice responds.

"Advance to the left flank," the German says. "Move all your troops to the left." He muffles a laugh.

"Who is this?" the voice asks.

"Give up all hope now. You will be defeated!" He laughs and throws the radio down. Craig shoves him on the shoulder. "C'mon!" he says urgently. "Time's wasting! Get up there with the driver and let's go!"

Although quiet, I am secretly pleased. I look forward to seeing where this adventure will lead. Craig sits back proudly once the other German takes his leave. Now smoking his own cigarette, Craig dangles an arm on the truck's ledge and settles in, returning to his story: "We ran into the Allied commander. Do you know Carl Letch?" he asks, referring to the Allied commander at this event.

"Yeah," I nod. "I know Carl."

World War II US reenactors pose with tank, 1996

"Okay. Well, we made our way to Allied HQ, which is way over near those woods. And we sneak up real stealthy and all, and we see that Carl's like sitting there with a big stogie in his mouth—he's listening to his runners give reports. But he sees us walking around the edge of the camp and he's like immediately ordering his men, 'Get 'em, they're Germans!'" Craig laughs. "So they kind of captured us."

"Wow. How did he know you were Germans?"

"Oh, 'cause Carl knows we are." Craig giggles.

"So what did they do?" Just then, I hear the truck start up, the engine roar, and a terrible grinding sound as we lurch forward a few feet and then stall.

"Carl's like, 'You motherfuckers!' He was totally pissed and we were just like, 'Sorry dude. See how easy it was to get here?'"

"So what did they do?" I ask again, meanwhile hearing the engine start again, followed by another grind, another lurch, and then silence.

"Oh," Craig says laughing. "They killed us."

"They did?"

"Yeah, and then they had to move out so they left us there. We waited around a little and then we resurrected ourselves and came looking for a ride back."

The small German returns. "C'mon," he says with a frown. "We're going to have to find another vehicle. That guy claims he can't drive the truck either."

"Oh, Jesus," Craig grimaces.

"Yeah," the German responds. "He keeps stalling it."

"Okay." Craig jumps out of the truck, stomps out his cigarette, and grins. "See you later, Jenny."

As quickly as they arrived, they're gone. I get out of the truck to find Brian still in the driver's seat. When he sees me he starts laughing.

"Oh, man!" he says.

"What happened?"

"That was so funny. That guy's telling me, 'Drive! Go!' and I pretended to be all confused and nervous and like, 'I don't know how to drive this thing!' So I was grinding the gears, letting it stall, and acting like I didn't know how. The guy's really getting frustrated and he's like, 'If you don't get going, I'm going to have to kill you.' So I'm like, 'Well, if you kill me, then this truck is still staying where it is, cause no one else can drive it!'" Brian is exuberant, clearly proud he outwitted our would-be captors.

"So they had to go?"

"What could they do?" Brian asks. "I wasn't going to let them take us into the German lines."

"Wow," I say.

After a minute Brian says, "When our guys come back, let's tell them we killed those guys." He looks at me and raises his eyebrows.

"That we killed them?" I am incredulous.

"Well, yeah," Brian says, turning the ignition and expertly putting the double clutch in gear. "Let's just tell them that." He pauses. "I mean, those guys put us into their scenario. So why shouldn't we finish it the way we want to?"

"Okay," I agree, not wanting to change the course of history in this event. "We'll tell them that."

Brian smiles as he steers the truck across the ground. Several American troops are marching back from action. One flashes a victory sign at me, and I nod my head and sigh. Why not? Does it really matter that the truth of what actually happened will differ from the way Brian has decided to represent it? Did it really matter, after all, that Craig and his companion were able to come back to life to continue their war exploits? That they lived to tell their own war stories just as Brian would tell his own?

Later that night, I run into Craig. He squeezes my arm and grins. "Now how about that!" he says, laughing. "Wasn't it fun to be hijacked?"

"Yeah, at least it would have been. But it didn't happen."

Craig, still grinning, looks pleased. "Well, we figured out what happened. That guy, the driver, he just didn't want to play. You know, he just wasn't into it."

"Were you disappointed?"

"Well," he shrugs his shoulders. "That's the kind of over the edge stuff I wish more reenactors would get into. But most guys can't be forced to do things like that. They get all bent out of shape. They're just fair-weather reenactors. But it was a funny story."

Later I realized the scenario had produced more than one story. Each of us could make up our own version of events—captured, killed, escaped, double-crossed—it didn't matter what had actually happened that day, or for that matter, what happened in World War II. What seemed even more important than history was what we would decide to tell everyone later, how we would choose to tell our own war stories.

Part of Our History

"People want to have their own stories and their own history," Scott Mies explains, "and sometimes they want to make their own history by going out and starting a war." Speaking about actual war, Scott makes a point that applies to reenacting as well. Not only do reenactors create authentic illusions and experience magic moments, but they also take away evidence of their war experiences. And, as Brian, Craig, and I would do, they tell war stories.

"He leapt forward," a reenactor wrote of a unit member's stunning exploits, "screaming as he drew near the Russian lines. Muzzles flashed as he entered the hellish hailstorm." Some stories have become folktales among certain reenactors, such as the account of Luke's orchestration of the intense Vietnam combat patrol when all of the members of the 1st Cav unit reported one of the best reenacting experiences they had ever had; the story of the reenactor who was hit on the head by a grenade three separate times at three different events, each time knocked unconscious (after the third and, so far, final blow, the reenactor received an honorary grenade for having survived such a curious fate); or the comical tale of the reenactor who, wildly running with the unit on attack, tore his pants, and burst out crying to his father, "Dad! My pants!"

Telling war stories is the verbal equivalent to an equally time-consuming activity at events: taking photographs. Nearly 70 percent of reenactors report that they take pictures with modern cameras during events, often in the midst of combat. Some even devote themselves entirely to the camera, donning the popular impression of war correspondent. In fact, so central is taking photographs to reenacting that one Vietnam War reenactment unit in France organizes events it calls "photo-reenactments," which are designed solely for the purpose of crafting realistic-looking war images, and often even involve the staging of scenes to replicate actual period photographs. While some reenactors argue that using nonperiod cameras is karma-blowing or inauthentic, most admit that they love to have their pictures taken in uniform. The visual richness of an event, particularly to a novice, is undeniable; one reenactor, a professional photographer, said that to anyone with a camera, an event appears as a series of endless images waiting to be captured.

Even so, the ubiquity of cameras at events surprised me. At my first reenactment, as if my encounter with the mass of World War I reenactors was not enough of a shock, when several reenactors drew cameras from their kits to take pictures of me in uniform, it left me dumbfounded. It seemed incongruous that they should engage in such a self-conscious act, ill suited to what I believed then to be their wish to time travel. But I soon realized that just like a well-told war story, a reenacting photograph that "captures," as Luke says, an event's "historical quality [and] could have been shot on the scene," testifies to their success at staging war. And often, they explicitly reveal their efforts to make the creation of such images possible: "We do not want to see visible, out of place, non-period/incorrect items," one event announcement read. "Anyone taking pictures of these areas should walk away with a photograph as it would have appeared in 1944."

Whether admiring their own images in their reproduction *soldbuchs* (pay-books) or posting reenacting photographs on a Web site, reenactors reveal their desire to possess an authentic (looking) representation of war that features them squarely in its center. Richard Paoletti told me he spent two days before our scheduled interview trying to think up an analogy to explain this fascination: "No other collection that I can think of—like stamps or coins—you can't just shrink yourself into a stamp and put yourself in the book and go, you know, 'Oh,

Reproduction World War II German *Soldbuch* made by Jonathan Krieger
(courtesy Jonathan Krieger)

look! I'm a stamp!' Right? I mean this is something that you can actually collect and actually show off. Be a part of it." Having invented a way to put themselves "in the book" of history, reenactors carve out a place for themselves in the
long history of war . . . representations.

And there is no doubt that reenactors have long been captivated by images
of war. Since 1855, during the Crimean War, when the camera was used for the
first time on a battlefield, photographs have become central components to war.
Since then, still and moving images, both documentary and fictional, seem magi-
cally to capture war's many facets of horror, devastation, fear, and even triumph.
From Timothy O'Sullivan's gruesome pictures of Civil War corpses to Steven
Spielberg's jittery images of Americans landing on Omaha Beach in *Saving Private Ryan,* images of war have been conveyed steadily to a public that remained
far beyond the borders of a battlefield. As ardent consumers of these war images,
reenactors are both fascinated by their realism and mesmerized by the limitations of their frames. After all, there is so much that even the best war image cannot convey. Only in a reenactment can reenactors truly imagine what lies beyond
those frames. And, more important, only in a reenactment can they place themselves within the frames of their own war images.

To be sure, reenactors place themselves in history quite literally. One reenactor uses his skills as a graphic designer to replicate period wartime magazine covers. On a computer, he copies the covers' original layout, removes the images of history's actual players, and replaces them with images of reenactors; others produce pseudo-documentary films shot entirely at reenactments. William Gregory described a video his unit made called *Men Against Blanks*: "We used the opening credits of an original German newsreel and the soundtrack which described the battle, then we edited in the Battle of the Bulge from one of the Ft. Indiantown Gap battles. We then added subtitles. . . . It was shot in black and white and really looks like one of the original films."

Alain Benson uses a 1942 Leica camera to take photographs that are, he says, "indistinguishable" from period war photographs. He showed me one of his prize examples, a black-and-white photograph of several reenactors standing at the side of a road, silhouetted by gray fog. He explained "wanting to create this image because, remember, two hours before this photograph . . . these guys were all wearing blue jeans and T-shirts and we were driving our Volkswagens and Nissans. So I sort of—I created this moment. So there was a certain satisfaction of bringing everyone together, organizing them, and then staging the shot, and then getting this end result."

With great pride Alan claims that he has even fooled some top publishers into thinking his images are authentic. Many reenactors even told me that authentic-looking photographs of reenactors have been reproduced in books with captions that tout them as actual war photographs. Further, contemporary war documentaries often blend footage of reenactors with historical footage, making it extremely confusing for viewers, who don't know when they are watching film shot during a war and when they are watching footage that a documentary crew shot a few months ago. Similarly, Morris Call's own carefully produced replicas of period World War II German documents—made for reenactors—have been sold on eBay at prices that only original pieces can command. Although Morris is vehemently opposed to passing off as authentic the documents he makes, he says that other less scrupulous militaria dealers sell them under the guise of being period. A reproduction document for a World War II German reenactor that Morris sells for eight dollars, for instance, can command as much as one hundred dollars in the hands of one of these dealers. Another reenactor once had an extremely authentic-looking formal portrait of himself taken when his unit awarded him the Knight's Cross. Years later, he came across the photograph at a militaria show where it was being sold as authentic. "That's me!" he told the dealer.

Reenactors are not the only ones creating war images at events. Veterans also create some of their own. Bryan Grigsby (his real name) already served one tour of duty as a photographer during the Vietnam War. But he has a chance to capture images he may have missed by attending Vietnam reenactments, where he does an impression of a combat photographer. Bryan's photographs are so gritty and unflinching that they have become legends in certain circles. The reenacting newspaper *Battle Cry* did a story featuring them, and many of those pictured in his photographs proudly display copies in albums, on Web sites, and on walls at home. On a similar note, at one Bulge event, a World War II American veteran once decided to pose with a German reenactor. The veteran took the German reenactor's pistol, told him to put his hands up, and posed for the camera with his prisoner. Everyone laughed as this veteran staged a moment from his own history, and I was left to wonder whether he was reenacting history or creating it for the first time.

Reenactors often use the evidence of their war experiences in the real world. During the holidays, Fred Legum and others send greeting cards straight from the trenches; others use email addresses that signify their personas (to give a hypothetical example: Britsoldier@anyoldISP.net) or business cards designed to resemble period imagery; others display formal portraits of themselves in uniform in their homes; and Tilden Scott shows videos of reenactments in which he has participated to his high school students when teaching them about history.

Aware, of course, that they are not really soldiers, they also signify their involvement in history in lighthearted ways. At one memorable mail call, Hal Zane received a letter from his "wife" on the home front, actually written by another 4th Armored member. Included in the envelope was a black-and-white snapshot, circa 1940, picturing a child in a stroller. To signify Hal's possession of this bit of history, a comical mustache, a tiny replica of Hal's own, had been imposed on the child's face. So hilarious was this little gem that to this day it is remembered by many in the 4th Armored, and Hal still tucks it in the lining of his helmet.

Whatever form their war stories take, reenactors reveal their desire to involve themselves in history and thereby "own" or possess history for themselves. And it is only through the hobby that a reenactor can "feel as though you are part of our history of the wars." "I have had a lifelong love of history," one reenactor explains. "But something was always missing. At my first reenactment, it all came together. . . . Reenacting lifts history off the page and makes it real." What was missing, of course, was themselves. Having viewed common soldiers for so long from afar with awe at their sacrifice and disdain for the ways they've been forgotten, reenactors can now enjoy a connection to history that they have long imagined or desired. Further, by appropriating history for themselves, they have also asserted their authority over the public, the academy, and the media. Such

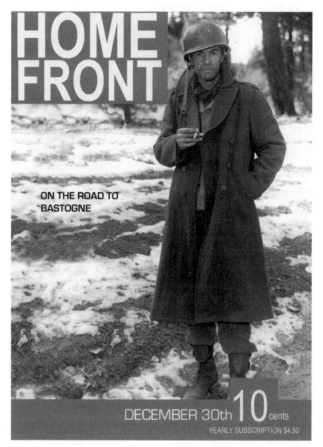

HOME FRONT

ON THE ROAD TO BASTOGNE

DECEMBER 30th 10 cents
YEARLY SUBSCRIPTION $4.50

Reenactor created wartime magazine cover featuring a reenactor and photograph by Wayne L. Pierce (courtesy Wayne L. Pierce)

power gives one reenactor "a sense of personal fulfillment and deep, internal joy that I never thought possible." And indeed, they delight in their ingenuity, often brimming with self-satisfaction and even arrogance as they describe their own roles in history.

No wonder they approach the hobby with little irony. "A lot of reenactors characterize themselves as grown men with toys," Patrick Hart concedes, "but it's very serious." And while they may dismiss the outsider-view of reenacting as "a drug-like escape from reality," privately they admit that pursuing an illusion is as strong as having an addiction. (Hence their descriptions of getting "hooked" on reenacting.) Alain Benson says his desire to experience a magic moment acts "like a drug in which you're trying to achieve that ultimate high."

In enjoying the fix the hobby affords, reenactors often remain high long after an event. Invariably, small and grand plans are made for the next event; photographs are posted on the Web; experiences are rehashed for weeks afterward. "I'm still telling stories," one 4th Armored member reported after returning home from an event, "even though [my wife] stopped listening after the Monday I got back." Dave Watkins describes how a postevent high helps him back in the daily pattern of a workweek. While his uninterested co-workers might look at a photograph or two, he has a feeling that "a lot of them don't approve of it." So, Dave says, "I keep it to myself and it helps me function in a mundane situation."

Another reenactor says that even if an event is miserable, and you "may not enjoy it when you are there," it still has benefits. "God, you have stories to tell your co-workers when you get back to the office," he declares. "I would not trade these experiences for any in the world." Perry Trent uses his war stories in his real-life job, which he describes as "a very tough, cut-throat-people-getting-screwed-left-right-and-center-kind-of-business." He laughed as he confided in me that he uses reenacting to intimidate people. "This nut collects tanks. What do you mean tanks? And then [I] pull out pictures and [they] see me rumbling down the road in an M36 with a 90mm cannon. . . . That can be very good in my business."

Others return home from events to find their appreciation for the common soldier has deepened. "It makes me appreciate what others have endured," one reenactor observes, "and makes me glad that I was not really there." Still others find that their appreciation for their own real lives is intensified as well: "It feels so good to stop," Craig Jones said after a tiring event. "Anyone who has been deprived of sleep, food, and is cold, wet, and miserable at an event," another says, "knows the joy of the experience when they get home."

But as much as they emphasize how fulfilling reenacting is, they also express an equal amount of frustration. In fact, most, maybe even all, suffer some degree of dissatisfaction and unhappiness because of the hobby. Through one cold winter, I spoke with an exasperated John Loggia several times. "When I started reenacting, I loved it," he said sadly. "Now it's just hard." By the time spring rolled around, Hank Lyle called up to tell me: "Reenactors are all fuckin' crazy. Seriously," he said grimly when I laughed, "You should put that in your research." And one summer day, Luke showed up at my apartment dressed in his GI uniform, filthy and exhausted after a private event at Fort Eustis in Virginia. "So much effort for such a disappointing event," he said pulling off his boots to reveal blistered feet. Perhaps only partially rhetorically, he asked: "Why do I do this?"

Much of this frustration stems from the fact that putting themselves into history is no easy task. The high of a magic moment may be seductive, but it is only a small and usually fleeting moment. In fact, most reenactors do not spend their time experiencing magic moments, but trying, and often failing, to create them. For, just as the slightest detail makes an illusion possible, it can also destroy it. A photograph that would otherwise appear authentic is spoiled by the slightest anachronistic detail in its frame; a moment of immersion is quickly disrupted by the sound of a cell phone ringing; and, for every war story a reenactor tells, another has his or her own, and the two do not always complement each other, as witness the stories Craig, Brian, and I would tell.

But in many ways, a single reenactor cannot achieve his or her goal alone. Not only is it impossible to reenact alone, as Luke observes, but "every reenactor affects every other reenactor." Thus, they find that even in private, they must work together, since "reenacting is a group effort." Or, as Luke puts it, an event "can only be as authentic as its least authentic members." In other words, a reenactor's claim to possess history is, to a large degree, legitimated by other reenactors—hence Brian's request that I agree to our fictional story.

Reenactors may have successfully gained control over war's representation by moving it into their private arena. As Lew McCarthy says of a private event, "the only ones you have to impress are one another." But their private use of history proves a double-edged sword. On one hand, it liberates them: they are able to represent war as they see fit—being able to commit atrocities, for example. On the other hand, their autonomy is tempered by their ability to reach consensus over authenticity: whether the atrocity would have been "historically authentic," whether it was performed authentically, and whether those who committed it looked authentic doing it. Thus, the question of ownership of history and its attendant issues such as authority and legitimacy that fuel debates over history's public uses rear their ugly heads even when they are "not really interpreting to people," as Patrick Hart says, but "interpreting to yourselves."

As they try to create their illusions, reenactors spend little time debating the question, how do we relive the past? Instead, they concentrate on trying to answer questions that will allow them to get to the magic moment and possess history for themselves. What happened in the past? What could have happened? When does one reenactor ruin another reenactor's experience? The intensity with which they pursue common answers, and the frustration such a quest produces, proves that the desire to claim personal possession of the past—to tell one's own war story—is a serious matter indeed.

Chapter 9

"I'm Dead! I Just Want to Party!"

Behavior Problems

"If this thing is going to work," one reenactor observes, "we need people not only to look like soldiers but act like them too." Indeed. Reenactors often describe their behavior in events as "role playing" and reenacting as "theatrical." And even though there's a lot of silliness and nonperiod activity during events, most reenactors argue that, in order to create a successful illusion, they must "play it as correctly as they can." Many advocate the need to assume what they call the authentic "mindset" of the common soldier, and many also believe that they should get in character before an event. Watching war movies, listening to period music, reading about a battle, or simply putting on a uniform can help. "When you put that uniform on," Paul Donald advises, "you better assume the demeanor of that person or you're betraying the uniform."

Reenactors may agree that they should somehow act like real soldiers, but there consensus ends. After all, what constitutes the authentic demeanor of a common soldier? Because each unit answers this question differently—even reenactors within units disagree—the aftermath of an event inevitably produces an endless stream of complaints. Whether harping on the "bad attitude of fellow reenactors," the "total disregard for authenticity," or the fact that there are just "too many yahoos [and] people not taking it seriously," they pour forth a rash of grievances about the ways the many bonehead reenactors ruined their karma

Firing in the field, the Bulge, 1994

or even an entire event. The object of their criticism is the primary cause of a failed illusion: the universally condemned farb.

"Farb," a noun used to describe a bad or inauthentic reenactor, and "farby," an adjective used to describe a reenactor's inauthentic behavior, attitude, or appearance, are both terms that refer to "something, someone, some idea, etc. that is different from historical reality." And nearly a quarter of all reenactors identify some version of farby behavior when asked what makes an event unsuccessful or not pleasurable.

From less egregious behavior violations (drinking a Diet Coke in the trenches) to the more overtly inappropriate (shouting in the middle of combat, as one reenactor once did, "I'm dead! I just want to party!"), reenactors aren't consistent in their levels of authentic behavior. "Some things are really outlandish," Greg Grosshans says. "You're like, ah, c'mon, nobody would have ever done that. But once again you're just reenacting."

But even the idea that they're just reenacting doesn't ease their frustration. "A lack of professionalism," Paul Harding said when I asked him what made a recent event unsuccessful. "No one seemed to have any clue or knowledge of the tactics, strategies." The charge that reenactors have no clue is only one in a long list of behavior complaints. From ignoring the rules to acting heroically, there are many different categories for a behavior farb. Other complaints over farby behavior include cheating, partying, showing off, being unsafe, being too serious, selfish, or overbearing, having a lack of appreciation for history, or simply being stupid.

But with so many different types of reenactors, reaching agreement on proper behavior is difficult. "There is a portion of reenactors who are living historians," Morris Call, an old-hand World War II German reenactor, says. "They want to present a picture. Then there are the tactical folks, into the game." Those less focused on the tactical (historians, poseurs) are derided as preferring to "stand around, look pretty, strike poses, and take pictures." They "don't want to get dirty," one reenactor believes, and are "worried about tearing their pants."

Then there are those who "want to do nothing but blast caps." These are the "trigger-time" reenactors (cowboys, yahoos, cappers) who "think they're John Wayne (or Steiner) and have no concept of what it was really like for the soldiers." Still others are derided as comfort lovers who are unwilling to suffer for authenticity's sake, but head for shelter at the first drop of rain or snow.

"To fully respect the suffering and sacrifices of those who were there," one reenactor argues, "you have to go 110 percent. What do you learn from sleeping in a camper or a motel?" Philip Moss agrees: "There is a high 'puss-factor' when it comes to bad weather. Not that I'm real thrilled at standing out in the rain or freezing my doo-dads off, it's just that I go to experience what they did if possible." "It's good to get out there and get dirty. Get your feet wet," Dave Watkins concurs. "I am miserable a lot. It's good to be miserable. . . . You have to do that if you really want to call yourself a reenactor."

But not all reenactors seek misery. "If I wanted to get that kind of experience," another says, "I'd be in the real Army. This is a hobby, and I am not into sadomasochism via natural exposure." Tim Gilbert agrees. "I do not feel that one must necessarily 'suffer' to experience a magic moment although a little misery occasionally reminds us of the tremendous ordeals that the World War II soldier endured." He concludes, "I have never been in favor of looking for agony just to get a better experience."

For my own part, I categorized myself as a definite comfort lover. After going to events for a couple years, I didn't worry about pushing myself to endure hardship. As I became more comfortable at events, I had no problem making life easier by, for example, bringing my coffee maker into the women's barracks at the Bulge event one year; leaving a World War I event early after spending a miserable, cold, rainy day outside; or, once, leaving the 4th Armored campsite in the middle of the night after trying for hours to fall asleep on a cot in the woods. (I slept in my car.)

Although I was definitely not alone in trying to ease the strains of reenacting (at that same event, Perry Trent also slept in his car), reenactors range widely in opinion over what constitutes a better experience. As much as they might prefer to devote their time telling war stories about their successes, they spend far more time recounting the ways farbs ruined their experiences.

Grace Hall became extremely annoyed at a World War I event when she was in camp cooking and, all of a sudden, "the Russians invaded our camp." She said they "started beating the women with rifle butts and prodding us and things like that." Since her unit's camp was in "the out-of-bounds area" of the Newville site, she "got really mad." Still, she said, she "played along with it" while "cussing at the guy in German."

Grace was able to incorporate her annoyance into period behavior. But Dave Watkins only grimaced when remembering his too-close encounter with some farbs at a World War I event. "Right in the middle of a raging battle," Dave recalls, "these guys were talking. A guy says, 'Oh, gee,' and he looked at his digital watch and said, 'It's getting late. I told my wife I was going to be home early, so I'll see you around.'" Before the guy left, though, the two farbs chatted loudly about their plans to watch next weekend's football game, discussing what they would bring to eat. "It really bummed me out that these guys kind of destroyed my little skull case," Dave laments, referring to his attempt to lose himself in the moment. "And I really disliked them doing that. . . . It was almost to the point where, well, why did you bother showing up?"

While Dave kept his feelings to himself, others make them public. German reenactor Greg Steel was livid after his run-in with some farbs who ignored an event's schedule. His unit was getting ready to go into battle, which was set to start at nine o'clock. At two minutes after nine, a unit of Allied reenactors poured into their camp on attack. "We didn't even bother to shoot back," Greg remembers. "We were pissed off!" His reaction to the unit's blatant disregard of the scenario's timetable was swift: "I told them to get the fuck out of my camp before I rearranged their faces."

Of all their complaints about behavior, though, perhaps the most vexing—and universal—concerns the farby failure to "take hits." Hank Lyle explains why this is such a problem. "You could kill a man at two hundred yards in war, but you can't successfully kill anybody at more than fifty yards in a reenactment because for me to take a hit from you, I have to see you shoot me. I have to know that you've shot at me." But, as Hank explains, a lot of the time reenactors have no idea that they're being shot. "If I'm in the woods and I hear people firing," Hank says, "I don't know that they're firing at me. So I keep going. So until I come around this corner and you're set up behind this tree—bang-bang-bang—then I know, okay, but you could have been firing the whole time when I was milling about eating my candy bar in the parking lot."

It is hard to know if you have been hit. I can testify to that fact. At several Eastern Front events, when I was involved in combat, things became so chaotic and crazy as we ran through the woods that I had no idea what was going on, much less who was shooting at me. I found it difficult even to remember to fire my own weapon, since I was usually trying to run away from the Germans. At other times, when, for example, our unit was ambushed, it was clear that I had been killed. But I always enjoyed taking a hit, since it meant that I could justify taking a nice rest. Others agree. One reenactor even admitted that during one event he took a hit and promptly fell asleep.

Still, being killed doesn't mean that one is out of the event for good. "The way that works," John Loggia explains, "when the fighting moves on, then you can resurrect yourself. But we ask people to not appear in your rear, you know, like they did something clever." (This is also known as "becoming a ghost.") But even with the promise of resurrection, many still refuse to die. One reenactor described an encounter with some "Kevlar" reenactors. "An MG34, a PPSH, and four MP40s plus many more rifles couldn't kill three airborne guys hiding in a small clump of bushes with scattered trees from fifty yards away. We had to stop the battle, walk over there and say, 'Okay, John Wayne, get up and get the @#!$ out of here—you couldn't be more dead. . . . You exemplify deadness.'"

"Calling a hit," or yelling to a target that you've killed him or her, is generally regarded as just as bad as not taking the hit itself. "When people don't fall dead," Terrence Scott explains, "the atrocities start to be screamed. . . . 'I got you, motherfucker! You're dead!' and they start yelling silly stuff." But Terrence thinks arguing over hits is "just wasted energy. I'm not here to argue with you—I got you or you got me—I'm here to do something entirely different and if you think you got me, great, I'll be dead. I'll be back alive in ten or fifteen minutes."

To be fair, most don't take hits because they aren't aware of being shot. "I can't tell you how many times my opponent has walked up to me, and said 'Will you please take your hit?'" one reenactor admits. "My truthful reply is always 'Okay. Gosh, I'm sorry, I had no idea anyone was shooting at me.'" But others create reasons to justify their refusal to respond. "Your gun [might not be] ze-roed, or the sights improperly adjusted, or the weather affecting the mechanical aspects," one reenactor offered by way of an excuse for not taking hits. Still others fail to take hits if they think an opponent is already dead. "I always die when I'm shot," Ben Sandler says earnestly. But he also admits that he won't die if he thinks the person shooting him is dead. "I shot a German several times," Ben recalls. "I emptied my clip into him, and he saw me shooting at him but he didn't die. And then he came around and started shooting at me, and I just ignored him."

Reenactors have promoted various solutions to this problem, from using referees and sensor systems to handing out "wound cards" prior to battle. These cards list fates such as "WIA: gunshot wound to the groin" or "KIA: grenade wounds." Others use referees to call hits, with one of the more elaborate referee systems awarding points for successes, such as inflicting heavy enemy casualties, and detracting points for failures, such as activating minefields. But most of the time, reenactors rely on the honor system. "What we usually do is tap your helmet," Ben explains, "and then you point at him. That means I shot you." They also issue rules for proper hit-taking procedure. "Scream, yell, and play out a good death scene," the GWA vice-president urges. Others spell it out more explicitly:

> When hit, fall (carefully so as to not injure yourself or others) lay dead for one minute. After your minute, remove all headgear and walk back to the C[asualty] C[learing] S[tation], sign in, wait your time, and then return from behind the front line, as if you were a replacement reinforcing your side, which in fact you now are! Do not argue at any time with one another. If in doubt over a mutual kill—"I got you first, no, I got you first!"—both parties shall retire fifty yards apart. If a said "hit" individual refuses to honor the kill, make note and report this individual to your unit leader. Do not under any circumstances take action into your own hands. Bad sportsmen and spoilsports we don't need.

Such procedures make the hit-taking process sound straightforward. And, if everyone followed them, reenactors wouldn't find themselves as frustrated as they usually are after an event. But as things heat up and chaos reigns on the battlefield, it is all too easy to ignore the rules. "It can be very disappointing and very disheartening," one reenactor says of the hit-taking problem. Others find that it "takes a lot of the enjoyment out of our hobby." While some blame particular nationalities for being the worst non-hit-taking offenders, nearly all assert their own willingness to die. "I take hits all the time, and you know why?" one reenactor rails. "Because it's the correct thing to do. I respect my opponents and the realities of the battlefield."

Taking a hit (and taking it well) is thus not only equated with acting au-

Dead French reenactors, World War I private event, 1993

thentically, but also with behaving properly and working together. It is seen as a way to respect one's opponent. It is a "courtesy" that is "expected to be theatrical as a tribute to the opposition." When opponents do respond to their fire, they're enthusiastic, often using the word "Hollywood" to describe particularly dramatic hit-taking performances. "Nothing is more satisfying as a target performing a good 'Hollywood' death," as one reenactor believes. Hank Lyle says he has "a lot of satisfaction in taking my hit." And he loves to really ham it up. "I'll run and get a couple steps and then I'll take a good theatrical hit and you can just hear people, 'Aw, man did you see that?! Did you see that guy take his hit?'" But Hank gets mad that so few are willing to return the favor.

Calling hits, ignoring each other, or screaming at each other to die are just some of the ways reenactors respond to farby behavior on the battlefield. When a scenario turns wholly inauthentic, for instance, John Loggia just refuses to play along, saying that he simply becomes "historically impaired" during particularly farby moments. "I'm at a World War II event," John explains, "and we end up fighting in a parking lot, like around Larry Cohen's Toyota. And I'm like, I'm not going to participate, this is stupid. . . . I'll walk away. I just will not do that. That's nonsense."

Others break character when confronted by behavior violations. It was nighttime at a World War I event when Rob Costi was captured and taken to a

German bunker for interrogation. All was going well, in rigorous period fashion, when a German offered Rob a sip from a bottle of schnapps. Rob abruptly refused, "came out of his impression," and took it upon himself to reiterate the GWA rule barring the use of alcohol during combat. "It's too dangerous," he told them, evoking the principle that "guns and alcohol do not mix." So disgusted were these Germans by their teetotaler prisoner that they ceased the interrogation and summarily released him.

Others become enraged. One German reenactor reported that he "almost killed (for real) a fat, farby-ass GI at the Yorkville event." The reason for his wrath: the American refused to die when a German grenade blew up next to his foxhole. His rationale for surviving was to tell the Germans that "it didn't fall in the hole, so I'm okay." One of the Germans approached him, and "started off nice and calm and tried to explain that the concussion alone would have killed him." But soon it turned ugly. "I eventually had to berate him so severely that he was compelled to drag his fat, sorry ass out of my line of sight for fear of his worthless life."

In an attempt to avoid what John Loggia sees as a potential for "anarchy" at events, he calls for the "active use of military discipline and professionalism." "The closer to the discipline, organization, and command and control tactics to the real thing (short of live ammunition)," another agrees, "the more successful."

But in a voluntary hobby, "policing themselves," as John Loggia says, can be very difficult. After all, how should they punish violations? Rarely is a reenactor kicked out of an event for improper behavior. Instead, unit commanders are expected to control their members, and the members are supposed to follow orders. "I was really confused," Ben Sandler said of his first event. "You try to stick with your squad leader. He'll hopefully show you what to do."

But not everyone is as well behaved as Ben. "Too many loud-mouthed, first-time-in-the-trenches privates took it upon themselves to continually scream orders at their fellow privates in total disregard of our safety and our NCOs' and officers' orders," one reenactor complained. Even within a single unit, a commander can have a hard time maintaining control. Greg Grosshans says it's tough just "trying to keep five guys together. Because you go out and someone starts shooting and one guy runs that way, another one this way." But Greg also says he doesn't "go so crazy with the command structure." "If one guy wants to go off in his little reconnaissance," he says, "then that's okay."

But others think it's anything but okay. "In real combat," Luke bitterly complains, "most reenactors would either die in their first fight or win medals for valor. Reenactors, unlike real soldiers, have no regard for the dangers of the battlefield." Along with others, Luke becomes furious at discipline problems, especially when troops run toward the sound of firing guns (clusterfuck), neglect mission objectives, flagrantly violate authenticity by, for instance, having a pizza delivered in the field in the middle of a battle ("Once on the base," Wilson Lyle recalls, "the delivery guy only had to listen to the sound of the blanks to find where the people were"), or, as a member of John Loggia's command staff once did, sitting in a trench in the middle of a World War I battle writing the unit's orders on a laptop computer.

Of course, part of their problem with enforcing discipline lies in the fact that officers have no real power. Morris Call cut to the chase: "Reenactor—the root word is 'ta-da!' Actor! No reenactment unit can enforce a state such as the real military. No unit has real consequences for disobedience aside from peer pressure. You can walk if you have the car keys." "You can't keep your foot on the necks of the men," Luke agrees, almost in disappointment, "because they're not enlisted men in the army subject to military discipline. You can't say, well, you know, shut the hell up and sit down."

In fact, reenactors deride authority figures, especially officers. Scott Friewald once joked about an impression he wanted to do at Vietnam events: In a clean, pressed uniform, he would sit in an air-conditioned trailer, his feet propped up on a government-issued steel desk, selling popsicles to dirty, sweaty grunts coming in from the field. Others found Scott's idea for a "REMF" (rear-echelon motherfucker, in military slang) impression endlessly amusing. This image of a chairborne official with little regard for the hardship of the common soldier reflects a realistic disdain for officers. "Bitching about officers is simply a part of a soldier's existence," as one reenactor observes.

But as an escape from real-life pressures, many want to relax and have fun at events, not be subject to a military system of discipline. "I have enough [responsibility] with my job," one reenactor says, "so when I go to a reenactment I don't want any." Greg Grosshans thinks striking a balance between fun and discipline is necessary. He's seen a lot of reenactors who "try to get really serious with it . . . they really push the commands out in the field." But in his unit, their main priority is to "go out there and try to have fun," Greg says. "If it isn't fun for us, it becomes work."

Those saddled with any level of responsibility at events—event hosts, commanders—often find their fun severely curtailed. The meetings, bureaucracy, arguments, and anarchy were just a few reasons John Loggia started to feel that going to events was "almost like going to work." Others, like Tom Schultz, become extremely unhappy in positions of authority. People complaining, not fol-

US officer reenactors confer in the field, the Bulge, 1997

lowing orders, and generally treating him poorly meant that he "was the loneli-
est guy out there," Tom says of his stint as GWA Allied combat commander. So
lonely, in fact, that he eventually demoted himself to private and handed over
the reigns of power to John, his successor.

Unlike some officers, John has a reputation as a fair leader who knows his
place. "You have to have some authority but you also have to remember that these
aren't really soldiers," John says. But many complain that too many officers are
on a power trip. Berating people, making unilateral decisions, and generally not
working well with others are just a few manifestations of a reenactor's suffering from what one reenactor calls a "self-appointed Caesar" complex.

"People enjoy having power and they take it to an extreme," Fred Legum remarks, explaining why he dropped out of a unit after the commander started to
act like an asshole. "People aren't getting paid to do it," Fred says. "You have
to realize that these are guys who paid for their own kit. They're taking time out
of their lives." Like others, Fred sees a fine line between disciplining someone
"within a fun level" and taking "it too far."

Whenever I saw an officer strutting around, ordering people to do things or
just generally acting like a jerk, I was incredulous. What was he thinking? I also
saw how such behavior can profoundly affect others, especially new reenactors.

"I was very eager to attend my first event," Donald Collins remembers. Upon arriving, he joined his World War II unit to practice drilling and found himself in the front line. "Immediately," he says, "I wished I wasn't." He didn't know how to act and wasn't clear on performing the rifle drill. "Suddenly," Donald recalls, "the 'commander' saw how I was behind and lashed into me like a real military man would on the first day of boot camp. After several minutes of yelling at me he told me to leave the group and to stay out of his sight." Donald was quite embarrassed and went off to practice on his own. "I never had the same enthusiasm," he says. But he was also mad that this unit of what he calls "extreme hardcore reenactors" had so "little patience for someone who was new and unsure of what to do." Donald concluded that there are simply too many units that take it too far when it comes to discipline. "I was obviously trying and would get better," he says. But "when I think back to my first event, I get embarrassed instead of remembering a good time."

There is another reaction to an officer who takes things too far—mutiny. Mark Lance reported an event where several 4th Armored men "fragged" one of the event's commanding officers after he acted like a total moron. At another event, an entire unit left in the middle of combat after finding the commander to be, as one recalled, a "fucking jerk."

Reenactors do enforce discipline within an acceptable level so that it can be fun for those involved. In his early days of World War I reenacting, Private John Loggia once ignored a sergeant major's orders by shirking sentry duty and leaving camp. "Upon my return," he recalls, "I was arrested and crucified." It was done authentically, John says, but, he also admits, "it was done in a tongue in cheek way." But at another event, one unit executed one of its own men for falling asleep on guard duty. Before the execution, the unit asked for volunteers to serve on the firing squad. "Everybody in our unit just said no," Fred Legum remembers. "It was bad juju to do that."

Whether bad juju or just taking things too far, "there are," as Greg Grosshans asserts, "certain limits." Even in trying to get to reenactor's nirvana, there must be a line between reality and fantasy, between the illusion and the real thing. One of the tricky aspects though is finding that balance. "Acting naturally is essential," Mark Sammons believes. "Some of the worst moments are when everybody tries to pretend to be real soldiers. It just looks bad. But there are other moments when people react real naturally to events without thinking that it becomes very real." But as they judge one another's behavior, they often have a hard time determining what is realistic-seeming and what is altogether too real.

"It Is Actually Kind of Sick When You Think About It"

"Two of my men had been killed down this road. And so I went down the road to investigate," Luke says, embarking on a well-loved reenactor tradition: telling a war story.

"My men had been giving the prisoners chocolate and treating them very well, giving them cigarettes and everything. Anyway, I shouted back up, I said, 'Hey, you know there's two men dead here, Sergeant Sharp and Sergeant so-and-so.' And I started walking up the road with my carbine and I was about twenty-five yards away, thirty yards away, and Private Rob Costi, nice guy, he's giving the Germans chocolate and I go, 'Rob, get away from them!' He looks up at me and said, 'Huh?' And I go, 'Get away from them!' And I start to raise my carbine and he's like, 'Oh!' And the two Germans, one of which has like chocolate in his mouth," Luke laughs, "they look up and they just have this expression like—" Luke makes a face of surprise. "And I shot five or six times. . . . That was Paul Wake, the best German prisoner of all. Both of them did a superb job. . . . They died well. But they thought they had been shot out of hand. But they took it. They took it like men."

"Why was the one guy giving them chocolate?" I ask.

"Oh, he was just being friendly to the prisoners. Being humane to them," Luke says casually. "And there was another time when I had shot some prisoners, too."

Still in the early phases of my research and trying to understand exactly how reenacting works, I ask, "What happened to those guys? They fell down and then you left and then you don't know what happened?"

"Exactly, we left and then we went on." Luke nods.

"But they would join their unit again and fight?"

"Yeah, they rejoined it later," Luke seems frustrated. "But that's what we did," he continues. "And actually I shot Greg Grosshans too because he'd been taken prisoner and George Ferraro, my runner, was keeping a gun on him, but Grosshans was shouting out instructions to his men and Ferraro wouldn't shoot him. And I said, 'Ferraro, shut him up!' Because Ferraro had his machine gun. He wasn't armed. And then I said, 'Ferraro, just get out of the way!' And I raised my rifle to shoot at him and Greg jumped behind a tree and Ferraro was behind the tree too! And I'm like, 'Ferraro! Get out from behind the tree!' You think that tree's going to stop a .30-caliber bullet?"

"Did he think you were going to shoot him?"

"Yeah, he did. Ferraro misunderstood. I don't know what the hell he was thinking. Anyway, Ferraro stepped out from behind the tree and then I shot three times at the tree. And Grosshans crumpled on the other side of the tree, dead. Quiet finally. . . . So as a result I have a reputation for killing prisoners."

"And didn't you say that . . ." I begin to ask Luke to explain how people know how to take their hits. But he interrupts me.

"Personally," Luke is emphatic. "So the commander has a reputation for killing prisoners."

"Right," I say, wondering why Luke is talking about his reputation as if he really had killed prisoners.

"So what kind of an example does that set for the men? That's pretty bad actually. So I swear I'll never do it again."

"But that's not really viewed as being a problem?" I ask, confused about why Luke is so emphatic on this point.

"Like that would be a very bad thing to do if you were an officer," Luke says with conviction.

"In real life, yes," I concede. "But, I'm saying, in a reenactment?"

"If you do that, then you can't tell your men not to kill prisoners if you kill them." He pauses. "It does happen though. It does happen in real life."

"But in a reenactment?" I ask again.

"In a reenactment, what about?"

"You said you have a reputation, but it's not a bad reputation?"

"Well, yeah, it's a bad reputation!" he says urgently. "They don't want to be shot!"

"Okay. But people don't dislike you because of that?"

"Some do."

"Because they think you're not playing fair?" I persist.

"Yeah, they think I'm hateful. Some people take this very seriously. Paul Wake didn't care but the other guy I shot—boy, I heard he was really mad about it."

"Because he felt that it was unrealistic?"

"I don't think he felt that it was unrealistic. I think he felt that it was wrong."

"Morally?"

"Yeah. That he shouldn't have been shot. And maybe he wasn't the guy that shot those two fellows down the road. Maybe neither of them were. But I thought it was a pretty realistic thing to do."

As happened many times interviewing reenactors, the lines between what did or could have happened in history and what happened in a particular reenactment became blurred. Was it a reenactment we were talking about? Or was it real life? But I soon stopped trying to get them to make such a distinction. In telling their war stories, they do not return from beyond with time-travel reports, but speak in the immediacy of their own voices.

As I heard more and more of their war stories, I was surprised to see how seriously they judge each other by their actions in the field. They can, as Luke said, take it "like men" or do a "superb job." But they can also get confused, misunderstand, or even be considered humane or hateful—all for their actions in a reenacted battle. However odd it may seem—and it did to me at first—reenactors earn real-life reputations as they reenact. I never once heard a reenactor dismiss another's behavior in the field as stemming from theatrics. Thus, with no real distinction between who they are in real life and who they are in the field, they view an event as "a battle where one can prove their merits and be recognized." Aside from sometimes being awarded medals for their accomplishments, they are primarily recognized with real-life congratulations, respect, or authority. For bad behavior, there may be mock punishment or a dose of discipline, but more often than not, there is derision and animosity. And a reenactor can easily earn a reputation of being a cheater, a loser, or an idiot.

Because behavior in the field has concrete repercussions in the reenacting world and in real life as well, it is not surprising that so many reenactors consistently stress the need to act properly. They even admit that it is sometimes necessary, even inevitable, that in trying to act authentically they often begin to "personify the units they're portraying," as John Loggia says. Fred Legum says there's no question that reenactors take on some of the personality associated with their historic units. "Some of the German units have that Aryan race kind of attitude," he observes. "I've gotten the impression that the French guys are just like the real ones, they have kind of a conscript kind of attitude. . . . And the British guys [are] just kind of sort of laid back. A lot of American reenactors, they have this savior type attitude, that they won the war. . . . They have that Sergeant York–Audie Murphy attitude."

A bit of personification may be inevitable. But at the same time, reenactors also recognize that there must be a line between acting authentically and going too far. Even in the best of magic moments, they shouldn't become so immersed in what John calls their faux war that they think they're really soldiers. And they constantly remind one another that they shouldn't forget that ultimately, they're only role-playing. "When you are passionate about your hobby and take it to heart you're cruising for a bruising," one reenactor warns. "We play soldiers plain and simple. We are not soldiers of the Reich, the King, or the US of A."

Successful ownership of history thus depends on maintaining a healthy distance between authentically performing in an illusion and thinking oneself to be truly part of history's reality. "This is a hobby," as one reenactor makes clear, "not real life." But Greg Grosshans finds that it can be very easy to cross the line

Morning safety briefing, World War I private event, 1996

between portraying a soldier and identifying with him. Especially after spending a lot of time researching a unit, it is easy, he believes, to start "internalizing some of the things."

I witnessed what I thought was evidence of this kind of internalizing quite often. Most of the time I saw it in the ways reenactors seemed to change once they put on their uniforms. They swagger, strut, or march with determination; they may hold their heads higher, stand a little straighter, shout a little louder than normal, or take on an intensely serious pose, intimidating, unflinching. Even Luke admits that when he puts on his uniform, he finds that he wears some of the attitude he associates with certain soldiers. "They're just so cocky," he says of Americans in World War II. Paul Donald agrees: "When you get dressed up in a World War I officer's uniform with your Sam Browne belt on and your leather leggings, you feel like you're something. You feel like you're a soldier. You feel the part. I don't know, there's something about putting on a military uniform that changes your whole bearing."

While some admit that their bearing changes in uniform, others seem to internalize history a little more intensely. At times, I ran into reenactors who caused me to wonder where they drew the line between fantasy and reality. Many reenactors spoke about the soldiers they represented with incredible passion, recounting actual war stories as if they were their own. In the most extreme case, a reenactor can even appear to believe that, in some ways, his persona is real. One World War II German reenactor I got to know pretty well was a prominent figure in the hobby, widely considered an expert on German militaria. Whenever we talked on the phone, he would refer to his German soldier persona, "Hans." He even sent me a photograph of Hans, which of course pictured the reenactor himself dressed in uniform. Although I knew that Hans wasn't a real person, I had an eerie feeling when this reenactor would begin to talk about Hans in the third person and tell me stories about what Hans was up to.

All reenactors argue that they understand the proper limits to reenacting. But they are quick to point out others who go too far—from the reenactor who built a sandbag bunker in his bedroom at home to those reenactors who proudly display their SS "blood tattoos" ("Mother of God," as one reenactor said of this tattooing trend among some German reenactors, "now that is a crazy idea"). These reenactors are said to have an "addiction" that is so out of control that they have lost the ability to "separate reality from fantasy." Further, the fact that they are so "into" the hobby earns them a real-life reputation: they have "no other life." "Reenacting," as Laura Paris says of these reenactors, "is their life. They live it. They eat it. They breathe it."

"Like I collect this stuff. I spend a lot of money on it and I am too much into it myself," Greg Grosshans admits. "But I have my own life and I go on dates and whatever, and, you know, I have other interests too." Greg seemed to delight in painting a picture of the large number of losers who are way too into the hobby. "A lot of these guys are like forty-something years old. They're single. They don't date. All they want to talk about is German stuff. And they don't have any other life." John Loggia calls such reenactors "walking anachronisms," and Hank Lyle has one sure way to identify them: whether or not they use the pronoun "we." "When reenactors talk about historical battles," Hank explains, "they say 'well, we kicked your ass there.' And I always look at them and [say,] what do you mean 'We?' You know? Who's this 'We?' They associate themselves so much with the books and the clothing and, you know, I wear this stuff; I am this, so to speak."

Hank insists that he's "never fallen into that trap." But those who have fallen, many argue, reveal symptoms of a reenacting pathology, a "deeper malfunctioning," as Sinclair Davis puts it. And most have stories of encountering others whose behavior proves that they have lost an "intelligent perspective on reality."

At a World War II event he hosted, Tim Castle ordered reenactors to hold their fire after midnight since people living in the area had complained to the police during an event the previous year. But late at night the sound of gunfire erupted. Unshod, without his glasses, Tim rushed into the dark night, winding his way through a forest, following the sounds. When he reached the offending unit's camp, he was told by the German reenactors there: "The Americans attacked our camp! We had to defend it!"

Tim stared at them in disbelief. "What the fuck are you talking about? This isn't real."

With visions of a lawsuit, the loss of his home, his job, and the end of his life as he knew it, he contemplated throwing the unit out. They "weren't worth it," he said. But when several unit members threatened to beat him up, he thought otherwise. Some reenactors, he concluded, are "living in an alternative reality."

When Tom Schultz proposed awarding a reenactor with the Victoria Cross, Fred Legum vigorously objected, arguing that bestowing such a highly esteemed award on a mere reenactor would "denigrate its honor." It's just a game, Tom responded, and it's not even a real medal. According to Tom, Fred's reaction was so inappropriate that he concluded that Fred was literally "touched in the head."

When Perry Trent ordered Leonard Lord to get the ambulance after someone had been hurt at a World War I event, Leonard refused, citing the rule barring nonperiod vehicles on the trench site during combat. After trying to persuade him—"C'mon, a guy's hurt. Let's just deal with the problem!"—Perry's patience wore thin. "You know," he erupted, "I don't care what the fuck you think. Just crawl back in your sick little world!"

And, at his first event, Sam Benevento lay on his cot fuming after Luke had "busted his balls" by forcing him to do KP while other unit members went on patrol. "I was lying there with my pistol was right beside me," Sam remembers, laughing. "I told my friend, if Luke comes in here, I'm going to shoot him." When Luke did stick his head in the tent, he saw the look on Sam's face and beat a hasty retreat.

All of these encounters earned those involved real reputations and damaged their relationships, so far beyond repair. Tom and Fred, Perry and Leonard, Luke and Sam have all ceased speaking to each other out of the conviction that the other is an asshole because he took things too far or not far enough.

Hank Lyle also experienced an eerie moment that crossed the line between authenticity and reality. He and his fellow Free French reenactors had been captured by several Germans during a night battle. "They surrounded us and [said] 'Get in a line! Get in a line!'" Hank remembers. All of a sudden, one of the Germans shouts, "Firing squad, ready!" Hank was shocked to hear that they were going to execute them, and immediately, he thought to himself, "Firing squad? Fuck that!" He recalls what happened next: "I turn around and I just start running. And then everybody else that was in the Free French, and there were probably about ten of us, just went bookin' haul-ass toward the wood line, which was a good hundred yards away." Hank laughs as he tells his story, delighted that he outwitted the Germans and escaped an untimely death. "I swear to you," he says, "I must have got seventy-five yards before the first shot was fired. Because they were so surprised that we ran and you know they're fumbling with their guns."

Confused about his reaction, I ask, "But they probably interpreted it as some Frenchman saying that, right?"

"Well, maybe so," Hank responds, "but my point, you know, Frenchman or Hank, you know, firing squad!? I ain't going to sit around and take a fucking round in the chest!"

When I ask him why he wasn't in the spirit of the game, Hank explains that this experience really made him think about what motivates some reenactors. He says that he "went around after saying, man, look, all you guys are saying that you're doing this for the veterans or you're nonpolitical. That was nothing of the kind. That was purely to reenact the joy of the slaughter." He started to feel uneasy with what happened because he thought that the motivation to reenact a firing squad came a little too close to what had been the real Germans' motivations in wartime. "Who's to say what would have happened if it had been the real thing?" Hank asks me with a deadly serious look on his face. "If they were a bunch of Serbians or something?"

This encounter prompted Hank to admit, "It is actually kind of sick when you think about it, dressing up to go pretend that you are slaughtering somebody else." It also made him wonder what motivates such a realistic performance. "It gets me to think well why is this guy reenacting at all? What is his hidden agenda? Or what is this fulfilling from his ego?"

As they read each other's behavior in the field, struggling to determine the limits of authentic behavior, they wrestle with the question of just how far one can go to "own" history, and history itself becomes the substance of their debates. The most contentious topic is the portrayal of World War II Germans.

On the World War II reenacting newsgroup, an SS reenactor once posted his fake intention of soundly defeating the Allies at an upcoming event. Writing as if he really were a Nazi, he leveled his phony threat: "We of the Hohenstaufen do not enjoy making wives into widows, or making innocent children fatherless. We do this because it is our duty, and it is in the interest of a greater Europe that a few must suffer. Join us, and your children shall reap the rewards of your sacrifices, oppose us, and you shall feel the crushing weight of God's will delivered to you by his army."

He ignited a firestorm. "Oh, please," Mike Sharp responded. "This stuff didn't work for the last guys that believed it." Another wrote, "Nazis; all mouth." The offending reenactor, now himself offended, wrote, "I do not portray a 'Nazi.' I reenact as an SS soldier who is fighting to protect his loved ones and his country. I'm sure you wrote it with tongue in cheek (as I do with all my postings), and I'm probably being too sensitive; however, I think I can probably speak for all German reenactors, be they Wehrmacht or SS, in saying that we detest having the 'N' word thrown at us. I expect that from John Q. Public, not from a fellow reenactor."

Reenactors often find themselves deflecting the charges that they are what they wear even from fellow reenactors. "I think we all realize that atrocities were committed on both sides," the SS reenactor continued, evoking the generic soldier theory. But he also asserted his capacity to distinguish reality from fantasy: "If my postings have a bit of overly dramatic flair to them, it's because I'm joking. . . . Some of you have taken it a little too seriously."

But they do take history seriously. And inevitably they expose their real life attitudes toward history—and each other. "Put a cork in it, Fritz," one reenactor erupted. "If it makes you uncomfortable to be called a Nazi, pick another impression." He continued saying that he wished the Americans "had nuked Dresden and Berlin along with it!" To this reenactor, the idea that the Nazis were just common soldiers like all other soldiers is ludicrous. And like many reenactors, he points to the Germans as being singularly evil. "Until you can come up with some Brit or American atrocity as bad as the 'Final Solution,'" he concluded, "just tuck your tail between your legs and dry up."

"It's really interesting," Patrick Hart offers. "A lot of guys, they still have those biases. They can't get over it. They just can't get over it. It goes back to that whole vilification of the enemy. Dirty Japs. Those damn Nazis." Scott Mies agrees. "There are quite a few reenactors who do World War II German who seem to think that Soviet reenactors should be held in contempt for doing Soviet." But Scott explains his own "healthy" attitude toward World War II German reenactors: "Anyone who's got living relatives that were victims [of the Holocaust] is naturally going to feel some animosity toward them. But the simple fact is I can't come to reenactments with the attitude of, 'Oh, I'm going to kill some Nazis this weekend,' because that's first of all going to make people nervous, and second of all it might get someone hurt."

Even if they are only role-playing, real-life feelings prove to underlie their actions in the field. And the idea that a reenactor might get hurt, whether through unsafe behavior or historic grudges, causes them to bar one thing from an event that might make it more authentic: hand-to-hand combat.

Sitting in the waterlogged farmhouse on the Newville site, a lackluster Phil

Fussel lamented the growth of the hobby. "It used to be that we all knew each other," he said sadly. "We could fight hand to hand, even in the trenches. Now everyone and his brother comes out, you've got a bunch of strangers out here, and it's too dangerous to fight like that."

In light of all the many arguments and animosities that exist among reenactors, they are ordered not to engage each other physically in combat. Their fighting at events should not erupt from disagreements, whether over hit-taking or the Final Solution. Instead, fighting is seen, ironically, as a symbol of their ability to work together. No matter how egregiously farby a reenactor's behavior is, how deep a pathology may run, or how painful the memories of history may be, there should be "no injuries or arguments during mock battle." Instead, they are expected to behave themselves. And not arguing, they say without any hint of irony, is necessary in order to fight with each other authentically. "We should not fight to be divided," one reenactor states, "but should fight to be united."

Such directives are easier said than followed. They may heed the call to work together in public, but in private, Dave Watkins says, they (metaphorically) "love to beat each other up." Charging each other with "living in an alternative reality," "thinking their way is the right and only way," being "Nazis," "crybabies," or "movie star wannabes with egos bigger than their abilities," or acting like "smug, arrogant snobs who know it all," they endlessly bicker over their failures and pathologies.

Reenactors may disagree about the precise reason their experiences are ruined, but they do agree on who ruins them. When, in my questionnaire, I asked them what makes an event unsuccessful, the majority pinpointed "other reenactors" as the number one source of a failed event, with another 20 percent listing "no cooperation." Citing problems such as "competing egos in command," "infighting among groups," "bickering and ego tripping," and "no cohesion," they made clear the importance of working together to achieve their goals and, seemingly, the near impossibility of achieving unity.

Still, they insist that their squabbles are an inevitable result of reenacting politics. Their penchant for in fighting, Hank Lyle believes, can be explained by the simple fact that the hobby has "people involved." But others seem genuinely puzzled by their seemingly intractable disputes. "There's just like no consensus," John Loggia observes. "Of course, that's understandable in coalition warfare. But isn't it odd though?" But after many years of service on the Western Front, John has a piece of wisdom to offer: "You can only try and work toward it, always keeping in mind that your perception of the way things should be is not always going to be what everyone else thinks it should be."

After finding the hobby to be an often merciless place where reenactors argue just as often as celebrate their fraternity, I came to view reenacting itself as a process, a trying to "work toward it." Given that they are surprisingly unconcerned with beating each other in combat, since, after all, everybody dies, their true conflict has almost nothing to do with tactical fighting. Instead, it lies in reaching consensus over the way things should be. As each attempts to place him or herself within an illusion, competition over defining authenticity is the central contest in their game.

Disagreeing over behavior is only the first battle in their authenticity war. They face another equally vexing question: what, exactly, constitutes an authentic visual representation of the common soldier? "We cannot control everyone's motives," Philip Moss says, but "we can control how they look on the outside so they don't ruin the event for the rest of us."

Chapter 10

"Farbs You Find Everywhere"

The Problem of Appearance

For all their arguing, reenactors tend to agree on one thing: their goal is to portray common soldiers authentically. "We are here to portray the normal look of the World War II soldier," as the World War II Historical Reenactment Society proclaims, "not the exception." Nothing, many reenactors say, ruins an event more than anachronisms. Although some believe that newbies should be granted "some latitude when it comes to authenticity," woe to those who start off looking inauthentic and never improve.

Some justify their concern with appearance in commemorative terms: they must "honor veterans' memories by showing up to [an] event in the proper kit." Others evoke the need to adhere to "historical reality." They must avoid "misrepresenting history," as Lew McCarthy says, "by doing crazy things like having a really atrocious kit." But most regard an authentic appearance as essential to an illusion. "The best description I've ever heard of reenacting," Patrick Hart says, "it's like you can't see yourself. So basically what you strive for is to make yourself look good, because when you look out in the crowd, and . . . you see somebody who's just atrociously a farb, you know, it just kills the whole thing for you. And it's almost like it keeps you—authenticity-wise—to make sure your stuff is good."

But appearing authentic is not achieved by wearing any old uniform. Often making a distinction between costumes that could pass at a Halloween party and their own impressions, reenactors regard an impression as a set of highly particular symbols. What an outsider might simply see as a German uniform is, to a reenactor's informed eye, a martial hieroglyph. From insignia and weaponry to the content of a gas mask canister, an impression speaks volumes about the precise type of soldier a reenactor purports to represent. Its messages reveal information concerning where the uniform would have been worn, when it would have been worn (often the precise year and season), as well as the rank, branch, and identity of the soldier who would have worn it.

With such emphasis on the details of their impressions, reenactors often struck me, especially as a male-dominated group, as being overtly obsessed with their appearance, as many doggedly cultivate their "look," as Greg Grosshans calls his impression. Some even admit to being "vain." Alain Benson forthrightly explains investing in his appearance: "You spend the year buying this and buying that, and visualizing that, you know, I put this whole image together. And then the end result will be dressing up in it, getting the right haircut, and then hanging out with other people who think the same way and then it's like, 'Wow, check it out.'"

As they check each other out, many evaluate appearance as an indication of one's symbolic commitment to the hobby. "Guys who go the extra mile (and dollar) for the correct stuff," one reenactor observes, "show respect for the players who have to look at them." On the other hand, guys who fail to have the correct stuff are quickly labeled farbs. Although farbs are identified by behavior, they are also—even foremost—identifiable by appearance. Farbs are, as Lew McCarthy says simply, "historically challenged." And reenactors abound with tales about how those with "marginal impressions" destroy their experiences.

With tremendous frustration, Michael Collins describes how a potential magic moment in a World War II event was ruined. "I was crawling through the woods and I was totally into this, and I looked over and the guy next to me had this reproduction watch that was actually from the Korean War and . . . it burst my bubble. It killed the whole thing."

Because of the importance of even the smallest, seemingly inconsequential detail, reenactors actively try to control their appearance. Organizations issue orders such as this: "All men and women will present a proper military appearance in representing a member of the Allied and Central Powers in World War I." Event hosts warn, "We do not want to see visible, out of place, non-period/incorrect items." To ensure no one makes any egregious errors, many event hosts even insist that they will conduct authenticity inspections at events. "Authenticity

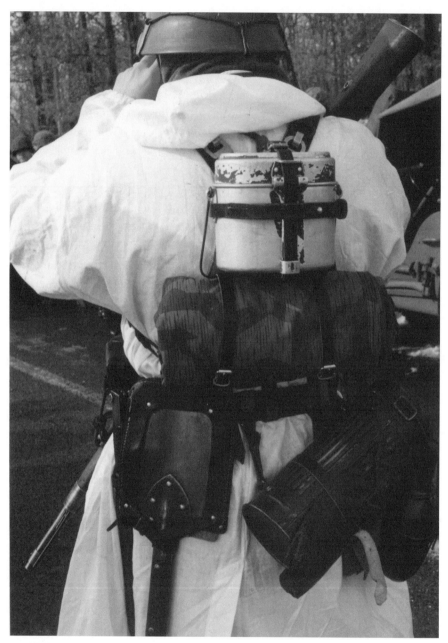

World War II German reenactor's kit, the Bulge, 1994

and haircut regulations will be enforced," each Bulge announcement states. "Those individuals with severe violations will be asked to leave the event and those with lesser violations will be noted in writing for inspection at the next event."

In a voluntary hobby, though, some think it is ridiculous to deny someone the right to participate because of a bad haircut. Others find it impossible to impose accurate authenticity regulations on the group as a whole. "I can understand setting up authenticity rules," one reenactor comments. "But can one say that they are realistically researched and thought out?"

I rarely saw an authenticity inspection conducted with any real impact. The GWA is far more aggressive than other organizations in trying to enforce regulations on its membership, and does in fact hold an inspection at each event before combat. But in general, regulations are left up to individual units. "Respective unit leaders," Wilson Lyle explains, "have their own . . . vision of the kind of appearance they want their unit to have." These visions are outlined in a unit's authenticity standards, which are defined and enforced by the unit's commander, authenticity officer, or committee; and they are set forth on unit Web pages or in handbooks, some of which number well over sixty pages. ("When a new member joins he receives a pound of paperwork," John Shampo, commander of the 3rd SS unit, wrote me in sending his unit's recruitment package. "We couldn't reenact without copiers and printers.") These standards include precise specifications for all elements of a unit member's basic kit. One World War II British unit's standards include an extensive list of required items by category, such as Footwear, Headwear, Equipment, Weapons, Paper Goods, and Personal Kit, which includes the following requisite items: "ID discs, period watches only, mess tin, tea mug (must be war time or proper post war type), housewife, ground cloth, underclothing (if not period, must be white cotton, à la long johns.)"

Although authenticity standards vary from unit to unit, most argue that they try to "adopt that which was most commonly used when choosing uniforms and equipment." They also argue that their standards are designed to reflect historical reality. To this end, John Shampo outlines his unit's minimum requirements for authenticity: "At a close up and personal distance, the reenactor should not be distinguishable from a World War II soldier."

Some units strictly enforce adherence to their basic kit requirements, and others even require accumulation of a more specialized "advanced kit" over time. "You must have all the items listed in the basic kit if you are going to look the part," the 4th Armored warns its newbies. "If you buy the wrong equipment or uniforms you will not be allowed to use them, so inform yourself and buy carefully."

Not only must the individual reenactor appear authentic, but the unit as a whole must also strive to achieve "a consistent, correct appearance." Thus, unit standards are designed to "eliminate any discrepancy" among members and guard against having "a unit full of exceptions." One unit commander instructs, "In assembling his personal impression each member should take care that [it is] compatible with that worn by the rest of the unit. It is of utmost importance that our group appearance credibly portrays the organized body we purport to be." He concludes: "By following our uniform and equipment guidelines we have a framework upon which individual and group impressions of the finest caliber can be built."

Some reenactors spend thousands of dollars on their impressions, and thousands more should they purchase a machine gun or vehicle. But even a basic kit costs several hundred dollars, if not more. "It costs between $1,500 and $2,000 to buy everything on our unit's current required equipment list," one reenactor reports. "And that does not include an SS *zeltbahn,* which is on our 'optional but recommended' list. . . . That's too much money." Some argue that "authenticity costs money, period." But others insist that "the cost between doing it right and doing it farby is not [as] expensive as people think."

Debates over the cost as well as definition of authenticity may be inevitable. But the difference between doing it right and doing it farby is not always very clear. Just as reenactors fight with each other over behavior, so too do they mightily disagree over what exactly constitutes an authentic representation of the common soldier. As a result, Wilson Lyle believes, "it's one big mess, and like it or not, it all affects why we can't all 'just get along.'"

"Farbiness Is in the Eye of the Beholder"

Many reenactors believe that everyone should achieve authenticity "as close as humanly possible to accurate (to the stitch)." Nothing less than perfection is acceptable to these reenactors, since "once you bow to mediocrity, then you are doomed to stay there."

One German reenactor describes how he strives for perfection with his haircut. Whenever he went to a barber, he would always have to explain the particular cut he wanted, a cut modeled after that of a World War II German soldier. "Long on top, short on sides," he'd say, sometimes even bringing along a photograph of his veteran grandfather. One day, at a new barbershop, the reenactor was surprised when, after he described the cut, the barber nodded, saying, "This is a typical *Wehrmachtschnitt.*" It turns out that the barber "was a soldier during Finland's Winter and Continuation Wars against Russia" and gave haircuts to both German and Finnish soldiers. Now this reenactor gets "the same treatment" as the Finnish barber gave soldiers in 1943. Not only is his haircut entirely authentic, but he also has the luxury of hopping in the barber chair and simply saying, "*Wehrmachtschnitt.*"

To the self-proclaimed hardcores such attention to detail is commendable, since they believe that reenactors with "sloppy inaccurate gear" or "modern obstructions" destroy any chance of achieving a magic moment. As Alain Benson observes, "It's not fun to drive four hours all the way to this event and then stand around with all these guys dressed in—yes, they're the Americans, yes, they're the Germans—but mustaches, sunglasses, long hair, bad uniforms, then it's like there's no fun in it because you can never achieve that experience you're looking for."

So virulent are these reenactors that the term "Stitch Nazis" was coined to describe them. (A reenactor doesn't have to do German to be considered a Stitch Nazi.) Many consider Luke to be a Stitch Nazi because of his relentless demands for perfection. "At mail call," Luke once observed, characteristically enraged by any lapse in authenticity, "I noticed some of these guys' kits and they needed improvement. And some of the things just should never have been allowed to happen. Like one of the new guys brought a plastic spoon out. For crying out loud! What did you bring a plastic spoon for?"

Stitch Nazis often make their complaints public, publishing diatribes in newsletters or posting them on email groups. At other times they internalize their outrage: At a small World War II event, two Stitch Nazis left before the event started after two reenactors showed up wearing HBT (herring bone twill) uniforms and not what the Stitch Nazis considered to be the more authentic wool uniforms required for the event. Disgust with poor authenticity can even drive a Stitch Nazi out of the hobby altogether—an extreme reaction that has occurred more than once.

Not all reenactors are Stitch Nazis however. An equal faction—what I came to think of as the moderates—admits that reenactors really can only be "authentic as far as practical" since "complete [authenticity] is not achievable." They, too, often use the term hardcore to describe themselves, but they decry the "hardcore ball-busters who *insist* on *maximum* authenticity from all participants." For them, the source of a ruined experience lies in the "pompous shits who look down and sneer at anyone or anything that isn't perfect." And they find that endless squabbling ruins an event more than the presence of farbs. Obsessing about trivial details turns events into "costume balls," consumes them with "bickering," or obscures their higher goal—commemoration. If a reenactor is "so wrapped up in being a World War II fashion statement and not remembering those who were a part of that struggle," one moderate argues, he should "get a job as a model." Further, they believe that Stitch Nazis "become so obsessed with relatively 'minor' issues in the big scheme of things that they do not have fun." Dave Watkins explains his more relaxed attitude: "You're always going to have new people in the unit," he says. "And a lot of them are younger guys, they don't have a lot of money, they're students, they don't necessarily look good for a while." Although Dave considers himself to be more allowing of others, he still holds to what he calls his basic rule: "You're better not having an item than using a bad item. If you don't have a bread bag that's good, don't use one at all. Certain things are tougher. Like footgear's always a problem. So you try to make that as innocuous as possible."

These two camps—the Stitch Nazis and the moderates—are "constantly at war with each other." But whatever side a reenactor is on, almost all agree on one thing: far too many reenactors are farbs. Whereas one thinks the hobby as a whole "suffers from a gross want of attention to historical detail," another claims "most people are too lazy or cheap to do it right." For Luke it is enough to say glumly, "Farbs you find everywhere." And most are not shy in pointing out each other's farby errors.

On the World War II Newsgroup, one reenactor recounted a "farbolio horror story" and encouraged others to tell their own. But Philip Moss couldn't bring himself to tell any farb stories, "as they bring pain and irritation to me and then I must go have a colon blow to relieve the irritation of such farbism."

In trying to understand what exactly farbism is, I knew that somehow a farb doesn't reflect the historical reality of a common soldier. But beyond that there seemed no clear definition, since the irritation of farbism manifests itself differently for each reenactor, and even moderates are quick to voice their own complaints.

For many, the tried and true sign of a farb lies in personal grooming: specifically, wearing a beard, wearing hair that is too long, or—unless one is doing, say, an impression of a World War I British officer—sporting a mustache. For others, a reenactor who insists on wearing modern glasses, despite what may be a scrupulously authentic impression, is a farb. To others, a farb is too clean; one reenactor complained that too few portray "soldiers who have been campaigning and fighting without rest for months." Others see farbs in those who wear improper footwear. One reenactor lamented "a steady decline in the overall state of uniform authenticity," noting as an example an American doughboy wearing "rubber-soled hiking boots." Still others identify farbs as reenactors who insist on wearing medals, for instance. (Most units prohibit wearing medals, since they believe that doing so insults real soldiers; and some permit members to wear medals only after earning them in events.) Farbs are also identified as those reenactors who violate an event host's or a unit's basic kit requirements, or as "atypical" reenactors who do elite, exceptional, or high-ranking impressions. Because rank is normally earned and not assumed, for example, many reenactors respond to self-promotion with little humor. When one unit member decided that he would wear a colonel's uniform, his commander reported that they "parted company on unfavorable terms."

But there is more. To others, farbs are those who simply fail to do it right. Whether out of laziness, ignorance, or an unwillingness or inability to invest in their impressions, farbs commit overt errors. They wear 1944 chinstraps when an event calls for an "early war impression." Or they are guilty of more ambiguous errors—carrying a sidearm, for instance, when doing a medic impression. (Many reenactors argue that medics would not have been armed in historical reality.) Others identify farbs as those who purposely use improper equipment but justify it with a concocted story, such as a US reenactor who carries a German weapon, explaining that he "captured" it from the enemy. (A Grossdeutschland member once told me that it would be okay for me to carry a German weapon in doing my Russian impression, even though his unit bans such "battlefield pickups," saying, "you could have just picked one up on the battlefield.") Farbs also make due with uniforms or equipment they judge to be "good enough." These are advocates of what is known as the "ten foot rule," (meaning an impression looks authentic from ten feet away). They wear poor reproductions, conversions (postwar items that have been reworked to look period), or items only close to authentic. Hank Lyle believes that for them, the concept of "'this is okay for reenacting' [or] 'this will pass and let you play'. . . is more appealing than 'this is how it has to be or it is not right.'"

Farbs are also those reenactors who use wholly anachronistic items. They wear digital watches, flagrantly smoke Marlboro Lights (filtered cigarettes are generally considered taboo in World War I and II reenacting), chow down on Doritos during mess, or sport postwar gear. Dave Watkins described one reenactor whom he called "a nefarious individual." "It was horrible," he grimaced. "He even had a bad rifle. He took a modern M1A and tried to make it look like a BAR." Luke, who was nearby as Dave and I chatted, piped in, "But that wasn't all, Dave," Luke said. "He had commando .45, whatever the hell they are, like a Thompson submachine gun sort of thing. So he had one of those, one thing in one hand and the other farby thing in the other hand. So if it wasn't bad enough with one farby weapon, he had a brace of them." Nodding in agreement, Dave concluded, "Well, he was a splendid example of what not to do. He was the antithesis of a good reenactor."

As I learned more about farbism, I feared that I was a farb! My World War II kit had improved greatly, as Luke and Tim assured me. During my first year in the hobby, I replaced most of the items that Tim had loaned me for my World War II impression with Women's Army Corps items that I found at flea markets and gun shows. I also acquired a Russian uniform and several items to round out my World War I impression. Still, I was guilty of an endless number of errors—wearing white socks and nail polish, using a modern Nikon camera, and bringing a contemporary pillow and blanket to my first field event. I was also subject to teasing every time I made a farby error: When Luke and Mike Sharp learned that I came to an event armed with my pillow and blanket, they delighted in my naiveté in bringing these "creature comforts" to an event. Referring to my "pillow and blankie," they teased me good-naturedly and told me to leave them in the car.

Another exceedingly embarrassing moment involving my overt farbicity occurred one year at the Bulge. Around midnight, I was on my way back to the barracks, carefully treading on the ice-covered road wearing my Arctic canvas overshoes, when I ran into Sam Benevento. We chatted for a while until he looked down at my shoes and began to laugh: I had mixed them up and was wearing them on the wrong feet.

I drew comfort from the fact that most reenactors—even Stitch Nazis—have some kind of farby or anachronistic item with them in the field—car keys, wallet, and the like. Ed Malthus always has his cell phone to check in with his wife and kids; another carries a small fire extinguisher for emergencies. But, of course, they don't use them flagrantly or during period scenarios. Still, I felt better about my own farbiness knowing that even normally hardcore reenactors can be caught in the trap of farbicity. John Loggia, widely considered exceptionally authentic, described his brush with farbdom when he made do with a nonperiod belt. "It looked exactly like a GI belt," John remembers, "same color, same style. The only difference was a tiny YSL (Yves St Laurent) on the buckle." He laughed, thinking he'd been sure "no one would notice." But on the prowl as always, Luke did notice, and John was forced to withstand a public critique.

Acts of public criticism make some reenactors angry. As one reenactor says: "Individuals are looking for a sock in the mouth if they criticize another guy without 'authority.'" But many more become confused. "We have a standard equipment list, standard uniform requirements, and the most stringent awards criteria in the country," one unit reports. "And I still hear from people . . . how farby we are." Others simply acknowledge the term's highly relative meaning. "Farbiness," as one reenactor observes, "is in the eye of the beholder." For this reason, many think no one is so authentic that he or she can criticize someone else with impunity. "When someone tells me my tunic has buttons on it that are 20mm rather than 19mm, it would mean a whole lot more if they weren't sitting on the tailgate of a Ford drinking a Coors when they said it."

Indeed. The contradictory manner in which some are derided as farbs and others championed as authentic was brought home to me time and again. Hal Zane, a much-respected World War I unit leader and 4th Armored sergeant, sports a mustache. But by all accounts, he's not a farb. On the other hand, I once saw Donald Kiev publicly berate a couple of reenactors for authenticity lapses. When I described this to Luke, he laughed: "Now that's the pot calling the kettle black. Donald Kiev, biggest damn farb of them all!"

Although they disagree about the term's definition, there is one unwritten rule regarding its use: farb is a label reenactors rarely, if ever, bestow upon themselves. Some admit to having been farbs, (before they knew better). But they generally reserve use of the term for others. In fact, in one of the strangest ironies of the hobby, the only self-proclaimed farb I ever met is the extremely amiable and hilarious, Scott Farb (his real name), who is not, despite the many jokes his name elicits, the word's etymological source. (When Scott and his wife were expecting their first child, much humor was enjoyed anticipating the child's first name. "Whatta" and "Total" were just two suggestions reenactors made.)

With no one owning up to being a farb, I used my questionnaire to ask reenactors to define the opposite of a farb: a hardcore. A small percentage considers hardcores to be assholes, but a vast majority looks upon being hardcore in a positive way. A hardcore reenactor, they say, is concerned with authenticity, takes reenacting seriously, and/or puts the most time, money, and energy into reenacting—though only a few equate spending a lot of money with being hardcore, quality of investment, not quantity, being the most important factor.

Using this model, I asked reenactors to rate other reenactors on a hardcore scale, from one to ten (least to most hardcore). Nearly a third of other reenactors were judged to fall somewhere on the lower end of the scale (1–5); almost half were placed in the moderate hardcore realm (6–7); and less than a quarter were granted high-end hardcore status (8–10). Next, reenactors rated themselves. A little over one tenth ranked themselves on the lower end of the hardcore scale (1–5); nearly a quarter ranked themselves at the moderate level (6–7). But the majority—61.6 percent—rated themselves as achieving high-end hardcore status (8–10).

These results show how reenactors tend to view others in the hobby as less hardcore—serious, authentic, devoted—than themselves. "They're just having fun," Alain Benson says, describing the great majority of other reenactors. "It's a weekend getaway. They're just [war] buffs in general. They probably have tons of books, tons of videos in their homes. They've probably built plastic models and it's a weekend getaway. They'll hook up with their buddies and drink some beer and dress in their uniforms and pretend."

After describing "these other people," Alain distinguished his own unit as "guys that are hardcore in the sense that they will wear all the original stuff and really go all out." But Alain isn't alone in thinking his unit is more authentic than others. Another who rated others at a "5" and himself at "10+" observes that in the hobby there are "a lot of mediocre units."

But just as the individual farb is not forthcoming, it is the rare reenactor who admits to belonging to a farby unit. Typically, reenactors talk about their units and say, "Compared to the other groups," as Alicia Mellon asserts, "we do have the highest standards." Or, as Scott Friewald says of 4th Armored, "We don't try to be egotistical about it [but] if there is such a thing as the reenacting elite then I would say 4th Armored is part of it."

Some attribute their unit pride and competition to historical reality. "Unit animosity," Fred Legum believes, "is very realistic." A commander of a World War II British unit agrees: "The only aspect that is true to life is how we react to each other. The Brits think the Yanks are hillbillies, the Yanks think the Brits are tea-sipping lollygaggers and the SS hates the [German] Army and the [German] Army hates the SS even more." But others, such as Morris Call, see their tendency to judge themselves as being more hardcore than others as stemming from "the very juvenile idea of look at my toys, they are better than anyone else's."

I interpreted their belief that they are better than others as stemming from more than egoism or arrogance. It is the product of the very question that lies at the heart of their debate over authenticity: How does one authenticate one's right to possess history? As they vie with each other over whose claim is legitimate, they become separated, as Michael Collins put it, into "two camps. The ones that really appreciate the history and the ones that are just out to have fun. And those guys, a lot of times, if you question them, have no link to the history."

Ultimately, I would come to believe, a farb is a reenactor who is judged as having failed to establish a legitimate link to history. They are the so-called yahoos, cowboys, and jeep jerks. They are the reenactors "who just want to burn blanks and don't care about the history." They are those who reenact for the "wrong reason." And they are those who violate the hobby's dignity, since, as Luke observes,

Loading a clip in a blank-adapted rifle, 1995

"a lot of them don't care. They can't aspire to anything higher than what they already do."

But all reenactors, I found, do aspire to some kind of dignity, and each is able to legitimate his or her claim or right to own history. Some do so by stressing the fact that they have done their homework. "I read and visit with vets," one reenactor asserts, "so my impression is top." Others derive credibility from a legacy (being a descendant of a veteran). "You might have some jerk," Michael Collins says, "that put his things together from a book, reading a book. I have my great-uncle's tunic . . . that he personally wore in Okinawa." For others, real military experience grants credibility and those who have none "look silly because they have no military background and no clue." Still others believe financial investment assures legitimacy. "If you can't afford to be as authentic as possible," one reenactor asks, "can you really afford to play? My feeling is no."

With such emphasis on creating a visual illusion, though, most simply equate a legitimate ownership of history with one's ability to appear visually legitimate. And although there are many ways a reenactor can establish credibility, the most obvious is through appearance. For this reason, many reenactors "despise people who look bad," as Dave Watkins admits, "just because they look bad."

Discrepancies

"The biggest problem with reenactors," Greg Grosshans declares without hesitation, is that "they're too old and way too fat." Greg's comment may sound cruel, but his complaint is echoed time and again by many reenactors. Some even argue, as Greg does, that "there should be a mandatory age when you have to retire from the hobby." Others advocate portraying age-appropriate impressions, arguing that once past a certain age, reenactors should give up their infantry impressions and do civilian, partisan, or *Volksturm* impressions.

But since the majority of reenactors are older than a common soldier would have been, the inordinate number of middle-aged foot soldiers is seen as less of a problem than the multitude, as Luke put it, "of ridiculously overweight soldiers." "You can't be fat," Luke states flatly, "and be a World War I or a World War II soldier. It doesn't work." Notorious for demanding that his unit members get in shape, Luke sets forth his recruiting guidelines: "We can be flexible on age if the man is in good physical shape, but we cannot be flexible on weight. (You can't tell a man is forty-five years old from one hundred feet away but you can tell he is thirty pounds overweight from five hundred feet.)" John Loggia agrees with Luke, saying that he finds something innately problematic about reenactors who "want to portray soldiers" but "don't look like the soldiers they're portraying."

When I asked John why there are so many overweight reenactors—a fact I'd noted long ago—he simply observed, "We live in a society of plenty."

Perhaps only in a society of plenty could reenactors expend their time, income, and effort on such a hobby. But therein lies one of the biggest hurdles to authenticity as they try to portray those who lived in times not so plentiful. The young, underfed, or even physically fit soldier is a model many cannot emulate. "A lot of reenactors tend to be older, fat guys like me," Dave Watkins says, and even some Stitch Nazis acknowledge they're not "in tip top shape," as Richard Paoletti willingly observes. "We're either overweight or we're not as physically fit as well as we should be or they were." "I don't consider my weight to be an easy thing to correct (wish it was)," another states. "It is a little easier to correct than another typical error, one I am also pushing, age."

For those who entered the hobby as young reenactors, over time they become less authentic as a result of living in the real world. "I remember ten years ago, before each World War II event, when I used to look in the mirror all suited up [I'd] see Audie Murphy!!" one reenactor lamented. "Now when I look, I see Benny Hill, fer Chrissake."

Older reenactors aren't usually criticized publicly about their age. But reenactors who aren't "off the racks" not only purchase higher-priced reproduction uniforms, paying what's known as the "FBT" or "Fat Boy Tax," but they also suffer humiliation. "Spare me the sight," one reenactor snarled, "of your wheezing, sweaty, about-to-have-a-coronary self in the field!" Another argued, "If you want to be authentic, you have to unstrap the feedbag, push away from the table, and exercise until you can wear a human size uniform that isn't made at Omar the Tentmaker."

Fit reenactors often champion their exercise regimens and receive praise for their dieting efforts. "Hats off to Phil Fussel and Perry Trent," Luke commended, "who lost at least twenty pounds each for the last event and looked great." But for others, particularly especially heavy reenactors, there's little praise. "There is no excuse for reproduction size 52 trousers," one reenactor railed. "Why not strap on a piece of sheet metal and call yourself a tank?"

Fat reenactors aren't the only ones whose claims are judged illegitimate. Women who portray male soldiers are just as likely to be considered farbs as overweight men, since they are also seen as assaulting historical reality. Many units require members to portray their own gender, a rule justified in commemorative terms. "To me," one male reenactor argues, "having a woman represent a World War I soldier is an insult to the sacrifice [the veterans] made." But to others, the insult is personal: "I have spent over $2,000 for my impression, and it is rather insulting to have someone come out in a totally unrealistic uniform (i.e., female infantryman.)"

Surprisingly, to me at least, many women reenactors agree. "If women are doing women's roles," Grace Hall believes, "and not trying to be involved in the

World War I Red Cross nurse impression

fighting, then it's fine." Another woman argues: "I do not agree with women reenacting as soldiers. Period. I think it is a slap in the face to the vets and I think it ruins the experience for the other reenactors."

But others think that a woman's claim to portray a male soldier is as legitimate as any man's. "You guys might get [your] panties in an uproar about how farby a woman in combat gear looks or how historically inaccurate it may be," one male reenactor argues. "But she has just as much right to play as you do!" Hank Lyle agrees; he thinks that if women "can pull off the impression of looking like a World War II soldier, [then] who am I to tell them that they can't try to get into the World War II experience via reenacting? If we can 'accept' some discrepancies for men," Hank says, "I don't see how we can refuse to admit a woman who meets the authenticity guidelines and goes the whole nine yards to look like a male soldier."

The question of who is a farb is thus a question of which discrepancies reenactors are willing to accept. "We are already pushing the limits of reality with regard to age and weight," one reenactor believes. "Women make the whole thing unbelievable." But another disagrees: "If I had to choose (and the real world is nothing but a series of choices, absolutes are non-practical) between a thin young woman in a Waffen SS uniform (who was making a real effort to look and act like a male) and a 350 lb. male tubster, I'll take the woman every time."

I always found it hypocritical that even those who roar loudest over farbs are usually guilty themselves of numerous farby errors. A unit of middle-aged, heavy reenactors is just as likely to object to women portraying men as is a unit of young, physically fit reenactors. But from dying gray hair (as a few reenactors do) to finding reasons for what could have happened in history, all reenactors can legitimate their own impressions regardless of any real-life discrepancies. "There were stocky and even chubby guys in the war," one reenactor rationalizes, while Mark Sammons justifies doing an infantry impression at age fifty: "In Germany things were so bad, you know, things were so desperate, you could be fifty and near the end of the war you might have even been in combat." Meanwhile, Dave Watkins once did an impression of an armored infantry captain. He was able to justify doing such a high-ranking impression despite the fact that, as he said, "some people didn't like" it. "Since I'm older than the regular infantryman," Dave reasoned, "I . . . felt that it was proper to portray an older person who would probably be an officer, and since I collect officers' equipment I wore that." But he remembers that "somebody remarked that I had the CIB [Combat Infantryman's Badge] and I'm really, in actuality, not qualified to wear that." In truth, Dave himself was not entitled to wear such a badge since he didn't earn it, but he rationalized further by saying, "the person who I was portraying was." "I did it properly," Dave remembers of his impression, "and if they had a problem with that, then that's, I think, their loss."

With each reenactor able to cite his or her own qualifications, the big question reenactors confront is "how much homage do we pay to the god of realism and how much to the god of reality?" Tim Gilbert offers his take: "I think my outward appearance should be exact to that of the World War II GI. But I also realize and admit that I am not 100 percent authentic and I am willing to bet that no one [is]!" Like many others, Tim sees a necessary line between pure authenticity and the reality of needing limits. "I know we all have non–World War II period 'thoughts' during these events," Tim continues. "Even worse, all of us have non–World War II period conversations during events! I don't know anyone who comes to an event without having bathed for a month and having worn the same clothes for that period of time. Does that make you a 'smell farb' because you do not stink sufficiently?"

Wilson Lyle, a self-proclaimed Stitch Nazi, sees it differently: "I will never win an argument with someone who has already embraced the philosophy that close is good enough." "Close has to be good enough," another reenactor, Steve Tilden, objects. "Absolute perfection is an impossible (and insane) obsession." Particularly angered by two Stitch Nazis on the newsgroup, Steve charged them with "driving yourselves (and the rest of us) crazy by pursuing it." He continued: "You may not like where we choose to draw the line, but rest assured that you are drawing the line somewhere as well, and that there is someone out there who no doubt considers both of you to be total farbs because of the tradeoffs and compromises you have made. It's all relative. . . . You may not think you are making any compromises at all, but you are. You're just making compromises that are acceptable (and thus transparent) to you. We're making compromises that are acceptable to us."

In fact, no one can help recognize the multitude of less-than-transparent compromises all reenactors make. The 17th Lancers portray cavalry impressions, with one glaring omission: they have no horses. Foreign soldiers speak English (often, for example, with a New Jersey accent); units participate in battles where their historic counterparts were absent; downed pilots have no planes. Combat lacks air bombardment and artillery fire. And, of course, no one really dies. Most acknowledge that their representation is inherently, and by necessity, relative. "The real military is good and bad," one reenactor admits. "We choose to portray just the parts we enjoy."

But enjoyment quickly fades when confronted by the myriad arguments over who is legitimate. And because reenactors view themselves not as actors or characters, but as themselves—who they really are—the arguments become intensely personal. As they refer to each other as "clowns," "assholes," or "idiots," they reveal the connection between their hobby and the real world. "Losers in reenactments," one reenactor surmises, "are usually losers in every other aspect of their life as well."

Historical Reality

My third Bulge event. I've paid my unit dues, donned my uniform, and spent the morning in the vehicle garage with 4th Armored waiting for the battle to start. When it's time to move out, Luke says curtly, "We're not taking all the vehicles. The roads are too icy and it's dangerous. So there's no room for you on a vehicle. If you want to come out, you're going to have to walk. It's probably three miles to the battle site. You can follow the other troops on foot."

But the 4th Armored is the last unit to leave. So I can see that following the other troops is no longer an option.

"If you go home," says Luke hurriedly, "drive safely." Without another word, he runs to his jeep, leaving me standing in the now-empty garage.

"Hey! Aren't you going out?" It's Tom Schultz.

"I was going to, but Luke just told me I couldn't come with them."

"Aw," says Tom. "No problem. Why don't you come along?"

I climb into Tom's car with Sam, a German reenactor. When we reach an intersection choked with cars and military vehicles headed to the battle site, we pull up behind one of 4th Armored's half-tracks. I notice one reenactor—who is not a unit member—sitting happily alongside the others on the truck. I grit my teeth when I see that there's plenty of room on board.

"Well?" says Tom. "You can hop out and follow the guys on foot."

"Sure," Sam offers. "Come with me. If anyone asks, I'll say you're my prisoner."

"I appreciate it, but I think I won't."

"Are you sure?" Tom asks.

"I'd rather go back to the flea market."

"Okay!" Sam pulls his pack and rifle from the car and waves before joining the mass of infantry heading for battle.

As we drive back to the barracks, I confide in Tom. "Luke said there wasn't enough room for me since they weren't taking all the vehicles, but there was plenty of room." Tears brimming in my eyes, I continue: "Plus there's a guy sitting on the truck who isn't even in 4th Armored. Why would Luke do that?" I brush the tears away, embarrassed to get so upset by what is, after all, just a game.

Tom sighs. I'm pretty sure he's noticed that I'm on the verge of crying, but he doesn't comment on it. Instead, he speaks gently. "Sometimes those guys—and I don't mean to insult them—a lot of them are really good guys—but they just get kind of, well, exclusive. Luke especially. A couple years ago, I had put on a lot of weight. I mean, I'd been heavy for a long time," Tom pauses. "Anyway, Luke kind of got bent out of shape and said a lot of things—not to me, but just things in the newsletter. And after a while, I stopped getting the newsletter at all. You know, in so many words, he made it clear I wasn't welcome in 4th Armored."

"That's terrible. You've been friends with them for so long."

"Yeah, but some really get into this and get out of control. They don't see it as, well, you're my friend, so it's okay. So I just thought, if you don't want me, fine. There are plenty of other units that don't act like that, you know?"

That night, I join the 4th Armored at dinner. I find myself seated at a table with Mike Sharp, Ed Malthus, and Luke, who is uncharacteristically happy.

"I don't think I made one person angry at me today," Luke beams.

"That's not true," I say. "You made me angry."

"What!?" Luke's eyes widen. "What do you mean?"

"You left me there. I paid my unit dues. And after everyone is already gone, you say, 'Oh, sorry, no room. Guess you'll have to walk.'"

Luke looks down at his plate. "Gee."

"For crying out loud," Mike says. "Jenny had every right to be out there."

I continue. "And then I saw that guy sitting on the half-track who wasn't even in 4th Armored! Why was he allowed on and I wasn't?"

"What guy?" Luke asks in disbelief.

"You know," Mike nods. "That correspondent."

"Oh, him." Luke says. "I didn't really know what his story was. I'm sorry. I wish you'd said something to me. You know how wrapped up I get. I've got a million things on my mind. You should've made your case with me."

"Everything happened so fast."

"Well, I'm sorry," Luke says. "I'm sorry."

Later that evening in the barracks, Ed Malthus and Mike Sharp ceremoniously present me with a 4th Armored unit patch.

"Luke's an asshole," Mike says apologetically.

"You're more a part of this unit than Lieutenant Wing-Nut will ever be," Ed agrees.

I was stunned. Just a few years back, I didn't even really know Ed or Mike. They were just two guys in the unit; and two men that I liked but judged to be fairly hardcore and rather tough. I would never have known them, I thought, if I hadn't come into the hobby. And now over the years, and after the many events we'd experienced together, somehow we'd all become friends. Their gesture might have been small, but it meant a lot. What they offered me that night was acceptance, and what they showed me, in however understated a way, was that they wanted me to feel better. Again I felt like I was going to cry. Instead, Ed broke out the beer. Mike started cleaning his rifle. And the three of us sat around and talked about nothing much at all.

Hemming the Loose Ends

That event was undoubtedly both the best and the worst I attended. Even though Luke and I discussed what happened, I didn't feel better after his apology. For, he admitted to being more than simply distracted. Earlier that morning, he had ordered the unit to conduct drills, and two new unit members refused. Luke reprimanded them, stating that their attitude was putting 4th Armored's stellar reputation at risk. Their retort: how authentic can you be with a woman in your unit?

Luke admitted that this challenge festered in the back of his mind as he confronted the day ahead. Although leaving me behind, he insisted, was not intentionally cruel, it may have been his knee-jerk reaction to the newcomers' challenge.

This experience gave me a sense of the high and low of the hobby all in the same day: On one hand, feeling the rejection that comes with being told I could not "play," and on the other, feeling the deep acceptance that came when Ed and Mike presented me with the unit patch. Curiously, I found myself making my own link to history through experiencing a form of overt discrimination that I wished belonged only to history. I soon found out that I was not alone.

Reenactors like Luke respond to the challenge of authenticity with utter seriousness. And, although they may not admit it, they largely perceive their real-life reputations as being dependent upon their success at being hardcore. Whether arguing against female or overweight reenactors, their call, as one reenactor puts it, for "greater exclusivity toward higher authenticity standards in private, invitation only events," is, they say, only an attempt to avoid historical inaccuracies. One reenactor explained that they "aren't anti-women. They just want to make sure that the impressions that they are presenting are historically appropriate."

These more conservative-minded reenactors find strength in numbers, and they bear clear resentment toward anything that they judge as disgracing or embarrassing their units. "Gee," one such reenactor, Alf Wanamaker, mused, "I thought the goal of this hobby was to accurately portray soldiers." Given what he finds to be the lax attitude of most reenactors in this regard, he sarcastically proposed, "Let's all gather for a group hug at the next battle."

Guarding against the indignity and femininity of being tolerant in a male hobby that prides itself on seriousness, these reenactors argue that creating what Alf calls a "kindler, gentler hobby" is not their goal. They believe that in order to dignify the hobby, they must avoid reflecting images of war contained within "slanted histories written by those who like to make things 'politically' correct." And they must take a stand against the "jackasses that wish to 'sanitize' World War I and World War II reenacting to allow women." These positions, they argue, are not personal, but historical. Often, they justify exclusion by asserting the need for typicality: a woman in a unit, for instance, would be a historical exception and not the common rule. "History," as Luke once wrote in his recruiting guidelines, "absolutely precludes us from allowing any women or blacks into the unit."

Sounding like an apologist relying on history to justify discrimination, Luke is certainly not agreed with universally. In some ways the 4th Armored members turn a blind eye to his exclusionary attitude because he's such a hard worker. After all, his efforts to improve the unit were hard to miss. Aside from doing things like silk-screening K-ration boxes, he worked to organize events, publish the newsletter, and orchestrate unit meetings. And although the unit members wanted him as commander, not all of them shared his attitude (witness Mike and Ed's effort to make me feel that I belonged). These more moderate-minded reenactors believe that exclusivity does "nothing but hurt the hobby." "You never turn out anybody," Sinclair Davis believes, "especially someone who's got his gear, his or her gear, and wants to turn out. It's a play, a show, it's a big game."

To these reenactors, there must be a line between pursuing perfection and "creating animosity and hard feelings." And even some Stitch Nazis can make exceptions for those reenactors they consider their friends. "My feelings about 'fat' guys," one reenactor states, "deals with the hobby on a different level. A human kindness level. . . . Anybody who bans overweight guys from his unit is plain cruel and short sighted because everybody has something to offer."

Others find extreme positions laughable, given that it's all fantasy anyway. "This is pretend," one reenactor wrote to the World War II newsgroup. "If we all really wanted to be authentic then let's restrict our recruiting efforts to those areas where units were actually raised. . . . Want to do the 29th I[nfantry] D[ivision]? Sorry, if you were not from Virginia, Maryland, or DC you are a farb. . . . It's a hobby and this isn't real, so where do you want to draw the line?"

Some reenactors are more intent upon drawing a strict line between those they consider farbs and the hardcores. To them, the concept of working together has a particular meaning. "We will have to work together to dragoon the farbs into shaping up," Luke proclaims, "or dragoon them out of the hobby." "We shouldn't cater to farbs," another agrees. "This is our hobby, not theirs. They are just temporarily trespassing on our property until such time as all the serious units and events get some backbone and stamp them out." Another argues for imposing restrictions against the comfort-loving "lawn chair rangers" and "motel militiamen." Such people, he believes, are the hobby's "loose ends" that need to be "hemmed."

But even some Stitch Nazis find hemming the loose ends difficult. Wilson Lyle sums up what he calls "the clincher" with taking this action: "The 'bad' units are filled with extremely likable guys. . . . Who am I to be the asshole that rains on their parade? I wish I could just tell them, listen, we're still pals and all, but in the field I don't want anything to do with you. But it's never going to be that simple as long as fragile feelings are at stake."

Others forsake fragile feelings and take on the task of hemming the loose ends themselves. One reenactor celebrated his unit's strict adherence to a no-farb policy. He recounted an event when an overweight German reenactor, who was accompanied by a woman dressed as a male soldier, asked if it was okay to "pitch their big farby tent" near his unit's camp. Their commander "looked him right in the eye and said, 'No way, it's too farby.' [The German] said that they could take it down in the morning, or throw a camo net over it. We replied that we don't allow farb in our camp—period. Authenticity doesn't stop when the sun goes down."

Many applaud such stringent dedication to perfection. But others quietly tell stories that are far less congratulatory of hardcore policies. Dave Watkins told me a sad tale about a reenactor who "failed to improve" and was ultimately driven out of the hobby for good. Dave remembers that this reenactor was "a nice guy" who had "done some work for the organization," and from "a long distance" he looked okay. But he had a bad uniform and "a huge handlebar mustache which he refused to shave off." When he asked if he could attend an upcoming event, he was told in no uncertain terms, "Well no, you can't. And the reason why you can't is you look bad . . . and the other people don't like having you around because of what you look like." He was also told that until he got serious with his kit, he wouldn't be welcome in the unit anymore. Dave says it was a shame that the guy soon "dropped out of the hobby." But Dave also justifies what the unit members did, since they weren't asking him "to do anything that the rest of us hadn't already done."

Others may not drop out of the hobby after receiving such treatment, but they do become aware of being excluded. After Michael Collins wore a First Infantry Division patch to several 4th Armored events in violation of the unit's basic kit requirements, he found no more invitations to join the unit forthcoming. Tom Schultz, aghast at Luke's very public opinion about fat reenactors, packed up his 4th Armored impression and joined another unit. And, after several attempts to portray a male soldier in a World War I German unit, Laurel

Moore, a strikingly pretty woman with long red hair, gave up entirely. "I don't look at all like a man," she said, "and it is hard to hide my femininity." Laurel still dresses in her German uniform and goes to events, but she now freelances without a unit.

With appearance being such a crucial part of the illusion, the question of whether or not to exclude someone because of his or her ethnicity has confronted reenactors several times. When a Korean American student expressed interest in joining the premier World War II German unit, Grossdeutschland, the unit commander, William Gregory, thought "it would be hard to justify a Korean in the ranks." But he also felt that "it would be something to consider." Turning to the others on the World War II newsgroup, he asked, "How would you handle this situation?"

Many rationalizations supporting the student came forth. One reenactor proposed justifying his presence, since there had been "a kind of exchange program with the Japanese in which a unit from Japan fought with the Germans." Another recounted hearing a veteran say he'd once seen "oriental-looking German prisoners." Another simply advised that they should let him join since "the Germans eventually used so many types of people in their military that you could find something for just about every case that comes up."

Others, though, were against these rationalizations. "I'd say 'no' to him," one reenactor wrote. "Although he might have his heart in the right place, he would be farb, and the unit would look so wrong. The vets would think your unit was a disgrace. Imagine Jackie Chan as the First Officer in *Das Boot*?" Insisting that "it's not about race, it's about a true portrayal," Philip Moss agreed. "I absolutely detest those organizations that buckle under to this PC bullshit," he fumed. While Philip felt that the student should be welcome in another unit, he didn't feel that he belonged in the elite Grossdeutschland. "Sometimes," he advised, "you just have to explain things and say 'We're gonna do it right!'" "Stick to your guns," he concluded, "and insist that whilst anyone may join your organization, they must do so in an authentic way."

But another countered Philip's position, reminding him: "You probably don't recruit only people of Germanic descent (although a pure impression looks great), so it shouldn't be a problem." Further, this reenactor thought the student "would feel the peer pressure and try to do his best as opposed to dragging your group down." He also said that his own Texas unit has several Latino members. "Nobody has ever asked if Mexicans fought in German [units]," he reported, "so it shouldn't be a problem with a Korean."

Many not only regard achieving a pure impression as impossible, but they also try actively to combat exclusion. When Donald Kiev, who is white, bought a World War II period staff car, he decided to use it to portray an all-black unit along with his friend Ray Sherman, who is black. (Ray would drive Donald around in the car.) "I could have done something like the 1st Division," Donald explained, "or one of the other more famous white units, but I wanted to portray the contribution made by black soldiers to the war because so often they're just overlooked." He also said that he also wanted to portray the historical reality of segregation in the American military.

Along with trying to include those who have been overlooked, some argue that discrimination is simply wrong. "This is America, and any minority can pretty much do what they want, that includes hunting their friends down in the woods in uniform. . . . If you don't believe me, go ask a lawyer." Another pinpointed the real-world liability of practicing exclusion. "As we all know," this reenactor warned, "left wing liberal groups, ACLU, NAACP et al love to get hold of this kind of well meaning type of guidance and screw it all round and then either a) hit you with a lawsuit, or b) go to the press, or even, c) do both!" He reminded others of the need to control their public image, saying: "That sort of publicity will kill this hobby stone dead! Sometimes it's better to bite the bullet, and go with something that is not 100 percent than to tempt fate!"

Even though a few of the more inclusive-minded reenactors sometimes practice their own more subtle forms of exclusion, usually in recruiting restrictions, they think others take the hobby too seriously. "Okay, guys, listen closely," one reenactor states. "This is a hobby. It is not a moral or religious crusade." Calling Stitch Nazis obsessive, they charge them with real-world character flaws. Stitch Nazis suffer from a "loss of perspective" and "use the hobby to bolster real-life inadequacies." "While most are quick to point out how they do this to honor vets and history," Morris Call remarks, "I see that it is not that at all, but an extension of ego or control of some part of their life." Another observes that "everyone is out there to fulfill a certain self-gratification or self-satisfaction." Larry Cohen agrees. Stitch Nazis "don't have a lot going on in their real lives and become king for the day when they're reenacting," he says. "They go from the mailroom assistant who gets yelled at all the time to a corporal in the 63rd."

One of the most levelheaded leaders in the World War II hobby, and commander of a widely respected American unit, Tim Gilbert finds the often-repeated argument that "farbs do not understand why the hobby was created" ludicrous. He thinks the reverse is true: Stitch Nazis "do not understand or have forgotten why we do this. The last time I checked it was a hobby . . . in other words, fun! The way some people get wound up in this hobby, I would hate to imagine how stressful their real life is, if this is how they relax."

Although reenactors insist that a boundary between real life and the hobby exists, their debates reveal how permeable such a border is. They may mask it with elaborate rituals, cloak it beneath the shroud of history, or bury it under their public mantra, but reenacting is directly related with their real-life concerns about their own social value, status, influence, and power. "Everybody wants to be the most impressive," as Michael Collins admits, while Gerald Lee simply observes that reenactors are "notoriously individualistic." Some even admit that they "secretly take pleasure in seeing something in someone else's unit that is messed up. . . . Imagine how boring reenactments might be without farbs to shake our heads at."

As reenactors compete with each other over who is most dignified, proper, humane, or closest to perfection, they vie for a place in the illusion and the right to declare themselves legitimate. But ironically, they escape from the public sphere, only to be plagued by many of the same concerns of their daily lives. Am I too fat? Too poor? Too female? The wrong color? Am I worthy of respect? Am I acceptable to others?

No wonder they become so frustrated. I once witnessed Ed Malthus turn red in the face, unleash a stream of obscenities, and storm off from an event after some farby Germans acted like assholes. At another time Craig Jones confided in me that in getting ready for events he sometimes gets so worked up and stressed out that he cries. I came to see the truth of one reenactor's observation that "feelings get hurt a lot in this hobby." But few men in the hobby acknowledge their feelings. Instead, they usually trace their disagreements to the purely academic issue of authenticity and the question of historical reality.

Wishing to avoid actual war, reenactors come together to fight with one another over issues with which their real lives confront them. But even after experiencing the hobby's lows and resolving to quit reenacting forever, as Luke, John, and Hank have done a number of times, something always drew them back. Perhaps the challenge of working toward it, the promise of aspiring toward dignity, or the lure of realizing perfection proves irresistible. With the cry, "Let history be your yardstick!" they turn to the evidence to authenticate their impressions and secure their places in history.

Chapter 11

"Preaching a Version of the Gospel"

Research

"As I sit and look at photos thru magnifying glasses, I'm seeing weird combinations of M36-43 features," writes reenactor Thomas Farley. "One guy is wearing a six-button blouse with point flaps and smooth pockets and dark green collar and pointed shoulder straps and Italian camo pants. Another guy has on what appears to be an M40 style, with point flaps and pocket pleats but with a six-button front. Two others wear . . . typical M43 jackets."

Whether using a magnifying glass to inspect photographs of World War II soldiers or subjecting a period garment to what's known as a "smell test"—period garments have a certain musty smell that can often be used, reenactors argue, to legitimate their age—reenactors are obsessed with historical evidence. But they're less concerned with issues concerning war's big picture than with identifying the typical details of a common soldier's kit. Thus, they subject evidence to relatively narrow research questions. On the World War II reenactor newsgroup, one reenactor once asked others which tartan members of a specific unit wore "on their Tams behind the Army Air Corps badge?" Meanwhile, another pondered if a 1944 Panzer crew jacket was "very green," "green gray," or, could it have been more of a "gray green?"

Answering such questions is not always easy. But in a hobby where studying history is the second most popular leisure activity (after reenacting), most look upon research as not only necessary but also enjoyable. Describing themselves as bookworms, history buffs, or historians, they believe that a good reenactor "honors and respects the history he is portraying by endlessly studying it." And, many argue, in order to be respected, a reenactor must base an impression on solid historical research—not on a farby Hollywood version of war.

In an effort to understand how reenactors use historical sources to define authenticity, I asked them, "Which sources have you used to put an impression together?" Their answers revealed that they use a wide variety of sources. But their answers to my next question, "Which sources are the most useful to put an impression together?" uncovered a hierarchy to the value they place on them. It turns out that historical sources, just like reenactors, range in value from farby to authentic. In sorting out this value, I found that forging a link between themselves and history, much less forging agreement over the way things should be, proves far more complicated than I'd ever imagined.

"The More You Look, the More You Find, and the More Confused You Can Get"

For a group that distrusts the media's portrayal of war—"anything the media touches turns to lead," as Scott Mies declares—I wasn't surprised that not a single reenactor reported using TV as a source for an impression. "That early TV stuff is pretty canned," Dave Watkins says of the war-related shows he watched growing up. "Shows like *Combat* and *The Rat Patrol* are now considered goofy," Alain Benson agrees, "with bad uniforms and real contrived action scenes . . . strictly for entertainment value."

Reenactors often make a distinction between entertaining and factual sources, and thus they judge fictional films as only slightly more valuable than television. To be sure, they're voracious war movie consumers, but they're also highly critical of them. War movies are almost universally considered farby, since they're "made with the intention to make money," as Alain says. "They have to appeal to a broad, general audience, and so lots was simplified." "It's just Hollywood show," Greg Grosshans agrees, admitting that he only watches war movies "for laughs" since there are "hardly any authentic World War II movies."

Many object to Hollywood's portrayal of soldiers as political ideologues. Greg, for instance, dismisses the portrayal of real-life Nazi Amon Goeth, the sinister German commandant in Steven Spielberg's film, *Schindler's List*, as "a stereotypical evil Nazi." Many wish that more movies would portray the common soldier more evenhandedly, since "only then will the intelligence-lacking public even consider the many commonalties between soldiers of all nations." But the majority of their film criticism focuses on what is most important to them: the details.

One reenactor offered a critique of the World War II classic *The Longest Day*: "The movie showed great numbers of US troops following field grade types using 'Hardees Tactics for Infantry' to move up from the beach through the draws," he observed. "In reality this would have been suicide, as the draws were heavily mined and pre-zeroed as obvious avenues of approach. The real troops, under the command of NCOs, used bounding tactics straight up the bluffs."

Aside from such a tactical error, the film also failed to achieve authenticity because the actors were wearing farby uniforms, including postwar jackets and trousers. One reenactor described the egregious farbiness of the actors' equipment: "They were wearing M-28 haversacks instead of M-36 musette bags [and] French khaki shirts instead of wool GI shirts." As if this weren't enough, he added: "Sal Mineo was wearing a cartridge belt, yet was carrying a Thompson [submachine gun]."

Reenactors often take along notepads when watching war movies to keep track of the farb quotient, usually finding that Hollywood fails miserably to reach their own standards of authenticity. "I do get a chuckle out of the dumbest farb stuff out there," one reenactor says, "like a movie where the Imperial Japanese are using No. 4 Mkls [British rifles] or the Germans are using Arisakas [Japanese rifles], or the Heer troops are wearing the wrong color, wrong gear, and carrying the wrong weapons." Even the eagerly awaited *Saving Private Ryan* (which reenactors universally celebrate as one of the best war movies ever made) was subject to weeks of criticism on the World War II newsgroup. Although they debated the film's plot and portrayal of soldiers, they focused mainly on the details: "The haircuts bugged us," one reenactor said. "They looked Russian! We also thought the pardoned MG42 crewman and the Waffen SS knife wielder looked, for lack of a better term, too British."

Whenever I watched war movies with reenactors, I heard the same run-on commentary, the voicing of complaints over incorrect belts, modern haircuts, postwar tunics, and anachronistic weapons. After a while, I found myself watching war movies with the same focus as I searched for the ever-present farby error. I always felt a little like an expert when I inevitably found one, and I understood why subjecting Hollywood to such minute scrutiny gives reenactors a sense of superiority. Their ability to pinpoint historical inaccuracies that most audiences would surely miss makes them feel that they indeed know more than most people about the details of war.

Even though reenactors universally condemn most movies as farby, they still love watching them, particularly to get revved up before an event. "I'm gonna watch *Tora! Tora! Tora!* tonight on DVD," one reenactor reported before an air show. "I like to blast the digitally enhanced sound really loud during the P-40 vs. Jap Zero Shooting Gallery scene." Many of them also love to quote dialogue from war movies in the field. *Kelly's Heroes* and *Cross of Iron* are two movies I've heard quoted endlessly at World War II events. The World War II classic *Battleground* is another reenactor favorite that provides quite a few good lines, such as, "He found a home in the Army!" The Stanley Kubrick film *Paths of Glory* provides a line popular among World War I Allied reenactors: "Ready to kill some Germans today, soldier?" But perhaps Vietnam reenactments are the most heavily influenced by movies. "I want every swinging dick in the field," Luke delights in saying at least once during every 'Nam event, poaching the famous line from *Platoon*. Phil Fussel reportedly quotes entire scenes from *Full Metal Jacket*, much to the dismay of unit members who think it's a little excessive. Quoting dialogue in the field, though, is done as a kind of ironic, even satirical allusion, not as an attempt to legitimate one's portrayal. Reenactors even quote from films that aren't war movies. At one event, a reenactor straddled the hood of a half-track, declaring, "I'm king of the world!"—quoting the famous line from *Titanic*.

Reenactors believe that documentary films are more factual than Hollywood movies, but only a few judge them a very useful source. Most are wary about the "origins of documentary footage," as Luke explains. And, given that many reenactors participate in the making of historical war documentaries, playing the parts of soldiers, their suspicion is warranted. But being suspect of any source is common among reenactors, and they are often merciless in evaluating even the most widely heralded war documentaries. "That was terrible," Paul Donald said of a highly touted PBS documentary about World War I. "They were speaking in generalities. . . . They haven't gotten beyond schoolbooks yet."

They place higher value on more direct sources, such as veterans' memoirs. About the World War II American paratrooper memoir *Those Devils in Baggy Pants*, one reenactor observes, "It is very anecdotal and is more of a character study than a narrative of the entire war. That's why it is so fascinating." It "very clearly indicated the typical state of mind of the average soldier," another says about the memoir *Inside the Battle of the Bulge*. "I personally could not put it down. Throughout I kept thinking what it pointed out that was wrong or right with my impressions."

Reenactors may rely on memoirs to determine right or wrong, but they also acknowledge that much can be lost in writing about war. "I think there's a tendency when you experience something to minimize it for the sake of readability,"

Luke explains. "If every detail was gone into, it would be an unreadable personal memoir." They are also aware that memoirs can be inaccurate or even fabricated. "Just because a book's cover says it's a true story," one reenactor warns, "does not necessarily mean that it is." Reenactors once argued for weeks whether the World War II memoir *The Forgotten Soldier*, by Guy Sajer, should be considered truthful—a debate that goes on well beyond the hobby's borders. William Gregory justified recommending Sajer's book to his unit's new recruits, especially since Sajer served in the Grossdeutschland Division. Moreover, William said that he liked the book because it doesn't "try to explain" the war in grandiose terms, but instead shows "what it was like for the common solider to fight and die for his country." But another reenactor cautioned against accepting Sajer's account as accurate: "I believe that many of us read this book when we were young and wanted to believe," he wrote. "Closer examination, of course, brings true details to light."

Armed with their own war experiences, reenactors often claim a newfound expertise as they confront historical sources. "Being able to wear the uniforms and use the same equipment, weapons, and tactics adds an extra dimension to understand these events that reading could never provide," as one reenactor asserts. Often they delight in disproving evidence touted in sources as true. For one reenactor, such a discovery "leads me to believe other things are false or incorrect and should be viewed with skepticism."

Perhaps because of such skepticism, few reenactors judge "written history" as one of the most useful sources—which truly astonished me. But for many, reading about war simply pales in comparison to reenacting. "No matter how many books I read," one reenactor says, "there are things they don't, or more likely, can't explain." "You can read all you want," another claims, "but true understanding is difficult until you experience something firsthand."

They also find that written history often raises more questions than it answers, since it is usually too generalized or watered-down for their highly-specific interests. "You read in a book about how tanks and infantry in the attack on the Siegfried Line are moving up to knock out pillboxes," Luke says. "Well, how does that work? How do you signal the tank? How does he know where to shoot? And that's not really gone into in the history books. They say the tanks and the infantry attacked the line and they broke it. Well, I kind of want to know how it's done."

They also argue that written history too often focuses on war's "leading personalities and grand operations," as Philip Moss observes, and not on the common soldier's perspective. Further, a lot of reenactors view written history with extreme caution, especially in light of their attempt to depoliticize their portrayals. The age-old claim, "history is written by the victors," is one reason that many of them "distrust some establishment histories." They place more value on sources that are judged not to have been "written by people with political agendas." Thus, nearly a quarter of reenactors say that primary sources such as military records and documents are one of the most useful sources; and they make wide use of training and equipment manuals, reports, and lists of issued equipment, often reprinting such documents in newsletters or unit materials.

But even with these primary sources at their disposal, authenticity debates are not always resolved. For instance, in an effort to determine whether US soldiers ever wore olive drab (OD) T-shirts in World War II, one reenactor stated conclusively: "nowhere in the US Army Quartermaster catalog does it describe a short sleeve undershirt in OD." Many others cross-checked sources and were on the verge of agreeing that an OD T-shirt was "uncommon, if seen at all, in the ETO." But others countered the emerging consensus and the sources: "Before you go relying solely on QM records," one reenactor warned, "let me say that . . . not everything they had is listed." Another introduced a possible rationale for wearing an OD shirt: "Could the OD T-shirt have been a private purchase item, either by the soldier or sent over by family stateside? That would explain its rarity and the fact it's not in the item lists."

The introduction of imagined possibilities means that even otherwise valued sources cannot always resolve authenticity debates. One reenactor points out the complexity involved in using period sources: "Look at the changes from the '42 to the '44 editions of the [Army field manuals]. What actually happened varied so much from unit to unit. . . . I would love to see all the variations on the norm written down someplace."

As they confront a multitude of variations on the norm, reenactors are often frustrated by the fact that "the more you look, the more you find, and the more confused you can get." For this reason, some think that information should always be cross-referenced, since legitimate sources can give different answers to the same question. But others advocate using a more flexible approach. One reenactor argues that "especially during the later years of the war adherence to uniform regulations was substandard. [They were] often ignored (or at least relaxed) in lieu of being comfortable and for purely practical reasons." Another agrees: "One should never say 'never' when discussing events affecting millions of people that spanned several years of time. One can always find one, and most likely several examples of absolutely anything." Still others take a hard line, stridently arguing against using imaginary information: "If they didn't wear it," one reenactor proclaims, "neither should we!"

Some reenactors think that arguing over minutiae is a waste of time. They become annoyed at the ceaseless efforts to identify "every trivial detail about every item of [a soldier's] issued equipment at the time, trivial details that have now become the source of a lot of silly how-many-angels-can-dance-on-the-head-of-a-pin arguments." These reenactors encourage others "to pay more attention to what was important, not what brand of prophylactics was best/most popular/issued most often." "God," as one reenactor lamented during the debate known as the "T-shirts wars," "I hope we do not start on whether we wear green or white boxer briefs!" Another sarcastically proposed: "Maybe we should institute underwear checks. . . . Everyone drops their trousers to see if their drawers are dated before May of 45." But another countered: "Underwear is only important to the wearer. But, when it is visible to others like in a barracks environment where others are forced to see you then you have crossed over into everyone else's business."

As they attempt to reach agreement on "what is acceptable," they have one source at their disposal that I initially thought they would value most: veterans. Indeed, most reenactors say that they use advice from veterans as a source, and nearly all report having interviewed veterans. Veterans can act as a "corrective," according to Luke, since "there are things [veterans know] that don't make the books, just because it's too much minutiae." Many champion veterans as an indispensable source that most other reenactors, such as Civil War reenactors, don't have. They also recognize that the veterans are "a diminishing asset." "Once they're gone," as one reenactor says, "we will be relegated to doing our research in books."

At the World War I veterans' convention that I attended with several reenactors, I had my first chance to witness reenactors making use of this resource firsthand. I was sitting with a ninety-year-old veteran after dinner. He was telling me about his experience as an infantryman in the US First Division. The man was quite morose and spoke with despair about what he had seen. I was upset, since I had met him earlier in the day and he had seemed very upbeat. But clearly, after a day spent with his fellow veterans conjuring up old ghosts, he was no longer cheerful. Then Luke and Scott Farb arrived. Polite and in genuine awe, they asked which unit the veteran had served in and where he was trained. Then Luke asked, "Did you use rifle-propelled grenades in the trenches?" Scott nodded encouragingly, "Were the men in your unit issued them as a rule?" The veteran stared back with a look of confusion, probably wondering why he was being asked such esoteric question. He looked at Scott and Luke with what I thought was annoyance. He had, after all, just been telling me about the terrible costs of war, his sense of loss after coming home, his friends who didn't come back, and now here were these young kids asking about his weapons. The veteran mumbled something about how unimportant their question was, and then he really got upset.

"Why are you asking me that? All them kids dying and suffering. All that war. That waste." He continued on this thread until Scott and Luke politely excused themselves. They later told me that they understood that some veterans get upset when they talk about their war experiences. Although I was upset myself about this encounter, it wasn't the last time I would witness the clash that can arise between those who use war as a pastime and those who really lived through it.

Still, reenactors are often persistent in trying to jog veterans' memories about even the smallest of details. Craig Bass described an encounter with several Royal Winnipeg Rifles veterans. "They practically got in a fight arguing over what color their webbing was," he remembers, and "not one of them would agree, and they were all in the same unit."

Because of such disagreements, many place limited value on veterans' advice. Although it outranked film, written history, and memoirs, veterans' advice was ranked by less than a quarter of reenactors as one of the most useful sources. Fred Legum explains why their intensive focus on details curtails the value of veterans' advice. He says that veterans are "not reliable to the extent where, you know, memory fades, they remember different things . . . and it all blurs together." Fred certainly doesn't blame veterans for not remembering the details. Instead he simply accepts that reenactors and veterans approach the topic of war differently. "When you're in the service you don't look at your equipment and take a lot of notice to it," he says. "You make sure it's polished or clean and that's it. But as collectors and reenactors, you know, you're looking at every little thing trying to get it straight, and these guys didn't pay attention to that."

Many also believe that veterans aren't always reliable, since they "repress so much of the memory of the war . . . and the details along with it." Thus, some offer a prescription for dealing with veterans. "There is an art and a science to pulling facts from vets," long-time reenactor Joseph Radway advises. "If you talk to enough of them, and are very cautious about finding out what they did, you can piece together some interesting things."

Whereas many reenactors accept veterans' advice only cautiously, others highly value veteran memory. After attending a World War II German Panzer veteran reunion, a reenactor shared his newfound knowledge: "Many vets looked at our [reenacting] pictures and told us that they were only issued the side cap, and never had the '43 model. This," he concluded, "amazed us." But, ever cautious of accepting memory as fact (and, not coincidentally, being forced to throw away their '43 models), another argued: "The veterans are wrong. I think it is too much to expect veterans to accurately answer uniform questions fifty years after the war is over."

Disagreeing with veterans may be uncomfortable at times, but there is also a more important dimension to it: Many reenactors think it undermines the hobby's commemorative aim. "Vets shouldn't be traumatized by members of the reenacting community," one reenactor asserts. Others agree: "Some [veterans] saw terrible things and would like to forget and work in their gardens and try to enjoy what's left of their life." These reenactors believe that veterans must be treated with respect no matter what information they offer. One reenactor took this position after his veteran grandfather's unpleasant experience: "He has spoken to a few reenactors at times and they always piss him off. They never seem to believe him when he says that he wore a prewar tunic at times during the war." Another fumed: "Nothing hacks me off more than for some clown to dismiss what a vet tells [him]. . . . These guys weren't running through artillery barrages counting how many men were wearing wool shirts over HBT trousers thinking, 'someday some goofy reenactor is going to ask me about this.' There were more important things to worry about."

Morris Call identifies what he believes to be the hobby's major hypocrisy: Reenactors tend to worship veterans "from afar" and "say they honor their memory," but they "don't want the firsthand info as it conflicts with their reality." For Morris, this only shows how "audacious and cruel" reenactors can be.

But for many reenactors, the most important thing to worry about is indeed whether or not soldiers wore wool shirts over HBT trousers. Unconcerned with replicating the veterans' experiences and only loosely following the script of history, they focus on getting the details right so that they can create their illusions. Many even privately admit that commemoration is the least of their concerns. Hank Lyle once told me about a time when a German paratrooper veteran attended an event with Hank's German unit. Hank said that "it was great talking to him and hearing all the stories and hearing all the stuff firsthand." But he also recognized that he doesn't reenact "because of him. You know, like this will make him feel better or—I think I need that explained to me again. That we do this because of the veterans, because of their sacrifice. I challenge people to tell me how often they're thinking about it."

Like Hank, I wondered how much reenactors thought about the veterans' sacrifices, especially when arguing over T-shirt colors. In fact, I'd seen reenactors get outright annoyed with veterans. One reenactor who is a veteran of the Korean War is certainly not treated with any more respect than anyone else, and some even say that he's an obnoxious know-it-all. And, once at a small private World War II event, I watched as two American veterans toured one of the campsites. Both were in their seventies, and one had lost his leg in the war. They were very friendly and seemed to get a kick out of the event. Lots of reenactors came up to say hello, and the veterans seemed impressed with all of the attention to detail. Still, one veteran wasn't shy in pointing out any lapses in authenticity. "We'd never leave a shaving mirror hanging anywhere," he said, pointing to a reenactor's mirror. "The reflection would give away your position." Later, after a reenactor ground out a cigarette under his boot, the veteran said, "Hey, don't you know how to field strip a cigarette? You're leaving evidence of your position, you know."

Both comments were met with polite smiles, but the reenactors seemed bothered by the criticism. Later in the day, the reenactor who had organized the event and invited the veterans came by. "Pain in the ass vets," he said, telling me that they were running him ragged and driving him crazy by pointing out what was wrong with the event. I know he didn't mean it literally, since he was the one to invite them, after all. But still, his attitude contradicted the reenactors' publicly proclaimed reverence for the sacrifice of veterans.

In fact, many reenactors seem perplexed by this part of their public mantra. Luke confided in me that he always thought that the idea of commemorating through reenacting was a "lie." Others agree: "I have never figured out how sleeping in the mud honors the World War II veterans. How about shooting ourselves with live ammo so we can really feel their pain?"

Some reenactors even go as far as arguing that they know far more about the details of war than the veterans themselves. One proudly declares that reenactors "really know more than the veterans of World War II whose memories are fifty years old." Another reenactor recalls talking to a German veteran who had served as a machine gunner. When the reenactor and his unit members "asked him specific details about the gun," they were delighted to learn that they had been "doing specific things that he did with the gun during the war." But they also determined that they had even more expertise since they "had been using it almost seven years longer than he had." Armed with the knowledge that their use of the weapon was entirely authentic, they concluded that "maybe in this limited sense reenacting mirrors reality."

Behind the lines in a German camp, World War I private event, 1996

Reenactors might like to believe that they mirror historical reality. But, of course, the reflection they cast is not a true replica of the past. Since they do not view history as being made up of an inert set of facts to be blindly replicated and called authentic, they don't always attempt to duplicate history as rendered in the sources. But at the same time, they do not always reject historical evidence as worthless, especially since they seek to replicate elements of authentic historical representations from the sources themselves. Thus, their desire for personal possession of a history that is often vaguely or even inaccurately rendered means that they must assert their own expertise in evaluating evidence. After all, these are the disgruntled consumers of history, whose dissatisfaction with available war stories compelled them into the hobby in the first place. With their "unique and bizarre approach to history," as John Loggia describes their research process, they exercise their own authority over the evidence, able to discount information, imagine undocumented possibilities, and "piece together" their own idea. This being the case, the two sources reenactors say they use most often—the same two sources they judge to be most useful—should come as no surprise.

"Everybody's an Expert"

I lost count of the number of times reenactors asked me to look at their reenacting photographs. After Greg Grosshans pulled out one of his albums during our interview, he guided me through it. "Here's some more photos. This was at the event you were at," he said, turning the pages and admiring the images. "Look how nice that is with the fog. And the black and white. There's me. These are some of those guys from California. They came out to it. . . . See, all of the guys pretty much wear real gear and whatever so we look good. There's Paul Wake. He's a member of our unit. There's me. There's Richard. That's me pointing out some things. You know, we all look pretty good."

Greg made sure to call my attention to two things as he showed off his photographs: himself and how good he and his friends looked. But really, such devotion to one's own image came as no big surprise. After all, a reenacting photo album (a staple in any reenactor's collection) is more than a chronicle of life in the hobby; it is a compendium of one's own historical expertise. And reenactors measure their own legitimacy by their capacity to mimic one source they value above and beyond all others: period photographs. Their faith in period photographs isn't hard to explain. They simply judge photographs as vivid documents that record moments from the past. "Pictures don't lie," as one reenactor declares. And they view them as a source that is least corrupted by interpretation. "You can never," Philip Moss claims, "look at enough old pictures when building or maintaining an impression." Judging themselves against old photographs, many believe that the height of authenticity is achieved when a reenactor is "able to look at a picture of a soldier from the war [and] look at yourself and . . . see nary a difference."

Often they turn to photographs as the final arbiter in determining authenticity. Scott Mies had read in period manuals that the brass buttons on World War II Soviet uniforms were always painted. However, after looking at period photographs, he no longer believed the written evidence. "I have yet to see more than two or three photographs from World War II Soviet that [show] painted buttons," Scott says definitively.

So valued are photographs that many believe one should not adopt an impression without photographic evidence to affirm its authenticity. "If another reenactor falls below another's expectations," one reenactor reasons, "that reenactor could be made to produce photographic evidence that his uniform and kit was actually worn and used in that fashion during wartime." Sometimes, however, finding the evidence is a challenge.

Calling it a "big bugaboo in our research," one World War II reenactor wondered if it would be authentic for his unit, the US 30th Division, to wear camouflage uniforms when portraying soldiers in the European Theater. His commander, Tim Gilbert, spent a day at the National Archives, where he and others sorted through a "collection of original contact prints hoping to find something on camo and the 30th Division." Tim reported that conducting the research "was like looking for a needle in a very interesting haystack." And although he said he "learned a lot," he was unable to "find anything on camo related to the ETO other than the previously published photo of the 2nd A.D. Engineers."

Though Tim's unit members seemed satisfied to conclude their research and give up the idea of wearing camouflage, others encouraged them to escalate their search. "Contact the Airborne museum at Ft. Bragg," Craig Bass directed. "Also ask the Imperial War Museum." But others expressed concern: If a single "needle" were found, would it be enough to legitimate the uniform's typicality? "Even if evidence was dug up about camo in the 30th," one reenactor argued, "I wouldn't think it viable to justify wearing that stuff."

"A picture is only one split second, a fraction of time," as Luke warns, "and it may be a tremendously atypical fraction of time." Thus even the trusted photograph must be used judiciously, since anything, even the exception, can be proven by a single image. "If a person looks hard enough," William Gregory believes, "he can find a picture of anything he wants."

As they try to avoid rendering war's uncommon details, many advise, "Don't pick out the extreme cases you may have seen once in an obscure photograph. We are portraying the average soldiers, not the one out of 100,000 who didn't have what everyone else got!" (Proving the authenticity of an impression based on a single photograph was the subject of one of Hank Lyle's witty performances.

"Oh, yeah," he said, mocking a farb. "It's totally authentic to dress as a big circus clown with floppy shoes, a red nose, and a fuzzy wig. One of those was on the beach at D-Day. Yeah, sure, I've got a photograph of one.")

As they debate questions of typicality, they also fundamentally disagree about how to mirror the historical reality of photographs themselves. Sam Benevento explains the debate. He once carried a contemporary replica of a 1944 knife at an event. When a reenactor challenged him, saying the knife was not authentic, but a mere repro, Sam replied that the knife was *more* authentic since it looked like those pictured in wartime photographs and not as an actual period knife, aged sixty years, would look today.

Some believe that ruining irreplaceable period gear for the sake of authenticity is a mistake, and for purposes of preservation, they should always use repros; as Dave Watkins says, "If you buy a pair of original German Y straps for 175 bucks, they're fifty years old and certainly getting them wet and getting abused isn't going to do any good. So you want to preserve your investment." Preservation issues aside, however, others side with Sam strictly out of a concern with appearance: Using period gear violates the "appearance" of authenticity. "The Wehrmacht as a rule did not issue fifty-year-old uniforms and equipment. It should look more or less new," Philip Moss asserts. "That means that all of you who delight in carrying or wearing crusty stuff are wrong." Still others believe that even the most "dead on" repros are fundamentally inauthentic, since only actual period artifacts are truly "real." For Greg Grosshans, wearing original gear "really makes a difference when you go out into the field. You can see a mile away what an original tunic looks like and what a fake one does."

The never-ending debate over facial hair is also fueled by photographs. As one reenactor argues, "I'm sure one guy out there will have a photo of a German with a beard in Southern France, so twenty guys [will] show up like that." Richard Paoletti believes they can resolve the hair problem by asking an important question when confronted by any evidence: "Is that the exception? Or is that the rule?" He says that he has seen photographs of unshaven soldiers, but usually they've been "out in the field a couple of weeks" with little time to devote to personal hygiene. "So we say, look, that's the exception." William Gregory instructs others how to handle the facial hair question: "One should take a look at pictures and see that the German Army was for the most part clean shaven. . . . Of course, you will find a picture or two with guys wearing [mustaches], but the majority will not. If your unit members insist on wearing mustaches, then you should limit it to about 10 percent of your unit."

Unit commanders usually hold the power to determine these limits, and re-enactors thus have their own internal hierarchy to affirm evidence. In fact, nearly all reenactors report that they rely on "advice from other reenactors" as a source; and almost a third rank such advice as one of the most useful sources, making it second in value only to photographs. This means that reenactors are more willing to accept each other's advice than they are to accept advice from films, written history, documents, memoirs, and even veterans. In ranking photographs and their own advice above and beyond all other sources, they reveal their intent to create an illusion that appears authentic, but is also valued as their own.

As they rely on each other to provide an authoritative filter through which confusing evidence can be authenticated and disseminated to the group, advice feeds the hobby like a central artery as information is pumped into the group's metaphoric veins in the form of authenticity regulations, newsletters, email, and conversations. Many even admit that they "learn more from friends [and] participants than . . . from reading [and] independent research."

Indeed, where but in the hobby could one get quick answers to questions such as: "What is the difference between the BC611 and the 617?" or "Does anybody have the regulations associated with footlockers and how they should be packed?" "It's a treat," one reenactor says, "to reap the benefits of [other reenactors'] knowledge, research, and experience and add it to your own."

With a concrete purpose to their eccentric pursuits—those long nights spent looking at photographs with a magnifying glass—they tackle the problem of unreliable sources, faulty memory, and imagined possibilities. Among them is a handful of "experts," also known as historians, who are often characterized by the following statement: "He's forgotten more about [insert war/battle/army here] than I ever knew." To be considered an expert is a high compliment indeed, and one reserved for those who have earned that reputation by running a top-notch unit, exhibiting a broad range of knowledge, or operating a reputable militaria business. Often these experts are cited as sources themselves—"My other reliable source, Craig Bass" and "the God of reenacting, Philip Moss."

Although a few experts are employed in real life professions that are history-related, such as teaching or museum work, one's job or degree does not necessarily translate into expert status in the hobby. One 4th Armored member, although having proudly earned a PhD, is not considered exceptionally knowledgeable. But John Loggia, whose profession is wholly unrelated to history, is considered the best-read person in the unit.

Morris Call earned his expert reputation by reproducing German items and publishing a series of books on German militaria. Watching him sell his wares at an event flea market, I marveled at his knowledge as two reenactors approached, asking to buy infantry assault badges. "You guys are in a Panzergrenadier unit, aren't you?" the unflappable Morris asked. "Yeah," they responded sheepishly. "Then you wouldn't be wearing those," Morris declared. "They're not correct for your impression." Such dictates are often heeded; these two settled for the more accurate bronze panzer badges.

Although nearly twenty percent of reenactors claim to use advice from sutlers, such as the advice Morris offered, as a source, only a tiny percentage considers such advice to be one of the most useful sources. Many believe that sutlers are motivated more out of concern for profit than authenticity. "We've got to separate the sutlers from the hobby," Larry Cohen remembers warning the GWA. "It's like separation of church and state. [A sutler] doesn't have the power to tell somebody this is okay to use."

But in Morris' case, he's seen as an expert first and sutler second. And because many reenactors have such high regard for experts, many argue that newbies should always rely on the sound advice of these expert reenactors when starting out in the hobby. But even the experts cannot always assume their advice will be followed.

One reenactor took on a question that had vexed reenactors for some time: was a World War II MP's web gear coated with white paint or a camouflaging paste called blanco? Relying on his real-life expertise as a chemist, this reenactor sought to resolve the debate for good. He issued the results of his experiment: "If you look closely at the white colored webbing and compare it to true blancoed webbing, one can notice a slight difference in film formation on the webbing's surface. This is due to the finer pigment grades, coalescing solvents, and dispersants in the paint rather than the primitive blanco coating." He went on to state conclusively, "Analysis of both coatings from several pieces using an infrared spectrometer showed that the white coatings on both British and American pieces were gloss alkyd paints, not blanco."

But even this chemist-reenactor knew that he could not rest easy, despite his mastery of an infrared spectrometer. "Even with all the work I've done," he speculated, "I'm sure someone will swear that his great-grand pappy painted his entire house with white blanco."

Indeed, regardless of one's reputation, almost all reenactors generously offer their own advice. Thus, they engage in a power struggle, competing over whose advice is most credible and therefore who has the power to define authenticity. And just as there is a hierarchy to the sources, so too is there a hierarchy to advice.

After the battle, the Bulge, 1994

As they evaluate each other's knowledge, reenactors judge one another by the sources their impressions seem to reflect. Farbs are not only unsafe, non-hit-taking, fat, old, or female, they're also "farby not-well-read individuals"; they "prefer 'Hollywood' looks to what is factual," or, as Scott Mies says, they "go with whatever the unit says without really looking into the historical reality of it." Luke describes a certain farb this way: "He was not the type of person to own a single scholarly book. He was a Ballantine series on World War II man, not even that actually. Not even a Time-Life series man. He was a documentary—a TV documentary man."

Luke says he almost never takes advice from other reenactors since there are "very few reenactors that have anything worthwhile to offer." He finds the whole business of relying on other people's advice to be unfortunate, since "most people who take advice from other reenactors should be reading and doing the research for themselves." Like others, Luke is proud to be able to say, "My kit exists because I've researched it that way. Not because somebody's told me, Oh, you should have this and you should have that."

Admittedly, some reenactors probably should not be considered credible, since they admit—as two reenactors admitted on my questionnaire—that their knowledge is derived from "my own imagination" or "common sense!" Clearly, some have done more homework than others; I was tremendously impressed by the breadth of knowledge that some reenactors possess. But in such a highly competitive hobby, many simply have a hard time being told what they should or should not wear or do, since they are so skeptical of know-it-alls. And many have no difficulty dismissing even the experts as "assholes that think they know all but don't." "I once had a guy try to convince me," a reenactor recounts, "that no one wore leggings and service shoes in Europe after 1943. He had gotten that gem from his dad. . . . That was one of those 'nod your head and smile, but don't say anything because he won't believe you' situations." Unfortunately, not everyone is so polite. "Do the words 'fuck you' mean anything to you?" Philip Moss artfully queried after receiving some advice: "Who the hell do you think you are to tell me how and why I should be doing any impression. . . . I hate self-righteous reenactors who feel that they have the answers to it all."

As they vie to earn respect and authority, reenactors can be downright competitive, especially as they champion their own knowledge as infallible. Thus, it was with great frustration that Larry Cohen recalled a disagreement he and Phil Fussel had over a seemingly trivial detail: the color of the belts US soldiers wore in Vietnam. Larry describes their initial exchange: "I'm like, 'Phil, I'm not trying to be a dick. . . . But I know for a fact that they were black. You know?' 'Well how do you know? What, do you think you know everything?' . . . 'Phil, I'm telling you, they're black. I mean it's like helicopters go up and down. . . . I don't have to prove it.'"

Larry was frustrated by this conversation, but not surprised, since, as he sarcastically says of reenactors, "everybody's an expert on something." But he didn't have to wait long before being proven right. "Sure enough," Larry remembers, "after bitching and moaning for two weeks Phil comes up to me and says 'I saw a few photos and they were black. You were right.' But it was like, I can't just say anything and be accepted at face value with some people." For Larry, not being accepted at face value was more than a slight from a friend; it was an insult to his legitimacy.

Given the fact that reenactors can always find a reason to ignore puzzling sources and accept or reject advice, many acknowledge that ultimately their "egos play a very big role" in defining authenticity, as Lew McCarthy believes. One reenactor thus considered the audacity of any reenactor declaring definitive truth: "It appears that in 1996 we think we know what is the correct re-creation of events and dress that occurred fifty plus years ago and a half a world away. Despite all the careful research, impeachable sources, and expert opinions the real truths stun our perceptions, and over such things as caps!" This reenactor reminded others about the sheer scale of history they confront: "We are dealing with millions of soldiers and events that spanned six years and yet we have the nerve to stand up on some ammo box and preach our version of the gospel."

With so many versions of the gospel being preached, reaching agreement would seem impossible. When someone suggested the commonsense idea of compiling a universal reenactor guidebook, nearly everyone dismissed it, since creating "an all-encompassing list of 'acceptable' and 'nonacceptable' items would be next to impossible." Another felt that such a guide "sounds nice on paper, but would be a general waste of time," since "virtually anything you put in your guide would be rejected by some regional group of reenactors somewhere." After nearly twenty years reenacting World War II, this reenactor says that he has come to accept that "it is nearly impossible to get a workable group of people to agree on anything." "In my entire life," he observes, "I have never been involved with any group of people who seem to have the same problems cooperating with others as World War II reenactors."

Indeed. According to Tim Castle, the hobby is like a "small town government." Reenactors vie for influence, seek to advance their reputations, grumble about lackluster leadership, complain about the high proportion of farbs, pledge allegiance to perfection, berate others for their failures, behave arrogantly, and dismiss each other as assholes, losers, and idiots. These are the "extracurricular exchanges" that some see as a natural result of a hobby that "by definition involves the simulation of armed conflict."

But in many ways, the reenactors' problems in cooperating are the result of their mutually exclusive goals: to be better than anyone else at being common or typical. "We are trying to do the average . . . armored infantry impression," as Troy Carnes says of 4th Armored. "We just happen to do it best." And yet, however much a reenactor might wish to declare him or herself to be the sole bearer of historical truth, such a claim must be legitimated by the very source that causes them so much frustration: "other reenactors." And ultimately, their success depends on their ability to create the very thing they fail to find in the long history of conflict: consensus.

Chapter 12

"How to Play Army without Everybody Getting Pissed at Each Other"

Camaraderie

"You are a brick in the wall of empire, and you shouldn't seek to rise in the wall lest you destabilize it." As we ate hamburgers in a Washington restaurant, Patrick Hart paraphrased the words of Sir Robert Baden-Powell, which he vaguely remembered from his Boy Scout days. Reenactors, he said, need to adopt a similar credo. We were marveling at the excessive amount of arguing in the hobby, and, like all reenactors I knew, Patrick agreed that reenactors seem to have a major problem getting along.

By the time this conversation took place, I had been studying the hobby for four years. My questions had evolved, my understanding had deepened, and I felt far more at home in the hobby than I did when I showed up at my first event. Still, I was confounded. On one hand, reenactors can be so intensely close-knit. On the other, they create so much animosity among themselves.

To be sure, many reenactors welcome good-natured competition. They are, after all, engaging in simulated combat. Others think that it is only natural for any group to have its arguments. "To expect that reenactors alone among the rest of society would be able to coexist without friction is unrealistic," one reenactor observed. But he also finds that "self-righteous pulpit thumping accomplishes little, or more likely exacerbates the problem." "What," he asked, "can we do to reduce the animosity?"

Some reenactors fear that their inability to answer this question could spell their demise. Deep-seated anger and unresolved fights pose dangers far more potent to their existence than any negative PR or public opposition. And the threat of self-destruction is real. Under the pretext of arguments over authenticity, units fold, organizations break apart, reenactors cease speaking to each other, and they trade an endless stream of insults: "Flame me, you fat little pogue," as one reenactor once wrote to another on a newsgroup. Another wrote, "You are such a waste of space on this planet that you're not even worth the energy it would take to tell you more about it." Even as they partake in this "unconstructive babble," they urge each other to act like adults, "stop bickering," "take a 'lude," and heed the rallying cry, work together!

After a particularly bitter argument between two 4th Armored members, Phil Fussel urged, "Remember we are all brothers and friends in this group. . . . That's how we started and that's how we will always remain." Scott Wawszyzki agreed: "If two 4th members have a problem with each other, fine. People will disagree. . . . We are men of honor and we are all adults. Got a problem? Settle it! . . . Let's keep the fighting towards the Germans!"

The call to settle disputes is not only sounded within individual units. "This hobby can only be viable if we unite," Donald Kiev declared to the GWA membership during his tenure as president. His successor, Perry Trent, issued his warning in starker terms. In his GWA newsletter column, Perry complained that although they "should be working together," they were spending far too much time "telling half-truths, undermining the work of others, [and] spreading false rumors." "I am not used to this kind of negative, destructive behavior," Perry fumed, "and quite frankly, will no longer put up with it."

Many scoff at the idea that they can ever cooperate. Some even seem set on escalating disputes. But there are others—particularly those who hold positions of power in respected units and organizations—who are dedicated to finding ways to reach some sort of collective agreement. These reenactors circulate drafts of basic kit requirements or rules of engagement asking others for feedback; they invite other units to event planning meetings with the idea that "all input has to be considered and weighed"; and they conduct surveys to pinpoint issues of concern. Perhaps most important, they institute official procedures for challenging authenticity regulations. "If a person can prove a unit or individual used a certain weapon, equipment, or uniforms by letters, photographs or film," one unit orders, "then use will be permitted." Another states, "If you feel that we are wrong bring proof, pictures, documents, etc. to prove us wrong."

By requiring documented proof, these leaders ostensibly grant authority in

On the battlefield, the Bulge, 1995

determining authenticity to the historical sources—however confusing they may be. But such procedures actually give final authority to reenactors themselves. Because reenactors often conflate the authority of historical evidence with their own power to decide a particular issue, what is sometimes deemed authentic is less a reflection of historical reality and more what those in power or a simple majority rule acceptable. "Authenticity is set," as one reenactor observes, by "leadership and peer pressure."

Morris Call willingly acknowledges that in this process, "history" is still "definitely a part of it," but "much gets rewritten to fit the bill." "The homogenization of history at a reenactment is offensive to the purist," Morris concedes. "But, with what is available reenactors must do what they can to play."

Of course, not all reenactors are satisfied by such procedures. "If you can't produce a (conveniently) required volume of evidence," one reenactor complains, "then the experts continue to stand their moral high ground." Some even evoke the principles of liberty: "As a fellow American, I don't have to believe what you believe nor accept what you feel is correct." But, as in the rest of life, objections to the realities of a situation are not always effective in changing them. Even some Stitch Nazis admit that authenticity by consensus may produce homogenized results, but within the hobby's big picture, they are acceptable.

When Craig Bass, who is widely considered an expert, manufactured reproduction World War I British cotton shirts, he admitted that they weren't truly authentic since the wartime originals were made of wool. But those who purchased the shirts argued that they passed the "ten foot rule," and, more important, they were preferable to the more authentic wool shirts, especially when attending events in hot weather. Some found this consensus intolerable. "If clothing versus climate is a major concern," Wilson Lyle argued, "then I think the answer is to host events with a scenario that matches the climate, not invent things for our convenience that never existed (like . . . 'wool' shirts made out of cotton)."

Wilson's challenge was not powerful enough to change the majority's will. Even those so outraged by farbicity often find that they must work together if only by default. They fail to heed the universal cry of reenacting banishment: "Go paintballing!" Still trying to raise standards and dragoon the farbs out of the hobby, even they must do "what they can to play." For Tim Gilbert this requires accepting what he calls the hobby's "bottom line": "You cannot control everyone else."

A reenactor's desire for control—whether over self, unit, the hobby, or history—proves to be restrained by the group itself. "Anyone out of the norm is shunned," Morris explains. "The norm being defined by the larger part of the group—straight out of grade and high school and the playground." Those who attempt to assert their own agendas, ignore the rules, or obstruct the will of the majority can be controlled if they go too far. And episodes far more controversial than debates over fake wool shirts show how some reenactors can be forced to work together.

A Collective Mindset

Longtime World War I reenactor Grant Holzer is a soft-spoken man in his forties. Raised as a Quaker, a virulent advocate of gun control, and a scholarly type who worked for many years for the National Park Service, Grant admitted that he found a deep dichotomy among reenactors: "In some respects," he observed, "reenactors do fit the stereotype of the armed and angry white man, at both his worst (racist, sexist, hardcore conservative) and at his best (strong sense of camaraderie, look out for each other) often simultaneously." For Grant, who counts reenactors among his closest friends, "this is what makes reenactors such a fascinating breed of people."

Grant's comment helped me understand the nature of the reenactors' struggles.

Yes, they can be petty, argumentative, sexist, and even racist. But at the same time, they can rise above such destructive positions and ultimately achieve a kind of harmony—even if only a forced harmony.

The first time I witnessed such a resolution came in February 1998, when the GWA issued an order to all "participants not falling into normal unit member status" that they must provide documentation to affirm the authenticity of their impressions. (This meant that all non-combatant reenactors—nurses, Red Cross workers, and so on—had to apply for special permission from GWA leaders to attend events.) Grace Hall reacted in outrage, saying that the order was aimed primarily at women, since most women in the GWA are registered as independents. "This is bullshit," she fumed. "There's nobody in the GWA that I think has enough knowledge of women's roles and women's fashions to be able to judge if something's appropriate or not." When Grace complained to GWA president, Perry Trent, she told him, "I'm not going to have anybody tell me that I can't be a member of my own unit." As a registered independent, I was also asked to provide documentation. When I spoke to Perry, he agreed that the rule was foolish. With his typical easygoing attitude, he told me to write up a paragraph describing my impression. I sent him a few sentences describing my Motor Corps impression, and Perry immediately deemed it authentic. I was now a legitimate independent.

In this case, Perry decided the issue himself, using his power as president to control those who wished to exclude women outright. I knew that Perry wasn't entirely sold on the idea of women in the hobby—he always marveled that any woman would choose to be in such a crass environment. But I also knew that he wanted to head off what might have become a protracted battle in the GWA. But this was only one controversy requiring reenactors to separate the overlapping threads of historical reality, personal agendas, and the need for consensus.

On another occasion, Ray Sherman suddenly appeared riding on Perry Trent's half-track during a combat scenario in a private event. Luke and a few other 4th Armored members were outraged. They weren't mad because Ray wasn't a unit member. And they weren't mad because he looked inauthentic; Ray always does excellent impressions. No, they were mad because, since Ray is black, he was committing a terrible breach in authenticity since American units in World War II, at least officially, were segregated. "You don't want to offend Ray," as John Loggia explained, "but historically, he could not have been there."

During the event, no one uttered an objection directly to Ray, and it was clear he had no idea about the controversy he'd caused. But he was also ready with a rationalization, based partly on historical reality and partly on his own impression. He told me later that Perry Trent had said to him, "Well, you don't have a Sherman tank, you don't have four blacks to get in it with you, so hop on this half-track." Perry also told Ray, "This half-track belongs to me and two other guys. We put our money in for this and we get to say who plays on it. . . . So jump on it. We're 4th Armored." Ray clearly knew opposition was possible, but he was ready. "In situations like that," he explained to me later, "when somebody wants to really pick on you, who says that's not authentic, [I respond,] 'Well, I'm with the 3rd Armored, my tank got blown up, and the unit was separated, so 4th Armored rolled through and an officer sees that I'm an NCO and told me to get on up there.' When an officer tells you to do something, you do it. . . . And that did happen a lot." Able to justify his presence on the basis of what could have happened in history—and because he was backed by Perry Trent, who literally owns part of history in the form of his half-track and whose status in the unit is quite high—Ray was allowed to play, however much he challenged some unit members' vision of the "way things should be."

I was disgusted by the episode. Not only was I reminded of my own experience of being excluded, but I was also particularly outraged knowing that most 4th Armored members knew and liked Ray. Later I spoke to Perry. Ray may not have known about the controversy, but Perry did, and he was mad. "I've been spat on because I am Jewish, and I don't care what you are," he said. "You're a decent human being, and if you're a decent human being you don't deserve that. And who the fuck cares if you're black?" Even John Loggia, who initially agreed with Luke, put the unity of the unit above all else. During the event, John said he tried to calm Luke down, telling him, "This is the Battle of the Bulge. Ray attached himself to us, okay? Can't we just settle it at that? What I have been told by some people is that Luke's got to remember that it's not his unit. That it's our unit."

Forced by peer pressure as well as the argument of mutual over individual ownership of history ("our unit"), Luke backed down during the event and let the controversy go. However, he later told me that he was mad that this corruption of historical reality had been allowed to occur.

Afterward, I was angry that so much energy had been expended on a racist argument. So what, as Perry said, if you're black? Ray is a good reenactor, a great person, and to a lot of unit members, a good friend. He was also doing an impression that I thought could be justified historically. Plenty of black Americans served in World War II, and I had read about instances where units had been de facto integrated on the battlefield. Ultimately, I also knew that reenactors cannot get around the fundamental hypocrisy of the pure authenticity argument. As soon as one reenactor makes a call on a cell phone in the field or takes a swig from a Pepsi, the whole argument is rendered moot. But along with my anger, I must admit that I felt a little admiration. I was impressed that somehow the issue was kept in check. It never became confrontational. They resolved it in the field. Right in the middle of combat, they achieved consensus of a kind.

This was not the only time that reenactors reached consensus over an important issue. Years ago, another controversy occurred in the GWA when Tim Reed announced that he wanted to form the first unit of World War I Russians, known as the "Russian Legion" or Legion Russe. Several GWA commanders thwarted his effort, arguing that no Russians had ever served on the Western Front. "They were not welcome at the event," John Loggia recalls. "There were people out there who were dead set against it. And, to be quite honest with you, I did not welcome a formation like that." When I asked why, John said, "Because I have maybe what you would call an anglocentric approach, and I like to see Yanks and French and British. These [Russian] guys were more of an exception rather than the rule."

In hushed tones, Paul Donald admitted that two of Tim's most vociferous opponents were self-declared anticommunists. Tim concurred, describing one of them as "a self-righteous, petty government bureaucrat out to save American democracy from the Cold War—no matter how much he tramples the Bill of Rights." Tim thought it was "blatant discrimination of the worst kind because of these two knuckleheads' political views." But he also thought it was absurd. "What makes it even more stupid is that it was a reenactment!" he declared. "They were acting as if it was 1918 and we were baby-eating Bolsheviks the good ol' USA needed to purge!"

Undaunted and somewhat amused, Tim was forced to prove the historical reality of the Russian presence by providing historical evidence to GWA commanders and then to the entire GWA membership at the fall 1990 event. As he stood before the membership prior to the start of the event, Tim made his proposal, citing a variety of sources to prove that Russians had indeed served on the Western Front. (For the record, a small number of Russian soldiers did serve on the Western Front during World War I.)

Once he did, though, the controversy only escalated. John Loggia remembers that a reenactor heckled Tim as he cited sources, saying, "Oh, what are they, in French?" John was horrified at the idea that sources would be considered invalid because they were written in a language other than English. He said, "It seemed to me that we had people who were practicing bad history and were being very ethnocentric. And because a source was French therefore it was invalid? . . . I mean, my goodness!"

Not willing to allow bad history to taint the hobby's reputation, John jettisoned his anglocentric vision and supported Tim's formation. After the entire GWA membership voted on the issue, the Russian impression was ruled acceptable and Tim's unit was allowed to play. Some championed the episode as proof of their adherence to historical reality, but many more celebrated it as evidence of their ability to work together. "The majority wins," Paul Donald states. "That's it. If you don't like it, leave." And, after the vote was cast, those most adamantly opposed to the Russians purportedly quit the hobby altogether.

Tim's unit was well received until it disbanded several years later. Ironically, the members of the new Russian unit that took its place were soon placed on probation. The reason: although a few of its members were actually Russian immigrants—the ultimate in authenticity!—"they don't understand English well enough," Grace Hall reported, "and they don't understand the rules."

"That's all it is, isn't it?" one reenactors asks. "A game with rules." And "why does anyone play by the rules?" another asks. "Because we want to have fun. And fun takes order." The importance of having order at a reenactment cannot be understated. Even far from the public eye, given all the freedom and privacy they desire, reenactors are dedicated to hammering out a "set of rules and regulations," as Patrick Hart explains. "That's what you want. There's no gray areas."

As reenactors seek an escape from the real world and a chance to experience chaos and isolation, they work hard to create a structure in which those experiences can flourish. In fact, I was surprised to learn just how important achieving order and consensus is to them. When I asked them what makes an event successful or pleasurable, most did not answer with "achieving authenticity," as I thought they would have when I first began my research. Instead, a majority cited variations on the theme of working together. Ideals such as "good sportsmanship," "teamwork," "friendship," and "cooperation" were ranked higher in importance than even achieving authenticity, since these are the ideals that must be realized before success can be achieved. The words "authenticity and cooperation," as one unit states, "are interchangeable."

"What I've told my guys," one commander explains, "is to be good sports and not argue, mind your own business, lend a hand when you can. It does work." "Play well together," Morris urges. "Build self and each other through interaction, make constructive criticism. Don't talk shit. Members use 'I' statements to talk about what they think and feel—all in the open."

Sounding more like therapists than reenactors, Morris and others speak to the primary problem in the hobby: "other reenactors." Even as they insist that their difficulty cooperating is the product of vague history and troubling research questions, more often, it's actually the result of enlarged egos, sexism, anglocentrism, anticommunism, political correctness, and prejudice. Thus, I came to believe that their emphasis on establishing a system to define typicality for the group as a whole reveals their desire to control the many competing ideas about, as John Loggia put it, "the way things should be." "It's all about having a collective mindset," as one reenactor aptly observed.

Clearly, reenactors value individual attributes that are also championed in the real world, such as youth, power, appearance, and knowledge. But they also value qualities that benefit the group as a whole. Thus, those who earn positive reputations may look good and know a lot, but they are also those reenactors who are seen as being team players. They are reenactors such as Ben Sandler and Sam Benevento, who don't behave arrogantly or escalate disputes. Instead, they "conform to authenticity" and "follow the rules set up by the consensus." Other reenactors with good reputations include John Loggia, variously described as a good man and a fair leader, and Perry Trent, whose landslide election as GWA president reflects the esteem others have for his willingness to work in the best interest of the group. On the other hand, reenactors who earn poor reputations may be good-looking or very smart, but they are also seen as being unable to work as part of a team. These are the reenactors who act on their own accord and "disagree with policy and try to break away." They are the reenactors known as misfits, exceptions, and free agents. In fact, the sheer number of terms reenactors use to identify "individuals" in the hobby underscores the importance they place on teamwork. As Morris observes, "extreme individualism" causes the "fragmentation of the hobby." And, ultimately, those individualists who try to reap personal benefits at the cost of others are seen as nothing less than "a cancer to this hobby."

Bill Lauter illustrated the effects of the disease of individualism after running into a reenactor at an event who was "walking around with a funky German-style uniform, with, get this, his breast eagle sewn on square! It was the worst thing you've ever seen!" But instead of ignoring him or laughing behind his back, Bill approached him. "I ask him if this is his first event and what unit is he with. What does he tell me? He heard about the event in the paper, never heard of World War II reenacting, and made his fucking uniform from pictures! But he said people had kinda been looking at him funny all day and I was the first person to even talk to him!" Bill said he "had the pleasure of squaring this intrepid soul away and hooking him up with some quality guys." But he also said that "it made me think quite a bit . . . without support from the organizations and common standards, the guys who don't give a shit really are giving a shit, all over you and your hobby."

Offering yet another definition of a bad reenactor, one reenactor observed: "A farb will never utter these words 'Say, that's very authentic-looking, where did you get that?' 'Can you help me do that?'" Since so much of the hobby is geared toward masculine behavior, it's no wonder that a lot of reenactors try to avoid what they might view as a feminine tendency of asking for help or accepting advice. They value their independence. Their stoicism. Their ruggedness. The same characteristics they associate with the common soldier. But at the same time, they sneer at the idea of the mythical hero-soldier, the maverick who gains glory by Hollywood-style behavior. Real soldiers needed to stick together. They needed each other. And those who didn't "give a shit" might get themselves or, worse, others killed.

With such value placed on the concept of teamwork, individualist reenactors can suffer a fall from grace—even within their own units. One British unit commander, reportedly after years of acting with little concern for his men, found himself attacked in the field by erstwhile members who had joined another unit. Meanwhile, Larry Cohen points to his weight gain as the reason he was largely shunned by Luke and others in 4th Armored. But others confided in me that they were tired of Larry asserting his own agenda. Whatever the reason, Larry expresses disappointment. "I kind of resent the fact that nobody's including me in anything," he said sadly. He told me that he heard about a Vietnam event that some members of his unit attended two weeks after it was over. "I was really pissed off," Larry said. "These guys got to ride in a Huey. They got to do all this stuff. And I'm essentially really pissed off . . . 'cause here are these guys that have professed to be my friends."

At the time, Larry said he was still trying to find his "niche" in the hobby, but he soon took a leave of absence from reenacting. When I caught up with him again in 2003, he told me he'd dropped out of reenacting for good. He seemed to try to put a good spin on the whole thing, but I thought he was disappointed. He seemed to feel cut out of the loop, even betrayed by his friends, and by Luke especially. But as much as Luke may have ostracized Larry, Luke soon got a taste of his own medicine.

In 1997 Luke stepped down as 4th Armored commander. Mike Sharp, a well-respected unit squad leader, took over. Publicly, Luke cited increased pressure from his real job, but privately, he admitted that he quit because he was disappointed with the unit. After the plans he had made for a hardcore invitation-only event fell through, he was angry because he felt that other unit members had dropped the ball. Admitting that he'd done all the "really difficult work," he then said, "Honestly . . . I am 4th Armored."

After Luke stepped down, though, a few of the rank and file began to criticize him, saying that he'd never really worked for the unit but was in it only for himself. When Luke got wind of this, he defended himself, stressing his devotion to the unit even to the detriment of his real life: "You have forgotten all that I do," he wrote to the unit in an email. "The newsletters and Web page entries and making the telephone calls to the men and doing all the work that you never see when you just show up for an event. I've been doing it for I don't even remember how many years. I was doing all I could to build up 4th Armored instead doing the things I should have done in my adult life and relationships and it was personally costly." He concluded by pledging, "I have never abandoned and will never abandon this outfit."

True to his word, Luke continued to serve as a private in 4th Armored. But I couldn't help noticing that after he stepped down, the unit began to reflect a less-exclusionary attitude: not only did Tom Schultz return, bringing a period staff car with him, and Sam Benevento, who had had his "balls busted" by Luke years ago, was invited to join, but the unit also welcomed its first black member.

Personally, I wasn't surprised that Luke relinquished his power. I did not agree with his politics or admire his hardcore attitude, but I also knew that he worked extremely hard for the unit. He was one of the most dedicated reenactors I had ever known, and although he opposed women in the hobby, he was also one of my most valuable informants. He helped me to attend events and make contacts, and he spoke openly and at length with me about his experiences. In a way, I was sad that he gave up. But I also thought that it was better for his mental health, quite honestly, since he was usually crushed when an event inevitably failed to live up to his standards for perfection.

With Luke's departure, however, things started to unravel. The 4th Armored stayed together through three successive presidents. But by 2002, all was not well. When two veteran members had a fight, a series of petty and mean jokes and arguments followed. Soon the unit split, separated into two groups loyal to each of the arguing members. Each group then formed its own new unit.

Later, I talked with a couple members who lamented the breakup. One long-time 4th member was particularly upset. He missed a lot of his friends who'd joined the other unit, and he was mad at several people for acting like assholes. Ultimately, though, he blamed the unit's demise on Luke's departure, saying that no one really appreciated what Luke had done for them. "He kept us together," he said. "He kept everyone happy." He also revealed that the old band of friends had self-destructed over something really stupid.

"What was the argument about?" I asked him.

"A chair," he said.

"A chair!?" I was incredulous.

Apparently, someone brought an incorrect chair to an event, and an argument erupted when someone made a nasty comment about it.

Sometimes a chair is just a chair. But I knew that more lay beneath the surface of this disagreement. How long were the hard feelings and anger simmering only to be unleashed at an inanimate object? I wondered. Whatever the answer, the original 4th Armored was no more.

"We should all bury the past, and pray for better times ahead," one reenactor declared, preaching from the ammo box. Like many others, this reenactor encouraged everyone to try to work things out before taking an extreme action like disbanding a unit. "I, for one," he stated, "like everyone I've ever gamed with (with very few exceptions). And like a tight-knit family, as all reenactors are, we are prone to squabbles and in-fighting. When the smoke clears, we would all fight and die for each other if this was real war."

After the smoke clears, reenactors return home from an event. They log on to the various reenactor newsgroups where the traffic continues to flow unabated. Old debates are recycled. New and old solutions to the problem of the failed illusion are proposed. Evidence is questioned. The insults and flame wars rage. They write their after-action reports, eagerly wait for their pictures to be developed, and begin to tell their war stories. To be sure, they recount how the many farbs ruined everything, the multitude of competing egos they encountered, or perhaps the rare magic moment they experienced. But once back in the real world, dressed in their late-twentieth-century street clothes and playing their other roles in America, they also tell another kind of war story. And it was this kind of story that made it clear to me just how much they really do want to get along.

"Our Home in the Trenches"

"I got separated from my squad and I wandered down to the road and then I ran into about twenty Germans down there, twenty SS, and I surrendered." Ben Sandler enthusiastically tells me about an experience he considers particularly successful. "First they took my weapon away and then one of the officers said something in German to one of the other Germans, and then they sent me in this ditch and they shot me." Ben pauses dramatically before continuing. "And then they posed with my dead body."

"Wow," I respond.

"Then they picked me up and they're like, ah, started talking. . . . They [said], 'Oh, you fell right in the mud'. . . And then they thanked me for playing such a good dead person, and then I walked back through the German lines."

Like many war stories, Ben's tale stresses how his actions contributed to the illusion—and probably provided some great pictures. But Ben's willingness to play "such a good dead person" did more than help create an illusion. It earned him the respect of his peers.

As I moved away from thinking about magic moments and authenticity and more about what reenactors gain through their events, Luke told me another story that helped me see that far more went on in their scenarios than I had first believed. It was during a small World War II event, when all hell was breaking loose. Luke was trying to keep his men together after an ambush and trying to figure out what to do with the German prisoners they'd just captured. "My first squad leader had been hit and was wounded. And there he was, lying on the road, feigning injury realistically," he recalls. "I shouted back to my staff sergeant, I said, 'I need a medic up here!' And he says, 'Well, there's only this German medic.' And the German medic had his hands up [and] he obviously was on the ball 'cause I said, *'Sanitäter!'* I said, 'I don't care if it's a German medic or not!'"

I'm thinking that I know what happens next, given Luke's reputation as a war criminal. Luke continues, quoting the German medic's response to his request for help:

"He's like, *'Ja, Ja.'* And I said, 'Come with me,' and I waved him over. And this German medic, he gave first aid to my wounded squad leader." Luke's voice softens and ends on an upward inflection, as if he were reciting poetry.

"And the German medic carried him away with the help of another man. And I thought, I wish I knew who this guy was because he did a fantastic job. And that's what the hobby is supposed to be about. That's the hobby at its very best."

Luke sits back, his tale finished. I marvel at the moral of this story: Even to hardcore Luke, at its best, the hobby finds reenactors looking good and behaving properly, but moreover, it is meaningful when they do a fantastic job by being willing to work together.

Fred Legum also told me a story about a meaningful moment he experienced with his friend during a World War I event. "We were at a trench raid at night-time," he recalls. "We had been running through the trenches on the German side and we were trying to get back. And he was out of pistol ammunition and I only had six rounds left. So we split up the rounds. I gave him three and I took three. And then we just stared at each other for a second and smiled and we said, 'That's what it's all about,' and we continued on our way."

I thought it odd at first that a hobby that so strongly emphasizes being macho, valorizes violence, and focuses on recreating war could also value so highly the rather touchy-feely aspects of human relations, like helping and sharing. But, to use Fred's words, "That's what it's all about." The small things, the details. These inconsequential, often anonymous, and even wordless exchanges establish real-life reputations and strengthen bonds. Could these also be the magic moments of the hobby?

During a World War II event, Dave Watkins experienced an unforgettable encounter. He was leading his German squad through the woods when they came upon some Americans who were "laying in this little copse of evergreen trees, obviously dead." Dave says that immediately he knew how to proceed, since "when that happens that's a good indication that they expect you to do something." Dave says he and his squad members "moved into the area, and we spoke only German with each other and we started to rifle them. We started to loot their pockets and pretend that we were taking their shoes off to replace our worn-out boots and looking at their dog tags and talking about their equipment." Dave remembers that "as we were doing it, they realized what we were doing and we could tell they really liked it. We kicked them over and rolled them over and went through their equipment. Of course we didn't take anything, but we feigned that we did. And I had some German candy bars in my bread bag and I put a couple candy bars in various people's pockets and then we moved off into another scenario and they didn't even know who we were. So it's kind of neat."

During their battles, reenactors capture, interrogate, punish, loot, rifle, and kill each other. They play out the violent acts of war, mimicking behavior associated with masculinity. Even if they are silent, as Dave and his men were, they use a kind of language learned after many years of consuming war stories. "Soldiers can talk to soldiers," as Morris says of the ways they communicate. "We . . . speak the language." In their attempt to appropriate war's language for themselves, reenactors clearly seek to connect with a tradition they've learned well. But with all their talk of wool shirts, facial hair, and the Russian Legion, their language is difficult to decipher, since its underlying meanings are masked by seemingly esoteric arguments. On the surface, it is a language for competitive, aggressive, and individualized male behavior. But underneath, it has a constructive effect. As they do things for one another's benefit, sharing, helping, and performing a host of other niceties, their war stories reveal another dimension to reenacting: it allows them to come together and help each other.

World War I German reenactors horsing around, private event, 1997

Perry Trent describes how this language functions. He had become angry at an event and was "burning." When his best friend, William Hoff, tried to calm Perry down and "put his arms on me and was just like, 'chill out,' I threw him up against the wall." The result of this act of violence? "We are the closest of closest of friends," Perry says. "We didn't lose our friendship because of that. It made us actually, I think, closer." Being able to "violate" each other, as Perry puts it, is a kind of glue that keeps their relationship together. Rather than create hard feelings or fear, it serves as a bond. "I've been able to violate him," Perry says, "and [he] still remains one of my greatest friends, and he's been able to violate me, and I think that's built the relationship."

The idea that a relationship can be built through violating each other goes a long way in explaining why reenactors use war as way to come together. What may appear contradictory—using conflict to unite—is in effect the ultimate constructive nature of the hobby, and it is a benefit that reenactors trace directly to historical reality. War creates "a big brotherhood that you never forget," as Sam Benevento claims. "I know I'm sounding touchy-feely here," Morris says, but "what has kept the veterans together? Not their love for the army or the combat—but the relationships."

Reenactors may wish to exercise control over war's representation in order to feel the joy and power derived from such an authoritative role. But they also try to find belonging and fulfillment. Their stress on consensus and cooperation, therefore, is not only about getting along and settling disputes, but also about making emotional connections with each other, about friendship.

Whether they describe themselves as solitary bookworms, who never joined teams or clubs, or as lifelong social butterflies, reenactors celebrate having found a community. In fact, nearly half of all reenactors cite camaraderie as one of their main interests in reenacting. "This is real camaraderie-building stuff," as one reenactor says. "I have more fun with the guys in my unit than anybody I know," another agrees. "We greet each other with hugs and warm handshakes and everybody is friends with each other." Even the often frustrated John Loggia concedes, "I just love those guys, and that camaraderie really develops."

Unexpectedly, I also found myself enjoying a kind of camaraderie I've seldom experienced, except in high school and college. In the real world, I lived the fairly secluded life of a graduate student and teacher, with its lonely hours of solitary work. It was wonderful to have a group of friends with whom I could retreat from the daily grind. And, oddly enough, even at times when I might have felt particularly vulnerable (when I was executed by those Germans or during the drive-by shooting, for instance), in a strange way, I always felt quite secure at events.

Reenactors seem to look upon the hobby as having the very kind of dual meanings that they also see imbedded in war: fighting and friendship, violence and bonds. Even Hank Lyle, who willingly admits to the sickness of pretending to slaughter one other, acknowledges reenacting's underlying worth: "If my brother falls down and takes a hit, I stop what I'm doing and go get him . . . because I'm not leaving him. And even though I can run off with the rest of the guys and he'll get up five minutes later, dead or alive, I'm going to stay there with him."

I came to see that in many respects reenactors use violence to work out a legacy of conflict. After all, reenactors have inherited the war story as a model for male behavior. Mark Sammons learned this model growing up with his veteran father: "I grew up in a house where there were all sorts of World War II mementos around. My dad put on his uniform once a week and went down to the reserve meetings . . . and it was just, that's what a man did, you know? To a little boy . . . this is the way it is."

But even growing up with the idea that "that's what a man did" didn't fully unlock the war story's secrets. They remained elusive, often guarded by the veterans themselves. And it is precisely such a difficulty in communicating that reenactors trace to historical reality. An authentic trait of a soldier is being unwilling to talk about his feelings related to his war experiences. You must be the stoic John Wayne type. "The keen sense of pain such memories bring back," as one reenactor says of the veterans' war experiences, "causes them to talk about the finer things of the war . . . wine, women, and song."

I came to believe that the reenactors' drive to find out for themselves what war was all about stems from an impulse to solve a riddle related not only to war, but, more important, to the feelings and experiences of men—especially their fathers. "I'm trying to kind of find out what he found out," Mark Sammons says of his father, while others admit that they grew up wondering what secrets their fathers kept to themselves. "My father was a great hero for me when I was young," one reenactor says. "He was a Navy pilot who saw years of service and I always wanted to know how he felt when in action." But like many others, this reenactor found his father unwilling to tell his war stories. Mark Sammons concurs, saying that his father "didn't always talk about the stuff" since "it was pretty upsetting." Another reenactor remembers watching a documentary with his veteran father at the age of fourteen. The two sat silently as some extremely gruesome footage was shown. "There was this scene when an American soldier rolls over a Japanese corpse . . . that was laying face down in the dirt," the reenactor remembers. "And when the Japanese soldier flops over, he is completely missing half of his chest, abdomen, and one arm. As the Japanese soldier's body comes to a stop, all of his intestines fall out. I look over at my father to see if he was still watching and asked, 'Was that what it was like, Dad?' He finished his martini and said, 'Yep' and left the room."

It's no wonder such minimalist encounters ignited a quest to find out for themselves. One reenactor, a therapist in real life, offers his theory concerning this impulse: "There may be a strong correlation between men who reenact and the disenfranchised [or] poor relationships they had with their fathers growing up."

Reenacting, then, may be as much about personal history as it is about history. Many reenactors admit that they had a hard time communicating with their fathers, and not just about war. "I had some problems with closeness with my dad," Mark Sammons says, while Sam Benevento remembers, "My dad and I fought and fought and fought when I was going through my teens and even my early twenties." But ironically, many also say that talking about reenacting can bring them together. "Now," Sam says about his father, "we sit around and we talk about this stuff and . . . I now understand where he was coming from."

From the reenactor who described with delight how his son had captured and shot him to the German reenactor who parades his twelve-year-old son in a Hitler Youth uniform at public events, the sheer number of father-son reenactors—and even many father-daughter reenactors—suggests that the hobby of-

Father and son World War II US reenactors, 1998

fers men a way to forge connections in their lives. And ironically, despite their violent trappings, these connections are safe. They're suitably macho, since they don't require openly grappling with communication issues or seeking the counsel of a therapist. Instead, they can be together—even if they aren't talking—while surrounded by the properly masculine symbols of uniforms, guns, and tanks. "A lot of men share sports with their fathers," as Patrick Hart says. "My father and I share reenacting and war movies. That's where we connect."

Sam Benevento also connects with his son through reenacting. In 1995, Sam started bringing his eleven-year-old son James to events. He explains how reenacting "gives us a common thing that we both like to do." He also admits, "I'm one of these people, I can't sit down and play a game with him—even when he was younger, I had a hard time doing that. But this stuff, we can do it together and he enjoys it and I enjoy it. And so it gives me an opportunity to spend time with him and then he gets an appreciation for what this is all about as far as what the veterans went through—what his grandfather went through."

As I considered the reenactors' dissatisfaction with their war encounters—whether through reading, watching movies, or talking to veterans—I realized that there was a broader context for their feeling disconnected not only from their fathers, but also from other men in general. Where else can they go to connect with other men? What other settings allow them to deal with issues related to their real lives without having to express their concerns or emotions directly? Only in the hobby can they act on a desire for respect or belonging, a need for control, or a wish to forget about daily life. Even in light of the hobby's frustrations and disappointments, a great majority of reenactors argue that the benefits of reenacting outweigh its liabilities since the bonds it affords are unavailable elsewhere. Mark Sammons doesn't know of any other place to find such connections, since in his life, as he says, "It's all kind of broken down to family and that's it." Fred Legum agrees: "I have a better level of camaraderie with the guys in the reenactment unit than I ever did in the Marine Corps." Larry Cohen was quite blunt about the hobby's value: "Reenacting fulfills something that's missing in people's lives," he told me. This is especially true, Larry believes, when a reenactor is feeling unsure of himself in the real world, especially with women. He described a reenactor friend: "When he was having like the worst life, when he wasn't like doing well with women or whatever, he would find himself going to reenactments every weekend." But the same was also true for himself. "When I was younger and in college and stuff, when I wasn't dating a girl, I'd be at every single reenactment." Patrick Hart also correlates an upsurge in his reenacting activity with a lack of real world commitments. "You did twenty events in 1996?" I asked incredulously. "At least," he responded. "My reenacting definitely goes up my times of being single." Others admit that pure dissatisfaction with their real lives compels them to the hobby: "Reenacting is an outlet for me," one reenactor says. "I have no social life so I use reenacting . . . as an escape from an arrogant and hostile society."

It's no wonder that imagining a world without reenacting is impossible for so many of them. When I asked why they might ever quit reenacting, almost 20 percent rejected the idea entirely ("won't ever quit") or saw the end of their lives as the only reason to stop ("death"). One reenactor laughed when we were catching up over the phone and I asked if he was still with Grossdeutschland. "Of course!" he responded. "Membership is for life." Mark Sammons also looks down the road to a future of reenacting, saying that he hopes to "give the last full measure of devotion to the hobby." "I kind of hope I kind of die out there," he told me. "I'd rather die out there than at the mall," he laughed. "They'd just drag you to the corner and go on with the sale."

Mark's comment reveals the divide some reenactors sense between their private world of reenacting and the real world of malls, relationships, and families. Many even express a desire to escape entirely into reenacting. "I wish I was retired," Richard Paoletti told me. "I'd spend more time on it." Meanwhile, Patrick Hart admits, "If I could make money at it, I'd be a full-time reenactor." Whether imagining a golden age of reenacting-filled retirement or a full-time job as a re-enactor, fantasies of unlimited participation abound. Paul Harding blissfully imagines what he calls "Reenactor World," a kind of Shangri-la for reenactors, where events would occur twenty-four hours a day. Morris Call has a similar dream: "I wanted to . . . get a large section of land. Then set up the National Re-enactment Center. . . . Of course it's a fantasy . . . but would that not be great?"

So great is the idea of somehow allowing the world of reenacting to be inte-grated with the real world that reenactors often try to bridge the two. When Ed Malthus asked his real children to write mail call letters to him, he experienced the joy of being missed and loved. "Oh man," he said after reading their letters at mail call during an event, "They wrote stuff like 'I love you, daddy. I miss you. When are you coming home?' I tell you, it damn choked me up out there. I thought I was gonna start bawling."

Another reenactor recalls "one of the best reenacting moments I have had in fifteen years of this hobby." During a World War I event, he and his brother were captured. "Things were looking very grim for our survival," he remembers. "We were taken to an underground bunker where a German officer was already interrogating a Brit sergeant. It turns out that the Brit also spoke German and the two were going at it in German very well. When it was my turn, the Ger-man spoke in broken English to me. He asked about my unit and so on, and then told me what would happen to me as a prisoner." But, as this reenactor explains, his captor didn't berate him or try to make him feel nervous. Instead, the two men had a rather sentimental conversation: "We talked about our wives and chil-dren and showed each other their pictures." This encounter didn't make this reenactor feel as though he was any closer to history. Instead, as he said, "It truly made me homesick for my wife and two kids."

Feeling homesick. Feeling relief. However much they mask their feelings and insist that there is a divide between the real world and reenacting, they escape from their daily routine only to try to fill the gaps of their real lives. In my own experiences, there were quite a few times at events when I had the satisfying sense of escape. At a World War I event, I sat in the Black Watch camp at dusk. A reenactor played his bagpipe as we sat around chatting and resting. As the wan-ing light played against the trees, I had a deep sense of being removed, if only for a while, from the real world. When I returned home, I felt as though I had truly been away; I was refreshed and energized as I returned to work.

Of course, I certainly knew that the world of reenacting wasn't for everyone; the joking and teasing would have been dismissed as juvenile and base by many of my outsider friends. But whenever I found myself back in the real world, at a

Reenactors pose after night combat, World War I private event, 1996

professional function for instance, I often felt so formal and way too serious. And I marveled at the divide that seemed to exist between the hobby and daily life.

But at the same time, given the more sinister side to reenacting—the exclusion, sexism, bigotry, and anger—I recognized that this divide was illusory and the hobby's sense of freedom from the real world was fleeting and dubious. The hobby may afford a temporary escape, but, to be sure, the reenactors' language doesn't always resolve the most important issues they confront. At the very least, it leaves much unsaid. At one point, Al Kingston and Ed Malthus excitedly told Ed's wife that they'd recently found out that a longtime 4th Armored member was a police officer in the same state as Al. "You never knew he was a cop, and how long have you known this guy?" Ed's wife asked in disbelief. "What do you guys talk about when you're together?" With a shrug, Ed turned the conversation over to me. I laughed as I tried to explain, "They tell stories. Tease each other." Ed's wife raised her eyebrows and snickered. "Okay," she said, "They don't really talk. I get it."

She was right. They didn't really talk about anything really serious, at least not as a group, anyway. Concerns about their jobs, relationships, money, health, any of the topics of conversation that might have been most important to them, seemed to be taboo in the larger setting of the group. I thought about all those nights sitting around the barracks and campfires. Telling stories. Telling jokes.

Each storyteller performed his piece in front of others, and then the next took over. They weren't really conversing. They were simply moving from one story-teller to the next. Just as in their scenarios, when they often communicate with-out speaking, there seemed to be so much unarticulated among them in a social setting. I saw how their own interactions dramatically differed, for example, from women's interactions of offering encouragement, asking questions, and show-ing support. That's not what a "man does," one reenactor told me. "You don't show your feelings." Or, as Luke once said, "The lives of great men are always kept private."

Although I knew that many reenactors had close, supportive relationships with each other privately, there were times when I saw how their general ten-dency to mask their feelings was harmful. Paul Harding found himself at a loss to explain why his closest friends had seemed to cut him out of the loop. "They said they didn't want to do Italian, so I sold all my stuff. Next thing I hear, they're putting on an Italian event. I'm like, thanks a lot guys."

"Why did they do that?" I asked.

"I have no idea."

I knew Paul was hurt by such a betrayal, but I also knew that he would do little to probe beneath its surface. This was only one reason I found myself won-dering about the personal value of reenacting.

For all the appearance of community and camaraderie, I knew that the hobby did not always offer reenactors a way to deal with problems in their lives. This point was underscored whenever I was singled out by a reenactor to talk privately about serious issues, which happened fairly often. Over the years, reenactors con-fided in me about very personal matters, a cheating girlfriend, a sense of fail-ure, a decision to marry, a divorce, a period of depression. But each implored me not to tell our mutual reenacting friends, reminding me that I was the only one who knew about these problems, and that's the way it should remain. The most intense of these encounters occurred when I visited one reenactor to watch the reenactor film favorite *Cross of Iron*. After the movie, our conversation turned to more real-life matters, and, to my shock, he broke down crying, admitting that he'd been terribly depressed, losing interest even in the hobby. He said he felt lost and broken, and that something was seriously wrong, but he couldn't say what. "Reenacting, all of this"—he indicated his reenacting paraphernalia strewn about his apartment—"is just a way to go back to childhood," he said, sobbing.

After this conversation, I was profoundly sad. For a group that so celebrates camaraderie and proudly claims to have "each other's lives in our hands," their bonds are sometimes clearly incapable of helping them face their lives. As I privately witnessed some of the real pain they feel, I knew that it wouldn't be allayed by the most well-conceived consensus, hardcore uniform, or proper behavior.

But I wasn't alone in making this assessment. "Most people that have started reenacting at a young age are all fucked up like myself," Hank Lyle told me after deciding to quit the hobby. "They spend their lives living in a fantasy while the real world passes them by. It has taken me a long time to realize this. I wish there was a recovery organization like AA for reenactors."

Hank was sick and tired of the arguments. He'd once said he thought reenactors were immature, ill equipped to handle real-life issues. As he faced the prospect of getting married and having to grow up, he wasn't sure if he could stay in a hobby that threatened to stunt his growth. Still, he struggled with the idea of quitting, especially since so many of his friends were reenactors. Like many others, Hank seemed torn by the hobby's contradictions.

Coming together to fight, reenactors often only barely mask the anger, aggression, and competitiveness that lies beneath their fake battles. Instead, they celebrate their capacity to achieve an unstated understanding among them. In one of the most dramatic war stories illustrating this point, Fred Legum recalled a World War I event at the old Shimpstown site. "We had some tentative fighting," Fred remembers. "And then—I don't even know how it all started—but somebody just started talking to the Germans and the Germans started talking to us and there was Christmas carols being sung." Fred continues with this amazing tale: "Before we knew it we were all up over the trenches exchanging chocolate and cigarettes. It was really neat. . . . We had soccer games out in no-man's-land. That was fun. . . . It got to be dark and some of the officers just started prodding us back. Basically, we really didn't fight anymore. When we left the trenches that was it for the day."

Nothing else need be said, I thought when Fred finished his story. "That was it for the day." I knew that history somehow lay beneath this story—an impromptu Christmas truce actually took place during World War I—but I also knew that the impulse to climb the fire step, walk into no-man's-land, and engage the enemy, singing, playing, and sharing did not stem from an attempt to repeat past victories or defeats. Nor was it derived from a desire to be a World War I soldier.

It was done in an effort to tell a war story to themselves and each other, using the language that is their legacy; it was an attempt to own history; to bridge the gaps of understanding that separates what a man does from who he is. But in this game, the players were seeking something that all the books, TV, movies and even some real-life relationships cannot offer. "The true secret of reenacting," one old-hand reenactor told me, "is not that it offers a hobby for history buffs but that it addresses the failure of modern society to provide social interaction on a human scale."

The reenactors' efforts to overcome such a failure, whether by building consensus or subordinating their egos, may not be successful in total. But the simple fact that they try to create a place for themselves based on martial masculine values, while at the same time trying to overcome the limitations of their martial tradition, suggests that these American men may be disappointed with their legacy and maybe even with the real world. Off they go to escape, to group together. There, they inhabit a place where tradition and history are respected, where consensus can be achieved, and where they are uniformed, unified, and understood. There, they may struggle for perfection, working toward the perfect illusion. But at the same time, even in their own created world, they may also experience disappointment, frustration, and failure. Ultimately, all of their efforts prove that "no hobby is an island," as Bill Lauter observes. History is not a remote place belonging to another time and another group of people. It is the foundation upon which real and common people write their own stories and live their real lives.

"Let's See What She's Writing"

The private battle has come to an early end, the result of sweltering temperatures, bonehead event hosts, and too many farbs. After an uproarious ice cream trip to a nearby town, all of us in uniform, riding in a couple of World War II jeeps, and receiving stares and questions from the locals, the 4th Armored returns to our secluded campsite to enjoy some downtime. Hal Zane and Phil Fussel trade jokes; Ted Shandy is busy in the woods exploding fake grenades; Luke drinks from a bottle of homemade wine; Warren Grace fiddles with his knapsack; I write in my notebook. Suddenly I notice Scott Friewald hovering over me.

"Hey," he calls out. "Let's see what she's writing!"

I look up in surprise. "No! You don't want to see."

"Aw, c'mon," Scott says.

"No. They're just notes," I insist.

"Hey, Margaret Mead had to go through this," Scott says.

Reluctantly, I hand over my notebook. Scott smiles and scans the page. He recites, thankfully—and incredibly—making up most of what he says: "Clearly, the reenactors' homoerotic tendencies are the most obvious of their characteristics." Everyone laughs.

"Homoerotic?" Phil Fussel says dryly. "Oh, she must be talking about you, Luke."

"Naw," Mike Sharp grimaces. "She's talking about you."

The familiar banter begins until someone points out that Ted has been conducting his experiments with the grenades, barefoot, in a clump of poison ivy.

"Medic!" someone yells.

Scott hands back my notebook. "See," he winks. "That wasn't so bad."

He was right. It could have been worse. After countless conversations and lots of time spent hanging out with reenactors, I never told them exactly what I would write. I did share some of my thoughts, but as far as standing up to proclaim my definitive take on the hobby, I was still working on it. I participated. I observed. I jotted down scenes and listened to them describe their interests, opinions, and experiences. But I didn't know if they were going to come across as weirdoes, commendable historians, or just people with a strange pastime. I also didn't really realize how much a part of them I had become. I may have started out studying them, but I ended up spending a lot of my time thinking about reenacting—which events to attend, the people I knew, what was happening in our lives. I was conducting research, to be sure, but unlike a scientist who puts on her white coat and steps into the lab, I conducted my work at all times, at all hours, while living my life.

I look at the page Scott had seen. Ironically, I had written "homoerotic tendencies," but only in quoting someone who had used it as a joke earlier. I was glad my ordeal was over. But a little while later, Mike Sharp returns to the subject of my notes. "Seriously," he says. "I mean no offense to you, Jenny, but any bad publicity and we're through."

After spending seven years hearing reenactors recite their public mantra and privately attack each other and argue over history, authenticity, farbs, and T-shirts, I felt a twinge of guilt knowing the publicity I would offer might not be entirely positive. "Thanks for being interested in us," one reenactor wrote on a photograph of himself he sent to me. "My sole concern," another stated, "is to have the hobby grow and be respected."

In the end, though, I did want to show them respect, not by minimizing their conflicts or avoiding touchy subjects, but by letting them tell their stories in their own voices. I wanted to represent them as I found them: complicated, contradictory, and human. Many reenactors said that they agreed with this approach. "You're not sugar-coating it are you?" John Loggia asked me as I was writing. Others echoed the same concern, urging me "to tell the whole story."

But as with any ethnography, the whole story cannot really be told. My experiences with reenactors constituted far more than a series of events and interviews. I'd seen and shared the difficulties and triumphs of their lives, just as they had shared mine. By the summer of 2003, as I finished the final revisions of this book, I was stunned to think that a decade had passed since I first met Luke Gardner, Tim Reed, Ray Sherman, and Perry Trent. "Ah, the old days," Dave Watkins commented in looking at some of the photographs for this book, "when I could hop over those sandbags like a kangaroo!"

In the decade that passed since I first came into the hobby, life seems to have changed relatively little for some reenactors. But for others, life has changed a great deal. Since I first met Tim Reed, he had gotten married, divorced, and moved across the country to embark on a new career. Luke got a job in a museum and moved with his new wife to the West Coast. Paul Harding became the proud father of a baby girl. Even without the help of an AA for reenactors, Hank Lyle gave up reenacting altogether after he and his wife moved to Canada for her new job there. His brother Wilson, now raising his own family, continues to reenact. Ray Sherman got married, changed careers, and still reenacts. Philip Moss moved with his wife to the Southwest. John Loggia, Bill Sharp, Hal Zane, William Gregory, Sam Benevento, Scott Friewald, and Phil Fussel, among others, continue to reenact. And Ben Sandler returned home after his four-year stint with the US Marines. During his service he'd written me from a ship steaming toward Okinawa: "I can't wait to do an event and use my experience as a Marine to be a better reenactor!"

As I was writing, I scaled back my participation, going only to an occasional event. Sometimes I went because I had a particular research-related question I needed to answer, but my interests had definitely shifted. Now I went just to see friends. In January 2000, I showed up at what was my sixth Bulge event in civilian clothes and spent the day at the flea market, chatting with Morris Call and the many others who eventually drifted past Morris's table of goods. Later in the evening, I went to the 4th Armored barracks to hang out. The 4th was still together then, and there they all were: Scott Friewald, Troy Carnes, the Sharp brothers, the old band of friends. As we talked and laughed that night, I remembered back to that first Bulge event when I arrived at the barracks. Of course, there was the same kind of joking and hilarity, but I also recognized another important element to our gathering that only the passage of time makes possible: catching up. One reenactor showed me photographs of his new baby; another told me about his new job; we recalled earlier events and happily made plans for others. Later that year, I went to the Frederick Air Show, but again I left my uniform behind and attended as a civilian. Despite all my earlier efforts to be part of the hobby and experience it from a reenactor's point of view, I now felt

The author with reenactors, the Bulge, 1999 (photographer unknown)

that I didn't need a uniform to be part of this world. One event in particular brought this point home to me.

In February 2000, Mike Sharp died of a heart attack. He was forty-two years old. Ed Malthus called me that grim morning with the news, his voice quaking, his shock and sorrow palpable. I spent that horrible day on the phone with several reenactors as we consoled each other and tried feebly to make sense of this tragedy. A few days later, Sam Benevento and I drove to the funeral. There, assembled in a beautiful stone church, were Mike's friends, colleagues, and family members. The members of the 4th Armored were there too, huddled together in several rows of pews. I was told that at the wake the night before, the line of mourners extended far outside the church door, as reenactors from various units, including Grossdeutschland, showed up to pay their respects.

During the service, people were invited to stand and say a few words. Ed Malthus stood. His whole face looked fallen. He started to speak, choking out a couple of sentences before being overwhelmed by his tears. Phil Fussel reached out and held Ed's arm. Ed was now unable to speak. He sat back down.

I, too, was crying. I was crying for Mike. I was crying for his family. But I was also crying because at that moment I saw how powerful our bonds were. These friends, a unit of men who look as if they would never let their emotions get the best of them, were now weeping like schoolkids. All that we seemed to share at that moment was the deep loss of a friend and the strength of our love for each other. I don't mean to be overly maudlin, but this experience underscored how close we all had become—all because of the hobby.

In many ways, that experience marked the symbolic end of my research. I had moved from stranger to friend, from outsider to insider. I had experienced the range of what the hobby offers: the combat, the hilarity, the anger, the magic moment, the exclusion, the camaraderie. But it was not until I moved to Chicago in 2001 that the real end of my participation came. I stopped reenacting purely because of the geographical distance that separated me from the friends and events I knew. But I also I knew that I would still be a part of this culture; after all, I was still in touch with people, and I hoped to go to an event some time in the future.

After I began writing this book, some reenactors started to ask with more intensity what my take was. "Why do I do this?" Perry Trent asked me. "You tell me," I laughed. But Perry didn't laugh. "I'm serious," he said emphatically.

And so it was that I began to offer some of my theories.

Reenacting war is not an effort to relive the past. It is a contemporary practice that hides its relationship to the present when someone dons an historical uniform. This is not to say that on some level reenactors do not want to understand what war was like or to represent it authentically. But on a deeper level, they seek a kind of gratification that stems from the power of creating and owning history themselves. After all, what could be more powerful—addictive even— than conducting a twilight trench raid against the Allies or storming the shores of Normandy? On an even more profound level, reenactors are looking for power, control, friendship, belonging, and approval. They may argue that they're escaping into history. They may try to maintain boundaries between reenacting and the real world. And they may use a language meaningful only within the hobby itself. But I would come to believe that, above all else, they use the hobby to fulfill the needs that go unmet in the lives of so many Americans.

From the outside, it might seem easy to dismiss reenacting as a subculture whose members have a bloodthirsty passion for war or to laugh at reenactors as extreme characters who have little connection with normal life in America. I, myself, had entered the hobby thinking that it was unusual. What was it about war and guns and uniforms that was so appealing to them? Initially, I thought I might find an explanation by exploring how disconnected from society reenactors must feel. But I found that the opposite was true.

The truth is that the hobby *is* a product of normal life in America. These are Americans. These are the people who process your credit card bills, fill your cavities, teach your kids, deliver your packages, and sometimes even perform in the movies you watch. They don't live on an island somewhere. They don't use alternative stores, roads, or schools. They're part of the real world in America. And, as American citizens not only have they created this hobby for themselves, but they have also chosen to be reenactors. Such a choice is made in response to what they confront in their lives on a daily basis. In the end, I would come to see that the hobby's own value system, its rules, successes, and failures, reflect the larger territory of American culture, and particularly, the concerns of men within it.

This is not to dismiss the importance of women in the hobby. Indeed, I believe that their needs and interests are similar to those of male reenactors. They, too, seek excitement, camaraderie, and approval, and they, too, are interested in war as history and as their own legacy. But given that the overwhelming majority of reenactors are male, making sense of the hobby partly relies on understanding issues related to masculinity.

Without question, the hobby is full of contradictions. But who would ever deny that American culture is rife with contradictions of its own? In general, we tend to view war as an acceptable subject for public entertainment, even, some would argue, as a legitimate tool of diplomacy, but we deride it as a personal pastime. We celebrate an increasingly powerful media that allows us access to the world and history, but we are highly critical of its limited or distorted perspective. We argue that we must be fair and work together, and yet we fight and inflict violence upon one another. We revere the individual while lamenting our extensive isolation and the loss of real, human connections. We are obsessed with achieving personal success, power, and dominance, but at the same time we pay homage to the ideals of democracy, community, and family. We value perfection—look younger, feel better—and yet we are constantly reminded of how insecure we feel in pursuing the impossibility of perfection. Finally, we argue that history is a public realm, not to be owned by anyone. And yet all of us, scholars, critics, the public, bitterly debate questions of historical representation and ownership.

It is within this context of contradictions that American men—and in particular, the white American men who make up the vast majority of reenactors—are being given specific messages concerning how to behave as men. Specifically, reenactors grapple with the contradictory meanings of one of the strongest and longest-enduring symbols of masculinity: the soldier. Each generation inherits its own ideas about war and masculinity, but reenactors are the most recent heirs to a lengthy tradition. Their avid interest in war partly stems from the fact that most of them never had their "own" real war to experience. And perhaps because of this, their fascination with war is intensified. Such a fascination only underscores how powerful and seductive the symbol of the soldier remains. Indeed, having grown up in a culture populated by the millions of veterans who became fathers, uncles, and grandfathers, reenactors were raised on war. They grew up in a culture—and a world—whose history has been marked by war after war, and they were reminded of those experiences continuously: they were given the means to experience the soldier's plight vicariously through an ever-growing archive of war representations.

But for these men born after World War II, the meaning of the soldier proves contradictory. What the reenactors reveal is that the soldier is a hybrid symbol, constituted partly from America's heroic ventures and tragic losses. He is the American patriot-hero of World War II who has been celebrated in countless books, memorials, and films, from the works of historian Stephen Ambrose to films like *Saving Private Ryan*. But especially after the Vietnam War and the subsequent reexamining of earlier wars, particularly World War I, the symbol of the soldier as well as the martial tradition in general, have also substantially changed, even weakened. War is no longer a grand story that can be described effectively with antiquated terms like "glory" and "gallantry." Instead, it is a newer kind of story told by historians like Paul Fussell, who attempt to dismantle the myths of a "Good War," or by TV shows like *MASH*, or through films like *Stalingrad* and *Full Metal Jacket*—all of which emphasize the inanity of killing, of war. In this respect, the soldier has simultaneously become another kind of symbol: he is a compassionate, common, antihero who suffers and endures; he is a forgotten victim, a pawn, canon fodder.

These shifting meanings of war and the soldier are reflected in the contradictions men are presented with in their daily lives. Being a man still means being strong, independent, and aggressive. Real men are reminded to take a stand against their enemies. They are unafraid to use violence. After all, they must defend tradition, and they should be proud of all the sacrifice and struggle that the common man has seen. Real men are America's heroes: Sergeant York. John Wayne. Audie Murphy. Rambo.

But at the same time, men are also reminded that because the world is different, they must change with it. They must be more accepting and open; they need to listen and negotiate; they should not be afraid to show emotion. They must pay more attention to the formerly feminine territory of personal concerns: appearance, youth, and fitness. And, as if this were not enough, they are reminded that they need to share history with others—women, black Americans, Asian Americans, for instance—whose new or rediscovered stories are just as important as their own.

With the tarnishing of the once-heroic war story, along with the continued celebration of war in American culture, reenactors look upon war as a story full of the very same contradictions they sense in their own lives. For them, the soldier has become their own contradiction; he is a hero and a pawn; a common, even universal figure whose identity and beliefs transcend national borders to exist somewhere in the gray areas. He is their legacy; he is the reenactors themselves.

In trying to resolve some of the issues related to their real lives and find out just how they should behave like men, reenactors have created a particular way to come together with other men in a safe, fun, and masculine environment that reinforces many traditional male characteristics: aggressiveness, competitiveness, strength, and stoicism. In the hobby, they can compete, act out their frustrations, and wield power. But they can also do other things not necessarily associated with traditional male behavior: they can learn how to get along and arbitrate; they can help each other; and they can create close relationships with others. They can also transcend the economic constraints of the real world and forge friendships that are not necessarily based on class.

Of course, they have also created their own set of contradictions. As they try to understand how they should act, what history means, and who they are, they seek legitimacy through a hobby that many outsiders see as marginal and even threatening. They rail against an ignorant public while trying to serve that same public and gain its recognition. They champion the common soldier as a hero, but they view him as a victim. They argue that war is hell and hope never to experience it, but they use war as a source of enjoyment. They pledge allegiance to historical evidence, but they often reject evidence as false or fundamentally alter it by crafting their own versions of authenticity. They reject the media as inaccurate, but they attempt to create their own mediated experiences. They identify with the common people of history, but they are entirely concerned with being themselves. Finally, they compete with each other over who is best or most legitimate, while at the same time seeking cooperation and consensus.

The fact that reenactors feel compelled to find fulfillment through things such as feigned violence is not altogether good. The attitudes some show toward women, nonwhite ethnic groups, and outsiders, as well as their drive to claim power over others, are certainly not positive. Further, their anger, disappointment, and sometimes immature ways of dealing with conflicts among themselves underscores how many of them are simply unable to cope with some of the social difficulties they face. But at the same time, the things that made me so uncomfortable in the hobby were often the very issues many of them seek to address through reenacting. Yet they address them in a ways that I never would have imagined. If they feel beaten down by real-life pressures or that they cannot achieve success or exercise authority, if they feel lonely or isolated, angry, or longing for friends, they can find a place in the hobby. And even if they do feel satisfied with their real lives, they can leave their daily pressures behind and feel excitement and fulfillment. Once in the hobby, they can assert that social rules no longer apply, since they are now disconnected from the real world. And the constraints of daily life are seemingly lifted as they play out their dramatic illusions, experiencing camaraderie, accomplishment, or the high of a magic moment. Whenever any real-world issues crop up, such as those concerning money, appearance, gender, or race, they can erect the defense of authenticity, arguing that theirs is an objective system designed solely for the purpose of imposing order on their game. But of course, their system only replicates many of the problems they attempt to flee. Even away from the real world, a reenactor can still feel terribly insecure; friends can betray each other; anger can destroy relationships.

In the end, though, I thought, all of this is worth it to reenactors. After all, the real world seems to offer few healthy escapes and opportunities to feel release. And in particular, for those reenactors who oppose women in their midst, they seem to feel that there are few places left that are "only" for men, few places where they can feel powerful and connected, and where they feel that they are doing more with their lives than, to use one reenactor's phrase, "driving a crooked nail."

As I somewhat cautiously presented a few of these ideas, reenactors reacted differently. Some listened politely, and said little in response. Others reacted more intensely. Over Chinese food, John Loggia nodded his head enthusiastically, "It is a social phenomenon!" he declared. And, after reading several chapters of this book, Luke returned from an event saying he was changed. "Now that's all I can see. Guys trying to own history."

When we talked about the book coming out, they were enthusiastic. "You can use that picture of me in my wife's underwear," Scott Friewald joked. "Just remember to give me proper credit." Others wanted me to use their real names. "I'm not ashamed of anything I said," John Ostroski told me. "Please feel free to use my real name. In fact," he urged, "I want you to use it."

I shouldn't have been surprised by their enthusiasm. After all, "reenacting is history," one reenactor proudly claims. "I mean, a hundred years from now, they're going to be saying, who were those nuts who were doing this in this weird part of American history?" I knew that they desired the recognition that a place within history's pages affords, but after Sam Benevento waxed poetic on the book's implications, saying that he hoped it would explain the hobby to outsiders and maybe even make it more accepted, I tried to temper his excitement. "It's not a cure for cancer," I reminded him.

"But for us," he insisted, "it kind of is."

I knew that some reenactors hoped this book would help them face their opposition. I also thought they hoped that they would finally be able to explain their hobby more comprehensively to outsiders, especially to their wives or girlfriends. But I also knew that outsiders might never be completely sold on reenacting. In returning to the question of the proper way to represent war, I found myself asking: What is it that people wish to achieve by opposing reenacting? To oppose war itself? Or to oppose the use of war as entertainment?

I came to believe that one reason people oppose the hobby lies in the fact that its very existence reveals something that some may find threatening: as a culture, we are not only largely shaped but also fascinated by war—or, more broadly, violence. However much we grandstand and take a position on our own ammo box to preach against violence, we promote, package, and profit from war. We fill our own heads with war stories; and to some degree or another, all of us experience it vicariously. "War is Hell," proclaimed an advertisement for the TV series *War and Civilization*. "So why do we keep fighting?"

Answering such a question might be achieved by shifting the debate. Rather than ask why we keep fighting or whether reenacting is a proper way to represent war, we may do better to ask about what contemporary needs our fascination with war fulfills. In particular, why are so many men so obsessed with it? They read about it, write about it, make movies about it, play games that focus on it, debate it in many arenas, including the media and the academy, and, of course, many enlist to serve in the military. Clearly, reenactors are not the first group of men to find something in war that attracts them. And it is not particularly shocking that they should take that attraction "one step further," as one reenactor says.

We might also ask ourselves whether the whole question of propriety related to uses of history stems from a similar desire to exercise control over the past and "own" it for ourselves. In fact, just as I came to see that using war as a pastime is not the sole territory of the hobby, I also came to see the underlying patterns of the reenactors' debates apparent in wider society in general. From authors to academics, social critics to members of the public at large, all of us engage in debates over what constitutes authenticity in both historical representations and contemporary knowledge. Who should be included in a representation of history? What is to be considered true? What is to be dismissed as illegitimate?

You don't need to look hard to see that debates over historical interpretations are everywhere; from the meanings of the Holocaust and the Vietnam War to the legacy of slavery and Thomas Jefferson, we constantly struggle to work out what's true. We argue over portrayals of history in movies—from *Birth of a Nation* to *JFK*—and we debate the proper uses of historical symbols, most notably the Confederate flag and representations of Native Americans.

These are not insignificant debates, since by determining the nature of who owns the truth, we shape contemporary notions of who we are today. And those who wield the power to provide answers to historical questions exert their own kind of "ownership" over history. Certainly, then, reenactors are not alone in wanting to judge historical authenticity and thereby claim control over history themselves. In fact, I couldn't help but notice how even some outsiders to the hobby, most notably male critics, get caught up in the reenactors' own debate. Even as they judge reenacting to be mere silliness, they are attracted to the spectacle, vying for a chance to have their say. Of course, they are careful to call attention to the divide that separates themselves from reenactors, but they aren't shy in asserting their authority and legitimating their own claim to the best kind of history (usually by comparing a reenacted version of history to what, they assert, really happened). In an essay on a 1998 Gettysburg reenactment, critic Christopher Hitchens calls himself an "intruder" in this "stubborn American culture," but has no qualms, after a single day before the hobby's public face, to offer definitive insight: "Those who can't forgive the past are condemned, not without pathos, to reenact it."

But others seem to understand the martial lure. Even Tony Horwitz, whose book *Confederates in the Attic* so angered some reenactors, admits to this draw: "As a child, the Civil War had formed a vivid fantasy world I could enter with the stroke of a paintbrush, or by clutching a stick and imagining it a musket. In part, my journey had been an attempt to rediscover that boyhood rapture. But my childhood fantasy kept colliding with adult reality—the reality of my dulled adult imagination and of the discomfiting adult questions that remembrance kept raising."

But the dichotomy between childhood "rapture" and adult "reality" need not be so starkly drawn. For, as the reenactors show, even for people without first-hand experience, war—or history for that matter—exercises more complicated and enduring effects. For reenactors, the power that war exercised in their childhood imaginations never waned. But as adults they found that war was not a subject to be resolved through "forgiveness." It was not to be relegated to a fantasy world. And it was surely not to be handed over to the official or popular realm. Instead, war was a subject to be personally appropriated, since reenactors feel their connection to its legacy so acutely.

For my own part, I find criticism of the hobby to be understandable, but pointless. After all, what does it mean to forgive the past? If reenactors made one point clear to me, it is that history was not fair to many who lived through it, nor is it fair to those who struggle with its legacies. As long as Hollywood rakes in money selling tickets to war movies and American culture celebrates war as an heroic formative epoch in its history, the responsibility for the hobby, as it were, lies everywhere.

I also came to see that simply condemning the unusual isn't truly constructive. Any kind of apparently marginal behavior that people engage in always has its own logic—from the behavior of fanatic sports fans with painted faces to the behavior of those who pay thousands of dollars to climb Mount Everest. We need not necessarily advocate such behavior by studying it, but perhaps we can move closer to understanding it, and therefore, learn something about ourselves.

As a scholar whose interest lies in the ways Americans have experienced and represented war, the hobby taught me many things. Even though I knew that perceptions of war have changed over the course of the twentieth century, I came to see that the practice of categorizing each generation's response to its own particular war might need to be reconsidered. As the reenactors prove, the meanings of war don't change in a clean, linear fashion from one postwar era to the next. Instead, meanings become intertwined; they shift and are reconstituted by several different generations at once.

I also knew that war has long exercised power over many lives. But the hobby allowed me to see just how extensive that power is. A war's reverberations are felt not only by those who personally experience it. They also echo through the lives of the children, grandchildren, and great-grandchildren of soldiers and victims alike, playing out even in the lives of those who only know war through all its many different depictions: novels, movies, photographs, games, reenacting.

In the end, I found myself somewhat saddened to think that the war story will most likely continue to be both represented and communicated across numerous generations. A photograph taken in the 1930s at a Confederate veterans' home shows more than a Boy Scout posing with ninety-year-old veterans. It illustrates the human connection among generations—men and boys—bonded by war. Almost half a century and several wars later, a reenactor would strike a sim-

Civil War veterans and Boy Scout, 1930s (courtesy Beauvoir, Jefferson Davis Home and Presidential Library)

ilar pose at the side of a World War I veteran. The Confederate veterans, the Boy Scout, the reenactor, and the ninety-five-year-old veteran of the Great War represent an abbreviated human timeline spanning more than a century.

As for their own part in this timeline, some reenactors will perpetuate war's tragic components—violence and prejudice—as well as try to defend a largely white, male image of history. But many also sow the seeds of a new tradition. Their need and desire for consensus as well as their stress on working together suggests that they wish to alter their legacy to some degree. In the end, I felt that overcoming conflict was perhaps their strongest desire—a desire that contradicts the greater society that enshrines the ideals of peace and diplomacy but still carries on its own tradition of war. Many reenactors are well aware of this contradiction. "As much as we recreate war and I think at some point we glorify it," Scott Friewald says, "you have to understand it's a terrible thing." Patrick Hart agrees, saying, "I would be happy if we had nothing to reenact. You know?" But he also believes that war is a bleak reality of humankind. "I'd love to see that. The world community," he told me. But "we can't get beyond our state borders at this point. But I'd love to see that. Man, a society of man. It won't happen in my lifetime."

Perhaps it is partly because reenactors do not feel capable of breaking with their martial tradition—a tradition that has been celebrated, represented, and replicated for decades, even centuries—that they instead turn their attention away from the big picture and focus on what they can control: the details. Through the hobby, they can at least imagine what will happen in their lifetime: their own continued quest "to work toward it," to pursue perfection, and to create their own legacies in the form of reproductions, mock documentaries, and authentic-looking images. Mark Sammons, who had struggled so hard with the question of why he reenacts, told me about the time he served as a reenactor-extra in the Civil War movie *Glory* (1989).

"Everything kind of converged at this one point, and there I am," Mark said. "And if I die, or when I die, something like that, I don't know, I don't have any kids and I'm not married, it's just like well, they made this movie, they used thousands of reenactors, and there I am in that role and that's what I do."

"It's your legacy?" I asked.

"Yeah," he responded after a moment. "That's sort of what I've done."

Marking their lives with their efforts, reenactors show just how vital history is. It is a series of stories that serve as the foundation from which people construct their identities. At the beginning of a new millennium, the past proves contemporary; it is with all of us, like those soldier-ghosts I sensed so long ago in the German barracks. The shiver that ran up my spine returns as I consider the lengths to which people go to give meaning to their lives. Neither governed entirely by the past nor trying to forge a completely new story, we all struggle somewhere in the gray area, a place that exists somewhere between memory and history, past and present. Maybe this was the place Alain Benson was trying to describe when he said, "We're here, we're there, this is it."

Glossary

advanced kit Items for an impression beyond those of a basic kit. Such items may include, for example, tents or rain ponchos.

After-Action Report (AAR) A military term for a written account of a battle or combat experience. Reenactors publish AARs in newsletters and post them on Web pages or email newsgroups.

age farb A reenactor who is well above the age of an average soldier. Some believe that reenactors should do chaplain, medical personnel, partisan, civilian, or correspondent impressions once they reach an age that precludes them from doing authentic infantry impressions.

airbornism A reenactor pathology that causes reenactors to portray only elite impressions such as paratroopers, pilots, or high-ranking officers.

Alter Hase A German term that literally means "old rabbit," but also means "old hand." Reenactors use the term to describe an experienced reenactor who helps new members put their impressions together and often helps them at their first events, teaching them the rules and guiding them through combat.

ammo inspection The organized, and often required, checking of all reenactors' blanks before the start of an event.

anachronism Any item that would not have existed in the period portrayed. Also known as a "non-period" item.

anachronistic farb A reenactor who uses, carries, or wears any item anachronistic to the period portrayed.

armored event Any reenactment in which tanks or other armored vehicles are present.

asshole magnet A tank, so called because it attracts reenactors who, for reasons of prestige, want to be near it during combat.

atypical farb A reenactor who chooses not to portray a common soldier, but an elite one, such as a high-ranking officer or a highly decorated soldier. (See Airbornism.) This category also includes freelancers who participate in events without belonging to a unit, such as the inevitable "downed pilot."

barracks event Event held on a site with a barracks. Reenactors stay overnight in the barracks and may do what is known as a "barracks impression," meaning that they set up their living quarters in period style.

basic kit The fundamental, often required, items of a reenactor's impression, such as a uniform and rifle.

basic kit requirement Standard set by an individual unit or, sometimes an event host, that requires reenactors to have certain basic items to complete their impressions. Usually includes type of uniform, weapon, and certain pieces of equipment.

battlefield pickup A weapon used by a reenactor that would not have been issued to a member of the unit being portrayed (for example, a Russian weapon carried by a German reenactor). A reenactor often justifies using a "foreign" firearm by arguing that he or she simply found it on the battlefield or took it from a dead or captured enemy. Some units, such as Grossdeutschland, specifically forbid the use of such pickups.

blank adapting Process by which firearms are converted to fire blanks in reenactments through the installation of a blank adapter, a metal device attached to a rifle muzzle.

The Bulge Annual event held at Fort Indiantown Gap, Pennsylvania, reenacting the 1944 Battle of the Bulge, a critical engagement in the European Theater. Also known as "FIG," "The Bulge Event," "The Bulge," or "The Gap."

cadre Group of unit members who serve under a unit commander as noncommissioned officers (NCOs).

call a hit To yell at your target that he or she has been shot or is dead.

camp followers Term used widely in the Civil War hobby to refer to women and children reenactors.

cap To touch hand to helmet to indicate to another reenactor that you have hit him or her.

capper A reenactor who is primarily interested in firing his or her weapon in an event. Also known as "powder burner" or "cowboy."

cheater A reenactor who ignores the rules of engagement by, for instance, "faking death in order to gain tactical advantage" or attacking units in out of bounds areas (Great War Association, "Rules of Engagement," October 1997).

clusterfuck Disorganized tactical event in which reenactors group together in nonperiod fashion, usually following the sound of the guns.

collection A reenactor's personal accumulation of militaria. The term often refers to a group of items that are high in value or quality and are not used in reenactments but may be used in static displays.

collector-grade Term referring to militaria in excellent condition. Also known as "collectible."

collector-reenactor A reenactor who is primarily a collector of militaria.

comfort lover A reenactor who generally wishes to avoid hardships at events such as long marches, exposure to inclement weather, and ditch digging. Also known as "fair weather reenactor."

conversion Any nonperiod item, usually a uniform, that has been altered to appear as if it were a period item. Converted items are usually postwar pieces that are similar to wartime pieces.

corpsman Term used during simulated combat to indicate a real injury or emergency and to call for medical assistance.

cowboy A reenactor who delights solely in "trigger time" to the detriment of authenticity or discipline. Also known as "capper," "yahoo," or "powder burner."

Dietz reenactor A new reenactor, also known as "newbie" or "recruit." The term derives from a character, Private Dietz, in Sam Peckinpah's 1977 film *Cross of Iron,* a study of German soldiers on the Russian Front in World War II.

do Verb indicating a reenactor's impression or period reenacted; for example, "I do German" or "I do World War I."

downed pilot A reenactor who does a pilot impression, justifying his lack of aircraft by saying that he had been shot down.

downtime In a private event, refers to the time before or after combat when reenactors are relaxing, usually not concerned with acting authentically. In a public event, refers to time away from spectators.

drive-by A method of inflicting casualties in an event while driving by in a vehicle.

early war/late war Terms reenactors use to distinguish the period of a given war being portrayed. In World War II reenacting, for instance, "late war" refers to 1944–45.

elitist A reenactor who portrays only "elite" impressions, such as high-ranking officers, paratroopers, or pilots. Such a reenactor is said to suffer from "airbornism." Also known as "atypical farb," "poseur" or "vain reenactor." (See "Flyboy.")

encampment A military term for a bivouac or camp. For reenactors, this refers to an outdoor assembly of reenactor camps where reenactors set up static displays of militaria and perform for and instruct members of the public.

event Any private or public gathering of reenactors for a tactical battle or display. An older term, no longer widely used, is "show."

event host Individual reenactor, unit, or organization that sponsors, insures, and usually profits from an event.

expert A reenactor who is widely considered exceptionally knowledgeable.

fantasy farb A reenactor who concocts some kind of fantastic story to legitimate use of an inauthentic item, particularly in the case of weapons.

farb A bad, inauthentic reenactor. Reenactors are judged by others as bad reenactors for various reasons, including inauthentic impressions, tactics, or behavior; poor attitude; and "improper" commitment to the hobby. The term is highly subjective, and one reenactor's authentic is often another's farb. The etymological origin of this term is something of a mystery, and many stories concerning its origin circulate. Two of the most often told are, first, that it comes from the German word for color, *Farbe,* and thus refers to the wearing of uniforms that are incorrect in hue; and second, the more widely accepted, that it is a truncation of the phrase, "far be it for me to criticize your impression" or "far be it from reality." Reenactors generally agree that the term was coined in the early days of Civil War reenacting. Also used as an adjective, "farby," referring to a reenactor's inauthentic impression, attitude, or behavior.

farbarella Derogatory term for a female reenactor who portrays a male soldier.

farbfest Any event at which a large number of farbs are present.

farbolio 1. A state of complete inauthenticity. Also known as "farbicity." 2. A reenactor in violation of one or more categories of authenticity. Such a reenactor reaches "the pinnacle of not even coming close to looking authentic." Also known as "Atomic farb."

Fat Boy Tax (FBT) The extra amount a reenactor must pay to purchase large-size reproduction uniforms.

fat farb An overweight reenactor. Also known as "Farbzilla."

field A military term referring to the site away from the comforts of civilization where soldiers and reenactors live and fight—as in "being in the field." Reenactors usually use the term to indicate being at a private event. Also used as a verb, "to field": "we fielded twenty of our members at the last event."

field event Event that does not provide use of barracks (see "barrack events") but instead requires reenactors to sleep outdoors in camps, bunkers, tents, trenches—or sometimes in their cars or nearby motels.

field impression A reenactor's portrayal of a soldier in combat.

first person Form of portrayal in which a reenactor acts and talks as if he or she were living in the period portrayed.

flea market Gathering of reenactors and dealers selling militaria at an event.

flyboy A reenactor who does only (or mostly) Luftwaffe, Army Air Corps, or Air Force impressions.

free-flowing Term describing unscripted action in an event in which units act according to their own choices and knowledge of period tactics.

freelance To participate in an event without being part of a unit.

freelancer Reenactor who does not belong to an established unit.

gapper Reenactor who attends large events only, such as "The Gap" (Bulge) event.

gate fee Participation fee charged by event hosts to individual reenactors. Also known as "event fee."

G-8 Governing body of elected officers of the Great War Association (formerly known as the G-7).

ghost A "dead" reenactor who resurrects himself or herself in combat without waiting an appropriate length of time.

hardcore Term derived from Civil War reenacting, referring to reenactors who are intensely focused on authenticity, put a lot of effort into the hobby, and are generally "serious." Reenacting events with strict authenticity standards are also referred to as "hardcore."

HBT Herringbone twill, a type of uniform made of cotton.

head farb A reenactor who wears his or her hair in an inappropriate way or wears nonperiod glasses. Reenactors commonly complain most about such violations.

hero A reenactor who acts heroically in combat, putting him or herself in dangerous situations that real soldiers would have avoided. Also known as "Audie Murphy" or "John Wayne."

historian A reenactor considered highly knowledgeable about history.

hobby A synonym for reenacting. Can also be used to refer to a particular period: "the World War I hobby."

Hollywood death A dramatically performed death in an event.

Hollywood mentality An inaccurate perception of war, usually presented in popular movies. Generally refers to renditions of war that are political in nature, melodramatic, or highly simplistic, with clear-cut heroes and enemies.

Hollywood rifle A gun a reenactor converts to fire blanks without using the telltale blank adaptor. The method of conversion is invisible to the naked eye.

honor system Method by which reenactors must choose to "die" in events without being told or ordered to do so.

impression A reenactor's portrayal of a soldier (or of any period military personnel, civilian, or partisan), which includes, uniform, equipment, personal items, behavior, and attitude.

karma A reenactor's period or authentic state of mind. Also known as "mindset." Also used to refer to the general authentic ambiance of an event.

Kevlar reenactor A reenactor who will not die no matter how many times he or she is hit. The term derives from the material, Kevlar, used to make military helmets. Also known as "Teflon reenactor."

kit A rather antiquated military term referring to a soldier's uniform as well as equipment worn or carried on his or her person. Also used as a verb, to "kit out," or to dress in one's period impression.

lazy farb A reenactor who is "farb-sighted": unwilling to upgrade or invest in his or her impression, instead settling on cheap, poorly reproduced, or incorrect equipment or uniforms despite the fact that he or she knows better. Also known as "nonprogressive reenactor."

living historian Reenactor who tries to re-create all aspects of the war experience with special emphasis on activities other than combat, such as cooking, conducting mail call, and various other camp activities.

living history Term coined by Carl Becker in the 1930s. The term is used today to describe a form of historical interpretation that involves dressing in period clothing and performing historical scenes or lifestyles or as historical characters. Reenactors use it to describe period activities other than combat that represent a soldier's experience, such as mail call. Also refers to the method through which they interpret war at public events.

lone wolf A reenactor who portrays a solo impression, such as a sniper or downed pilot.

magic moment The elusive pinnacle of the hobby, when a reenactor experiences a completely "authentic" moment while reenacting. Often described as involving the sensation of time travel.

mercenary reenactor A reenactor who conforms too much to the demands of outsiders such as event hosts. Often refers to reenactors who work as film extras without pay.

militaria Military items, including equipment, firearms, uniforms, and personal items.

mindset An "authentic" state of mind that a reenactor tries to assume in seeking a magic moment in an event. (See "Karma.")

minty Variation on the adjective "mint," used to describe militaria items in near-perfect or perfect condition.

newbie A novice reenactor. Also known as "recruit" or "Dietz reenactor."

nonperiod Any item that would not have existed in the time portrayed. Also known as "anachronism."

off the rack A reenactor who is small or slender enough to fit into period uniforms.

old hand An experienced reenactor. Also known as "veteran reenactor" or *Alter Hase.*

paintballer A participant in the competitive game of "paintball," in which players shoot at each other with guns loaded with color paint. Reenactors use this term as a derogatory label for a reenactor who is not serious or authentic, but simply wants to run around and fight.

partier A reenactor who prefers the drinking/socializing part of an event.

pathological reenactor A reenactor who is said to live in an alternate reality and cannot separate an impression from his or her real-life identity.

period Term describing the time reenactors portray, for example, "World War II period." Also refers to the historical accuracy or chronological derivation of an item, such as a "period" stove.

persona A reenactor's period character, which includes elements of personal life history.

postwar Term usually describing an item made and used in the period following the war being reenacted, such as a "postwar" helmet. The use of postwar gear, which often looks quite similar to period gear, is generally considered farby.

POV Privately owned vehicle.

powder burner Reenactor primarily interested in firing a lot of blanks at events. Also known as "capper," "yahoo," or "cowboy."

power lover A reenactor, typically an officer, who goes too far in attempting to exert authority.

prewar Term usually describing an item made and used during the period prior to the war being reenacted, such as a "prewar" tunic.

primary impression The impression that a reenactor does most often, and is usually his or her favorite.

public General term reenactors use to refer to those outside the hobby, especially people who attend public events. Also known as "spectators," "visitors," "tourists," or "touronz."

public event Any event in which members of the public are present. Such events include air shows, mock battles, parades, encampments, historical timelines, and commemorations.

reckless A reenactor who is unsafe for a number of reasons, such as the improper use of a weapon or vehicle or drunkenness.

recruit A new reenactor. Also known as "newbie" or "Dietz reenactor."

reenactor grade Term describing items or equipment that are less than minty and thus may be used in the field "consumptively" without concern for damage.

reenactor organization A group of reenactors or reenacting units that sponsor events, such as the World War II Historical Preservation Group (W2HPG) and the World War II Historical Reenactment Society (HRS). These organizations often have nonprofit status and are run by an elected body of officers. They usually charge membership fees and issue reenacting rules and standards.

referee A reenactor who serves to call hits during an event.

registered independent A GWA reenactor who does not belong to a unit but receives permission to "freelance."

repro Any militaria item that is not period but is a reproduction. Also known as "repop."

resurrect To bring oneself back to life after being killed in a reenactment.

Rev War Revolutionary War reenacting.

scenario Portion of an event that constitutes a period of self-contained action. The term can refer to a battle, an attack, or an ambush, as well as to a smaller action such as a prisoner interrogation.

script Device used to plan a course of action in a reenactment, primarily used to orchestrate fighting in public events.

secondary impression Impression a reenactor does less frequently than his or her primary impression.

Silly War Term reenactors use to describe the American Civil War reenacting hobby.

Soldbuch German term for a soldier's paybook. Also used as identification.

starter impression A reenactor's first impression, usually consisting of only the most basic elements of a soldier's kit.

static display Form of historical presentation that reenactors use in public events to display militaria and represent camp life.

Stitch Nazi Term used in both praise and derision to describe a reenactor who is obsessed with the authenticity of the smallest details of his or her own as well as others' impressions. The term does not necessarily refer to a German reenactor, but to any reenactor who is intent on achieving complete authenticity. Often such a reenactor is not shy in publicly correcting or berating others for lapses in authenticity. Such a reenactor tries, as one reenactor joked, to be authentic down to his or her "period belly button lint." Incidentally, the term was coined by reenactors long before the *Seinfeld* episode featuring the infamous "Soup Nazi."

sutler A reenactor who sells (and often makes) militaria through a store, Web page, catalogue, and/or flea market; any dealer who sells material to reenactors.

tactical A private event; also used to refer to the portion of an event that is devoted to combat: "tactical battle." A somewhat older term for a tactical reenactment is "show."

take a hit To respond to another reenactor's fire during combat by falling and, if not dying, at least feigning injury.

ten-foot farb A reenactor who advocates looking authentic or passable from a distance, but upon closer inspection is revealed to have a number of farby elements.

ten-foot rule Authenticity standard by which reenactors are deemed authentic if they appear so from ten feet away.

touronz Tourists, satirically. Used to refer to visitors at public events.

trench party A gathering of World War I reenactors at the Newville site for work on trench sectors. Such a gathering usually takes place over a weekend when the site is open to any units that wish to improve their trench sectors, build bunkers, and the like.

trench pass Card handed out to all registered GWA members before the start of an event, which must be shown to officials on demand.

trigger time Combat portion of an event in which reenactors fire blanks.

undisciplined A reenactor who does not follow orders.

unit Reenactor's primary method of organization.

unit impression Collective impression of reenactors formed into a unit modeled after an actual, historical military unit. Also refers to the general reputation or image of a reenactor unit.

vain reenactor A reenactor who prefers to parade around in uniform and pose for pictures.

vehicle people Participants in reenactments whose primary interest lies in period military vehicles, including both the owners of such vehicles and their crews. Also known as "jeep jerks."

walking-out impression Noncombat or dress uniform intended for wearing at a public display or at period dinners and dances.

wound card Card handed out to a reenactor before combat, describing the type and nature of injury, including death, that he or she must suffer in the impending scenario.

yahoo A reenactor primarily interested in the combat portion of an event but who is not historically minded. Also known as "powder burner," "capper," or "cowboy." The most extreme yahoos are marginalized (and marginal) because of extreme politics or dangerous behavior—or simply because they are "weird."

Zeltbahn A German tent.

Introduction: "Those Guys Need Therapy"

xiii   [As early as 1822 . . . troops at Lexington.] Edward T. Linenthal, *Sacred Ground: Americans and Their Battlefields* (Urbana: University of Illinois Press, 1991), 13.

[in 1902 . . . Sheridan, Wyoming] Ibid, 134.

xiv   [twentieth-century war . . . and Vietnamese troops, for example.] Throughout this book I use the word "Russian" to refer to both World War I and World War II impressions. Although technically a World War II soldier from the USSR should be known as a Soviet soldier, most reenactors use "Russian" when referring to soldiers of both wars.

xv   [what one reenactor calls its "public face."] Eric Sanders, "Public versus private events," email posted to the subscribers of a listserv for World War II reenactors, hereafter referred to as WWII Newsgroup, 8 April 1996.

xvi   ["Americans . . . and commemorate the past."] G. Kurt Piehler, *Remembering War the American Way* (Washington, DC: Smithsonian Institution Press, 1995), 9.

["How do you tell . . . ethical problems."] Tobias Wolff, *In Pharaoh's Army: Memories of the Lost War* (New York: Random House, 1994), 207.

["are nothing but mere . . . and trivialized past."] Kevin Walsh, *The Representation of the Past: Museums and Heritage in the Postmodern World* (London: Routledge, 1992), 102–103.

["battle reenactments are . . . war's terrible effects."] Dwight F. Rettie, *Our National Park System: Caring for America's Greatest Natural and Historic Treasures* (Urbana: University of Illinois Press, 1995), 60.

xvii   ["We do somewhat trivialize . . . whizzing by you."] Greg Grosshans, interview with the author, March 1996. Unless otherwise noted, most quotes attributed to reenactors by name within the text are drawn from my interviews with them. Other quotes from unnamed reenactors without specific citations are drawn from their open-ended, written responses to questions on my reenacting questionnaire.

Although some reenactors I talked with and interviewed said that they did not mind if I used their real names, others asked that I not identify them. In order to be consistent, and with four exceptions (for which I received written permission), all reenactor names used here are pseudonyms. I have also altered some details of their personal lives (jobs and home-towns) to protect their identities.

xvii   ["I can understand . . . their own as heresy."] Morris Call, email to the author, "Thoughts on reenacting," 14 January 1997.

["narrow minded . . . don't know either."] Luke Gardner, interview with the author, September 1995.

["lies outside the boundary . . . thrives on independence."] Jay Anderson, *Time Machines: The World of Living History* (Nashville, TN: Association of State and Local History, 1985), 191.

1. "Hazardous Activity for My Own Recreation, Enjoyment, and Pleasure"

3   ["I, the undersigned . . . injury such activity involves."] World War II Historical Preservation Federation, Battle of the Bulge reenactment, "Waiver of Liability," 1997.

11   ["Barter . . . makes the hobby go round."] Barry Lott, "Brits," WWII Newsgroup, 25 June 1996.

2. "This Must Be Something They Do in California"

30   [Only two years had passed . . . war's centennial.] The last known Civil War veterans both died in 1959: John B. Salling, a Confederate veteran, was 112 years old when he died in March, and Walter Washington Williams, also a Confederate veteran, was 117 when he died in December. Jay S. Hoar, *The South's Last Boys in Grey: An Epic Prose Elegy* (Bowling Green, OH: Bowling Green State University Press, 1986), 35–36.

31   ["carnival of tents . . . innocent refreshments."] "Confederates Carry Day Again at Bull Run," *New York Times*, 23 July 1961.

["accurate as to sequence . . . interesting or critical turns."] Ibid.

["As the artillery batteries . . . to the fearsome fray."] "Manassas Incidents Add Realism," *Washington Post*, 23 July 1961.

["chased the Union . . . woods in panic."] "Confederates Carry Day Again."

[An estimated 175 spectators . . . temperature.] "First Manassas Ends with 175 Casualties," *Evening Star*, 24 July 1961.

[this first centennial reenactment . . . Gettysburg in July 1963.] "1,000 to Act in Battle Fete at Gettysburg," *The Morning Herald*, 29 May 1963; see also James Birchfield, "Pickett's Charge Ends 1963 Battle," *Evening Star*, 4 July 1963.

[One disgruntled observer . . . "grisly pantomime."] "Civil War Games Assailed," *New York Times*, 29 July 1961.

["this silly business . . . indescribable tragedy of war."] Editorial, *Evening Star*, 23 July 1961.

32   ["men and boys . . . Civil War games."] "Confederates Carry Day Again."

["The gaudy show . . . you're dead."] Editorial, *Washington Post*, 30 July 1961.

["real ammunition . . . our society."] Letter to the editor, signed "Disgusted," *Washington Post*, 27 July 1961.

["I hope the social psychologists . . . this type of activity."] Letter to the editor, *Washington Post*, 29 July 1961.

["Be slow to criticize . . . our faith in America."] Letter to the editor, *Evening Star*, 27 July 1961.

33 [Four years later . . . commemorative activities.] US Civil War Centennial Commission, *The Civil War Centennial: A Report to Congress* (Washington, DC: Government Printing Office, 1968), 44–45. For more on the Manassas reenactment and the Civil War Centennial, see John Bodnar, *Remaking America: Public Memory, Commemoration, and Patriotism in the Twentieth Century* (Princeton, NJ: Princeton University Press, 1992); Richard M. Fried, *The Russians Are Coming! The Russians Are Coming! Pageantry and Patriotism in Cold-War America* (New York: Oxford University Press, 1998); and Robert G. Hartje, "The Civil War Centennial," in *Bicentennial USA: Pathways to Celebration* (Nashville: American Association of State and Local History, 1973).

["The brevity and . . . years of centennials."] Owing to the negative publicity the Manassas event and other centennial reenactments generated, spectators at Appomattox were not treated to a reenactment but witnessed the great-grandsons of Generals Grant and Lee inaugurating a newly built courthouse. William Chapman, "Appomattox Centennial Rites Subdued," *Washington Post*, 30 April 1965.

["when and how the reenactment craze began."] Tom Carson, "Battlefield Potemkin," *Village Voice*, 9 July 1996.

["occasionally performed . . . youth."] Tony Horwitz, *Confederates in the Attic: Dispatches from the Unfinished Civil War* (New York: Random House, 1998), 136.

[Historian George Mosse . . . "noble" enterprise.] George L. Mosse, *Fallen Soldiers: Reshaping the Memory of the World Wars* (New York: Oxford University Press, 1990).

34 [The Boy Scouts . . . entered its fold.] Robert H. MacDonald, *Sons of Empire: The Frontier and the Boy Scout Movement, 1980–1918* (Toronto: University of Toronto Press, 1993), 189.

["junior militia companies . . . performing mock battles.] E. Anthony Rotundo, *American Manhood: Transformations in Masculinity from the Revolution to the Modern Era* (New York: Basic Books, 1993), 36.

[Groups . . . flourished.] At the close of the nineteenth century, over a quarter of American adult males were members of fraternal groups. Mark C. Carnes, *Secret Ritual and Manhood in Victorian America* (New Haven, CT: Yale University Press, 1989), 1. Veterans organizations such as the Society of the Cincinnati, founded in 1783, and the Grand Army of the Republic, founded in 1866, established the tradition of drawing together veterans in service to both national and individual needs. Jennings Hood and Charles J. Young, *American Orders and Societies and Their Decorations: The Objects of the Military and Naval Orders, Commemorative and Patriotic Societies of the United States and the Requirements for Membership Therein* (Philadelphia: Bailey, Banks, and Biddle, 1917), 38.

So numerous were veteran groups that in 1936 students at Princeton, anticipating another world war, founded the Veterans of Future Wars and demanded payment of their benefits before performing services to the nation. Fifty other universities soon founded chapters and female students followed suit with organizations such as the Future Gold Star Mothers. Richard Seelye Jones, *A History of the American Legion* (Indianapolis: Bobbs-Merrill, 1946), 15.

[Sons of Union Veterans . . . first year of existence.] In 1925, the Sons of Veterans changed its name to the Sons of Union Veterans of the Civil War. Virginius Dabney, *The Last Review: The Confederate Reunion, Richmond, 1932* (Chapel Hill, NC: Algonquin Books, 1984), 28.

[By 1901 . . . 163,000 members.] Wallace Evan Davies, *Patriotism on Parade: The Story of*

Veterans' and Hereditary Organizations in America, 1783–1900 (Cambridge, MA: Harvard University Press, 1955), 76.

34   ["Memorial and Union . . . memories of their fathers."] Grand Army of the Republic, *Cleveland: Official Souvenir of the Thirty-Fifth National Encampment of the Grand Army of the Republic* (Cleveland, OH: E. W. Doty, 1901), 12.

["the modern embodiments of age-old traditions."] Mary Ann Clawson, *Constructing Brotherhood: Class, Gender, and Fraternalism* (Princeton, NJ: Princeton University Press, 1989), 21.

[At parades . . . in contact with veterans.] Rotundo, *American Manhood*, 234. By 1919, World War I veterans formed their own organizations, such as the American Legion (founded 1919), whose members also took part in events hosted by the Civil War veterans and their descendants. Directly after World War I, the Grand Army of the Republic reported the presence of "World War I boys" who joined ten thousand Civil War veterans and their descendants in their annual parade. Grand Army of the Republic, *Final Journal*, 24. The American Legion also spawned its own veteran-descendant organization in 1932: The Sons of the American Legion, which sponsored "Citizens Military Training Camps" for young boys, including Boy Scouts. According to Marcus Duffield, the Legion encouraged boys to cultivate a "martial spirit" in response to the belief that "American youth . . . are not sufficiently military-minded." Marcus Duffield, *King Legion* (New York: Jonathan Cape and Harrison Smith, 1931), 253–262. For a discussion of veteran and descendant organizations' politics and efforts to establish universal military training, see Mary P. Dearing, *Veterans in Politics: The Story of the G.A.R.* (Baton Rouge: Louisiana State University Press, 1952).

[Together . . . historical pageant.] This discussion of the pageant movement in America relies on Naima Prevots, *American Pageantry: A Movement for Art and Democracy* (Ann Arbor: UMI Research Press, 1990), and David Glassberg, *American Historical Pageantry: The Uses of Tradition in the Early Twentieth Century* (Chapel Hill: University of North Carolina Press, 1990). Richard M. Fried's book provides a thorough history of the continuation of pageantry in the United States.

So popular were these historical pageants throughout the late nineteenth and early twentieth centuries that a national organization, the American Pageant Association, was founded in 1913 to guide communities from California to Vermont as they were caught up in the craze. Prevots, *American Pageantry*, 2.

35   [And having real veterans . . . history.] See Glassberg, *American Historical Pageantry*, for a detailed discussion.

[While the pageants . . . for new immigrants.] Ibid., 53.

["The players may not . . . inspire a finer fellowship."] Ralph Davol, *Handbook of American Pageantry*, 2d ed. (Taunton, MA: Davol Publishing, 1914), 28.

["displayed the gallantry of war without the violence."] Glassberg, *American Historical Pageantry*, 209.

["a stream of social sewage . . . pageant field."] Davol, *Handbook of American Pageantry*, 108–109.

[Through sequential scenes . . . heroically returned home.] Glassberg, *American Historical Pageantry*, 211.

36   [By World War II . . . died out in the United States.] Carnes, *Secret Ritual and Manhood in Victorian America*, 151; Clawson, *Constructing Brotherhood*, 263.

[In 1943, one of the few . . . of public history.] Glassberg, *American Historical Pageantry*, 276. [By the time historian Carl Becker . . . founded 1947.] In his seminal study of living history, *Time Machines: The World of Living History* (Nashville, TN: American Association for State and Local History, 1984), Jay Anderson attributes the coining of the phrase "living history" to Carl Becker, who used the term in a 1931 presidential address to the American Historical Association.

[new groups began . . . veteran encampment.] This history of these early living history groups is informed by and primarily draws from my discussions with members of the North-South Skirmish Association, Steve Meserve and Dan Grekitis; from interviews with reenactors, Mark Sammons and Grant Holzer; and from Jay Anderson's *Time Machines*.

[In 1933, the National . . . used Civil War weapons.] The NMLRA is still in existence.

["primitive rendezvous."] See the NMLRA Web page for more about the group and its activities: www.nmlra.org/nmlrapage.html.

[Many of these early events . . . attended the skirmish.] Steve Meserve, executive secretary of the North-South Skirmish Association, email to the author, 23 April 1998.

37 [In 1958 . . . continue to take place.] Steve Meserve, email to the author, 24 April 1998.

[Coming together . . . and Canada.] North-South Skirmish Association, Recruitment flyer, 1998. In 1992, N-SSA members amended their by-laws to allow women to become active participants and members of skirmish teams. Steve Meserve, email to the author, 24 April 1998.

[Many are direct . . . and Sons of Union Veterans.] The Sons of the American Legion (SAL) is also still operative. In 1997, the SAL reported an all-time peak of 201,302 members. Membership in the SAL is restricted to male descendants of veterans of World War I, World War II, the Korean War, the Vietnam War, the Persian Gulf War, and all conflicts since 1991, as well as those who served in Lebanon, Grenada, and Panama. *National Update: The Official Newsletter of the Sons of the American Legion* (March 1998): 4.

["Becoming a part . . . the N-SSA Recruitment Officer."] North-South Skirmish Association, Recruitment flyer, 1998.

[Along with other regional . . . of the American Civil War.] Other groups included the Maryland Black Hats and the Civil War Skirmish Association in California. Although the N-SSA publicly distinguishes itself from the reenacting hobby, according to N-SSA member, Dan Grekitis, it also struggles with the same accusations of trivializing or glorifying war that are leveled at reenactors. Dan Grekitis, telephone conversation with the author, 14 April 1998.

38 ["two schools . . . question of authenticity."] Steve Meserve, email to the author, 24 April 1998.

39 [With cash or credit . . . reenactor handbook.] Handbooks range from self-published manuals to more commercial works, such as R. Lee Hadden's *Reliving the Civil War: A Reenactor's Handbook* (Mechanicsburg, PA: Stackpole Books, 1996).

[As the Civil War hobby . . . fee-paying reenactors.] At the 1997 Antietam reenactment, for instance, the cost of admission for a spectator was fifteen dollars. Event Program, 135th Antietam Commemorative Reenactment, September 1997. Reenactors themselves are also often charged admission fees in order to participate in reenactments, and usually they must register with the event host prior to participating.

42 [the officers of the first . . . governing body, were elected.] The G-7 includes the GWA offices of President, Vice-President, Secretary, Treasurer, Allied Representative, Central Powers Representative, and Allied and Central Powers Combat Commanders. In 1998, "G-7" was

changed to the more accurate "G-8" after the office of Secretary was added. Officers serve two years before ballots for new elections are sent to all GWA members, along with the group's quarterly newsletter, *On the Wire*. World War I reenacting also takes place at sites in Wisconsin, Oklahoma, and California. Other groups, such as the Great War Society on the West Coast, were founded after the GWA.

42   ["troglodyte fever."] Larry Cohen, "President's Message to the Troops," *On the Wire: Official Newsletter of the Great War Association* 4 (fall 1993): 3.

[five- to ten-year lease . . . for their own training.] Perry Trent, "Updated Information on Proposed Sites," 14 October 1993.

43   ["This site . . . enthusiasts forever."] Reginal Holmes, "Caesar Krauss: The Man Behind the Memorial," *On the Wire: Official Newsletter of the Great War Association* 8 (spring 1997): 21.

44   ["We need not be visionaries . . . which we all strive."] Donald Kiev, "President's Address to the Membership," *On the Wire: Official Newsletter of the Great War Association* 7 (spring 1996): 3.

["for us—not for the Publick . . . the love of it."] Philip Moss, "Ramblings from Atop the Soapbox," *On the Wire: Official Newsletter of the Great War Association* 8 (spring 1997): 6.

[Parallel to the development . . . grew in popularity.] This history of the early days of World War II reenacting relies on several interviews with old-hand reenactors. I am particularly indebted to Alain Benson, William Gregory, and Walter Tannen for sharing this history with me.

[Many of the members . . . Pearl Harbor and Hiroshima.] Piehler, *Remembering War*, 144. See also C. R. Chandler, "World War II as Southern Entertainment: The Confederate Air Force and Warfare as Re-enactment Ritual," in *Rituals and Ceremonies in Popular Culture*, ed. Ray B. Browne. (Bowling Green, OH: Bowling Green University Popular Press, 1980), 258–269.

45   [In 1980, the HRS . . . across the country.] "Treasurer's Report," *The Point: Journal of the Historical Reenactment Society* 6 (May/June 1980): 2. Throughout the 1980s, reenactors were required to pay annual membership fees and join organizations such as the CHG, HRS, or the MVCC to attend reenactments.

[The HRS continues . . . Federation.] National WWII Historical Reenactment Federation President, "World War II Reenactments: Problems and Considerations," *The Frontline: The Official Publication of the National WWII Historical Reenactment Federation* 2 (spring 1981): 18. The Federation is now known as the World War II Federation.

46   ["We have many splintered . . . began with the HRS."] Philip Moss, "Enough," WWII Newsgroup, 8 November 1997.

49   ["to accurately and respectfully . . . connection with the past."] Infanterie-Regiment Nr 63, "Purposes of Our Organization," September 1997.

3. "Something a Little Strange"

52   [During my first . . . members of the GWA.] Jack Hunter was one of the GWA's "benevolent dictators." Although several others were a part of the dictatorship, it was Jack, according to Tim Reed, who "basically ran the whole operation" before its democratization in 1990. Tim Reed, email to the author, 1 July 1999.

["is extremely difficult . . . Irish offended by the British?"] Ralph Hanson, "CW vs WW2," WWII Newsgroup, 10 September 1997.

53   ["I'll be the first to . . . think it's cool."] Greg Steel, "Hollywood opinions!" WWII Newsgroup, 20 July 1998.

54   ["The members of . . . not political science."] Infanterie-Regiment Nr 63, Web page.

["a place to sound off on one's political agenda."] Jessie Powell, "Eisenhower," WWII Newsgroup, 12 November 1998.

["there is no change . . . Americans at heart."] Morris Call, email to the author, 10 April 1997.

[In fact, some reenactor organizations . . . un-American group."] Liebstandarte Adolf Hitler (LAH), "Membership Information—Disclaimers and Notes," 1998.

[The 20th Century Tactical . . . Nazi, or hate group."] 20th Century Tactical Studies Group, Inc., "Bylaws," 1997.

55   ["That is part of . . . what we want!"] Philip Moss, "The Allies are sellouts," WWII Newsgroup, 16 July 1998.

56   ["I am definitely not . . . reasons for reenacting."] Leonard Lord, letter to the author, 26 March 1997. I received only one other blatant rejection of my survey: "Not interested in responding," a World War II German reenactor wrote in returning his unanswered survey. "Once I saw questions about politics I decided this was not a study I'd like to be associated with."

57   ["Most people are naturally stupid . . . is a f^&*'n Nazi."] Chris Turner, "Mercenary reenactors," WWII Newsgroup, 1 August 1996.

58   [Others with jobs . . . keep quiet.] Warren Tate, [no subject], WWII Newsgroup, 5 December 1996.

["A lot of guys like . . . innocent rebellion."] Larry Mayon, "SS motives," WWII Newsgroup, 9 September 1996.

60   ["too many tribes and too many chiefs."] Craig Bass, "What's up," WWII Newsgroup, 7 October 1997.

["still have a long way to go in communication."] Tim Gilbert, "On recruiting, blowhards and such," WWII Newsgroup, 11 September 1997.

[Communication among reenactors . . . highly informal.] Thus far, there has been only one truly national twentieth-century war reenacting publication. *Battle Cry: The Newspaper of Reenacting* premiered in the winter of 1995 and covered a broad range of reenacting periods across the country. Reenactors loved its content of reenactor-related articles, photographs, event announcements, and classifieds. But the publisher/reenactor found it too difficult to solicit articles and folded it in 1998.

61   [Almost 70 percent . . . Korean War to the list.] Of twentieth-century war reenactors, more than 40 percent choose World War II impressions as their favorite, with World War I following at over 36 percent.

62   ["When you go to . . . our equipment off the shelf."] William Gregory, "CW vs WW2," WWII Newsgroup, 10 September 1997.

[Some reenactors found it . . . often recruit new members.] The commander of a World War II German unit described his unit's recruitment efforts at public events: "We set up a table . . . with our photo albums, displays of our MG34s and MP40s, wear our uniforms, and as of late we have a video on our unit that we can play." Barney Sugarman, "Recruiting new men," WWII Newsgroup, 9 September 1997. Over the last few years, with the rise of the Internet, many units increasingly recruit new members through their Web pages.

63   ["Dietz reenactors" . . . decidedly green soldier.] With a mixture of Dietz reenactors and "old hands" (veteran reenactors), the hobby is populated by several generations with varying levels of reenacting experience: Old hand reenactors, who've been reenacting for twenty-one to thirty-six years, comprise roughly 13 percent of reenactors; roughly 12 percent have been reenacting for sixteen to twenty years; about 20 percent have been reenact-

ing for eleven to fifteen years; more than 25 percent have six to ten years experience; and more than 25 percent have been in the hobby for less than five years.

64   ["Getting younger kids . . . in favor of it."] Barney Sugarman, "(The truth about) young recruits," WWII Newsgroup, 12 September 1997.

["I don't want . . . Screw that!"] Philip Moss, "Young recruits," WWII Newsgroup, 12 September 1997.

65   ["limited number of applicants."] First Panzer Division, classified advertisement, *Battle Cry: The Newspaper of Reenacting* 4 (spring 1998): 21.

[Units range . . . twenty members.] The largest unit I identified is the Midwestern World War II German unit, Liebstandarte Adolf Hitler (1st SS LAH) with 250 members. The LAH is also one of the oldest, founded in 1976.

[In both world wars . . . German units coming in second.] Of the thirty-four units in the World War II reenacting organization, the Historical Reenactment Society (HRS), for instance, American units rank first in number, constituting more than half of existing HRS units. German units come in second at less than a third, with British Commonwealth units ranking third at over 10 percent. Among the GWA's thirty-five units, German units are out-ranked by Allied units. German units constitute a little less than a third of recognized units. American units constitute more than a quarter of all GWA units, with British following closely at nearly another quarter and Canadian coming in at less than 10 percent; Russian, French, and Australian units are equally represented, at roughly 3 percent each.

66   [They also oversee . . . keeping members informed.] Unit dues are spent on newsletters, unit mailings, vehicle upkeep, or purchases of items owned jointly by all members.

[More highly organized units . . . nonprofit status.] Both units such as GD and reenactor organizations such as the Federation have nonprofit, tax-exempt (501-C3) status.

["After you sign up . . . in a unique hobby."] Infanterie-Regiment Nr 63, Web page.

67   ["Our philosophy is simple . . . together himself."] William Gregory, "On recruiting, blowhards and such," WWII Newsgroup, 9 September 1997.

68   ["A lot of reenactors do SS . . . top-notch soldiers."] Mayon, "SS motives," WWII Newsgroup, 9 September 1996.

[Another reenactor, who . . . never happen!"] Alf Sample, "Jews in reenactment units," Wehrmacht Newsgroup, 21 December 1999.

[Others have what they call . . . "secondary impressions."] Secondary impressions are done less frequently than primary impressions. Along with "combat" or "battle dress" impres-sions, reenactors also do what they call "walking-out" impressions, which are uniforms worn for dinners or other noncombat occasions. Some also refer to impressions done strictly for performance value at public events as walking-out impressions.

71   [Add to these costs . . . can rise dramatically.] Based on the median number of events re-enactors participate annually (4.5), the average cost of participating in a single event is just over eighteen dollars.

[On average . . . five events a year.] For example, a total of fourteen events were on the 1998 annual calendar of the National Military Historical Association. *The Command Post: The Official Newsletter of the National Military Historical Association, Inc.* (April 1998): 7–8. Unit and individual participation at events ranges widely. Some unit calendars are packed with events throughout the year; others come together for only a few events, and not every unit fields all its members at a given event. Nearly a third of reenactors attend three events or less in one year; another third attend an event roughly every other month; about 20 percent attend up to one event per month; and nearly 10 percent attend up to two events per month.

[For Fred Legum . . . sixteen hundred (fake) grenades.] Most reenactors make their own grenades for World War I events. These grenades cause no damage, but they do make a small explosion. Most are made using plastic film canisters or Easter egg shells.

["I have about fifty firearms . . . probably outshine."] Fred's collection consists of British infantry equipment dating from 1890 to 1945.

72   ["You can get addicted . . . like shooting heroin!"] Phil Herr, "Idiots on eBay," WWII Newsgroup, 13 January 1999.

[Compared to the general . . . are divorced or separated] According to data from the US Census Bureau, in 1997, 8.7 percent of males 18 years old and older in the United States were divorced. I chose to compare divorce statistics from 1997 with the reenactors' own divorce statistics since my questionnaire was conducted in 1997. US Census Bureau, 1998 Statistical Abstract of the United States, No. 62, "Marital Status of the Population, by Sex and Age: 1997"; www.census.gov/prod/3/98pubs/98statab/sasec1.pdf.

73   ["thinks I'm completely out . . . being a reenactor.] Patrick O'Hara, email to the author, 2 July 1996.

4. "I Lead Two Completely Separate Lives"

77   ["Gay, straight, married . . . the range of reenactors.] In conducting my fieldwork, I never met an openly gay reenactor, but I certainly heard from others, and would expect, that there are gay reenactors in the hobby.

79   [They have a broad . . . type dominates among them.] Almost half occupy managerial or professional jobs; almost 20 percent are employed in technical professions, sales, or administrative support; nearly 15 percent work in service-sector jobs; nearly 10 percent are laborers, operators, or fabricators; approximately 5 percent work in precision production, craft, or repair, and approximately 10 percent are students. Although no single profession dominates among them, the top professions include managers (8.3 percent), police and law enforcement agents (6.3 percent), self-employed or small business owners (5.2 percent), teachers (4.5 percent), salespeople (4.5 percent), and engineers (4.2 percent).

[Their annual income . . . to $400,000.] Less than 8 percent report incomes under $20,000, and nearly the same number report incomes over $100,000; about 30 percent report incomes falling between $20,000 and $40,000; another 20 percent report incomes up to $50,000; roughly 10 percent range up to $60,000; another 10 percent range up to $70,000; and the rest, 8 percent, report incomes of $80,000 to $100,000.

[And people with all levels . . . participate.] Roughly 10 percent of reenactors have high school degrees only. Near one third have completed some college or earned associates' degrees; about 40 percent have college degrees; and about 17 percent have graduate or professional degrees.

[They're overwhelmingly white (97.8 percent).] Those who identified themselves as black (0.3 percent); Asian or Pacific Islander (0.3 percent); Latino (none); and "other" (1.6 percent) account for only 2.2 percent of reenactors, a percentage decidedly disproportionate to the US population.

["Membership is open . . . religious preference or handicap."] California Historical Group, World War II Living History Association, "Statement of Purpose," 1998.

82   [Despite the high proportion . . . support gun control.] When some GWA members proposed buying an insurance liability policy backed by the NRA and encouraged reenactors to join the NRA in order to decrease their premium, many objected. Indeed, much debate followed the proposal and many, such as Grant Holzer, made their objections public.

83   ["I used to be a Republican . . . the Commie Left's BS."] Philip Moss, "Refrain from outside politicking," WWII Newsgroup, 7 July 1997.

["I have always wondered . . . 'characters' come and go."] Duane Kit, "Dos centavos," WWII Newsgroup, 5 July 1996.

85   [As members of a general . . . turn-of-the-twentieth-century society.] To be sure, children played games involving types of simulated warfare—whether tin soldiers or "Indians versus settlers"—before the turn of the twentieth century. But the advent of the industrialized means of producing war toys and games formalized such games and made them widely available. For more on the production of war-related games and toys for children see, George Mosse, "The Process of Trivialization," in *Fallen Soldiers: Reshaping the Memory of the World Wars* (New York: Oxford University Press, 1990), 126–156.

[Whether born at . . . if only vicariously.] According to my 1997 questionnaire, only 2.5 percent of reenactors were born before World War II; 4.6 percent were born during the war; and only 0.3 percent of reenactors were born after 1979. It is important to see reenactors as part of a larger generation. The tendency to make sharp distinctions among groups separated by only a decade or even several decades seems to overplay the concept of generational difference. There is far too much overlap among people alive at the same time, even though their childhoods may have been separated by twenty years. Thanks to the media, historical events that "belong" to one generation may also be "experienced" by the next.

["Our heads were filled with war stories."] Tilden Scott, letter to the author, 27 February 1997.

90   [Nearly all units impose . . . their mid-twenties or older.] Most units require members to be at least eighteen years old. Some allow sixteen-year-olds to join with written permission from a parent or guardian.

91   [Nearly 98 percent . . . informed about history.] More than 70 percent of reenactors think Americans are both misinformed and underinformed about history. A little more than 23 percent think Americans are underinformed; and just over 4 percent say Americans are misinformed.

92   ["I doubt very strongly . . . the Right to Party."] Al Adams, 4th Armored Newsgroup, 14 April 2000.

93   [They do this through . . . and air shows.] Living history displays usually involve setting up period "encampments" that are toured by visitors. Popular reenactor encampments include a World War II event held at the Eisenhower National Historic Site in Gettysburg, Pennsylvania, and one held at the Jefferson Barracks in St. Louis, Missouri. Air shows popular among reenactors include the Frederick Air Show in Maryland; the Mid-Atlantic Air Museum's World War II Weekend in Reading, Pennsylvania, also called the Reading Air Show; and the Dayton Air Show in Ohio. Other popular public events are historical timelines such as "Military Through the Ages" at the Jamestown Settlement near Williamsburg, Virginia; the "Timeline" in Vermont; and "Marching Through Time" at the Marietta Mansion in Maryland.

5. "Dog and Pony Shows"

95   [The CIA . . . for various events.] Some reenactors have played "OP-4" (enemy) forces in US military training exercises. The CIA asked for volunteer reenactors to do a "Check Point Charlie impression, ca. 1971" for a CIA Family Day in Virginia. No compensation was offered. Interested participants were instructed to supply their names and social security numbers before being put on the event roster. Luke Gardner, letter to 4th Armored members, CIA Event, September 1997.

[Hollywood production . . . *The Battle of Shaker Heights* (2003).] Members of a World War I French reenacting unit performed as extras in the World War I combat scenes in *12 Monkeys*. In *Saving Private Ryan*, several World War II reenactors worked as extras on location, while others provided reproduction gear for the production. A World War II German unit based in California provided the vehicles, uniforms, and reenactors for *The Battle of Shaker Heights*. And for many smaller, independent and student films, reenactors have been recruited to play the parts of soldiers and serve as technical advisors. The fact that reenactors constitute a pool of ready-made volunteers is widely recognized among event hosts and especially among those in the film industry. Silver Screen Soldiers, a company that recruits reenactors as movie extras, describes reenactors as "a proven asset for the film industry. Unlike extras who must be trained and costumed, reenactors may be hired complete with their own authentic period uniforms and weapons. They arrive on location already trained in the tactics of their time period, and tend to have a natural flair for film work." Advertisement, Toyland Combat Vehicles and Silver Screen Soldiers, 1998.

[And even the National Park Service . . . known as Eisenhower Farm.] The National Park Service bars "battle reenactments" and bans the use of blank ammunition on its sites. Reenactors are, however, allowed to "demonstrate tactics." Richard E. Lemmurs, letter to Living History Volunteers, Eisenhower National Historic Site, WWII Public Event, 21 July 1998.

[Event hosts . . . direct mailings.] The park ranger at Eisenhower Farm explained how he "received tips on World War II units by searching the Internet and just talking to people." Once a contact is found, that reenactor will often provide hosts with lists of units or will agree to advertise the event over email subscriber newsgroups, the telephone, or in newsletters. Letter to the author from Richard E. Lemmurs, Park Ranger, Eisenhower National Historic Site, 1 October 1998.

96   ["This is a call for troops . . . remembrance ceremony."] Rosehill Cemetery and Veterans Museum, invitation to reenactors to attend the April 1997 Great War 80th Anniversary Commemoration and Battle Reenactment, Chicago, December 1996.

["knowledgeable reenactors . . . military vehicles."] Richard Lemmurs, National Park Service Ranger, letter to Luke Gardner inviting him to attend World War II encampment event at Eisenhower National Historic Site, Pennsylvania, February 1998. Like almost all other professions, historical site managers, National Park Service guides, and interpreters are found among the hobby's many members. This often spurs a working relationship between reenactors and public event hosts. One reenactor, who worked for the NPS for nearly ten years, observed that: "the parks have become more living history friendly, at least that's what I've observed. And it's probably because you've got people working for them who have been reenactors. I think they become more friendly to us because of that."

96   [Finding people . . . quite a bit of revenue.] The Rosehill World War I event, for instance, offered no compensation to reenactors, but promised them a "complimentary breakfast on Sunday morning, and remuneration for powder expenses." Sometimes reenactors are even charged event registration fees to attend public events.

[The Mid Atlantic Air Museum . . . commemorative weekend.] The annual budget percentage figure refers to the June 1998 event. Fred Pierce, publicity and promotions officer of the Mid Atlantic Air Museum, telephone interview with the author, 18 July 1998.

[This event draws up to . . . World War II reenactors.] Event program, "Living History, WWII Airfield," Eighth Annual WWII Commemorative Weekend, Mid Atlantic Air Museum, Reading, Pennsylvania, 6–7 June 1998.

["to provide a learning experience for park visitors."] Richard Lemmurs, letter to Luke Gardner, February 1998.

[A World War I encampment . . . larger audience."] Rosehill Cemetery and Veterans Museum, invitation, December 1996.

["living history volunteers . . . feel of a past era."] Owen Findsen, "Old-Time Weekend Warriors," *Cincinnati Enquirer*, 24 April 1998.

["The encampments before you . . . past to life."] Event program, Marietta Mansion's "Fifth Annual Marching Through Time," Glenn Dale, Maryland. Sponsored by the Maryland-National Capital Park and Planning Commission, April 1997.

[Ranging from the elaborate (a reenactment of Pearl Harbor)] The Pearl Harbor reenactment, also known as "Tora! Tora! Tora!" is a mainstay of the annual Frederick Air Show in Frederick, Maryland. It is performed by reenactors on the ground and by planes overhead which are flown by members of the Commemorative Air Force. Event program, "Wings of Freedom Air Show," Frederick Municipal Airport, Frederick, Maryland, 24–25 August 1996.

[In June 1994 . . . anniversary.] At the same time, another D-Day reenactment was staged at Montrose Beach in Chicago. In 1982, a small D-Day reenactment took place at Fort Story, and other D-Day reenactments in Chicago had also been conducted on a small scale before the fiftieth anniversary.

[A reenactment group . . . to host the event.] The US Army appointed an official liaison to handle the many reenactor groups who would participate in a variety of World War II commemorative activities from 1991 to 1995. Steven E. Holtzinger, US Department of the Army, Office of Education and Public Affairs, "Memo to Re-enactment groups on 50th Anniversary of World War II Commemoration Committee," 3 March 1992. The Department of Defense and reenactor groups worked together to organize various events. WWII 50th Anniversary Commemoration Historical Advisory Council, "Fact Sheet," 1991.

97   [Eight landing craft . . . reenactors to shore.] Event announcement, Fiftieth Anniversary Battle Announcement, D Day Normandy: Commemorative Celebration, 1–5 June 1994.

101   ["History . . . dry pages of history books."] Matthew Bowers, "Simulation Fleshes Out History Texts," *The Virginian Pilot and Ledger-Star*, 5 June 1994.

102   [At another D-Day . . . chaos of the invasion"] Robert Becker and Jan Ferris, "City Gives Big 'Thanks' for D-Day," *Chicago Tribune*, 5 June 1994. The D-Day reenactment in Chicago was staged on the shores of Montrose Beach on Lake Michigan. Four hundred allied reenactors assaulted the beach from landing craft, while one hundred German reenactors defended it. According to the *Chicago Tribune*, hundreds of thousands of spectators, including many veterans, "jammed the lakefront" to watch the reenactment.

102   [1. The first twenty men . . . the program to a close.] "Operation Overlord Procedures Manual," D Day Reenactment Event Rules, June 1994.

104   ["I don't worry so . . . we have to work within."] Wilson Lyle, "Living history," WWII Newsgroup, 18 June 1998.

      ["When the Allies clear . . . Follow the script!"] "Operation Overlord Procedures Manual," 14.

      ["The whole point . . . impress the spectators."] Steve Tilden, email to the author, 12 April 1996.

      [But there is another . . . a "static display."] "Static display" is a term commonly used by reenactors as well as military and museum professionals.

      ["explain the display to the curious public."] Gerald Lee, "Zing? Moi?" WWII Newsgroup, 16 September 1997.

      ["living history . . . more realistically than the latter."] Wayne Adams, "Back to early war," Great War Newsgroup, 21 December 1999.

      ["Welcome to the Jamestown Settlement's . . . role in history continues."] Event Program. "Military Through the Ages." Jamestown Settlement, Virginia. March 1998.

105   ["experience three centuries of history in just one day!"] Advertisement for the James River Plantations in *Richmond: The Metropolitan Richmond Visitor's Guide* (Richmond, VA: Richmond Metropolitan Convention & Visitors Bureau, 1995), 34.

      ["Beat a Path to the Past!] The Chrysler Museum, Norfolk, Virginia, visitor pamphlet.

      [Museum employees . . . the gift shop.] This description is based on my 1998 visit to MTA.

107   [A well-loved . . . "antitank dog" impression.] When the sweet, elderly Toby passed away in 1999, reenactors mounted a dedication site on the reenactor net Web site, with photographs, stories, and a condolence book. He was, and still is, sorely missed.

108   ["We teach the public . . . during World War II."] American Military Medical Impression flyer.

      ["living historian . . . explain yourself as a reenactor."] William Gregory, "UK newspaper article," WWII Newsgroup, 19 March 1996.

109   ["For a public display . . . to be photogenic."] Bill Mason, "7 September 1996 Kirksvi," WWII Newsgroup, 14 August 1996.

      ["A personal story . . . for the average viewer."] Ford Hendricks, "Veterans Museum/displays," WWII newsgroup, 25 July 1996.

      ["Most of the equipment . . . and very rare."] American Military Medical Impression flyer.

      ["bring all your best . . . battles/public displays."] "Commander's Briefing," *Propblast: Newsletter of the 82nd Airborne Division, WWII Historical Reenactment Society* (April 1997): 3.

110   ["We have consciously set . . . any obvious fault."] Paul Tate, "Perth Tactical: After the battle," WWII Newsgroup, 27 October 1997.

      [Presenting themselves as real . . . veterans tour their camps.] Plenty of World War II veterans, including Russian, British, and German veterans, attend public events, but rarely do World War I veterans show up. At the 1998 World War I encampment at the Eisenhower Farm, for instance, several made an appearance. But meeting these increasingly rare veterans usually requires attending their reunions, such as the 1993 World War I Veterans Convention, which I attended with several reenactors.

111   ["Whenever I'm involved . . . now applauding us."] William Gregory, "Living history," WWII Newsgroup, 18 June 1998.

112   ["The public really appreciates . . . box to the top."] William Gregory, "Reading Air Show," WWII Newsgroup, 16 June 1998.

112   ["I don't mean just . . . folks on the home front."] Homer Thomas, "Reading (long . . . sorry),"
        WWII Newsgroup, 18 June 1998.

113   [An SS reenactor was . . . just lookin' at this guy."] Mark Wilson, [no subject], WWII
        Newsgroup, 25 June 1996.

        ["Some vets get ticked . . . when they see us."] Ibid. Several reenactors have told me about
        an occasion when some World War II American veterans reacted so badly to seeing German
        reenactors that a fistfight broke out. I have heard this story a number of times, but I was
        unable to confirm it or learn any further details.

114   [In one case, an elderly . . . dressed as a Russian commissar.] Shawn Birt, "Reds," WWII
        Newsgroup, 6 June 1996.

115   ["Learning to credibly . . . has the knack."] Philip Moss, "On recruiting, blow hards and
        such," WWII Newsgroup, 10 September 1997.

6. "We Must Police Ourselves Constantly"

117   ["work together."] Stephen Paul, "Clarification of my last posting," WWII Newsgroup, 18
        November 1997.

        ["Together! United! . . . or not!"] Nathan Wills, "SS controversy," WWII Newsgroup, 29
        June 1996.

        [One alerted . . . saviors by the public at large."] "Streamwood, Illinois Event Canceled,"
        Battle Cry: The Newspaper of Re-enacting 4 (summer 1998): 17.

118   ["tried, convicted . . . before the fact."] Whitman Ford, "Educating people," WWII
        Newsgroup, 13 March 1996.

        ["amateurs in the strictest sense."] Dennis Hall, "Civil War Reenactors and the Postmodern
        Sense of History," Journal of American Culture 17, no. 3 (spring 1994): 11. Because twentieth-
        century war reenactors have not been the subject of academic study, criticism of reenact-
        ing is primarily aimed at Civil War reenactors.

        ["tends to be . . . impressionistic, and imprecise."] Michael Kammen, The Mystic Chords of
        Memory (New York: Knopf, 1991), 666.

        ["sincere and meaningful . . . and after the war."] Jim Cullen, The Civil War in Popular Culture:
        A Reusable Past (Washington, DC: Smithsonian Institution Press, 1995), 196.

        ["to replicate . . . production of particular simulations."] Richard Handler and William
        Saxton, "Dyssimulation: Reflexivity, Narrative, and the Quest for Authenticity in 'Living
        History,'" Cultural Anthropology 3 (1988): 243.

        ["almost pathologically doomed . . . in [their] enterprise."] Ibid, 251. For another critique,
        see David Lowenthal, The Past Is a Foreign Country (New York: Cambridge University Press,
        1984). For an analysis of institutionalized living history practices, see Richard Handler and
        Eric Gable, The New History in an Old Museum: Creating the Past at Colonial Williamsburg
        (Durham, NC: Duke University Press, 1997). For more positive views on reenacting, see
        Rory Turner, "Bloodless Battles: The Civil War Reenacted," The Drama Review 34 (winter
        1990): 123–135; Randal Allred, "Catharsis, Revision, and Re-enactment: Negotiating the
        Meaning of the American Civil War," Journal of American Culture 19 (winter 1996): 1–14; and
        Dale Jones, "Living History in the City," History News: The Magazine of the American
        Association for State and Local History 50 (summer 1995): 13.

        ["it's hard to tell . . . and skinheads."] Patricia Holt, "Still Fighting Mad Over the Civil War,"
        review of Tony Horwitz, Confederates in the Attic, San Francisco Chronicle, 27 April 1998.

119   [A well-known English professor . . . "dimensions of twelve-year-olds."] The quote comes from a letter the professor wrote in response to a reenactor who had written asking for a critique of some reenacting photographs he was trying to publish.

["development of mock-combat . . . not in itself surprising."] James William Gibson, *Warrior Dreams: Violence and Manhood in Post Vietnam America* (New York: Hill and Wang, 1994), 126.

["began to dream . . . and reorder the world."] Ibid., 11.

[Nat Handler reported . . . wished us good luck."] Nat Handler, "Public events and good press," WWII Newsgroup, 19 March 1996.

["It just takes believing . . . a lot of honesty."] Ibid.

120   ["I guess I'm of the . . . survivor, to be sure!"] Edward Stewart, "Public events and good press," WWII Newsgroup, 19 March 1996.

["I myself do not . . . a little self-conscious."] Bill Mason, "Response to Steve Tilden," WWII Newsgroup, 18 November 1996.

["discount, low budget or freebie work"] Gerald Lee, "Mercenary reenactors," WWII Newsgroup, 31 July 1996. This feeling is common among reenactors, especially when working as extras for films.

121   ["The vast majority of public events are a real hassle."] Wilson Lyle, "Reading Air Show," WWII Newsgroup, 18 June 1998.

["The vast majority . . . educated."] Ibid.

["I for one . . . it isn't fun."] Philip Moss, "Reading Air Show," WWII Newsgroup, 19 June 1998.

122   [Meanwhile, Perry Trent railed . . . think that we're idiots."] Perry was not alone in his reaction to Horwitz's book. Other reactions ranged from mild amusement to outrage, and most reenactors were quick to point out that Horwitz focused on only one reenactor type—the extreme hardcore, leaving unexamined the great majority of others.

[In October 2001 . . . to "non-mission" oriented activity.] Walt Owen, "Cancelled: HRS National Battle—Ft. McCoy, WI," WWII Newsgroup, 25 September 2001.

[Further, "in view of recent . . . run around playing war games."] Charles Milton, "Odessa???" WWII Newsgroup, 13 September 2001.

123   ["We must police ourselves constantly."] Duane Kit, "Liberal bias against reenactors," WWII Newsgroup, 6 June 1996.

["I do feel strongly . . . do not involve reenactments."] Tim Gilbert, "CW vs WW2," WWII Newsgroup, 12 September 1997.

["Obviously, we can and should . . . completely different animal."] Wilson Lyle, "Public events and good press," WWII Newsgroup, 20 March 1996.

[Nearly half of reenactors . . . both positive and negative ways.] Nearly 20 percent believe the media's portrayal of reenacting is primarily positive, whereas more than 15 percent find the portrayal to be strictly negative.

["The media hasn't done . . . problems as possible."] Mark Wilson, "SS controversy," WWII Newsgroup, 27 June 1996.

["because [an upcoming event] will . . . let's take it!"] Event announcement, "Across the Rhine," event sponsored by the WWII Historical Preservation Association, Historic Chestertown, Maryland, May 1995.

124   ["Regardless of what uniform . . . something to exploit."] Jim Laurel, [no subject], WWII Newsgroup, 1 July 1996.

124   ["Reasoning with them . . . is the only solution."] Mark Wilson, "Media," WWII Newsgroup, 16 July 1996.

[An event is about "honor and preserving . . . what those soldiers did."] News story on the 50th Anniversary of the Battle of the Bulge Reenactment, WPHL-TV, Philadelphia, January 1995.

["There can be a hundred . . . the six o'clock news."] Scott Silver, "SS reenacting," WWII Newsgroup, 27 June 1996.

[Wilson Lyle calls all events . . . foot in his mouth."] Wilson Lyle, "UK article as it applies to us," WWII Newsgroup, 19 March 1996.

["Make the calmest . . . send them to that guy."] Bill Mason, "Handling the media," WWII Newsgroup, 20 March 1996.

["Just remember . . . you're fucked!"] Greg Steel, "Public relations tips," WWII Newsgroup, 11 September 1997.

125   [And there's no question . . . the Waffen SS impression.] Many German reenactors make the distinction between reenacting regular German army (Heer) units and reenacting SS units, which are far more controversial. Those who reenact the regular German army often say that because such units comprised "average" Germans, they were far less sinister and politicized than the infamous SS units. Of course, this subject elicits much debate among reenactors, just as it does among historians.

["I don't think that's all . . . a little innocent fun."] Larry Mayon, "SS motives," WWII Newsgroup, 9 September 1996.

[Although these extreme types . . . not the majority.] Because the hobby as a whole is so large and made up of so many different types of people, any kind of true and extreme transgression, such as neo-Nazism, is not tolerated, nor is there any real place for it. In fact, reenactors often make distinctions between those who wish to reenact World War II German and those who put on a German uniform in order to advance a political agenda. I have heard a couple of stories of reenactors or sutlers who were banned from events because they were identified as neo-Nazis. Thus, anyone in the hobby who might be radical politically in their identification with the ideology of the Nazis must either keep it to themselves or deal with the vast majority of other reenactors who take pretty quick action against such transgressions. Still, reenactors can often be judged to go "too far" in their identification with the soldiers they represent, a phenomenon I discuss in chapter 9. But, as I argue, there is a major difference between identifying with the soldiers and turning that identification into political action.

["a high level of authenticity . . . a reason to wear a swastika."] Jesse Hill, "National Battle— WW2 Superbowl," WWII Newsgroup, 4 March 1998.

126   ["If this hobby is . . . those who are beyond hope."] Greg Wylie, "I couldn't agree more," WWII Newsgroup, 5 June 1997.

[When one hapless reenactor . . . Historical Reenactment Society.] The reenactor was pulled over for driving the wrong way on an airport road (he was lost). After finding a trunk containing World War II rifles and an AR-15 rifle, the police charged the reenactor with a misdemeanor: illegal transport of a semiautomatic weapon. Alicia Mellon explains that the HRS decision to ask for his resignation was "regrettable" but "necessary" given the press the incident inspired. Eric Zorn, "For Military Buffs, Being 'Farb' Means Uniform Rejection," *Chicago Tribune*, 23 May 1995.

["I would sooner eat . . . murdering bastard's farm."] Philip Moss, "Eisenhower," WWII

Newsgroup, 12 November 1998. In a letter to reenactors, the Eisenhower Farm park ranger asked reenactors to "organize a scenario [in which] German soldiers are captured or have surrendered and are then processed on their way to the enclosure." Richard E. Lemmurs, letter to Living History Volunteers, 21 July 1998.

126   ["For a 'German' reenactor . . . less obscene response in the future."] Jessie Powell, "Eisenhower," WWII Newsgroup, 12 November 1998.

["the eventual elimination . . . SS impression imposes on reenacting."] Mark Wilson, [no subject], WWII Newsgroup, 5 June 1996.

["To eliminate Waffen SS . . . would be revisionism."] Greg Wylie, "Oops I stirred the pot!" WWII Newsgroup, 5 June 1996.

127   ["We need to stand our . . . uniforms in closets."] Barry Lott, "SS reenacting," WWII Newsgroup, 26 June 1996.

["Early horsehair backpacks . . . 'We are the World.'"] Gerald Lee, "Liberal bias against re-enactors," WWII Newsgroup, 6 June 1996.

["There were two . . . rate of the First World War."] Bruce Young, "Irvine Park time-line," WWII Newsgroup, 21 November 1997.

["tasteless antics are ill-afforded."] Greg Wylie, "I couldn't agree more," WWII Newsgroup, 5 June 1997.

["Executions do not play well . . . can get carried away."] Rob Tremaine, "Unit count," WWII Newsgroup, 10 January 1999.

128   ["There is, after all . . . events, experiences, and processes."] Mike Wallace, "Visiting the Past: History Museums in the United States," *Radical History Review* 25 (1981): 88.

[In a newsletter report . . . and late war packboards."] "Memorial Day Display in Cary," *The Old Hickory Chronicle: Newsletter of the Old Hickory Association* (July/August 1997): 3.

129   ["Since it was Memorial Day . . . a moment to remember them."] Ibid.

["World War II tactics and weaponry . . . losses were not quickly restored."] Luke Gardner, script for 4th Armored public demonstration at Pickatinny Arsenal, Armed Forces Day, n.d.

130   ["the German Army uniform . . . the last fifty years."] Philip Moss, "Living histories bite," WWII Newsgroup, 18 June 1998.

["Reenacting pays . . . reenactors choose to emulate."] Author unknown, WWII Newsgroup, 10 July 1996.

["My main reason for . . . the Hollywood hype."] William Gregory, "Reading," WWII Newsgroup, 17 June 1998.

131   ["between the good guys . . . and the bad guys."] Duane Kit, "SS controversy," WWII Newsgroup, 13 July 1996.

["The bad incidents . . . but not glorified."] Author unknown, WWII Newsgroup, 10 July 1996.

132   ["History is history . . . avoid offending people."] Nathan Wills, "SS controversy," WWII Newsgroup, 29 June 1996.

["It certainly wasn't . . . would like to believe."] James Beaton, "Reality check," WWII Newsgroup, 31 August 1996.

["There is a tendency . . . were to the Jews."] Mark Grove, "Black G.I.s," WWII Newsgroup, 30 August 1996.

["Your religion alone . . . list goes on, my friends."] Gerald Lee, [no subject], WWII Newsgroup, 10 July 1996.

132   ["Unlike some narrow imbeciles . . . Calley and My Lai?"] Philip Moss, "The Allies are sell-outs," WWII Newsgroup, 16 July 1998.

133   ["Judging years after . . . is pointless."] James Comer, "The evil Nazis," WWII Newsgroup, 16 July 1998.

        ["It was war . . . a crooked nail."] Greg Wylie, "The evil Nazis," WWII Newsgroup, 16 July 1998.

137   ["So maybe you don't . . . need your expertise."] Max Terrell, "Reading Air Show," WWII Newsgroup, 18 June 1998.

        ["Do you get wet . . . that uniform hot?"] Horace Sanders, "The Things Spectators Say," *Battle Cry: The Newspaper of Re-enacting* 3 (summer 1997): 17. "It did get tiresome quickly," one reenactor noted about the endless stream of "stupid" questions at a public event. "On one occasion a woman asked me 'Aren't you hot?' and I replied 'We think so, thanks for noticing!' I couldn't resist the opportunity." Tad Tracey, [no subject], WWII Newsgroup, 5 July 2000.

        ["We get asked questions . . . view of history to the public."] Brian Terrence, [no subject], WWII Newsgroup, 2 July 1996.

138   [their "splendid performance . . . laugh or move. Well Done!"] Gdsm. Terria, "On Public Duties at the Roosevelt Mansion," *Broad Arrow: The Irish Guards* (July/August 1996): 9.

        ["The next morning . . . until well around noon."] Ibid.

        ["a bonus battle . . . the crowds go home."] "May events," *The Command Post: The Official Newsletter of the National Military Historical Association* (April 1998): 1.

        [According to a reenactor . . . the reenacting world."] Greg Steel, "Great WW2/timeline event!!!" WWII Newsgroup, 5 February 1998.

        ["a full day's work . . . questions for the public."] "Warning order," from Luke Gardner to 4th Armored unit members, December 1995.

139   ["inform the public about . . . additional revenues."] GWA, G-7, Board Meeting Minutes; *On the Wire: Newsletter of the Great War Association* (spring 1998): 4.

        [With the benefits . . . for the very first time.] "GWA Summer Living History/Combat Event to Be Held June 14–16 2002," *On the Wire: The Newsletter of the Great War Association* (summer 2002): 1. The GWA combined its open house with a private reenactor–only tactical event. The public was welcome on the site on Saturday afternoon. Reenactors allowed them to tour the site, watch demonstrations, and look at displays. Once the public was gone, the reenactors engaged in a private combat scenario. Suggested donations for the event were $5 per person and $10 per family.

        ["When handled tastefully . . . to 'legitimize' our cause."] Wilson Lyle, "Reading Air Show," WWII Newsgroup, 18 June 1998.

        [And in fact, when a local California . . . to kiss goodbye."] Bill Mason, "The climate of the San Francisco Bay Area (and I don't mean temp)," WWII Newsgroup, 12 September 1997.

140   ["A different set of hows . . . sitting alone in a trench."] Karl Seldes, "Reading Air Show," WWII Newsgroup, 18 June 1998.

        ["I personally enjoy . . . very different."] Steve Tilden, email to the author, "Studying re-enactments," 12 April 1996.

        ["the public will never be invited."] William Gregory, email to the author. "Studying reenactments," 11 April 1996.

7. "It's Not on the Page Anymore"

141   [I'm standing somewhere . . . World War I reenactment.] The 1993 Fall GWA event took place at a secluded Boy Scout Camp in Farmington, Pennsylvania, during the GWA's trenchless phase. This site was used once by the GWA and attracted only a portion of the GWA membership. The following event, in the spring of 1994, took place at Fort Pickett, Virginia.

145   ["go over the top . . . chance to find out!"] Twentieth Century Tactical Studies Group, recruitment flyer, n.d.

        ["The History . . . the weight they used to."] Black Watch Unit, Web page, 1998.

149   ["War is very uncomfortable . . . at all possible."] Quote attributed (on the sign) to Fritz Nagel, a German lieutenant who served in World War I.

150   ["make it look as real as possible."] Patrick O'Hara, email to the author, 30 June 1996.

        [Virtually all reenactors agree . . . and its participants."] Only a tiny percentage of reenactors view the concern with authenticity as somewhat important; and less than one percent thinks it is somewhat unimportant or not important at all.

        [But achieving . . . is "not easy."] John Shampo, "Unit Commander's Letter to Potential Recruits, HRS, 3rd SS Division, Totenkopf," March 1997.

        [For the reenactor groups . . . announcements and registration materials.] Having insurance coverage for an event is necessary given the possibility for injury. Organizations and units that host events often go through great pains to secure coverage. The GWA, for instance, holds a million-dollar liability policy; other units secure insurance policies for the events they host. All participants are required to sign waivers of liability.

        The GWA often hires Combat Caterers, a company that specializes in providing food for reenactors to cater their private events. In other events, food may be provided by an outside vendor or by the hosts themselves. Grossdeutschland often serves dinner at its invitation only events, usually consisting of beans and hot dogs. Other meals are provided by units themselves, and individual reenactors always bring along their own food.

        [For participants, preparation . . . off from work.] Reenactors are instructed to file "Applications for Transfer Interstate NFA Weapon" (Machine Gun Transfer Form 5320.20) whenever transporting automatic weapons across state lines to attend an event and are often required by event hosts to show proof that they have done so.

        [Some GWA reenactors host . . . weeds before each event.] The defoliating process takes place twice a year, making the Newville site "authentically" free of vegetation throughout the trench sectors.

        [Sam Morse, Allied Trench . . . dig new trenches.] Sam spent $4,000 of his own money to purchase a back hoe solely to service the Newville trenches and help with the defoliation of the trench site before each event—no small investment, since Sam has a limited income as an assistant in a nonprofit foundation. For his work, GWA officials pay him a small fee, and, as a symbolic gesture, they named a segment of trench after him.

152   [In World War I events . . . designated trench sectors.] The trench sectors at Newville are permanently assigned to different units, grouped by nationality. Each unit is responsible for maintaining its sector. Some of the more elaborate sectors include wooden walkways, bunkers, and command posts.

153   ["Can the Allies force . . . find out for yourself!"] Event announcement, World War II "Italian Campaign 1944," World War II private reenactment, Virginia, sponsored by Hampton Roads Historical Reenactments, June 1998.

153   ["The historical time frame . . . France, Belgium or Holland."] Event announcement. "Odessa '97," World War II private reenactment, New York, sponsored by Fusilier Kompanie 272 and W2HPG (the World War II Historic Preservation Group, a reenactor organization run by Grossdeutschland). Most World War II events are set in the Western Front of the European Theater of Operations, and a few in the Eastern Front or Italy. GWA events are strictly Western Front battles, divided between what reenactors call "early war" and "late war" combat. Traditionally, early war combat scenarios excluded American reenactors, since the United States was not involved in World War I until 1917. Early war scenarios also require variations on impressions and equipment. Late war combat requires all participants to wear steel helmets and use gas masks.

["We are bound . . . creation of our scenarios."] Frank Aylward, "Nominations for Allied Combat Commander of the GWA," *On the Wire* 4 (fall 1993): 5.

[attempting to replicate historical . . . as "counterproductive."] Morris Call, "Small survey," WWII Newsgroup, 23 September 1997.

["Scripted scenarios are okay . . . death for a tactical event."] Steve Tilden, "Small survey," WWII Newsgroup, 24 September 1997.

154   ["cheapen the actual . . . a lame-o parody."] William Samuel, "Small survey," WWII Newsgroup, 23 September 1997.

["I don't believe in letting . . . will be more realistic."] Mark Henry, "Nominations for Central Powers Combat Commander of the GWA," *On the Wire* 4 (fall 1993): 6.

["implement the appropriate . . . for a given situation."] GWA, "Rules of Engagement," October 1997.

["Being given realistic goals . . . people on a stage."] Bill Mason, "Small survey," WWII Newsgroup, 23 September 1997.

155   [to behave with "some degree of control."] Derrick Harris, "Unit count," WWII Newsgroup, 9 January 1999.

["Remember . . . and *no live ammo!*"] Event announcement, "Duel on a Dutch Levee," World War II private reenactment, Chesapeake City, Maryland, sponsored by Tim Castle, June 1996. Safety inspections vary depending on event. Usually they involve checking ammo (blanks) and listening to speeches regarding safety procedures. The GWA's requisite safety inspection occurs on Saturday morning before combat begins. Various commanders give speeches, reiterating the rules of engagement. Then, each reenactor who plans to use "grenades" must detonate one of his own while standing over it, legs spread apart. This is designed to ensure that should a reenactor have charged his grenades too much, he will be the first to suffer the consequences.

["Do not aim and . . . just yell, Bang!"] Tim Robb, "Enlightenment from the GWA Vice President," *On the Wire* (spring 1996): 7. The "bang" rule was revoked by the GWA in October 1997.

["Don't start talking about . . . having a heart attack.)"] "Warning order," from Luke Gardner to 4th Armored unit members, 1994.

["Please do not stand . . . we are trying to accomplish."] World War II Historical Preservation Federation, memo "To all reenactors and veterans of the Battle of the Bulge from the Federation Staff Officers," 26 January 1996.

["No use of controlled . . . No drunkenness."] W2HPG, "Rules," n.d.

["I lost my hearing . . . concrete bunker and firing."] Joseph Radway, "Dangers of reenacting," WWII Newsgroup, 4 December 1996.

["broken femur, broken pelvis . . . with no ground guard."] Steve Tilden, "Dangers of reenacting," WWII Newsgroup, 5 December 1996.

[All action must cease . . . way to the scene.] Historically, the GWA hired a local paramedic unit to bring an ambulance to the Newville site and stay the weekend. A few years ago, however, the G-8 decided not to spend the money on the ambulance and instead to rely on several reenactors trained as emergency medical technicians to serve as designated emergency personnel. At some World War II events (such as the Bulge), ambulances are present, but at some smaller, more exclusive events, there are none.

156   ["the injuries were entirely . . . respect for the rules."] GWA, "GWA Spring Combat Info-Brief," event announcement, 1997.

["John Wayne stuff has no place here."] Fourth Armored Unit newsletter, Company A, 51st Armored Infantry Battalion, December 1993.

["The idea is not so . . . being killed yourself."] Ibid.

["The life of an infantryman . . . scared out of your wits."] Tim Gilbert, "Digging foxholes," WWII Newsgroup, 21 August 1996.

157   [In all types of private events . . . replicated over and over.] An Eastern Front event, for example, may differ from a Western Front event due to differences in tactics, uniforms, and equipment, but in general each will have the same types of scenarios.

[Many use period names . . . or create historical personas.] Most reenactors who do American impressions use their real names or nicknames unit members have given them. One reenactor is known as "Manchild" because of his youth, another as "Needles" because of his tailoring skills. Reenactors who portray foreign soldiers usually adopt names appropriate to their impressions. Most simply "germanify" or "anglicize" their real names.

158   ["I think of myself . . . fifty-four years earlier."] Craig Bass, "First person," WWII Newsgroup, 1 July 1997.

159   [For instance, there is no scenario . . . end of a war.] In determining which kinds of scenarios took place most often, I was interested to note that as far as I could tell, reenactors do not reenact certain scenarios such as a troop mutiny or an individual soldier's "breakdown." After I talked with Fred Legum about such scenarios, though, he said that he thought the mutiny idea was a great one.

160   ["Who will yours be . . . carrying your child?"] Luke Gardner, "Intelligence Report," *Name Enough! 4th Armored Division Reenactment Association Newsletter* (January 1999): 1.

[During one event . . . father of their children.] Mail call letter to Lt. Luke Gardner from "Robert M. Connolly, Lt. Col. USA, G-1 4th Armored Division."

["It rained on our original *zeltbahn* . . . repeated during the war."] Greg Wylie, "Why I reenact," WWII Newsgroup, 20 November 1996.

162   [According to my questionnaire . . . not important at all.] Roughly 60 percent of reenactors say that winning in an event is not important at all; about 11 percent say it is somewhat unimportant; less than 5 percent say that it is either vitally or very important; and a little more than a quarter say that winning is somewhat important.

["Who cares who wins . . . expensively dressed paintballers."] Burt Johnson, "Referees," WWII Newsgroup, 18 November 1996.

163   ["If you haven't spent . . . a 100 percent accurate re-creation."] Bob Shore, [no subject],
         WWII Newsgroup, 22 November 1996.

         ["I would never begin . . . to God we never do."] Bob Still, "MILES for Reenactors," WWII
         Newsgroup, 21 November 1996.

8. "Look! I'm a Stamp!"

173   [What he saw . . . *Great War and Modern Memory.*] Paul Fussell, *The Great War and Modern
         Memory* (New York: Oxford University Press, 1975).

177   ["He leapt forward . . . entered the hellish hailstorm."] William Azari, "After Action Report:
         North Vernon-17-2-96," *Third SS Zeitung: The Official Newsletter of the Re-enactment Group
         "Totenkopf"* (April 1996): 18.

178   [In fact, so central . . . actual period photographs.] Grunts: French Vietnam War
         Reenactment Society, unit Web page, http://grunts.free.fr.

         [events it calls "photo reenactments"] Unit Listing, Reenacting Units, US and Allied Forces,
         www.reenactor.net/korea_nam/vietnam.html.

         ["We do not want to . . . would have appeared in 1944."] Event announcement, "Anzio:
         Breakout from the Beachhead," World War II private reenactment, Massachusetts, spon-
         sored by the 3rd Panzer Grenadier Division, August 1998.

180   [William Gregory described a video . . . of the original films."] William Gregory, "Men
         against blanks?" WWII Newsgroup, 31 July 1996.

183   ["I'm still telling stories . . . the Monday I got back."] Paul Sciora, "Spare musette bag?"
         4th Armored Listserv, 10 May 2000.

         ["may not enjoy it . . . for any in the world."] John Haneke, "Addressing some concerns,"
         WWII Newsgroup, 14 January 1999.

         ["Anyone who has been . . . experience when they get home."] Ibid.

184   ["every reenactor affects every other reenactor."] Greg Steel, "The ultimate stitch 'food'
         nazi," WWII Newsgroup, 21 November 1997.

         ["can only be as . . . least authentic members."] Luke Gardner, letter to the editor, *On the
         Wire* 8 (fall 1997): 5.

9. "I'm Dead! I Just Want to Party!"

185   ["play it as correctly as they can."] Paul Harding, phone conversation with the author,
         July 1996.

186   ["something, someone, some idea . . . from historical reality."] Hank Lyle, "British wool
         shirts," WWII Newsgroup, 24 July 1996.

187   ["don't want to get dirty . . . tearing their pants."] Bob Still, [no subject], WWII Newsgroup,
         18 November 1996.

         ["think they're John . . . like for the soldiers."] James Turk, "Morris' FIG 2000?" Wehrmacht
         Newsgroup, 19 April 1999. "Steiner" refers to Sergeant Steiner, a character in Sam
         Peckinpah's film *Cross of Iron.*

         ["There is a high 'puss-factor' . . . they did if possible."] Philip Moss, "Weather. . . ." WWII
         Newsgroup, 13 January 1999.

         ["If I wanted to get . . . via natural exposure."] Steve Tilden, "On zeltbahns," WWII
         Newsgroup, 5 November 1997.

["I do not feel . . . get a better experience."] Tim Gilbert, "Reenacting 'What it's really like,'" WWII Newsgroup, 22 August 1996.

188 [German reenactor Greg Steel . . . rearranged their faces."] Greg Steel, "Yorkville battle summary," WWII Newsgroup, 26 October 1997.

189 ["Kevlar" reenactors.] Philip Moss, "Men against blanks," WWII Newsgroup, 6 July 1997.

["An MG34 . . . exemplify deadness.'"] Greg Steel, "Men against blanks," WWII Newsgroup, 6 July 1997.

["I can't tell you . . . anyone was shooting at me.'"] Steve Tilden, "Referees—reply," WWII Newsgroup, 19 November 1996.

["Your gun [might not be] zeroed . . . affecting the mechanical aspects."] Lawrence Beal, "Germans not taking hits?" WWII Newsgroup, 4 February 1997.

190 ["Scream, yell, and play out a good death scene."] Tim Robb, "Enlightenment from the GWA vice president," *On the Wire* 7 (spring 1996): 8.

["When hit, fall (carefully . . . spoilsports we don't need."] Craig Bass, "Rules of Engagement," *The Front: A Quarterly Publication of the California Historical Group World War II Living History Association* 20 (summer 1995): 6.

["It can be very disappointing . . . disheartening."] Scott Silver, "Germans not taking hits?" WWII Newsgroup, 4 February 1997.

["takes a lot . . . of our hobby."] GWA, "Rules of Engagement," October 1997.

["I take hits . . . realities of the battlefield."] Greg Steel, "Canadians taking hits," WWII Newsgroup, 5 November 1997.

191 ["courtesy" that is "expected . . . to the opposition."] W2HPG, "Tactical Rules of Engagement," n.d.

["Nothing is more . . . 'Hollywood' death."] Bill Mason, "US Units and appearance," WWII Newsgroup, 10 September 1997.

192 ["guns and alcohol do not mix."] Tim Scherrer, "Dangers of reenacting," WWII Newsgroup, 5 December 1996.

[One German reenactor reported . . . fear of his worthless life."] Greg Steel, "Canadians taking hits," WWII Newsgroup, 5 November 1997.

["Too many loud-mouthed . . . NCOs' and officers' orders."] Lon Santo, "November 1990 GWA Show," *Gas Attack of the New York Division, 27th Div. USA* 4 (winter 1991): 2.

["In real combat . . . the dangers of the battlefield."] Luke Gardner, letter to Vance Hollee critiquing reenactment video, fall 1997.

193 ["Once on the base . . . where the people were."] Wilson Lyle, "Pizza delivery," Wehrmacht Newsgroup, 23 November 1999.

["Reenactor . . . have the car keys."] Morris Call, email to the author, 15 April 1997.

["Bitching about officers . . . a soldier's existence."] Bob Still, "At ease servicemen," WWII Newsgroup, 26 May 1998.

["I have enough . . . I don't want any."] Gorden Harris, "Occifers," WWII Newsgroup, 7 December 1997.

["almost like going to work."] One reenactor sometimes brings a bit of his real work to events. A real-life chiropractor, and GD member, he will often provide free back adjustments to unit members during downtime. I once had the opportunity to have my back adjusted by him at an Eastern Front event.

198   ["a battle where one . . . be recognized."] Vic Mossar, "Commentary #1 (long)," 25 May 1999.
        ["When you are passionate . . . the King, or the US of A."] Craig Bass, "Truce," WWII
        Newsgroup, 19 January 1998.

200   ["Mother of God . . . is a crazy idea."] Norman Rabon , "Blood group markings," Wehrmacht
        Newsgroup, 10 December 1999.
        ["separate reality from fantasy."] Ernest Tagg, "Craig [Bass]," WWII Newsgroup, 5 December
        1996.

202   ["It is actually kind of . . . slaughtering somebody else."] Hank Lyle, "Why reenact," WWII
        Newsgroup, 20 November 1997.
        ["We of the Hohenstaufen . . . delivered to you by his army."] Phil Herr, "Allied company
        assignments, FIG '98," WWII Newsgroup, 18 January 1998.
        ["Oh, please . . . last guys that believed it."] Mike Sharp, "Allied company assignments, FIG
        '98," WWII Newsgroup, 18 January 1998.

203   ["Nazis; all mouth."] Willard Samuel, "Allied company assignments, FIG '98," WWII
        Newsgroup, 18 January 1998.
        ["I do not portray a 'Nazi' . . . from a fellow reenactor."] Phil Herr, "The 'N' word," WWII
        Newsgroup, 19 January 1998.
        ["I think we all realize . . . a little too seriously."] Ibid.
        ["Put a cork in . . . legs and dry up."] Willard Samuel, "The 'N' word," WWII Newsgroup,
        19 January 1998.

204   ["We should not fight . . . to be united."] Johnny Schoenfield, "Armor safety," WWII
        Newsgroup, 22 May 1998.

205   ["We cannot control . . . for the rest of us."] Philip Moss, "Thoughts," WWII Newsgroup, 7
        November 1997.

10. "Farbs You Find Everywhere"

206   ["We are here to portray . . . not the exception."] HRS, "Safety and Authenticity Rules," 1996.
        ["some latitude . . . to authenticity."] Greg Wylie, "A possible rationale for a farb," WWII
        Newsgroup, 16 November 1997.
        ["honor veterans' memories by . . . in the proper kit."] Anzio event announcement, August
        1998.

207   ["Guys who go the extra . . . to look at them."] Tim Marcus, "My 2 Pfennig," WWII
        Newsgroup, 23 July 1996.
        ["All men and women will . . . in World War I."] Twentieth Century Tactical Studies Group,
        Inc., "Rules and Regulations," 1998.
        ["We do not want . . . non-period/incorrect items."] Anzio event announcement, August 1998.
        ["Authenticity and haircut regulations . . . at the next event."] World War II Historical
        Preservation Federation, "Event Rules and Regulations, Battle of the Bulge: 50th Anniversary
        Commemoration," November 1994.

209   ["I can understand . . . researched and thought out?"] Ralph Hanson, "Battledress, think
        about it," WWII Newsgroup, 7 November 1997.
        ["Respective unit leaders . . . their unit to have."] Wilson Lyle, "Brit groups/national units,"
        WWII Newsgroup, 13 December 1996.
        [One World War II British unit's . . . a la long johns.)"] First Airborne Division, No. 4 Cdo.
        C Troop, "Lonsdale Force," "Authenticity Guidelines," 1996.

["adopt that which was . . . uniforms and equipment."] Infanterie-Regiment Nr. 63, "Regulations," September 1997.

["At a close up . . . a World War II soldier."] John Shampo, "Unit Commander's Letter to Potential Recruits, HRS 3rd SS Division, Totenkopf," March 1997.

["You must have all . . . and buy carefully."] Fourth Armored Web page, 1997.

210   ["a consistent, correct appearance."] Stephen Paul, "Comments on WW2 reenacting," WWII Newsgroup, 18 December 1996.

["eliminate any discrepancy."] Fifth SS Panzer Division, Unit Manual, "Uniform Regulations," 1990.

["a unit full of exceptions."] Tim Marcus, "Authenticity," WWII Newsgroup, 24 July 1996.

["In assembling his personal . . . can be built."] Infanterie Regiment 63, "Guidelines for 3./Infanterie-Regiment Nr. 63," September 1997.

["It costs between . . . too much money."] Steve Tilden, "On zeltbahns," WWII Newsgroup, 5 November 1997.

["authenticity costs money, period."] Whitman Ford, "Reenactmentfare," WWII Newsgroup, 6 November 1997.

["the cost between . . . as people think."] William Gregory, "Alter hase," WWII Newsgroup, 15 November 1997.

["it's one big mess and . . . all 'just get along.'"] Wilson Lyle, "Brit groups/national units," WWII Newsgroup, 13 December 1996.

["once you bow . . . doomed to stay there."] Philip Moss, "On zeltbahns and farbicity," WWII Newsgroup, 5 November 1997.

[One German reenactor describes . . . saying, *"Wehrmachtschnitt."*] Felix Schurz, [no subject], WWII Newsgroup, 6 July 1996.

211   ["complete [authenticity] is not achievable."] Bob Still, "Original vs. acceptable," WWII Newsgroup, 18 December 1996.

["pompous shits . . . anything that isn't perfect."] Hugh Carville, "Something to chew on," WWII Newsgroup, 2 June 1998.

[If a reenactor is "so wrapped . . . job as a model."] Stephan Paul, "Comments on WW2 reen-acting," WWII Newsgroup, 18 December 1996.

212   ["become so obsessed . . . they do not have fun."] Tim Gilbert, "Good enough—reply," WWII Newsgroup, 12 November 1997.

["constantly at war with each other."] Greg Steel, "Farbs vs. Stitch Nazis," WWII Newsgroup, 5 November 1997.

["most people are too lazy or cheap to do it right."] Philip Moss, "Survey," WWII Newsgroup, 13 June 1997.

[But Philip Moss couldn't . . . irritation of such farbism.] Philip Moss, "Farbolio horror stories," WWII Newsgroup, 13 September 1997.

[one reenactor complained . . . without rest for months."] Paul Strauch, "In the field," Wehrmacht Newsgroup, 8 January 1999.

["a steady decline . . . rubber-soled hiking boots."] Letter to the editor, *On the Wire* 8 (spring 1997): 5.

[Most units prohibit . . . earning them in events.] One unit awards gold close combat clasps only to members who serve "for 150 consecutive tactical combat days at TMHS tactical battle events." Other higher awards, such as the German or Knights Cross, are given only for "continuous and outstanding leadership, both on and off the field of battle, over a period of years, and require unanimous consent of everyone [in the unit.]" Steve Tilden, "Awards," WWII Newsgroup, 30 December 1996.

213   [When one unit member . . . on unfavorable terms."] Myron Beal, "Awards," WWII Newsgroup, 1 January 1997.

[the concept of "'this is okay . . . or it is not right.'"] Hank Lyle, "Farb vs. Stitch Nazi," WWII Newsgroup, 6 November 1997.

214   ["Individuals are looking for . . . guy without 'authority.'"] Greg Steel, "Small survey," WWII Newsgroup, 23 September 1997.

["We have a standard equipment . . . how farby we are."] Frank Lieberman, "Lawsuits, women, and farbs!" WWII Newsgroup, 3 February 1999.

215   ["When someone tells me . . . a Coors when they said it."] Shawn Birt, "My 2 Pfennig," WWII Newsgroup, 23 July 1996.

[A small percentage . . . a positive way.] Most reenactors define a hardcore by identifying more than one characteristic. About 60 percent say a hardcore is "concerned with authenticity." Roughly a third say a hardcore "takes reenacting seriously." One third say a hardcore "puts the most time, money, and energy into reenacting." Nearly one third identify a hardcore as having all of the above characteristics. Less than 10 percent define a hardcore as one who simply attends a lot of events.

[Using this model . . . hardcore status (8–10).] I asked reenactors to rate themselves and each other on my 1997 questionnaire. A 1997 survey conducted by the HRS confirmed my own results in terms of how reenactors judge themselves and each other. HRS members rated their own unit's authenticity level at 89 percent, while the authenticity level of other HRS members was rated at 67 percent. HRS, "Membership survey," 1997. Thanks to Alicia Mellon for sharing the HRS survey with me.

216   ["The only aspect that . . . hates the SS even more."] Craig Bass, "Units getting along?" WWII Newsgroup, 7 October 1997.

["the very juvenile idea . . . anyone else's."] Morris Call, email to the author, "Thoughts on reenacting," 14 January 1997

218   ["If you can't afford . . . My feeling is no."] Whitman Ford, "Reenactmentfare," WWII Newsgroup, 6 November 1997.

["We can be flexible . . . overweight from five hundred feet.)"] Luke Gardner, Fourth Armored, Headquarters 51st Armored Infantry Battalion, "Recruitment of New Members," n.d.

219   ["I don't consider my weight . . . also pushing, age."] Lou Rockefeller, "Big vs. thin," WWII Newsgroup, 2 June 1998.

["I remember ten years ago . . . Benny Hill, fer Chrissake."] Al Adams, "Reenactmenapause," Fourth Armored Newsgroup, 27 April 2000.

["FBT" or "Fat Boy Tax."] Andrew Haig, "Garrison (overseas caps)," WWII Newsgroup, 11 October 1996.

["Spare me the sight . . . coronary self in the field!"] Willard Samuel, "Big vs. thin," WWII Newsgroup, 2 June 1998.

["If you want to . . . made at Omar the Tentmaker."] Alf Wanamaker, "Bigger problems than uniform delivery," WWII Newsgroup, 1 June 1998.

["Hats off to Phil Fussel . . . and looked great."] Luke Gardner, Fourth Armored, Headquarters 51st Armored Infantry Battalion, "Recruitment of New Members," n.d.

["There is no excuse . . . call yourself a tank?"] Scott Silver, "Focus on authenticity," WWII Newsgroup, 13 May 1996.

[Many units require members . . . in commemorative terms.] Units such as the 4th Armored and Grossdeutschland do not allow women to portray men. The issue of women portraying male soldiers has long been debated in the hobby. In 1991, a female Civil War reenactor filed a lawsuit against the Department of the Interior after she was barred from an event when it was discovered that she was a woman dressed as a man. She won her lawsuit, and now the National Park Service is prohibited from excluding women reenactors from combat. For more on the woman who filed the lawsuit, see Amy Dockser Marcus, "When Janie Came Marching Home," *New York Times*, 23 March 2002.

["To me . . . sacrifice [the veterans] made."] Gorden Harris, "Ladies in WWII reenacting," WWII Newsgroup, 21 January 1998.

["I have spent . . . (female infantryman)."] Matt Nelson, "Women in reenacting," WWII Newsgroup, 12 February 1997.

220   ["I do not agree . . . for the other reenactors."] Margaret Kitteridge, "Ladies in WWII reenacting," WWII Newsgroup, 20 January 1998.

["You guys might get . . . to play as you do!"] Mark Reiser, "Lawsuits, women, and farbs!" WWII Newsgroup, 3 February 1999.

221   [if women "can pull off . . . look like a male soldier."] Hank Lyle, "Why not women?" WWII Newsgroup, 21 January 1998.

["We are already pushing . . . unbelievable."] Paul Myer, "Women in feld grau," Wehrmacht Newsgroup, 9 March 1999.

["If I had to choose . . . take the woman every time."] Steve Tilden, "Why not women?" WWII Newsgroup, 21 January 1998.

222   ["how much homage do . . . the god of reality?"] Karl Clift, [no subject], WWII Newsgroup, 3 February 1999.

["I think my outward . . . not stink sufficiently?"] Tim Gilbert, "Authenticity solution—reply," WWII Newsgroup, 8 November 1997.

["I will never win . . . good enough."] Wilson Lyle, "British 'wool' shirts made of cotton?" WWII Newsgroup, 23 July 1996.

["Close has to be good enough . . . acceptable to us."] Steve Tilden, "On zeltbahns," WWII Newsgroup, 5 November 1997.

225   ["Gee . . . group hug at the next battle."] Alf Wanamaker, "Kinder, gentler hobby," WWII Newsgroup, 2 June 1998.

226   ["slanted histories written . . . things 'politically' correct."] Max Terrell, "The question of minorities," WWII Newsgroup, 31 October 1998.

["jackasses that wish . . . to allow women."] Philip Moss, "Being PC and smut," WWII Newsgroup, 8 February 1998.

["History . . . blacks into the unit."] Luke Gardner, Fourth Armored, Headquarters 51st Armored Infantry Battalion, "Recruitment of New Members," n.d.

[exclusivity does "nothing but hurt the hobby."] Tim Marcus, "My 2 Pfennig," WWII Newsgroup, 23 July 1996.

226   [there must be a line . . . animosity and hard feelings."] Harry Pirandello, conversation with
       the author, January 1997.

       ["My feelings about 'fat' . . . has something to offer."] Steve Tilden, "No standards?" WWII
       Newsgroup, 2 June 1998.

       ["This is pretend . . . draw the line?"] James Comer, "Minorities in ranks," WWII
       Newsgroup, 31 October 1998.

       ["We will have to . . . dragoon them out of the hobby."] Luke Gardner, letter to the editor,
       On the Wire 8 (fall 1997): 5.

       ["We shouldn't cater . . . stamp them out."] Greg Steel, "Keep out the farbs," WWII
       Newsgroup, 8 February 1998.

       [Another argues for . . . need to be "hemmed."] John Haneke, "Authenticity—it's simple,"
       WWII Newsgroup, 17 January 1999.

227   [Wilson Lyle sums up . . . fragile feelings are at stake."] Lyle, "Brit groups/national units."

       [He recounted an event . . . sun goes down."] Steel, "Keep out the farbs."

228   [When a Korean American . . . handle this situation?"] William Gregory, "Minorities,"
       WWII Newsgroup, 30 October 1998.

       ["a kind of exchange program . . . fought with the Germans."] Sam True, "Minorities,"
       WWII Newsgroup, 30 October 1998.

       [Another recounted hearing . . . German prisoners."] James Turk, "Minorities," WWII
       Newsgroup, 30 October 1998.

       [Another simply advised . . . every case that comes up."] Peter Locke, "Minorities," WWII
       Newsgroup, 30 October 1998.

       ["I'd say 'no' to him . . . the First Officer in Das Boot?"] Frank O'Hara, "Minorities," WWII
       Newsgroup, 31 October 1998.

       ["it's not about race . . . in an authentic way."] Philip Moss, "Minorities," WWII Newsgroup,
       30 October 1998.

       ["You probably don't recruit . . . problem with a Korean."] Barry Lott, "Minorities," WWII
       Newsgroup, 30 October 1998.

229   ["This is America . . . go ask a lawyer."] Mark Holtstein, "Women in feld grau," Wehrmacht
       Newsgroup, 9 March 1999.

       ["As we all know . . . than to tempt fate!"] Hugh Carville, "Minorities," WWII Newsgroup,
       30 October 1998.

       ["Okay, guys . . . moral or religious crusade."] Steve Tilden, "On zeltbahns," WWII
       Newsgroup, 5 November 1997.

       [Tim Gilbert finds . . . this is how they relax."] Tim Gilbert, "Thoughts on authenticity
       debate," WWII Newsgroup, 7 November 1997.

230   ["notoriously individualistic."] Gerald Lee, "What to do," WWII Newsgroup, 14 June 1997.

       ["secretly take pleasure . . . shake our heads at."] Adam Granger, "Adam's letter," WWII
       Newsgroup, 11 December 1997.

       ["feelings get hurt a lot in this hobby."] Haneke, "Authenticity—it's simple."

       ["Let history be your yardstick!"] Greg Steel, "Authenticity solution," WWII Newsgroup,
       7 November 1997.

11. "Preaching a Version of the Gospel"

231   ["As I sit and look . . . typical M43 jackets."] Thomas Farley, "German uniform questions,"
       WWII Newsgroup, 8 June 1996.

[On the World War II reenactor . . . Army Air Corps badge?"] Lawrence Sams, "5th Scottish Light Infantry Battalion, 1st Airborne Div.," WWII Newsgroup, 3 December 1998.

[Meanwhile, another pondered . . . more of a "gray green?"] Scott Silver, "Color, colour," WWII Newsgroup, 9 January 1997.

232   ["only then will the intelligence . . . of all nations."] George Lapin, "SPR reactions," WWII Newsgroup, 26 July 1998.

233   ["The movie showed great . . . straight up the bluffs."] Thomas Farley, "The Longest Day," WWII Newsgroup, 26 January 1997.

["They were wearing M-28 . . . carrying a Thompson."] Matt Nelson, "The Longest Day," WWII Newsgroup, 27 January 1997.

["I do get a chuckle . . . the wrong weapons."] Gerald Lee, "Movie trivia," WWII Newsgroup, 1 August 1996.

["The haircuts bugged us . . . too British."] Greg Wylie, "German haircuts," WWII Newsgroup, 26 July 1998.

234   ["I'm gonna watch . . . Shooting Gallery scene."] Al Adams, "Wara! Wara! Wara!" WWII Newsgroup, 16 August 2000.

["It is very anecdotal . . . is so fascinating."] Walter Littman, "Devils in Baggy Pants," WWII Newsgroup, 27 January 1997.

["very clearly indicated . . . right with my impressions."] Bob Still, "Follow-up on reference to a book," WWII Newsgroup, 19 November 1996.

235   ["Just because a book's . . . mean that it is."] Steve Tilden, "The Forgotten Soldier," WWII Newsgroup, 15 July 1996.

[Moreover, William said . . . die for his country."] William Gregory, "The Forgotten Soldier," WWII Newsgroup, 25 November 1996.

["I believe that many . . . true details to light."] Felix Schurz, "The Forgotten Soldier," WWII Newsgroup, 16 July 1996.

[For one reenactor . . . viewed with skepticism."] Tim Marcus, "SS controversy," WWII Newsgroup, 10 July 1996.

["You can read all . . . experience something firsthand."] Greg Wylie, "Why I reenact," WWII Newsgroup, 20 November 1997.

["leading personalities and grand operations."] Philip Moss, "WWII German Reenactor's Reading List and Research Tips," 1997.

236   ["nowhere in the US . . . sleeve undershirt in OD."] Joe Estefan, "T-shirts," WWII Newsgroup, 23 December 1998.

[Many others cross-checked . . . in the ETO."] Joe Estefan, "T-shirts," WWII Newsgroup, 26 December 1998.

["Before you go relying . . . had is listed."] Sharp Hammond, "T-shirts," WWII Newsgroup, 24 December 1998.

["Could the OD T-shirt . . . the item lists."] Frank O'Hara, "T-shirts," WWII Newsgroup, 26 December 1998.

["Look at the changes . . . written down someplace."] Joseph Radway, "TO&E slavery is bad," WWII Newsgroup, 14 June 1996.

["the more you look . . . confused you can get."] Lawrence Beal, "Pictures," WWII Newsgroup, 31 October 1996.

[For this reason, some . . . to the same question.] Lawrence Sams, "5th Scottish Light Infantry Battalion, 1st Airborne Div.," WWII Newsgroup, 3 December 1998.

236   ["especially during the later . . . purely practical reasons."] Walter White, [no subject], WWII Newsgroup, 20 December 1996.

["One should never say . . . of absolutely anything."] Steve Tilden, "The Forgotten Soldier," WWII Newsgroup, 15 July 1996.

237   ["If they didn't . . . neither should we!"] John Pallacci, "T-shirt wars," WWII Newsgroup, 27 December 1998.

["every trivial detail . . . on-the-head-of-a-pin arguments."] Steve Tilden, "On zeltbahns," WWII Newsgroup, 5 November 1997.

["to pay more . . . popular/issued most often."] Ibid.

["God . . . or white boxer briefs!"] James Comer, "T-shirt wars," WWII Newsgroup, 26 December 1998.

["Maybe we should institute . . . before May of 45."] Bob Still, "Original versus acceptable," WWII Newsgroup, 18 December 1996.

["Underwear is only . . . into everyone else's business."] Joe Estefan, "T-shirts," WWII Newsgroup, 26 December 1998.

["what is acceptable."] Bob Still, "Ten foot or ten inches rule," WWII Newsgroup, 20 December 1996.

["a diminishing asset . . . our research in books."] Homer Thomas, "Reading (long . . . sorry)," WWII Newsgroup, 18 June 1998.

238   [Craig Bass described . . . all in the same unit."] Craig Bass, [no subject], WWII Newsgroup, 26 July 1996.

["repress so much . . . details along with it."] Mark Wilson, "War and remembrance," WWII Newsgroup, 9 July 1996.

["There is an art . . . interesting things."] Joseph Radway, [no subject], WWII Newsgroup, 5 August 1996.

[After attending a World War II . . . amazed us."] Mark Wilson, "Authenticity," WWII Newsgroup, 24 July 1996.

239   ["The veterans are wrong . . . the war is over."] Mike Ceynowa, "Authenticity," WWII Newsgroup, 25 July 1996.

["Vets shouldn't be . . . the reenacting community."] Adam Granger, "Uniforms," WWII Newsgroup, 29 January 1997.

["Some [veterans] saw terrible . . . left of their life."] Craig Bass, "War and remembrance," WWII Newsgroup, 26 July 1996.

["He has spoken to . . . at times during the war."] Matthew Crell, [no subject], WWII Newsgroup, 23 July 1996.

["Nothing hacks me off . . . things to worry about."] Author unknown, WWII Newsgroup, 27 July 1997.

[Morris Call identifies what . . . reenactors can be.] Morris Call, email to the author, "Vets and reenacts," 4 June 1997.

240   ["I have never figured out . . . really feel their pain?"] Steve Tilden, "On zeltbahns and far-bicity," WWII Newsgroup, 6 November 1997.

[Another reenactor recalls . . . reenacting mirrors reality."] Paul Verros, "Questions," WWII Newsgroup, 16 February 1998.

242   ["Pictures don't lie."] Greg Wylie, "Good enough revisited," WWII Newsgroup, 14 November 1997.

["You can never . . . maintaining an impression."] Philip Moss, "From Mount Olympus," WWII Newsgroup, 13 September 1997.

["able to look at . . . see nary a difference."] Alan Schaeffer, "Grosz," Wehrmacht Newsgroup, 19 April 1999.

243 ["If another reenactor falls . . . that fashion during wartime."] Walter White, [no subject], WWII Newsgroup. 20 December 1996.

[Calling it a "big bugaboo . . . the European Theater.] Edward Stewart, "US camo photo ETO," WWII Newsgroup, 18 August 1996.

[His commander, Tim Gilbert . . . of the 2nd A.D. Engineers."] Tim Gilbert, "US camo ETO," WWII Newsgroup, 19 August 1996.

["Contact the Airborne museum . . . Imperial War Museum."] Craig Bass, "A question for you all," WWII Newsgroup, 17 August 1996.

["Even if evidence was . . . wearing that stuff."] Edward Stewart, "US camo photo ETO," WWII Newsgroup, 18 August 1996.

["If a person looks . . . anything he wants."] William Gregory, [no subject], WWII Newsgroup, 21 December 1996.

["Don't pick out . . . everyone else got!"] Hampton Roads Historical Reenactments, "Purpose and Authenticity Guidelines," 1993.

244 [Preservation issues . . . concern with appearance.] With such an emphasis on the "appearance" of authenticity, reenactors coined the term "Hollywood rifle" to describe a reenactor's weapon that lacks the telltale blank adaptor since it has been internally altered to fire blanks. Such a procedure irreparably alters the weapon—it can never be used for live fire—but in terms of an illusion, or the appearance of authenticity, many believe it is extremely authentic-looking.

["The Wehrmacht as . . . crusty stuff are wrong."] Philip Moss, "Survey," WWII Newsgroup, 13 June 1997.

["I'm sure one guy . . . show up like that."] Bill Mason, "Focus on authenticity," WWII Newsgroup, 14 May 1996.

["One should take . . . 10 percent of your unit."] William Gregory, "A small survey to stir the pot," WWII Newsgroup, 13 June 1997.

245 ["What is the difference . . . BC611 and the 617?"] Charles Seed, "BC611 and 617 difference," WWII Newsgroup, 24 December 1996.

["Does anybody have . . . should be packed?"] Bill Mason, "Question about footlockers," WWII Newsgroup, 1 October 1996.

["It's a treat . . . to your own."] John Shampo, "Unit Commander's Letter to Potential Recruits, HRS 3rd SS Division, Totenkopf," March 1997.

["My other reliable source . . . Philip Moss."] Greg Steel, "Philip [Moss] is a god," WWII Newsgroup, 26 July 1998.

246 [One reenactor took on . . . alkyd paints, not blanco."] Scott Silver, "White blanco query," WWII Newsgroup, 21 October 1996.

["Even with all . . . house with white blanco."] Ibid.

248 ["I once had a guy . . . won't believe you' situations."] Gorden Harris, "T-shirts," WWII Newsgroup, 23 December 1998.

["Do the words . . . answers to it all."] Philip Moss, [no subject], WWII Newsgroup, 12 July 1998.

248   ["It appears that in 1996 . . . our version of the gospel."] Duane Kit, "Authenticity," WWII Newsgroup, 24 July 1996.

249   [creating "an all-encompassing . . . next to impossible."] Hampton Roads Historical Reenactments, "Purpose and Authenticity Guidelines," 1993.

[such a guide "sounds nice . . . as World War II reenactors."] Mark Wilson, "Guide," WWII Newsgroup, 17 March 1997.

["extracurricular exchanges . . . simulation of armed conflict."] Wade Mantegna, "FIG rubbish—reply," WWII Newsgroup, 31 January 1997.

12. "How to Play Army Without Everybody Getting Pissed at Each Other"

250   ["How to Play . . . Each Other."] Bill Lauter, "National battle," WWI Newsgroup, 7 March 1998.

["You are a brick . . . lest you destabilize it."] In 1909, Baden-Powell, founder of the Boy Scouts, wrote: "Being a fellow among many others, you are like one brick among many others. . . . If you are discontented with your place or with your neighbour's or you are a rotten brick, you are no good to the wall. . . . If the bricks get quarreling among themselves the wall is liable to split and the whole house to fall." Quoted in Michael Rosenthal, *The Character Factory: Baden-Powell and the Origins of the Boy Scout Movement* (New York: Pantheon, 1986), 9.

["To expect that reenactors . . . reduce the animosity?"] Wade Mantegna, "FIG rubbish—reply," WWII Newsgroup, 31 January 1997.

251   ["Flame me, you fat little pogue."] Bill Lauter, "Quit whining!" WWII Newsgroup, 25 February 1998.

["You are such . . . tell you more about it."] Greg Steel, "Why you shouldn't join 2nd Panzer," WWII Newsgroup, 11 March 1998.

["unconstructive babble."] Jesse Hill, "Quit whining!" WWII Newsgroup, 25 February 1998.

["stop bickering."] Willard Samuel, "Yep!" WWII Newsgroup, 28 December 1997.

["take a 'lude."] Greg Steel, "Personal attacks," WWII Newsgroup, 26 February 1998.

["Remember we are all . . . we will always remain."] Phil Fussel, "Now that that's over with," 4th Armored Newsgroup, 6 August 2000.

["If two 4th members . . . towards the Germans!"] Scott Wawszyzki, "A Laurel and Hardy handshake," 4th Armored Newsgroup, 5 August 2000.

["This hobby can only . . . if we unite."] Donald Kiev, "Words from the GWA President," *On the Wire* 8 (fall 1997): 6.

[In his GWA newsletter . . . put up with it."] Perry Trent, "From the G-8," *On the Wire* (spring 1999): 4.

["all input has . . . considered and weighed."] Greg Wylie, "National battle," WWII Newsgroup, 7 March 1998.

["If a person can . . . will be permitted."] 20th Century Tactical Studies Group, Inc., "Rules and Regulations," 1998.

["If you feel that we . . . prove us wrong."] William Gregory, "German authenticity for the [1997] Gap," December 1996.

[By requiring documented proof . . . to reenactors themselves.] For example, the GWA's authenticity committee, co-chaired by the Allied and Central Powers Representatives, has the power to "review all newly forming units and determine their historical correctness."

GWA, "Bylaws of the Great War Association," ratified 1990; revised 1995, p. 6–7. Meanwhile, the HRS by-laws outline an extensive process for appealing authenticity decisions: "Appeals on matters of authenticity may be made by the submission to the chairmen of the Authenticity Committee in writing, with six (6) photographs; three (3) of the items used by the re-enactors and three (3) photographs taken during World War II period. These pictures must be proven original and/or copies from a published source and must show the disputed item in use by troops of the same unit, type, and rank as the re-enactor. A majority vote by the members of the Authenticity Committee shall decide the issue." Historical Reenactment Society, "Safety and Authenticity Rules," 1996, p. 4.

252   ["Authenticity is set . . . and peer pressure."] Mike Brown, "Ten foot or ten inches rule," WWII Newsgroup, 19 December 1996. Even Luke agrees that peer pressure is one of the best ways to hem any loose ends: "I have less than exceptional characters in my unit," he says, "but I think that being around the other guys kind of buoys them up, and it kind of shows them what's right and what's wrong." Dave Watkins agrees: poor reenactors, he says, "can be worked on. If they're willing to stick with the hobby, it will rub off on them."
[Morris Call willingly acknowledges . . . rewritten to fit the bill."] Morris Call, email to the author, 16 January 1997.
["The homogenization of . . . they can to play."] Morris Call, email to the author, "Thoughts on reenacting," 14 January 1997.
["If you can't produce . . . moral high ground."] Duane Kit, "Odds and sods," WWII Newsgroup, 24 July 1996.
["As a fellow American . . . what you feel is correct."] Gil Rausch, "Women in feld grau," Wehrmacht Newsgroup, 9 March 1999.

253   [When Craig Bass, who . . . events in hot weather.] Craig described the shirts as being the "same cut and color as the originals," and justified them on a number of grounds: one, the original wool was expensive and rare; two, repros allowed for making larger sized shirts for larger-sized reenactors; and three, wearing originals would leave them "tattered." Craig Bass, "British 'wool' shirts made of cotton??" WWII Newsgroup, 23 July 1996.
["If clothing versus . . . shirts made out of cotton.)"] Wilson Lyle, "British 'wool' shirts made of cotton??" WWII Newsgroup, 23 July 1996.
[For Tim Gilbert this . . . cannot control everyone else."] Tim Gilbert, "Authenticity solution—reply," WWII Newsgroup, 8 November 1997.
["Anyone out of . . . school and the playground."] Morris Call, email to the author, "Thoughts on reenacting," 8 January 1997.

254   [in February 1998 . . . authenticity of their impressions.] Letter from GWA president and vice president to participants not falling into normal unit member status, "Complying with the Bylaws of the Great War Association," 25 February 1998. The GWA bylaws define registered independents as "non-combatants and individuals who do not fit in regular member units, such as nurses, chaplains, pilots or medical impressions." GWA women reenactors, who usually portray nurses or Red Cross workers, are considered "friends of the trenches," loosely allied with and sponsored by a given unit, but technically, not official unit members. Women such as Grace Hall, who considers herself an active member of her World War I German unit, find such a distinction ludicrous.

256   [Tim concurred . . . needed to purge!"] Tim Reed, email to the author, "GWABWA," 1 July 1999.

256   [Tim was forced to . . . the fall 1990 event.] Lon Santo, "November 1990 GWA show," *Gas Attack of the New York Division, 27th Div. USA* 4 (winter 1991): 2.

257   [Ironically, the members . . . placed on probation.] In August 1997 the G-7 put the Russian Legion on probation, which meant that any further violations would be the grounds for ejection from the GWA. Philip Moss described their behavior: "Two members of my own unit were shot in the face by members of the Russian Legion. This and their steadfast refusal to take hits is growing thin!" Philip Moss, "Ramblings from atop the soapbox," *On the Wire* 8 (fall 1997): 3.

["That's all it . . . game with rules."] Greg Wylie, "National battle," WWII Newsgroup, 7 March 1998.

["why does anyone . . . fun takes order."] Alan Schaeffer, "Big armor battle—shoot and skoot!" WWII Newsgroup, 7 July 1999.

[The words "authenticity . . . are interchangeable."] Grossdeutschland Division, "German Authenticity Guidelines," 1996.

["What I've told my . . . It does work."] Craig Bass, "Units getting along?" WWII Newsgroup, 7 October 1997.

["Play well together . . . all in the open."] Morris Call, email to the author, "Changing the way it goes," 2 April 1997.

258   ["It's all about having a collective mindset."] Karl Brady, "Attitude," Wehrmacht Newsgroup, 19 April 1999.

["conform to authenticity."] William Gregory, "FIG 98 authenticity inspection," WWII Newsgroup, 17 December 1997.

["follow the rules set up by the consensus."] Greg Wylie, "National battle," WWII Newsgroup. 7 March 1998.

["disagree with policy and try to break away."] Mark Wilson, "National organization," WWII Newsgroup, 20 December 1996.

["extreme individualism . . . fragmentation of the hobby."] Morris Call, email to the author, "Old vs new," 10 April 1997.

["a cancer to this hobby."] Greg Steel, "What's up?" WWII Newsgroup, 8 October 1997.

[Bill Lauter illustrated . . . over you and your hobby."] Bill Lauter, "Standards! The War & Peace version," WWII Newsgroup, 9 March 1998.

259   ["A farb will never . . . help me do that?' "] Bill Rodriguez, "The definition of a farb." n.d.

260   ["You have forgotten . . . abandon this outfit."] Luke Gardner, email to 4th Armored members, 2000.

261   ["We should all bury . . . if this was real war."] Tim Marcus, "Laundry apology," WWII Newsgroup, 10 May 1996.

263   ["Soldiers can talk . . . speak the language."] Morris Call, email to the author, "Vets," 8 June 1997.

264   ["I know I'm sounding . . . but the relationships."] Morris Call, email to the author, "A thought," 4 September 2000.

265   ["This is real camaraderie . . . friends with each other."] Greg Steel, "Yorkville battle summary," WWII Newsgroup, 26 October 1997.

266   ["The keen sense of . . . wine, women, and song."] Pat Goodman, "Genug!!" Wehrmacht Newsgroup, 27 August 2000.

[Another reenactor remembers . . . left the room."] Burt Carson, "Guadalcanal/Americal Div.," WWII Newsgroup, 24 June 1997.

269   ["I wanted to . . . not be great?"] Morris Call, email to the author, "Thoughts V," 31 January 1997.

[Another reenactor recalls . . . homesick for my wife and two kids."] Sherman Lake, "The Battle of Neuville, France, November 1998," *The Shell Hole* (spring 1999): 5.

271   [Each storyteller performed . . . next took over.] Linguist Deborah Tannen describes this phenomenon in *You Just Don't Understand: Women and Men in Conversation* (New York: Ballantine, 1990), 76–77.

272   [an impromptu Christmas truce . . . during World War I.] See Stanley Weintraub, *Silent Night: The Remarkable Christmas 1914 Truce* (New York: Free Press, 2001). The truce is also discussed in Modris Eksteins, *Rites of Spring: The Great War and the Birth of the Modern Age* (New York: Anchor Books, 1990).

Epilogue: "Let's See What She's Writing"

275   ["My sole concern . . . grow and be respected."] Greg Steel, "Look at these guys," WWII Newsgroup, 9 March 1998.

276   ["I can't wait to . . . a better reenactor!"] Ben Sandler, letter to the author, June 1999.

279   [In the end, I would . . . concerns of the men within it.] Scholar John Caughey argues that a form of imagination-based experience, such as fantasy—and, I would add, reenacting— is not "completely an escape." Instead it is "partly determined by the particular cultural norms it attempts to transcend." John L. Caughey, *Imaginary Social Worlds: A Cultural Approach* (Lincoln: University of Nebraska Press, 1984), 186. Such experiences, Caughey argues, "reflect problems in the wider social system, including the disruption of traditional social relationships and the erosion of value systems" (247).

[It is within this context . . . behave as men.] For more on contemporary masculinity see, Susan Faludi, *Stiffed: The Betrayal of the American Man* (New York: Morrow, 1999).

280   [But at the same time . . . must change with it.] For more on the shifting values of masculinity see, William Betcher and William Pollack, *In a Time of Fallen Heroes: The Re-Creation of Masculinity* (New York: Macmillan, 1993.) There's no doubt that women have long struggled with their own cultural contradictions and mixed messages concerning how they should behave, and for years they have grappled with the insecurity that arises as a result. I couldn't help but feel that male reenactors are caught up in a similar set of contractions, and perhaps this is just one reason that I came to identify with so many of them, even as a woman.

284   [In an essay on . . . pathos, to reenact it."] Christopher Hitchens, "Rebel Ghosts," *Vanity Fair*, July 1999.

[Even Tony Horwitz . . . remembrance kept raising."] Tony Horwitz, *Confederates in the Attic: Dispatches from the Unfinished Civil War* (New York: Random House, 1998), 387.

Index